RAINBOW WINGS

When no human would help,
heavenly help was sent.

R. R. Ford *and* C. T. Ford

Exulon
ELITE

Rainbow Wings
When no human would help, heavenly help was sent.
by R. R. Ford and C. T. Ford

Printed in the United States of America

ISBN 9781498453899

www.xulonpress.com

Feb 3, 2017

To Carmyn

    Hope my daughter's
true story touches
    your heart!

        God Bless you

        CT Ford

Prologue

C hildhood: Separate the compound word and you have "Child" and "Hood". Child: A person of young age; youth. Hood: A covering: to protect, shield from harm, injury, or danger. Put the two words together, "To protect a child from harm". The Webster dictionary knows the definition of childhood, yet verbally abusive, mentally ill very disturbed parents and caregivers do not! It is these specific mentally ill people causing lasting damage to children and the courts are allowing it. A non-breathing "book" has more knowledge and caring feelings than these people. The "Emotional" well being of a child should be protected just as much as the "Physical" well being of a child.

My memorable "childhood" was split into two totally different worlds. The one provided by my loving mom was happy, safe and secure. The other one was miserable and maliciously controlled. It was this childhood that caused so much havoc in my life that it nearly destroyed me. Those memories; scary, hurtful, cruel memories, now a permanent part of me, because of the one who was supposed to be my protective covering during my childhood, failed to do so. In fact, the one who did this injury and harm to me was my "DAD"!

From age eight to ten, I cried myself to sleep every night at my dad's. I cried because I wanted to be with my mom. I didn't understand why she wasn't protecting me. Every time I had to go with my dad, I would hold on to Mom's clothes with the strongest grip my body could produce.

I would cling so tight to her neck, digging my fingernails deep into her skin. I even kept my legs hugged around her waist, begging her to please not put me in the backseat of my evil dad's car. No matter how hard I cried, begged, punched, kicked, or screamed, nothing helped, absolutely nothing! Once, I even got away from Mom and ran to the backyard, but that didn't work either. I didn't understand how she could put me in "that" backseat and watch me scream and cry until I was out of sight. How could she do that to me?

Then I realized it wasn't at all my mom forcing me to go with someone who would hurt me. It was "The Law". To be more specific, it was those two evil, worthless judges' decision. Mom told me she had to follow what the judges ruled on or she would get in trouble. My courageous and determined mom fought over and over trying to protect me. She went to court twelve times plus two mediations. Fourteen times Mom spoke with many "supposedly" intelligent adults and still no helped my situation. Why?

Those excruciating long, long years, I endured my dad's abuse, which consisted of pinching, poking, hitting with the hand and objects, screaming, cussing, degrading hurtful words, insane punishments and biting. Yes, I said, "biting"! I witnessed many vulgar things young eyes should have never seen. So much abuse!!

Physical abuse is always very damaging. That's obvious! The visible scars and bruises leave a lasting feeling of emptiness and shame. As bad as the physical abuse was for me, the verbal and emotional abuse was far worse. It almost destroyed my soul. My mom told me that this kind of combination-secretive abuse was rarely mentioned in family courts, because you couldn't prove it. Are you kidding me? You can't see pain, sadness and fear in a kid's face. Seriously? My mom told me that the law didn't recognize this form of abuse as abuse. She said that unless a child was almost beaten to death and hospitalized or even worse, the court forced these children to endure this abuse until they could walk away, if they were still alive!!

Verbal abuse never leaves any physical bruises or marks. It leaves a different, more damaging kind of scar. A scar consisting of name-calling, belittling, insults and constant put-downs, all which I endured! These scars never completely heal. They stay with you for the rest of your life, having the most serious long lasting effects of all.

Emotional abuse carries a more intentional, calculated evilness to it. This premeditated form of abuse can also haunt you for life. It's like those scary creatures you vividly remember in a Halloween movie, which you chose to watch. You can't remove them from you brain. They can lurk under your bed or in the closet, so close to you that a good night sleep is impossible. These terrifying memories can attack you anytime of the day, but at night they seem worse because you cannot distract them from your mind. You try to fall asleep but they won't leave you alone. They never truly leave your brain.

I tried talking to God every night. I prayed and prayed and prayed, but never heard from Him. I didn't understand. Then I thought that maybe God was taking care of kids worse off than me. The summer I was ten, Mom sat me down and told me I was court-ordered to start spending fifteen days, twice in the summer, with my monster dad. He was even allowed to pick the days. Who came up with that crazy, insane, sick idea? My mom went to court and tried to stop it, but once again, no such luck.

I prayed some more. The night before I had to start my first dreaded fifteen days of "legally-enforced confinement", I decided to write God, thinking maybe I could get through that way. Don't get me wrong, I know God hears my prayers, but I wanted Him to read my "Help" letter NOW! I was so stressed, that same night after losing a front tooth, I even wrote to the Tooth Fairy. A letter to Santa followed. Forgive me God, I was desperate and I thought they could get word to you faster.

Then it happened! God answered my pray and letter. Two long years, but help finally arrived in a storm and a "Rainbow". Storms use to scare me, not anymore. I still remember this particular, violent storm because it peeked my interest. It was a Saturday. The storm started in the afternoon and lasted all night. I was awakened to a bright light and the most incredible rainbow I had ever seen.

My name is Rachel Rene and this is *my* true story of how I survived those early years while being with an abusive, mentally ill parent. My life greatly improved, all because of God, not because of all the loser adults who did nothing to help me. There were "26", because I kept a record of their names. Can you believe that? "26" adults allowed a child (ME) to be injured by a bad parent, in more ways than one. You will see the complete list at the end of the book. I suffered through every weekend and summer that I had to spend with my dad. The two sorriest on the "adult list" came around during this time. I would just glare at their miserable, lying faces during the uncomfortable "forced" visits.

I wasn't the only one suffering. Constantly dealing with the unsympathetic, "finish before lunch time" family court and their lifeless, elected judges was slowly destroying my mom emotionally, physically and financially! She screamed and cried and screamed some more every time she returned home from that so-called "honorable" courtroom. The judge's decisions didn't make a bit of sense. I knew Mom felt helpless, because I witnessed it. Going through this "legal" nightmare about killed her! She survived the years of stress trying to protect me because of her steadfast relationship with God. There WAS no other explanation!

My mom never stopped praying. I would hear her nightly crying out to God. Crying, I thought, was supposed to help stress go away. It didn't help my kind of stress. My stress was my dad and he's still around! I believe 100% in my heart I endured and survived this painful part of my life so I could share it with other victims. I wanted them to know, they were not alone! For every child that has been terrorized or tormented mentally, verbally or physically, I strongly believe they will identify and even connect with what happened to me.

After my first traumatized visit with my dad, my mom decided to keep a detailed journal of the abuse that had occurred. I also kept one. For over three years, our journals stayed by my devoted mom's bed-side. At the time, we never realized that keeping a dated, documented record would provide accurate material for this book.

Finally, I hope my story will inspire all the "RIGHT" adults in the government to find a better way to protect kids, because the today's court system is *NOT WORKING!!* The court system failed me, and many, many others. I'm sure of it!

When no human would help, heavenly help was sent!

My story begins. . . . .

Introduction

"It's time. S TOR MY, call for R A IN."

"R A IN, you have been chosen to go to Earth. The child and her mother are at the ends of their rope. God has been waiting and hoping for the dad's behavior to improve, but it looks like that will not be happening anytime soon, if ever. Instead, we will focus on the child and mother. We cannot lose them! There is still hope in the mother's soul, but the child's faith is beginning to fade. The desperate child has now sent a letter. She has even drawn you. You are in her thoughts and broken heart. A first meeting is to take place. We will see how it goes. R A IN, Be your unique self and the great listener that you are! The child will fill in the rest. We will stay in constant contact. There is no time to lose. So, travel to earth and seek out the young lost soul any way you can. Pique her wonderful curiosities, interests and fears, and in time you will gain her trust. God will be with you. Good luck on your journey!"

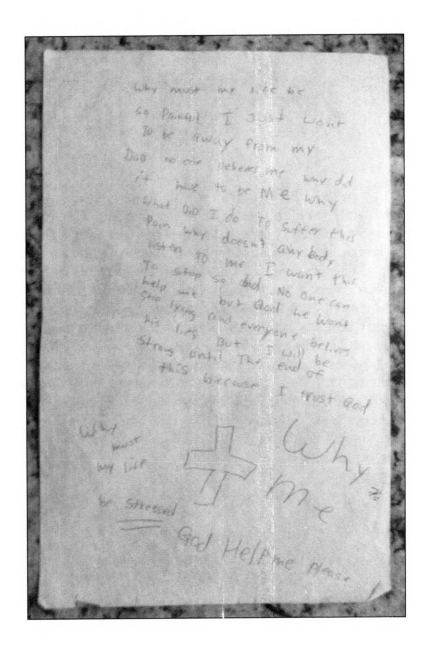

*Fathers, do not embitter your children or
they will become discouraged.*

Colossians 3:21 (NIV)

Chapter 1

D ark, gloomy, scary, intense, violent, anxious, and loud! Sometimes predictable, sometimes not! I was not only describing the approaching storm outside my window, but also the one I heard coming down the hallway. How ironic, exactly the same words described a storm and a monster, a monster of a dad.

It was a summer Saturday morning, a day I would never forget! "Get your "F" n ass out of bed," the monster screamed from the hallway. I shot up fast. I learned the hard way, you did exactly what the monster said, or you would be sorry. Nervous tension and fear instantly filled my young body. *He* was approaching. I was always a nervous wreck at my Dad's condo, now you understand why. I slept like a dolphin, one eye open all the time. It was that terrifying. He always yelled and screamed and said bad words. Bad words at me! I mean every time he opened his mouth.

That particular Saturday morning, the screaming and the cussing were louder than ever! My body was literally shaking. Now, just outside my door, the monster screamed again, "I said, get your lazy, "F" n ass out of bed, this instance!" My door flew open. He added, "Do I have to get my belt out?" He turned and stormed out of my room. If he was trying to scare me, it was working. So here you have it! This was my morning greeting, at Dad's.

He was always screaming about something or someone. The words he used hurt me badly! I was only ten years old. My dad had been yelling and cussing at me, since I was eight. He was taking all his anger out on me, instead of Mom, because she filed for divorce. It all started the first weekend I was forced to be alone with him. Mom wasn't around to stop it, so he said and did whatever pleased him. My dad treated me horribly! Why? What did I do to suffer this pain? I guess he chose to be down right "MEAN"!

I quickly jumped out of bed before he came back with that very thick belt. I got up, went straight to the bathroom, and then to the kitchen for some breakfast. He arrogantly walked in carrying his 'chosen' weapon shouting, "See what I'm holding! Never forget it!" As the monster stormed out he growled, "You better not make a mess, missy!" He was wearing only underwear and a devil face. Why didn't he ever wear more clothes in front of me? I saw things shaking I should have never seen, his privates! He was a man and I was a little girl. He even stayed dressed like this when his mom came over. Gross! Double Gross!!

I poured myself a bowl of his yucky cereal. I had to eat something! My "*so called*" dad never would buy me anything I like, only what he liked. Once, I asked him why he didn't buy the orange juice without pulp. I never liked those icky pieces in my mouth. He glared at me and said he liked the pulp and I wasn't around enough, so what did it matter. So that meant, I didn't matter. So mean and cruel!

I carefully got out the milk and slowly poured it over the cereal, making sure none spilled on the counter. I put the milk back in the refrigerator making sure the label was facing forward and was perfectly straight. I quickly ate my cereal leaning over the kitchen sink. This was the only place I was allowed to eat. I constantly kept checking after every bite making sure nothing dropped from my mouth. I finished as fast as I could, before my dad came back in the room. I put the cereal back in its exact place and cleaned the bowl and spoon spotless.

After I put the dishes back up in their correct position, I wiped out the sink with the dish towel until it was completely dry and then used it to wipe the counter and refrigerator handle for fingerprints. I hung it back on the "specific" hook, left the room turning the lights off. This was my insane routine every other weekend at the condo. Mom told me that Dad suffers from OCD. She explained that basically meant everything had to be in perfect order. "NO MESSES"!

I headed to my room to gather up all my summer homework. When I reached my door, Dad barked, "Get on your homework, NOW!" I hurried as fast as I could and straightened up my bedroom and bathroom, just like the kitchen. I did the best I could at my age. My dad's mother would be coming over later to clean. Dad made her clean his condo every weekend. She was his maid! Sounded more like his slave to me. I knew what a slave was, because last year in history class, I read all about slavery during the Civil War. That was a very disgraceful period of time in our country. My dad was just as bad as some of the people I read about, maybe worse. I think my monster dad enjoyed ordering us around, why else would he do it?

I decided to stay in my cat T-shirt and pajama bottoms, because they are so comfortable. Carrying all my books and binder, I tiptoed quietly to the kitchen table. I didn't want my dad screaming at me again. Walking to the table, I took one last inspection of the kitchen to make sure it was perfect.

I sat down, spread out all my books and homework as neatly as possible. I was about to start on the math problems, when the loudest sound came from outside. It was so loud I almost fell out of my chair. I jumped up and ran onto the balcony. From the distance, a storm was approaching. I saw dark clouds moving towards me. As I was watching, lightning shot across the sky. My already trembling body jerked, it was so loud. I quickly raced back inside. I turned and was about to slide the glass door shut, when I looked up at the storm one more time. A frightening sound loudly rumbled inside the clouds. Thunder, along with lightning, was now in control!

The door was almost closed, when I witnessed a bolt of lightning coming straight through the black clouds, striking the ground. It was such a powerful hit, that it immediately shot back up into the clouds, like a bouncing ball. The lightning instantly lit up black clouds! I stood there frozen, right by the glass door, not moving an inch. I mean it, I couldn't move! I was terrified of the vicious storm and at the same time I couldn't take my eyes off it.

Then I saw something incredible! Rainbow colors were slowly drifting in and out of the storm clouds, as though they were secretly showing themselves to me. I ran back to the balcony rail. Instantly, calmness took over my trembling body. My eyes stayed fixed on the black clouds lighting up. As I kept watching, the colors red, orange, then yellow, green, blues and purple appeared.

As the colors were winding in and around the black clouds, I could have sworn, on my Bible, I saw some sort of figure attached to them. I whispered so quietly to myself that only the ears of God could hear me say, "Did I just see a person in the storm? I must be seeing things". I stood there still as can be, hoping to see the figure appear again. The lightning and thunder continued. I needed to get back inside, but I just couldn't take my eyes off the mysterious black clouds.

The sky continued to light up. I wanted to see the colors just one more time. I moved to each corner of the balcony rail, looking in all directions. I didn't know how long I had been out there; 5 minutes, 20 minutes. I didn't care. I just patiently stood there waiting and hoping. Finally when I decided to go in, the colorful movement reappeared. I watched it move right along with the storm, as though it was supposed to. I kept saying to myself, "No way is there a person in the clouds, unless it's an angel, an angel with colors."

It continued to flow in and out of the clouds until it was gone. It was so beautiful and a little scary at the same time. Beautiful rainbow colors attached to a dark and ugly storm! How odd the two mixed together! Then I thought maybe it was just the beginning of a rainbow, peeking through the storm. It was preparing to completely show itself, after the storm ended. That was what rainbows did! I learned that from my mom and school.

Watching the sky, I drifted off thinking about all the fun story-telling times I have had with Mom. Every time there was a bad storm, she would lie beside me until it ended or I fell completely asleep, which ever came first. She knew storms scared me. Telling me a story always calmed me down. I can still remember the first time Mom told me the Bible story of the rainbow. She told me all about why God sent a rainbow after flooding the Earth.

It was the story of Noah and his Hotel. I knew it was an ark but Mom called it a "Hotel" to make me laugh, just like her dad (my grandpa) told her when she was a young girl. I think she was just seeing if I was really paying attention. Anyway she told me that in the Bible, in the book of Genesis (6:8-9,17), there lived a man named Noah. He was a good man who loved and obeyed God. God told Noah to build this boat (an ark) for his family and 2 of every kind of living creature. I told Mom that must have been a HUGE boat!!! One interesting fact about the ark, it had only one window (Genesis 6:16).

After the ark was completed, all boarded. Everyone was on the ark for 7 days before it began to rain. It rained 40 days and 40 nights before it stopped. The water covered the earth for 150 days. Now, while waiting for the rain to dry up, Noah sent a raven and a dove to search for dry land. The dove returned, so he waited a week and sent it out again. This time the dove came back with an olive leaf in its mouth. Noah waited one more week and sent the dove out one last time, but it did not return. The land must be dry.

They had been on the ark for 370 days, from the time Noah closed the door, until God told him to open it and leave. When Noah and his family stepped off the ark, they, the animals and the fish were the only ones to survive the awful flood. Mom said that the fish lived because God only destroyed what was on dry land. Maybe that's why the fish became a symbol among the early Christians!

Anyway, that was a long time to be on a boat, I mean an ark. Mom agreed. Then Mom said that God made a promise to Noah and all living creatures. He sent a rainbow that would appear in the clouds. Mom said that the rainbow was to remind us of God's faithfulness, a special covenant our Lord made between Himself and all of mankind. The bow shape represented the glory of God. The seven colors represented the seven covenants God gave Noah. There were seven colors because our eyes could only see light in that spectrum. God already knew this.

Mom has always believed the rainbow is a holy, sacred reminder of God's authority and grace, no matter how many other ways it may be represented. It was God's symbol, FIRST!! It should always be remembered as "Holy", because God is Holy. God told Noah, He would never again send the waters to become a flood to destroy all life. God kept His promise. I told Mom I was glad God kept His promise, because storms and lots of pounding rain really scare me. I think it scares most kids.

Thinking about our story times together brought a smile to my face. Noah and the rainbow is one of my favorites! Mom also shared with me an interesting fact; Noah's grandfather was the oldest man who ever lived on the earth. His name was Methuselah and he lived to be 969 years old (Genesis 5:27). I'm glad I have a mom who knows and loves the Bible! My dad has never told me a Bible story. I don't think he even knows one. He doesn't even own a Bible. I miss being away from Mom.

I came out of my daydreaming and remembered all my homework waiting for me. I took one last glance at the storm. Whatever I thought I saw was no longer there. So, I went in and shut the door. I sat down and began working mainly on math. Every summer I have required homework. I had to get busy, before mean dad came back into the room. It was hard, though. My thoughts kept going back to the storm.

I would do a few math problems, then stare at the storm, then a few more math problems. I then leaned far back into my chair to get a better look at the sky.

My eyes started wandering around the den and kitchen area. As they were roaming, I noticed everything was perfectly in place, no trash or food or anything lying around. You wouldn't think anybody lived here. The whole condo looked like one of those show homes I visited with Mom. It was almost creepy how clean this place was. I bet it was cleaner than a hospital room! It had to be the OCD Mom said that Dad suffered from!

I sat the chair back down and pulled it closer to the table. It's a fairly nice looking table. The wood is light-colored brown. There are four chairs, completely covered in dark green fabric. Sitting there, I placed my elbows on the table, with one fist under my chin. I was staring across the table, when my mind stumbled onto an incredible discovery. The only thing I did at this table was homework. I had never been allowed to eat at this nice table. So crazy! Something WAS very wrong with my dad! My mom NEVER acted like this. I ate all my meals at our kitchen table, because that was what it was for. When I was with Mom stress was never present. Life with her was fun, easy and VERY QUIET! No screaming or cussing! No bad words ever came out of her mouth! I was beginning to understand why Mom kicked Dad out of the house!

I went back to my math of multiplying and dividing number problems. I stopped for a brief moment and glanced at the storm. One more deep thought, wondering about the rainbow colors in the clouds, filled my mind. The doorbell rang. I could hear Dad growling in the hallway at Martha, Dad's mom. Guess she was here to do her chores!

"You are not only responsible for what you say, but also for what you do not say."

Martin Luther

Chapter 2

I stayed seated at the kitchen table. I was still working on my math, when my nose smelled food. Sure enough, Martha (Mama) walked in, carrying a pan of brownies. Yum!!! She immediately started with the usual baby talking. "Hi Tweetie, how's my itty-bitty precious itty baby doing? Look what Mama brought my baby." It drove me bananas! I politely said, like I always do, "I'm not a bird so please stop baby-talking me." Mama answered, "Okay, I saw-we." (For those who don't know the baby language, "saw-we" means "sorry.") She couldn't help it. According to my mom, Mama had been talking like that as long as she had known her. She had grandkids now in their 30's, and she still baby talked them. Mom would tell me to try and not let it bother me, because it would never change. I had learned to ignore it.

My "baby-talking" grandmother headed to the kitchen. As she turned and walked away, I noticed her pale pink jogging pants and pink top. She was wearing only one of the three colors I had ever seen her in; pale pink, white or cream. That was it! In the few years I have lived, I never saw another color on her, except those three. So odd! With her short gray curly hair and those dull colors she wore, it made her look so pale and almost dead. She was already old, so why would you want to make yourself look dead?

My other grandmother was older than Mama, but she looked much younger. Maybe because she wore bright and rich-looking colors! Us kids notice more than you grown-ups think! We're usually not allowed to talk much, so instead of using our mouths, we would use our eyes. Always so amazing how much you learn, just by watching!

Anyway, Mama only wore pale colors, to match her pale life. She was short in height, just like my dad, very meek and quiet. She had been a widow for some years now. Mom told me "widow" meant that Mama's husband (my grandfather) had died. I didn't remember meeting him. I was only two years old when he passed away.

Mom said that he was a nice man, "Too nice to be a parent". (Those were her exact words). He was soft spoken like Martha (Mama). She said that they were as quiet as a pair of mice. Maybe that was why they married each other? I had to ask myself, "How did these two quiet and nice parents have such a loud and mean son?" So bizarre! For some strange reason Mama put up with my dad because he was her only child still living." I think she came over a lot because it made her feel needed, regardless of how her son treated her. She did bring food over from time to time. The only thing I liked she made were the desserts. The rest of the food wasn't very tasty. I know that sounds bad to say, but it was the truth.

This time she walked in carrying one of my all-time favorites, brownies. I think she cooked for me, because my dad never did. She tried her best to be a good grandmother to me, but she wasn't! I blame her for not raising my evil dad better. She NEVER stopped him from screaming and cussing. He always screams and cusses at her and now screams and cusses at me!

Dad would never get away with screaming at me in front of Mom. No way!! I would never scream and cuss at my mom or anyone. So disrespectful! My mom taught me better than that. I really didn't get Mama! Why didn't she stop it the first time her son screamed and cussed at her? I just didn't get it! Mama claimed to be a "God-fearing" Christian, as she always put it. She was supposed to fear God, not her son. She should have been a parent and not a wimp!

Mom told me that Martha babied her son to death and never disciplined him at all. She never set standards for him. I asked Mom what that meant. She said that Martha didn't have rules and never said "no" to her precious baby, because she didn't want to make him cry. Now, I'm the one who cries.

I found out when Dad was young he would bite other kids and relatives and Mama would say, "He's just playing!" Now he was biting me and it was NOT playing! Playing is not supposed to hurt. She should have stopped it, but she didn't! My dad's mom was a horrible parent! Mom also explained to me that parents are supposed to raise their children according to the Bible. I guess Mama just didn't care how her son turned out or she didn't have a Bible. Either way, it's now too late.

He became mean because she didn't make him nice. Now I had to be around "Meany" Dad. Thanks a lot Mama!

This reminded me of something Mom shared with me. A few years ago, she told me a true story about two families that lived in a nice neighborhood. They lived side by side for over twenty years. They lived in the same kind of house, drove the same kind of car and had kids about the same age. It looked like they were about the same in every way. As the years went by, one family started having so many problems.

This family's problems were their kids; dealing with drugs, alcohol, cussing, dropping out of school, disrespecting their parents, fighting all the time. The police came to their house so many, many times over the years. Then their children grew up and had children without marrying. Mom said the list went on and on.

Now, the other family's kids finished school, didn't do drugs or get drunk. They respected their parents in every way. There were no bad words coming out of their mouths. No police ever came to their house. Now these kids grew up, married and then had kids. Mom asked if I could tell her what made the two families so different. I thought for a few minutes and said it was the parents. I looked at Mom and asked if I was right. She said I was. Then Mom added that she truly believed the outcome would have been different if God had been in their home.

After hearing about those two families, boy, Dad's parents messed up badly. Maybe they were asleep for a lot of years. When they woke up, it was too late, because their son, my dad, became a monster, right in front of their eyes. One of the first Bible verses I ever memorized for school is Proverbs 22:6 (NKJV). It says, "Train up a child in the way he should go: and when he is old, he will not depart from it". Parents can make all the difference. It's their job to teach their kids to behave. I firmly believe if they had raised my dad to live the way God says, he wouldn't have become so mean. I see it with my own eyes. I'm living it!

After thinking all about this, I went back to my math, because it wasn't as exhausting on my brain! Mama came out of the kitchen. She was walking towards me, when Dad yelled out to her. He was having another hissy fit, but this one sounded much worse. Mama was now standing right beside me, when Dad walked up. I could see she was in trouble. "Martha, you dumb "F", if you had a brain you would be dangerous," Dad screamed. "What? What? What's wrong?" Martha nervously asked?" "Shut the "F" up!" Dad rudely answered.

I stayed quiet as a mouse. I pretended to be doing my math. Kind of hard to work during this one-sided "screaming match!" I wasn't about to but in. Martha tried to speak. She didn't know what her 'precious' son was so upset about "this time" He wouldn't stop screaming. You can never get a word in when my dad was "vomiting" from the mouth!

He yanked her by the sleeve. I got up from my chair, and watched him drag her down the hallway. I saw them go into his bedroom. I couldn't see them anymore, and didn't want to, but I certainly heard them. It was mostly dad screaming. While he was screaming at his Mom "over who knows what", I decided to get a brownie. When I got to the kitchen door, I stood there. I could now hear the reason why my dad was screaming and cursing at his mother. It was the way she had folded his socks and underwear last weekend. At the top of his lungs he screamed, "Sit your lazy worthless ass down on the bed and refold them, like I have shown you time after time. Are you a retard or just plain stupid? Get busy!"

I quietly snuck all the way into the kitchen. The brownies were there waiting on the counter. I peeled back the foil. They were still warm. Yum! I got a knife and started to cut from the corner of the pan. Then I thought it would be fun to cut one in the shape of a triangle. So I did. I carefully lifted it out with the knife, balancing it with both hands and carried it over to the kitchen sink only a few feet away.

Leaning over, I started to take my first bite, when evil dad stormed in. I quickly looked at him and said that I would make sure I cleaned up after myself. He was red in the face, I guess from screaming at his mother. He walked past me and went straight to the pan of brownies. He rips his mother to shreds and then comes and gets a brownie that she made. Wow!

I was trying to eat my brownie when all of a sudden he started screaming and cursing at me. "What the "F" is this," Dad yelled. I spun around so fast, dropping the brownie in the sink. He was mad!! Rage was coming out of him. It reminded me of a cartoon character, but he wasn't funny, not at all! I was scared. With fear in my eyes I asked, "What's wrong?" He got right in my face and screamed, "What did you do to *"MY"* brownies?" I quickly asked, "What do you mean?" He grabbed a hold of my T-shirt and pulled me over to them. I was terrified! "Look what you have done. You have ruined them," he yelled. "What?" I asked. Then my dad lost it, I mean really lost it.

He started screaming and screaming and screaming at the top of his lungs, because I had cut a brownie in the shape of a triangle and not a square! He was so loud throughout the condo Mama came dashing into the kitchen to see what was going on. Dad turned to her and screamed, "She ruined the brownies. I need you to make a new batch." Mama looked confused.

While she was standing beside him, Dad yelled, "Get to your room and stay there for your punishment." He hurtfully added, "I better not see your fat ass missy, or I'll get my belt out, you got that?" I burst into tears. With my back up against the refrigerator, I started slowly moving. I had only taken two steps when Dad raised his hand above his head. I screamed, "No Dad, please don't hit me, please, pretty please! I'm hurrying." He just screamed again, "Get your ass to your room, NOW, I don't want to see your ugly worthless face for two hours."

Finally by him, I ran to my bedroom, tears pouring down my face. I shut my door and plopped down on my bed. I put a pillow over my ears trying to drown out the violent noise, because he started screaming and swearing his mother, worse than before. He was saying horrible things to her. I was crying, gasping for air, crying and gasping for more air, while trying to make sense of it all. What did I do that was so wrong? I cut a brownie in the shape of a triangle and he went berserk!! Why? I didn't understand! I was in total shock. What hurt the most was his mom, my grandmother, stood there and did NOTHING, ABSOLUTELY NOTHING!!! She didn't even try to stop him. It was because she was scared of him, scared of her own son.

I rolled over on my back and just stared at the ceiling. My thoughts went back to the madness that had just happened in the kitchen. I was crushed over Mama allowing her insane son's abusive behavior on a child, his child! From that moment on, I no longer cared for her. I had no respect for her. She was no longer my grandmother. She was just "Martha" and that was all! I now had only one grandmother, my mom's mom. Dad's mom could have helped me and didn't. I will NEVER as long as I live, EVER forget about the triangle brownie!! I stayed on my bed and continued crying. I couldn't stop. I wanted to go home and be with Mom. I wanted to be so far away from this cruel and evil condo. Sadly, that was not going to happen anytime soon.

Some time went by. Finally it was dead calm, outside my bedroom door. Here, that could be just as scary. It was like the saying Mom told me "The calm before the storm." I heard a door slam. Martha came to my door and quietly asked if I was okay. She said my crazy dad went to steam. Steam! That was all he ever did, besides screams. Screams and steams! When insane Dad lived with Mom and me, he would go to the spa and stay gone for hours. It was as though he never wanted to come home. I said nothing back to Martha. There was nothing to say.

I turned over onto my side to try and rest. I heard rain coming down hard and loud. The storm outside had arrived. Lying there, I kept wishing the rain would wash away my dad for good! I got up and walked over to the window just to watch. Standing there, I decided to finish my homework because I wanted to be in bed sound asleep before "Mr. Evil" (that was Dad's new name) got back. I left my bedroom and saw Martha quietly doing her chores. I glanced at the balcony. Boy the rain was really coming down, along with lots of thunder and lightning. Mom always says "The storms talking tonight". It wasn't just talking tonight, it was yelling!

I went into the kitchen to make myself a sandwich. While I was in there eating it over the kitchen sink, the lights started flickering off and on several times. Then they went completely off. Martha came in to see if I was okay. I said I was fine. I got the flashlight from under the sink. I turned it on so I could see my sandwich. About ten minutes later the lights came back on. I cleaned up the few crumbs and drank the milk I had poured myself in the dark. Thank goodness the power came back on before Mr. Evil got home, because some had spilt on the floor. I turned the flashlight off and put it back in its "*exact*" position. I made sure the kitchen was spotless. I turned the lights out and headed to the kitchen table, where the math was waiting for me.

Sitting there, I kept staring at the storm through the balcony glass door. The sky was very dark. All I could see was black, no rainbow colors. I finished all the math problems, gathered up all my homework and binder and headed back to my room. Martha came out of the office, I guess to check on me. I said I was going to take a shower and get ready for bed. She said back, "Okay Tweetie." I just rolled my eyes. Baby-talking again! Oh well. She asked if I needed anything. I simply said no.

The thunder and lightning was so loud! Too scared to take a shower, I decided to just wash my face, brush my teeth and climb into bed wearing what I had on all day. It was so comfy. Just as I turned off the bathroom light, I heard the front door open. Mr. Evil was back. I leaped into bed and pretended to be asleep. It didn't matter. He abruptly opened my door and started in on me again. He yelled,

"If you ever ruin any of "*MY*" food again, you will be sorry." I was shaking. I kept praying secretly to myself for God to make him stop.

He came over to my bed and raised his hand to me. I curled up into a ball and put the pillow over my face. Big mistake! He grabbed the pillow and told me to never ignore him when he was talking to me. "Talking!" That was what dad called talking! Martha walked in. Mr. Evil turned to her and said, "What the hell do you want, Martha?" It was so sarcastic. She started to say something, almost as though she was going to help me, when he got in her face. He told her to mind her own "GD" "F" n business, because this matter didn't concern her.

He then asked her if she wanted his fist in her face, again. Did he just say AGAIN? I wondered if Mom knew about this? Martha said nothing. She turned and quickly left the room. Mr. Evil then told me to go to sleep and think about what I did wrong today. He threw my pillow at me and in the most evil voice said, "Boo hoo all you want missy. Your "F" n bitch mother can't help you!" Then screaming at the top of his lungs he added, "No one can help you!!!" He stormed out, slamming the door behind him.

I was shaking-scared and sick to my stomach. I felt like I was going insane. Something was seriously wrong with my dad, but what? Why did he go so crazy over a pan of brownies? He was even meaner to his own mom, than I have ever seen before. I actually felt sorry for her. If my dad could hit his mother, who was old, he was going to hit me. It was just a matter of time. I cried under my pillow so my evil dad wouldn't hear me. I cried out to God to please help me. I told Him, "I don't know how much longer I can take this. Please my Heavenly Father HELP ME!!!! I sent you a letter. Didn't you get it?"

I was emotionally exhausted from the day. Crying as much as I did, took a lot out of me. Thankfully the storm in the condo ended, but the one outside was still going strong. The rain was beating against my window. It was kind of calming me. I got completely under my comforter, with my stuffed kitty hugged tightly in my arms, keeping my pillow over my head for protection. My body and soul was beaten down. I remembered the last part of the Bible verse in Isaiah (41:13). Mom would recite it all the time. She knew it by heart. She knew a lot of Bible verses by heart. It says, "Do not fear, I will help you." I kept saying it over and over until I dozed off. My mind was traveling to a peaceful place. I was so relaxed. Was I dreaming or was I dead? Either way I was away from my cruel dad. I could see something colorful in the distance. I didn't want wake up!

29

"Pay attention to your dreams. God's angels often speak directly to our hearts when we are asleep."

Eileen Elias Freeman

Chapter 3

Dreaming, wonderful dreaming, the kind of dreaming you refuse to leave. Mom always told me that closing your eyes was a lovely way to be, because your soul became aware of things it was meant to see. She was right! This dream I was definitely meant to see. It was very vivid and colorful. I wanted it to continue, but something deliberately kept waking me up. It was so bright! I couldn't keep my eyes closed. I tried everything. I completely covered my face with my pillow, but it was hard to breathe. I threw it on the floor and covered up with just the comforter. That didn't work either.

Then, I put the pillow and comforter back on top of my face. Nothing helped! I threw both of them to the side of me. The brightness was driving me crazy. I squinted my eyes and saw it was coming in from the balcony. It seemed to be purposely shining straight into the bedroom. It was most certainly demanding my attention! I closed my eyes for a moment. Then, I peeked again and saw a perfectly straight line of light coming towards my face. It was so bright I couldn't see anything else.

I stumbled out of bed and felt my way to my toy chest. It was at the foot of my bed. When I reached it, I had to cover my eyes with one hand while the other hand rummaged through the toys, looking for my florescent yellow colored spy glasses. I knew they were in there. That was where I kept all my favorite stuff. I found my visor that I got on a trip to Disney World last summer. I quickly put it on. It blocked the bright light enough so I could use both hands in my search. I started getting frustrated looking for those darn glasses, excuse my language. I kept digging and digging, pushing my toys over to both sides, when I felt them. Finally, thank goodness, they were in my hands. I cleaned 'um with my T-shirt, for smudges. Spy glasses were great to wear when you wanted it dark!

I slipped them over my hair and did some adjustments. Now, I got a better look at the annoying bright light. Yep! It was coming straight down from the sky. I walked out onto the balcony to get a better look. My spy glasses kept slipping down on my face. I turned away from the bright light to adjust the strap again. While fiddling with them, the strap slipped out of the groove. They dropped right between two balcony bars. I quickly grabbed them, before they fell to the street below. Dad lived in a high-rise condo that was located right smack in the busiest section of the city's downtown.

As I was still bent over, I put the glasses back on. When I came up, the bright sky was so blinding, I lost my balance and dropped the glasses, a second time. This time they fell, hitting the ground below. Hope they didn't break! I leaned over the rail to see exactly where they landed. No such luck! I looked up and glanced at the light. Oh my goodness gracious! I could see a rainbow. It was right under the bright beam of light.

It was so close to me, I just had to reach out to touch it. When I did, I lost my balance and fell off the balcony. I started screaming and screaming at the top of my lungs. I just knew I was going to die. Then I realized, I wasn't falling to my death, I wasn't falling at all. I was traveling up, not down, higher and higher, into the clouds. "Was I going to Heaven?" I asked myself. For some odd reason, I didn't feel scared. I was flying away from Dad. That was all that mattered!

I went through several dark clouds. Then suddenly I stopped, but not for long. I started going back down. I dropped through a few more heavy clouds. I looked down and saw the rainbow. Within a few seconds, my feet landed on it and then my butt. I took off sliding downwards. There was nothing to hold on to. I kept both hands by my legs to balance. My body was leaning in every direction. I curved to the left and then to the right, then to the left once more. Twisting back and forth until finally going straight down!

"Woooooooh, Oh, Yikes, Woooo, Wo, Helppppp,," I screamed the whole way, until kerplunk!! Oh! Ouch! Oh! Ouch! I landed hard on my butt. Stunned and shaken-up I lied back on the ground keeping my eyes closed. I was way too scared to open them. I thought to myself that I had to be dreaming, even though it sure seemed real. As I was lying there completely flat and perfectly still, the tips of my fingers started investigating the soft ground. It felt and smelled just like grass. It was just tall enough to twist in and out of my fingers. I stayed still as a statue, with only my fingers moving. My eyes remained tightly closed. I wasn't about to peek!

I couldn't get over how soft and thick the grass was. It was softer than my favorite blanket Mom bought for me, earlier this summer. I was completely resting, still in a daze of what just happened, when my nose started itching. I slowly reached up to scratch it. Something was flying around my face, tickling it, badly! I kept blindly swatting at it, but it didn't seem to help. The tickling caused me to sneeze so big! It was driving me bananas!! It wasn't going away, so I had to look.

I bravely peeked with one eyelid. I couldn't tell what was tickling my nose and now my forehead because of the light. Taking my cautious time, I opened one eye and then the other just a little more. Was I really seeing a face? Now, I HAD to get a better look. I opened my eyes wider. I gasped out loud! I saw colored pigtails dangling over me. I was so startled, that I jerked my body back, by my heels and elbows. Now, several inches away, I got a better look. It was a girl, not much older than me. My mouth dropped and stayed completely open. I couldn't stop staring at her and her pigtails. They were rainbow colors. I mean every color of the rainbow, long and perfectly braided! They blew me away! That's what was tickling my nose, not a bug, pigtails!

When she stood up straight, those incredibly looking pigtails hung clear down to her waist. Wow Wee! They were something to look at. Her fair-skinned face was covered with freckles and a bright smile. She spoke first, cheerfully saying, "Howdy, my name is R A IN, and you are?" I timidly answered, "I'm Rachel, Rachel Rene." "Hi there Rachel Rene. Sorry about my pigtails hanging down in your face. They kind of have a mind of their own. Didn't mean to frighten the 'jitters' out of you!" R A IN vibrantly, but politely answered.

I stayed on the ground in shock, not scared, just in shock. R A IN reached down and said, "I have a hand for your hand." I grabbed hold of it. Her hands were unusually warm. She pulled me straight up. Standing, facing one another, I noticed we were just about the same height and both slender in size. Her hair was vivid colors. Mine was just regular dark brown, matching my eyes. This girl had on a colorful short-sleeved shirt and light blue jean shorts. She was barefoot just like me. We just kept staring at each other. R A IN looked at what I was dressed in and genuinely said, "I love your cat T-shirt." I smiled

33

and said, "Thanks a bunch. My mom took a photo of my cat to a place where they know how to put it on a T-shirt. When I got home from my dad's, she surprised me with it. She told me I could keep it with me at all times. I wear it a lot at my dad's. It reminds me of my mom. I love her and my cat T-shirt! Sugar is now with me all the time." R A IN said, "Oh, her name is Sugar. That is a terrific name for a cat!"

I smiled and nodded. I paused for a moment, and then asked, "What did you say your name was?" She said again, ""R A IN." "I'm sorry I can't seem to say it. It's a tongue twister." This well-adjusted girl seemed to be okay with me not being able to pronounce her name. We took a few steps towards a house. "Welcome to my home Rachel Rene!" R A IN proudly announced.

I looked all around checking my new surroundings. I'm telling you, this was the most beautiful place I had ever seen. The colors! It reminded me of the movie *"The Wizard of Oz"*. Dorothy got up from her bed after the tornado and opened the front door. That was when the movie went from black and white to color. This girl's home was that colorful, maybe even more. She was colorful!! I stared at everything, then at her again.

I remarked, "I'm sorry, but I just can't take eyes off your hair. It has every color of the rainbow. I just love it!" She chuckled, "Yeah, my rainbow pigtails are a gift from God. My freckles too!" I was standing close enough to her face to notice her freckles also had a little bit of color in them. She said, "I love your beautiful dark brown hair. It has such lovely long curls. You love my hair and I love yours." We both laughed at the same time.

There was a short pause of silence. The colorful girl abruptly shouted, "My goodness! It is time to get busy!" I asked, "Busy doing what?" She said, "I have to show you lots, here at my home". I eagerly replied, "I would love to see everything." My interesting companion quickly responded, "Why thank you my dear, you are certainly a very kind and polite young lady." I liked the way this girl talked. It was so grown-up like Mom, not baby talk like *"you know who"!*

She gently took my hand and said, "Come with me." We took several more steps. I saw the back of her home. It was small, but very cozy looking, just like a quaint cottage. Why would you need anything bigger when you have this kind of outdoors? I glanced over her shoulder and saw a rainbow attached to the right side of her home. It looked like what I had been rapidly riding on. It DID resemble a slide!

I looked back to my left, trying to take it all in. The cottage was painted a grass-green color and covered in white and green ivy. I had the same ivy at home in flowerpots and in the ground. I even remembered Mom telling me that ivy represented faithfulness and eternal life.

On each side of the cottage were medium-sized lemon trees. I asked if I could take a closer look. She said that it would be just "Lemony." I walked from one end to the other. Both trees were chugged full of lemons and smelled wonderful. I wish I had a lemon tree. Just a ways out, there was another tree. It was a peach tree. I strolled over to it. The mysterious, but kind girl yelled out, "The peach symbolizes good works." I didn't know that. I turned and walked back to the girl, who was now leaning against the cottage. How did she move without making any noise? Mysteriously weird!

The warm, vibrant green color of the cottage was breathtaking. I took a couple of steps back. The roof was made of Spanish tile. I know because I have seen it one of my friend's roof. The tiles were a mixture of soft brown and burnt reddish color. Very pretty, I might add! The front door was huge, much larger than my front door. It was jet black. I looked even closer and noticed a long, slender sign, hanging over it. It was slightly swaying back and forth by thick, silver metal chains, holding up each end. It read, "First Door of R A IN E Rainbow's Cottage." I looked at her and curiously asked, "Is that your name, R A IN E?" R A IN said, "Why yes!" I exclaimed, "Your name spells "Rain." Is the "E" your middle name?" R A IN just smiled and giggled. I respectfully asked, "Since you name spells "RAIN" and your middle name is "E", would it be okay if I called you Rain E?" R A IN looked straight up to the sky, then at me. She gladly answered, "Of course you can my dear, that would please ALL just fine. I mean that would please ME just fine!"

I graciously thanked her. Then I began telling Rain E that her name reminded me of the book in the Bible named "Job." I stated, "It can be said two different ways. "Job": a man from the Old Testament and "job", a way of making a living. When I was younger, my mom told me it was pronounced both ways. That was a bit confusing for a kid. I finally got! I learned about Job in the Bible from my mom and at my Christian school. Now I know another person with a very special name."

I was looking around when I blurted out "Wait a minute, shouldn't the sign read, "Front Door" not "First Door"? Did you misspell it?"

Rain E giggled some more and said, "No, my friend, it is spelled right, right for you!" "What do you mean, *for me?*" I curiously asked. She added, "You will see at the end." "End, end of what? End of the visit?" I kept asking.

Rain E never answered any more of my questions. Her lips stayed together and just became a smile. The way Rain E smiled, reminded me of a saying "A smile is a curve that sets everything straight." A lady named Phyllis Diller first said it. Mom told me she was funny and clever with words. I loved the saying so much, I memorized it. Rain E was wearing that kind of smile, because I felt at ease and safe with her. I just stood there now smiling too, looking at a perfect cottage and a delightful, but mysterious girl with rainbow pigtails.

*The wilderness and the solitary place shall be glad
for them; and the desert shall rejoice;
and blossom as the rose.*

Isaiah 35:1 (KJV)

Chapter 4

M agical! Just Magical! That was the best word to describe Rain E's home. I was enjoying taking it all in. Twisting and turning my body in every direction took some effort. I was twisting so much my back popped. It made the loudest noise. Troubled by what she heard, Rain E asked, "You okay? That sounded dreadfully painful." I giggled, "I'm okay. My cousin Matt showed me how to do it. It scares my mom too."

After looking around for several minutes, Rain E cheerfully said, "Come on, no time to waste." She held on to my left hand. They were still warm, much warmer than mine. We started slowly walking, swinging our arms back and forth. Then, our feet started moving faster, and then a little faster. Then within seconds, Rain E and I were running so fast, I was sure we would leave the ground like an airplane. There was one step when we left the ground together, and stayed in the air longer than normal. I mean for a brief moment we defied all the laws of gravity. I learned about Newton's Law of Gravity in my science class.

Back on the ground, Rain E and I took off! She turned to me, gasping for words. "We need to run fast enough so we can leave our troubles behind. Then and only then, can we start having a grand old time!" I like the way Rain E says things.

After the vigorous run, we both stopped, still holding hands collapsing to the ground. When we hit the ground our hands let go of each other. My hand that had been holding Rain E's hand was now toasty. So much warmth in her and now in me! I felt loved. While we were on the incredible thick grass, I took my extra warm hand and held it with my other hand. The strangest thing happened next. The moment I put my hands together, I could feel the warmth heating my entire body as though I had a humongous electric heating pad wrapped around me. There was something very unique about this new friend of mine. I wanted to know more about her.

I was exhausted from the run, but felt great inside. I looked over to Rain E to see how she was feeling. She didn't look tired at all. She looked back at me and started rolling side to side, so I joined in. I wanted to do everything Rain E was doing. We were rolling so fast we kept bumping into each other. Rain E started chanting. "Two little girls in a row, one rolled over and said "Oh No!" Two little girls back in a row, the other rolled over and said, "Time to GO!" I giggled first, then Rain E. The happiest of laughter followed. It felt good to really laugh. We said the chant again together and then again. This went on for several minutes.

Suddenly, Rain E bolted up in a seated position and shouted, "Oh my, I almost forgot! There is something special I want to show you. Something I must show you!" "Show me! Show me!" I said with excitement. We helped each other up and took off walking down a small hill. I looked all around. There was so much beauty in every direction.

On my right side was a row of Palm trees and many bushes in front of them. Rain E told me all about the plants and trees. She said the trees over to the left were pine trees. I knew those trees, but not the bushes around them. Rain E said they were a combination of sweet cane, sage and blackberry. They smelled wonderful. We slowed down, so I could take a closer look at my surroundings.

Rain E's outdoor environment was awesome! Her place seemed to be perfect. The weather was perfect, not too hot or cold, just right. There was a light breeze. The sky was a pale blue color with puffy white clouds perfectly in place. I loved being a part of it. Rain E's outdoors reminded me of happy times with Mom. I told Rain E, "I love being outside with my mom, because she lets me help her plant flowers all year long. I always stay right next her, helping dig holes. She would tell me the names of each and every one. To this day, I still remember them." Rain E commented, "Your mother sounds wonderful!" I told her, "She is!"

We kept walking down the hill. There were some magnificent oak trees straight ahead. They were gigantic! The trees reminded me of a recent discussion my science class had. I told Rain E I learned that trees were the longest living organisms on earth. Rain E nodded her head. I think she already knew this, but seemed happy to hear again.

Everything I saw was beautiful and so clean, I never saw a weed. It was very well taken care of. When we got to the bottom of the hill, I looked straight ahead and saw flowers, lots of flowers.

I let go of Rain E's hand and tore off running. I reached the flowers and immediately noticed they were all roses, red roses to be exact. Rain E caught up to me and said, "Well, how do you like my flower garden?" I answered, "I love it, but there are only red roses here." Rain E took one step back. I stepped back too and saw a huge sign hanging over the front gate. I didn't notice it when I blew right by. It read, "The Flowers of the Week Garden." I told Rain E I had never heard of such a garden, but loved it. Rain E said that it was a very special garden only to be seen by special people.

I got choked up because she thought I was special. I slowly strolled up and down looking, smelling, and gently touching the beautiful red roses. They were not in full bloom, still buds, but they were beautiful. I walked around in amazement! I caught up with Rain E and thanked her for letting me enjoy the red roses. I told Rain E it was my favorite flower. I even told her that my mom said roses are related to apples and almonds. Rain E looked straight at me, smiled and said, "Imagine that!" I smiled back. Kind of weird that she seemed to know what my favorite flower was! Maybe she would eventually tell me how she knew these things.

We stood outside the gate for a moment. Not too far away was a beautiful pond. Rain E grabbed my hand and said, "Come on!" We walked right up to the edge of it. The water was a dark blue ocean color, but clearer. There were grassy plants sticking up out of the water, gently swaying in the light breeze. The thick plush grass was all the way to the edge of the water. We stood for a few minutes, just looking across the pond. It was so peaceful.

Rain E put her hands on my shoulders and slowly turned me around. There was bright red colored bench a few feet away. We walked over and sat down. I sat on Rain E's right side. I expressed, "Sure is bright red!" Rain E stated, "Yes, red is a strong and bright color. You know, colors can represent things and even stir up emotions. Rachel, what does the color red mean to you?" I thought for a minute and said, "Blood, because of the red blood of Christ and His sacrifice. I have been learning about Christ at my church and school, but mostly from

41

my mom". Rain E contentedly smiled. She must have been pleased with my answer.

She added, "The color red can also stir up feelings deep down inside you, like anger, fiery temper and rage!" I sat there in silence just listening to how wonderful Rain E explained things, just like my mom. She was right. I shared, "The fiery red anger, reminds me of my dad! He gets red in the face when his anger comes out and that's every weekend." Rain E quietly said, "I am so sorry for what you are going through."

As we sat there talking, I started reliving the horrible insane night at the condo. Rain E was quiet. Then it just came out, "I hate being at my dad's. I hate it so much!" Rain E stayed silent. I could sense she wanted me to get it all out. Tears filled my eyes. Rain E gently touched my arm. I continued, "My dad is so mean and hateful to me. What did I do to deserve this, Rain E, what? I don't understand his mean ways, especially towards me. I dread every time I have to be with him. It breaks my mom's heart. She has gone to court so many times trying to protect me and the judges don't listen, nobody listens. I'm sorry for talking so angry, but I am and I don't understand these judges? What's wrong with them?"

I was waving my arms in every direction, spouting out angry words. I almost hit Rain E in the face, I was so angry. She stayed seated and ducked when necessary. Rain E patiently listened while I exploded! I told her how much I worried about my mom. I finally finished by dropping my head into my hands and cried.

Rain E touched my back. I could feel the heat shoot through my body. I raised my head and screamed up to Heaven, "My dad won't stop hurting me! He pinches and pokes me, all over my body. He even bites me. I mean bites me hard for no reason, leaving marks mostly on my arms. Rain E, my dad screams at me and calls me mean and ugly names. Why? No one helps me! No one helps my mom! Why doesn't anyone help us? Whyyyy?"

Rain E let me spill my guts. She WAS a great listener, better than that court-appointed man therapist I was forced to talk to. Mom listened to me, but it caused her so much pain that there were times I didn't even tell her how bad it really was. Then I told Rain E, "I hate when my dad calls me fat girl, dummy or piggy. Fat girl hurts me the most." All of a sudden, Rain E abruptly interrupted me, "You're not fat! Is he sick in the head?" I started giggling along with crying. "Yes, my dad MUST be sick in the head! Dads are supposed to make you feel good about yourself, but my dad just wants to hurt me! My mom said that he's mentally ill and needs help. I think she's right."

Rain E said, "It sounds like you have a very smart and compassionate mother." I told her, "She is smart and beautiful! I thank God everyday that she's my mom." I finished yelling. Rain E leaned towards me and softly whispered in my ear, "I know what you are going through." My eyes bugged out spooky. "How did she know what I was going through?" I curiously pondered. A moment went by. We were both quiet. There was now such a comfortable silence that a little bit of peace found its way inside me.

A few minutes later Rain E started moving her body and legs back and forth as though we were sitting on a porch swing. I joined her. Suddenly, the bench started moving back and forth, then high into the sky, swinging freely in the air. Calmness now joined my inner peace. The floating bench was helping take my mind off of my dad. The bench stayed in the air for a short while. I think it was supposed to help me feel better inside. It worked! I was feeling better. I got a lot of my bad feelings out. I thanked Rain E for listening to me.

At that precise moment, we floated back down and landed softly on the ground in the same spot. That was beyond cool! Rain E spoke, "I'm glad you now have some peace and calmness in your body." How did she know what I was feeling? Wow! What a magical and mysterious friend! We stayed seated.

I looked out over the pond and the green grassy hills. It reminded me of one of my favorite Bible verses I learned at school. Since first grade, I have been memorizing Bible verses each week. I'm glad I have learned many. Learning the Bible changes you in a very good way! I started quietly saying one to myself. Rain E heard me and asked if I could say it a little louder. She very much wanted to hear it.

I said, "Alright, it's from Psalm 23, but I just want to say my favorite part." Rain E said, "That's fine, Rachel, any word or phrase of the Bible is always worth speaking. Please share your words with me." I started reciting. "He makes me lie down in green pastures. He leads me beside still waters. He restores my soul." I abruptly stopped. Then quietly whispered to myself, "I wish He would restore my soul." I couldn't say anymore. Rain E tenderly placed her hand on top of mine and answered, "He will." How did she hear what I said to myself? I was too emotional to ask her. Somehow she knew.

Rain E spoke, "That was beautiful, just beautiful. You said it with such sincerity and conviction." Still too emotional to speak, I just nodded my head with thanks. I didn't know what sincerity and conviction meant, but I think it was a compliment. Rain E knew I was choked up. My insides felt a little better I just couldn't speak. Instead, I gently removed my hand and placed it on top of Rain E's. My palm squeezed my new friend's hand!

At that moment, I remembered my mom telling me about the word "Psalms." She said, "If you removed both 'S's from "Psalms", you would have the word "Palm". The 'S's were gone and you would be in the "Palm" of God's hand. He loves holding them, close." Rain E and I just sat there quietly.

Then, out of nowhere, a few sprinkles fell from the sky. I raised both hands over my eyes to look up. It began to fall a little more. Raindrops hit my cheeks and the tip of my nose. As I was watching, the raindrops became a light shower. I turned to Rain E to tell her we needed to find a place to stay dry. She was gone! Just like that.

A bolt of lightning covered the sky. It was loud! The lightning along with the thunder scared the 'dickens' out of me. I abruptly woke up. I was in my bed. I looked over at my window. The storm was still going strong. I stayed flat on my back and covered my ears with my pillow. I curiously started thinking, "Was I dreaming?" Was Rain E just a dream?" I tried to fall back to sleep. I wanted to go back to her. I closed my eyes tightly, trying to make myself go back to sleep. I wanted to be with Rain E not my dad. I quietly listened to the storm. I called out to Rain E. No physical answer, but I did feel peaceful inside. My left hand even felt extra warm.

It was quiet until, "Get your ass up!" It was the monster. "It's eleven, almost noon, and you've slept long enough. If I'm up, you're up too!" I quickly got up, changed into a pair of jean shorts, but kept my cat T-shirt on. I went to my closet, got my drawing pad and set on my bed. I grabbed my colored pencils from my desk and put them in my backpack. I went to the kitchen to find some breakfast.

Just before I got stuff from the pantry, my dad walked in and said he was taking me back home. He said he had to get ready for a trial that was going to be in another town. My dad was an attorney: a short, mean, cruel and very loud attorney! I was beyond thrilled. This summer visit was shortened. I do believe this WAS a miracle from above!

I hurried back to my room to get my flip-flops. I gathered up my homework and my personal stuff and shoved it in my backpack. I put my drawing pad between two schoolbooks. Dad would just think it was part of my homework. I came back out in a jiffy and said, "I'm ready." I didn't even take time to see if Martha was still there. I didn't care. I was going home!

Off we went. I threw my stuff in the backseat and then climbed in. Dad had just rolled out of the garage when I screamed, "STOP!" He slammed on his breaks and said, "What the "F"? I said, "I see one of my toys in the bushes. It must have fallen off the balcony during the storm." I got out and rushed over.

Oh my, goodness gracious! There they were! I reached in and grabbed my florescent yellow colored spy glasses. I jumped back into the car. Dad took off. Whatever he was bitching about, I wasn't listening. I couldn't believe what I found. I was holding my spy glasses! I wiped away the grit left from the storm and held on to them, tightly. Mom was wrong. The storm came before the calm. A huge grin covered my face. It wasn't a dream. Rain E was REAL!!!!!!!!

Chapter 4.5

The light shower ended. R A IN was still seated next to Rachel on the red bench only now invisible to her. R A IN touched Rachel's hand one more time. Rachel couldn't feel it. R A IN felt it. R A IN felt everything Rachel had stored inside her beaten down body. Her sorrow, her sadness, her emptiness, her tucked-away love, her frustration and her ANGER!

A bolt of lightning separated them. Rachel was gone. She made it back to her Dad's. It was heartbreaking watching her go back to so much unnecessary cruel abuse. R A IN deeply felt Rachel's pain. She prayed and patiently waited on the red bench. The sky became a crystal blue color, with the brightest sunshine. S TOR MY whispered in R A IN's right ear, "The child's crushed spirit has latched on to you. The first and crucial meeting surpassed all expectations. I must also add, miraculous, absolutely miraculous in your angelic performance!"

"Taking hold of this special child's life and guiding her on the right path will be a challenging, but rewarding job. The next visit will be soon. There will be close and distance interaction as needed." R A IN answered in spiritual thoughts, "Thank you S TOR MY. I will do everything to help this precious child. I want to restore her lost faith. Some of her needs and wants are already emotionally vocal. All the rest need to surface! I know I am up to the task. I know my strengths. Where I fall short in the "weak" department, help will ALWAYS be there. Rachel's happiness is locked away. Time to find the key."

A moment passed by. R A IN patiently waited, looking up to the Heavens in continuous prayer. The clouds opened and allowed a beam of light to appear. A huge smile covered her face. R A IN looked across the pond. All at once, the beam of light struck the pond. The light shimmered in every direction. She knew the main and final approval arrived. The job was given to her. R A IN knew the amount of work required, but wanted the opportunity. Her soul was filled with over-whelmingly joy. She knew there was no greater satisfying job on the face of the earth than helping a child discover who they are.

A child is capable of accomplishing so much if given the encouragement early on in life. R A IN nodded with grateful thanks. She stayed seated on the red bench sending messages in silence. R A IN knew she would need help from Rachel's mother. Quietly listening, she smiled. God's help would be there and not to worry. All would fall into place. Glowing with a satisfied smile, R A IN was off preparing for Rachel's next visit.

As R A IN headed to her cottage, she passed by "The Flowers of the Week Garden". There was a bright shiny gold and silver clipboard hanging on a large gold hook, near the entrance gate. It read, "The Seven Self-Help Chart". Under those words, was written in bold print, "RACHEL RENE"! There was a slender, rainbow-striped pen attached by a gold chain dangling on the right side of the clipboard. R A IN studied the notes. More loving warmth filled her heavenly body! The same heavenly warmth Rachel felt, would continue, but now with extra approval. R A IN had a lot of work ahead of her. She wanted to help Rachel and Rachel wanted her help! They would be together again soon, very soon. R A IN started brainstorming over Rachel's second and exciting visit! What unique and clever way would bring Rachel back? Hummmm???

"I remember my mother's prayers and they have always followed me. They have clung to me all my life."

Abraham Lincoln

Chapter 5

I could hardly sit still. Those reliable, now rescued spy glasses, stayed hugged around my left leg the whole way home. I couldn't take my eyes off of them. My mind wandered back to the bright light and Rain E. Wow! I met a girl with rainbow pigtails. Absolutely amazing! It was mind-boggling! What an incredible home she had. I wondered if I would see her again, maybe tonight? We would see. If not, it was wonderful meeting her. I was just thrilled to be coming home early.

My evil dad pulled into the driveway. He tried saying bye. How disgusting, after this brutal visit. I got out so fast, with all my stuff, then slammed the door. I didn't hear or care what he had to say. As I was heading to the house, I heard the tires screech. I never turned around. I just kept walking straight to my front door, with a long overdue smile covering my face. Dad was not going to see it. My new and very unique friend Rain E helped bring it back. I knew things would still be bad at my dad's, but now I have someone extra special on my side. For the first time in two years, I found some hope.

I was almost to the door, when Mom opened it. She stretched her arms out. I dropped my spy glasses, backpack, drawing pad and schoolbooks and ran to her. We hugged a long time. She kissed my forehead. I looked up at her and we smiled big at each other. Mom had an odd look on her beautiful face. She stated, "My precious Rachel, you look different." "How?" I asked. Mom continued, "I can't put my finger on it. You just seem happier." I wanted to tell her about Rain E. I just wanted to wait a while. She was my new friend. I don't want to share her, yet. I know that sounds selfish, but I can't help it. I finally had something wonderful in my life, all to myself. I know Rain E will get me through the bad times with Dad. I hope I see her again, soon.

After Mom and I hugged and hugged, I ran back and got my stuff. Mom helped me. She was so happy I returned home earlier than scheduled. I dashed upstairs with everything piled high in my arms. I dumped it all on my bed. I happily called out to Mom, "Be right down in a jiffy!" She hollered up, "You're in a good mood! Anything interesting happen this weekend you want to share with me?" "No, just happy to be home and excited about camp next week!" I yelled back. Mom added, "Let's go eat as soon as you are ready."

While I was unpacking, I started thinking about summer camp. I was so glad it fell on Mom's time. My dad told me at the beginning of the summer, if the camp fell on his time, there was no way he was going to let me go. He didn't just say "No!" He said, "Hell No!" Can you believe how mean and cruel he was, saying that to me?

I changed clothes to get rid of the awful smell of my dad's cologne. He wore so much it stunk up his car, making it smell like a perfume store. I still remember when Dad lived with us he wore so much it would stink up the house. After he left for work, Mom would have to open the windows and doors for an hour, to get the smell out. Now I had to smell it at the condo, plus in his car. It was gross!!

While I was unpacking my clothes and stuff, I noticed my spy glasses tangled up in my backpack handle. I guess it happened outside, when I dropped everything. I untangled them and sat them on top of the skirted table, right beside my bed. I wanted to remember Rain E each night, before I fell asleep. I kept my drawing pad and colored pencils near the headboard slightly under the decorated bed pillows, so I could start drawing Rain E Rainbow's home when we get back from dinner

I washed my face to get rid of the rest of the cologne smell. I gathered up the stinky clothes, headed downstairs and took them to the utility room. Mom was sitting at the kitchen desk and watching *Wheel of Fortune*. She loved that show. Her other favorite shows were *Big Bang Theory* and *Criminal Minds*. Both so different! Mom never missed an episode of either one! She even recorded them.

One time I asked Mom why she liked those two specific shows. She told me that *Criminal Minds* was not only good but it also dealt with crazy and evil people, and that intrigued her. I think it was because my dad was crazy and evil and she got information from the show on how to deal with him. She said that *Big Bang Theory* made her laugh out loud and she needed that! Most the time, Mom would watch *The*

History Channel or Hallmark. She loved watching history, especially if it was about presidents, England or real life people. *Hallmark* carried the old reruns of some of her favorite TV shows. I preferred my cartoons.

"You ready," Mom asked? I quickly answered, "Sure am! Hey, where's Grandma? Did she want to eat with us?" She stayed in her room a lot, but usually greeted me when I came home. Mom said, "She's away visiting her friend for several days." I said that was nice and that she needed to get out of the house. Mom agreed. I was glad I have some alone time with Mom, before I leave for camp.

We got in the car and headed to the restaurant. When we arrived, the hostess sat us immediately. During dinner, we talked mostly about camp. Mom told me about her first camping trip, when she was a Camp Fire Girl. She said the camp was near a prison and her friends were always making up scary stories about crazed prisoners escaping. Mom said that she went there four years in a row. I hoped I could do the same and make-up scary stories too! I should ask her if she remembered one? Camp was going to be a blast. I just felt it. Mom was excited for me. She said that camp was a "fun" first for kids to experience.

We finished dinner and headed to our car. Right when Mom and I stepped outside, we noticed the sky. "It looks like rain," Mom stated. I agreed. You could smell it in the air. Yeah! Rain was coming! Would I see Rain E again? I couldn't wait to go to sleep tonight to find out!

When we got home, I told Mom I was going to take a quick shower, before the rain showed up. I barely wet my front and back body and quickly got out. I slipped on my favorite pajamas. I could hear footsteps coming up the stairs. I quickly shoved my drawing pad and pencils under my bed. I got in bed and grabbed my pillow. Mom walked in and sat down beside me. Thunder crackled outside. Mom commented, "The sky is talking loudly tonight! Boy, I just had a flash-back of the worst storm I've ever lived through!" "Tell me! Tell me! I love your stories, ever since I was young. The scarier, the better," I shouted. Mom climbed up in the bed next to me.

She started, "I remember it like it was yesterday. I wasn't much older than you. The year was 1970. The date was May 11th. A day I have never forgotten. I got home and completed my homework. My Mom was making dinner, when Dad called. He worked for a local television station. He told her to turn the TV on. It was around 6:00

pm. He said he would be home shortly. My three brothers and I gathered in the den, with Mom. All our eyes were glued to the TV. Heavy thunderstorms were in the vicinity and within hours would become a severe storm, including baseball size hail near the airport."

"My dad walked in and said the weatherman was predicting a tornado. When you live in "Tornado Alley," you're always on alert. I still remember the look in my Dad's eyes. He was frightfully concerned! He stayed in the den, while everyone else quickly ate dinner in the kitchen. After the meal, I got up from the table and went into the den to join him. Dad was eating with one hand, while the other was holding the phone to his ear. He wanted to stay in constant contact with the TV station."

"I remember walking outside to the front yard. The sky was an eerie green, yellow, brown color. The air was silent and still. I never even heard a bird or any animal. A few minutes went by. Dad walked out. Then we heard it. From a distance, the storm sounded like a freight train. The sirens started going crazy. We ran back in. I was terrified. Dad had news of a tornado touching down near the airport. My whole family ran across the street to the neighbor's storm shelter. There were two other families already there. Inside you could hear the hail pounding on the metal door. An hour or so went by. The sirens finally went off. Everyone climbed out of the shelter and went back to their home."

"Dad heard from the station, there were reports of a second, even larger and more destructive tornado that had touched down on 19th street and traveled downtown. The reports were coming in of severe damage to downtown, the country club and the close surrounding area. He left in the car to go check it out. I got ready for bed. It was late when Dad came home. I heard him talking with my mom in their bedroom because my room was next to theirs. They were whispering loud for a long time. I knew it was about the tornado. The city would know about the destruction tomorrow, but I wanted first hand news that night."

"I walked into my parent's bedroom and asked my dad what he saw. He said that there was a large percentage of smashed glass everywhere and that the tallest downtown building was literally twisted, impossible to go in. Dad stopped for a moment and sat down on one corner of the bed. He looked up at us. It looked like he had seen a ghost. Mom asked him what he saw. Dad said, "I stood on one corner of the church we attend and saw nothing but mass destruction on

54

the other three corners. Our church was not touched. There wasn't a single broken window or tree branch laying anywhere. God HAD a hand in this."

"The next day at school one of my cheerleading friends said a pick-up truck landed in her grandmother's living room. She was blessedly lucky. She had just moved from the living room to her bedroom when the truck came through her roof. The college campus lost almost all of their trees."

"The next year a man by the name of Theodore Fujita developed a scale to measure the strength of a tornado. The higher the number, the more devastating the damage! My hometown suffered damages of a F5 tornado. To this day there have only been 5 others in the state since 1953. The next that occurred after 1970 was in 1997. I remember that one too, but only from the TV news. To this day, I have the utmost respect for ALL of nature, as do many, who have lived to tell their tragic real-life nightmares. How's that for a scary story?" I swallowed big and said, "That was good!"

After the story, we said our nightly prayer, alternating the verses. I said an extra prayer thanking God for protecting Mom when she was young! Mom kissed me on my cheek and whispered in my ear, "I'm glad your back home safe and sound." She walked out adding, "Don't stay up too late. We have to pack you for camp, tomorrow." I said, "Okay, night, love you!" I waited for Mom to turn all the lights out and walked downstairs before secretly turning on a light.

The house was quiet as a mouse, unlike Dad's. I turned on my table lamp and pulled out my drawing pad and colored pencils. It was getting so loud outside I went over to my window to check it out. I slowly lifted it, without making a sound. I took a deep breath, filling my lungs with the smell of rain, then one more. Wonderful!

The lightning lit up the sky. I counted to 15, when the thunder roared. A few minutes went by. The lightning struck again. This time, I only made it to 10. The thunder was louder than ever causing my body to jerk. The storm was getting nearer. That was how you could tell, by slowly counting. Learned it from my mom and a scary movie! I gently lowered the window, leaving it open just a crack. I wanted to listen to the storm. Hopefully I wouldn't hear any sirens go off!

I jumped back into my extremely comfortable bed and started working on my drawing. I first drew the rainbow slide because that's how I arrived at Rain E's home. Then, I drew the hill and thick grass.

Next, I started drawing Rain E and those pigtails. I looked up at the storm. It was making me sleepy. I stopped and hid everything back under my bed. I would work on it tomorrow. I yawned big and fell back onto my fluffy pillow, thinking about Mom and the tornado she lived through. I finally crashed, never being disturbed by the storm.

The next morning I woke up to rain tapping on my window. It must have rained all night. I love sleeping when it rains. I think most people do. It was nice sleeping in. All that rain last night, but no visit from Rain E. I was okay with it. I was with my mom. Everything was happy and quiet around here! Stretching across my comfy bed I heard a wonderful sound, my mom's voice. "Rachel, are you up? I made homemade biscuits". I excitedly hollered, "I'm up. Be right down!" I grabbed my robe and slippers and flew downstairs. I loved my Mom's biscuits. They were always Yummyyy!

We sat down at the table, ate and just talked, mostly about camp. Mom reminded me we had to be at the church at 5:00 am sharp. The bus had to drive three to four hours to get to the campsite. I remarked, "I can hardly wait. I bet I won't sleep much tonight." Mom replied, "I didn't either the night before my first camping trip." We finished our breakfast. Mom helped me pack early. We watched TV and relaxed all day, until it was dark. I got ready for bed. Mom came upstairs to say our nightly prayer and to tuck me in. She sat there on my bed after we prayed. Mom started stroking my hair, pushing it away from my eyes staring at me the whole time. It felt nice. I asked her if anything was wrong.

Mom paused for a few minutes, then softly said, "Rachel, do you remember when you were little and I would sing to you my version of *Hush Little Baby?* I told Mom, "I've never forgotten it. There have been times at Dad's when I felt scared and would softly sing it to myself." Mom kept looking right at my face. She had tears forming in her beautiful "cat" green eyes. I asked her why she looked so unhappy. She said, "I am so sorry honey for everything you are having to go through, at such a young age. I am so very, very sorry." I kept looking at her sad face and said, "Mom, you had to leave Dad. He would have destroyed you. He's already destroyed his own mom and now he is trying to destroy me. I will be okay, I promise you. I remembered what you told me, "Trust in The Lord." That's what I'm doing." Mom leaned over and hugged me. One of her tears fell on my cheek. I asked her if she would sing the lullaby to me tonight. I laid my head down and closed my eyes.

Mom softly began singing, "Hush little baby, don't you cry, Momma's gonna bake you a pumpkin pie. And if that pumpkin pie's too sweet, Momma's gonna buy you a frozen treat. And if that frozen treat does melt, Momma's gonna buy you a shiny belt. And if that shiny belt's too small, Momma's gonna buy you a bouncing ball. And if that bouncing ball goes flat, Momma's gonna buy you a garden hat. And if that garden hat's too big, Momma's gonna buy you a baby pig. And if that baby pig can sing, Momma's gonna buy you a diamond ring. And if that diamond ring fits well, Momma's gonna tell you "ALL IS SWELL"!" All is swell with Mom. I wished I could say the same about Dad. Those were my last thoughts before I fell asleep.

The next morning, Mom woke me up at 4:00 am. I slept better than I thought I would. I knew it was the lullaby that did the trick. I was so excited! I was going to camp with my best friend. I quickly got ready and headed downstairs with all my bags. Mom was waiting there with her camera. "Smile" she said. "Mom!" I grunted. Mom added, "I have to have a memorable photo of your first camping trip, silly."

Mom grabbed one bag and I grabbed the other. As we were going out, I hugged and kissed Sugar, sleeping on top of the den chair. We threw the bags in the backseat and drove to the church. We arrived early, so Mom drove back to a fast food restaurant. I got a yummy breakfast burrito and some orange juice. When we pulled up in the church parking lot, several kids were there, including my best friend. I rolled down my window and screamed out to her. She screamed back with excitement!

Mom parked and unloaded the bags. The youth pastor was already loading them on the bus. Mom took a photo of my best friend and me. We smiled big. Then she took another one of us smiling goofy. Mom hugged both of us. We climbed on board and went straight to the back of the bus, so we could watch everyone. She blew me a hand kiss.

After everyone was securely on the bus, we took off. I waved back at Mom one last time. I was going to have a blast! I *will* temporarily block Dad out of my mind. I knew I was going back to him as soon as I returned, but for now I would be full of happiness for three days. That was something! This was my own vacation because of Mom!!!

*"Who would ever think that so much went
on in the soul of a young girl?"*

Anne Frank

Chapter 6

I got home safe and sound from summer camp. It was a blast! A blast! A BLAST!!! I would definitely be going back next year. Sure hope it falls Mom's week! Going to church camp made up for some of the bad times at Dad's. I was so happy I got to do something just for me! I will always remember my caring mom made it happen.

Summer was almost over. I had only one more long 'forced' visit with my dad, before school started. Thanks a lot judge! I wondered how many other kid's lives you ruined? As far as I was concerned, you were a horrible judge. I never knew exactly what went on in court. I just knew I was the one suffering!

It was two days before I had to go back to Mr. Evil. I rested, watched TV and played on the computer. I was trying to keep my mind on other things. Every time I have to go with my dad, I had to emotionally prepare myself, even if it was only for a weekend. The summer time was the hardest.

The dreaded start of the final two weeks required summer visit had arrived. I changed into the clothes I only wear to Dad's. They are my long jeans and a long sleeve T- shirt. I was always afraid of being hit. If he struck my body, I would be able to hide the bruises under my clothes. I would definitely keep them covered up until healed! This way Mom wouldn't see them! I didn't want to add to her worries and sadness. I worried about her as much as she worried about me. Mom stayed upset with everything bad my dad did to me. I would feel the same if it my child being hurt.

I brushed my hair, grabbed my backpack and headed downstairs. I had only an hour or so before my dad would be rudely honking his horn. Mom was sitting at the kitchen table, so I joined her. She had that worried look on her face again, so I started telling her more funny camp stories. We laughed and laughed. She was so happy I got to go to camp with my best friend.

While we were sitting, I heard the Grandfather clock start chiming. "Hey Mom, the chime sounds different." I asked. Mom said, "I changed it this morning." We got up and walked over to the clock, gracefully standing in the living room. Mom opened a small panel on the left side. I got a small stool to stand on. Now I could really see inside this grand clock. "Hey, this IS a grand old clock. Maybe that's why they call it a "Grandfather" clock," I remarked. Mom said, "Actually the name "Grandfather" evolved around a spooky story." "Tell me!" I nicely begged. "I love scary and spooky stories, especially if they are true!"

Mom first told me to watch inside the clock, to see it chime. There was a funny looking key in a compartment. Mom explained that it was used to keep the clock running, by winding it up. She told me to look at the front of the clock. I got off my stool and saw the long hand was past the two, almost to the three. Mom told me that it would chime on the three, then on the six, and then again on the nine and finish up the twelve. It chimed every fifteen minutes. I never realized that. You learn something new every day. She said that it chimed a little bit longer each fifteen minutes and completed the entire chime when the hand reached the twelve. I asked if I could change the chime to a new song, when I came back from Dad's. Mom grinned at me and said, "Of course you can!"

We moved to the sofa and waited for the long hand to get to the six. Mom started the spooky clock story. "A long time ago in the mid to late 1800's in North Yorkshire, England, lived two brothers by the name of Jenkins. They managed The George Hotel. A floor clock stood in the lobby. It kept perfect time. The townspeople even set their watches and clocks according to the precise time of this amazing clock."

"Then one day, the first of the two Jenkins brothers died. The townspeople noticed the clock lost a few minutes a day. Then it began to lose up to an hour a day. When the remaining brother died at the ripe old age of 90, the clock stopped all together. Many tried to repair it. The new manager, of the hotel decided to not work on the clock anymore. It was meant to remain on the exact time of the second brother's death."

"Word spread of this spooky phenomenon. An American song-writer by the name of Henry Clay Work visited The George Hotel. He heard all about the clock from the locals and composed the song "*My Grandfather's Clock*" based on their stories." "Wow! That *"WAS"* spooky! Is the clock still there? Maybe we could go see it?" I asked? "That would be cool!" Mom said, "I'm sure it is. I'll read more on it and let you know. I have a friend who lives in London. Maybe we'll visit her soon."

I looked up at the clock again. It had struck the six during Mom's story and I didn't even realize it. While watching, it struck the nine! I knew the long hand was the minute hand and the shorter hand was the hour hand. I learned how to tell time when I was in first grade and again in second. The teacher never mentioned the chimes. I guess 'cause not all clocks had them. Now I knew!

While waiting for the clock to strike twelve, I started daydreaming how wonderful it would be if I could stop the time on the clock, and not have to go with my dad. I knew that was impossible, still it was nice to think about. The clock finally struck the twelve. I was getting fidgety, still sitting by Mom. She could see the nervousness in me. My wonderful mom leaned up against me and quietly spoke, "Rachel, it seems like I never know what to say to you anymore. I just want you to try to be strong and to let you know I love you more than any other person. You are my child, but more importantly you are God's child. He IS watching over you. I know that's hard for you to believe at times, with everything happening to you. All I can say is to not give up on God."

Sometimes it was hard for me to believe, because my dad treats me so badly. I asked Mom, "Why is God allowing this to happen to me? Why? What did I do to deserve this?" Mom quietly said, "Honestly, I don't know the answer to that question. All I know is God allows bad things to happen in our lives. He wants us remember who is in control. He is testing our faith. He wants us to lean on Him. I believe God will never allow more to happen to you that He cannot help you get out of."

It was sort of peaceful listening to Mom's reassuring words. She added one more important reminder, "Just remember Rachel, we are on God's time, He is not on ours." That word "time"! Mom and I just finished talking about it. Right now in my life "time" was an ugly word. I had to spend "time" with a person who hurt me. "Time" drug on at Dad's and flew by with Mom. I would have to wait until a lot of "time" passed before I was old enough to make my own decisions.

I hugged Mom and whispered in her ear, "I'll always remember everything you say to me, even when I'm grown up. You are the best!" Mom held both of my hands together. She leaned over and kissed them for a long time. After the kiss she raised herself up and smiled at me. My hands were wet from her tears. I didn't mind. Mom was a part of me.

It was now after six. Dad was late. That was a first! We stayed seated, just waiting, when all a sudden, the thunder and lightning exploded outside. Mom and I both jerked and bumped each other at the same time. She said that the news had predicted rain. The lightning crackled again, this time even louder. I got up and quickly ran out to the back porch. I looked up and saw the black clouds approaching. It WAS a storm, a thunderstorm. I was so excited. All I could think about was Rain E. No matter how bad it would be at Dad's, hopefully Rain E would be nearby.

I turned back to Mom, now sitting at the kitchen table. She had turned on the small TV. I commented, "Yeah, looks like a terrific storm." Mom remarked, "I thought you didn't like storms. The storm is terrific? That's an odd way to describe it, silly." I proudly announced, "They don't bother me as much anymore. Actually, their kind of pretty with all the different colors mixed in the clouds. Mom, quick! Come look at the sky." Mom walked out and stood by me. We could both see the storm right in front of us. She said, "I love storms. You know, rain is my favorite weather." I said, "Rain E, I mean rain is now my favorite weather!" Boy that was a slip of the tongue! Mom didn't notice, or did she?

We came in and moved to the stairs. We said our prayers. It was now 6:15 pm. I asked when Grandma was coming home. Mom said that it would be this coming Sunday. I wished I had seen her before going back to Dad's. I told Mom to give her a big hug and kiss for me. I picked up Sugar, laying behind us and hugged her hard. I kissed her head over and over, before letting go. I looked at Mom. She was trying to look brave for me, but I knew deep down inside she felt helpless. Her eyes were sad looking.

Here came *the honks*. If I didn't open the door within seconds, my dad would continue honking one right after another, until I reached the car. So rude! I held on to Mom's hand all the way out the front door. I didn't want to let go, but had to. We said our goodbyes. About halfway to the car, I turned and sign language "I Love You". Mom signed back, then hollered, "Don't forgot your guardian angel is watching over you!" I gasped! That was insightfully creepy. Maybe she did hear me say Rain E? I got in the back seat. I kept waving until I was out of sight.

Dad turned a corner and abruptly stopped the car. Here came his hand, "Give it to me Missy," Mr. Evil growled. I promptly pulled my phone out of my pocket, and slammed it into his evil hand. I kept my mouth shut. Dad took off. I turned away and pressed my face up against the glass window. I watched the storm follow us, as though it had legs. I tried keeping happy thoughts inside me.

Rain was coming. Rain and Rain E, what a wonderful pair! "Oh God, I do hope I get to see her again," I whispered to myself. Dad stayed pretty quiet, which was weird and very suspicious. The surprisingly quiet was nice though. I know it never lasted but I cherished every peaceful moment that came my way. I thought about what Mom said about my guardian angel watching over me. I wonder what she knew? Moms knew everything!

We pulled into the garage and parked. Mr. Evil and I headed to the garage elevator. I never said a word. My dad tried to make a little conversation. I ignored him. I thought for sure he would start yelling at me, asking what the "F" was wrong. He didn't say another word. The elevator door opened and we rode up to the fifth floor, in complete silence. Out we came and quietly walked to his condo, only a few feet away. Mr. Evil knocked on the door. His mother immediately opened it, like the doorman in the lobby. She was already there doing her chores. As usual, she babied talked me. I said, "Hi." and headed straight to my room.

As I was walking down the short hallway, I heard Martha ask her evil son if everything was okay. I slowed down. He snapped back, "Yeah, the "F n" brat was quiet the whole time we were driving. Maybe she learned her lesson the last time she was here and now knows how to behave." Then there was silence. I stood by my door, waiting to see if Martha would defend me for her son calling me an "F" n brat. She said nothing. I wanted to barf. I went into my room and never looked back. I closed the door behind me, but could still hear the yelling. My crazy dad was losing it, over me being quiet in the car. My insides started getting nervous. I just wanted him to stop yelling.

Mr. Evil continued hammering away at his mother. I carefully cracked open the door. I stood there and clearly heard him tell Martha, "I've just about broken her in like you, as long as I can get that "B" mother out of the picture. You females are only good for one thing, to serve *me*, and Martha you can't even do that right. I'm gonna have to find a younger maid to replace your sorry ass. Now get busy cleaning, I have work to do on my computer. I want this place spotless."

I peeked out and saw my dad briskly walked to the study. When he reached the door, I saw him slightly turn his head and yell out, "Then you can fix dinner for your "F" n granddaughter. I don't want to hear a word come out of your mouth. You got that, you worthless piece of "S". You are the reason my two brothers are dead, and don't you ever forget that! I blame you and no one else!! You have been the sorriest excuse for a mother." Martha didn't even respond.

Finally, he closed the office door. I started thinking about the stuff Dad said. Was he really going to kill my mom? What was all that screaming about his brothers? Did Martha kill her other two sons? I wondered if Mom knows about this? I would most certainly asking her about this, when I get home. I had to tell her Mr. Evil wanted her dead. I immediately prayed to God, "Protect my mom and me. God, I want to live with my mom, just my mom, but no one will help me get away from my evil dad. I hope those judges and therapist rot in hell. Forgive me God for thinking such a horrible thing. I know it's wrong to feel this way, but it's just as wrong to not help a child in need."

I knew something was seriously wrong with my dad. Normal, decent people didn't act like this. How did Mom stay with Dad for so long? I could now see why she finally kicked him out. Dad WAS destroying her. Her life was better, just having him out of the house. If I could just get away, my life would be ten, a hundred, a thousand, a million times better.

I was laying on my bed daydreaming about my last visit with Rain E, when I heard a soft knock at my door. Martha quietly asked if I was hungry. Before I could answer, she said she brought over a cooked chicken and rice. Cooked chicken! Yuk! That was all she ever had for a meal. I was hungry. It was better than starving, but not by much. I hollered that I would be there shortly. I rested another 5 minutes or so still thinking about Rain E. She was real I just felt it! I rolled out bed and went to the kitchen. I saw Martha in the den, dusting. She said my dinner was in the microwave. I thanked her and walked into the spotless, hospital-looking kitchen.

I carefully lifted my dinner out of the microwave, grabbed a fork and went directly over to the sink. The first bite went into my mouth. A couple of more and I stopped. It was awful. I mean something awful! I spit out what was still in my mouth. I cleaned up my small mess and put away the dishes. I wiped down everything, including inside the microwave. I neatly folded the dish towel, straightening all the edges. It had to be *perfect*. I hung it back on the designated hook, straightening it once more. I secretly grabbed an apple to save for later.

Many times I snuck food to my room to enjoy when Dad was asleep and couldn't bother me. I always would put the leftovers in my backpack, and clean it out when I get home. One time, Mom was pulling out my lunch containers. She saw rotten food and asked why it was there. I told her the reason. She just looked at me and said that she was so sorry for what I was going through.

I was leaving the kitchen, when Dad walked in. I stayed quiet and headed to my room, with the apple under my shirt. That was a close call! He almost caught me carrying *his* food out of *his* kitchen. I was in the hallway, when I heard screaming. I thought, "NOW WHAT!" I hurried on to my room. I stayed right up against my door to hear everything. I nervously cracked it open, just enough for one eye to watch, in case Mr. Evil came after me. He was definitely in another one of his rages. I *had* to secretly watch his every move.

While spying I heard "Martha, get your ass to the kitchen, NOW!!!" From the corner of my eye, I saw Martha quickly rush by. She was hauling it fast! The condo was small and Dad's loud voice carried. He has had several complaints from neighbors. Go figure! The moment Martha reached the kitchen door, my dad's violent screams got louder. I already had some idea of what this fight was going to be about, the "Chicken Dinner".

In her soft, pathetic voice, Dad's mother asked her precious son, "What's the matter?" Boy, I had seen that ugly, scary look many, many times. Here it came. Dad screamed, "This is disgusting! You have got to be the world's worst cook. Why don't you buy a cookbook, if you can even read? Martha if you had a brain you'd be dangerous." That's my Dad's famous line! What did that even mean? Was my mean dad saying that everyone who had a brain was dangerous?

Martha apologized and said she was sorry he didn't like her cooking. She apologized, not my dad! I have never understood, to this day, why she lets her only living son treat her so badly. The hateful things he says to her. I think my dad enjoys hurting people and making them feel bad, because it makes him feel good. I would never say such degrading words to my mom. I knew it was disrespectful to say bad things to your parent or parents. My evil dad was the one who was disrespectful, to his parent. Maybe if *my* dad *didn't* have a brain, he wouldn't be dangerous. Just a thought!

Mr. Evil continued screaming at the top of his lungs, until he couldn't speak anymore. The monster was losing his voice. Ha! Ha! Too bad! I saw him walk out of the kitchen and head straight to his bedroom. He went in and slammed the door, hard. I didn't move. I kept waiting for him to come out. About ten minutes passed, then he did. I wasn't sure where Martha was. I couldn't see her anymore, and wasn't about to open my door. Dad walked to the kitchen and screamed, "Hey, dumb ass, I'm going to steam, you watch the kid, if you think you can handle that." He stormed out, slamming the front door behind him. He would be gone for at least a few hours. Finally, peace and quiet!

I went back into the kitchen to eat my hidden apple. I leaned over the sink, ate every bit of it then wrapped up the core in a paper towel to put in my backpack. I took my shirtsleeve and wiped the sink dry. There wasn't much water, and I didn't want to use the dish towel. It takes too long to fold it to suit my dad. My sleeve and shorts were just a little wet.

Martha walked in and said, "I'm sorry you had to hear all that." All I could say to her was, "I'm used to it. You should be too. You caused it. You never made your son behave when he was young. Now it's too late!! He'll never change. You created a monster, a monster born on Halloween." The look on Martha's face said it all. She knew I was right. She was the reason for his bad behavior. I passed by her and headed back to my room. I stopped at the doorway, turned around and stated, "I'm going finish my book for school. Reading helps take my mind off being here at the "Damn Evil Tower". That's what I have named your son's condo." She stood there in shock. I didn't care. It was how I felt! So here at the "Damn Evil Tower", lived Mr. Evil and sometimes ME! HELP!!!!!!

I closed the door behind me, took the wrapped apple core out and placed it in the front of my backpack. I put some pencils on top and zipped it up for safekeeping. I went into the bathroom, got out my blow dryer and dried my wet sleeves and the front of my jean shorts. I took extra special care of this specific long-sleeved T-shirt, because it was from my very first summer camp trip. It was army green with orange letters across the front, spelling out the camp's name. It would always be one of my favorite T-shirts, thanks to my mom for letting me go.

After getting my clothes dry, I pulled out my required reading book. We have to read two books this summer, before the start of school. I was allowed to choose one from a reading list. I chose "Treasure Island", with Mom's help. I have only a fewChapters left to read. It was very good and very adventurous. Mom knew I would like it. I scrunched up my two pillows, grabbed my kitty stuffed animal and I was just about ready to relax on my bed, when I heard loud thunder outside. I rushed out onto the balcony. You could smell the rain in the air. Storms had their own unique smell, and I thought it was a wonderful smell. The thunder started roaring even louder. I saw a bolt of lightning with long monster-looking fingers dip down from the sky. It was eerie, yet familiar sight to see. Rain E first appeared in a similar, scary storm. I watched the sky hoping to see her again. Several minutes passed. No Rain E!

I went back in and climbed on top of my bed where "Treasure Island" was waiting for me. I needed to finish it tonight, because I still had more summer homework. It was almost 9:00 pm when my reading was completed. I was about to get up, when I heard the front door open. "HE" was back! I quickly turned off my lamp and got under my comforter. I was perfectly still, pretending to be asleep, in hopes that he would leave me alone. I held my stuffed kitty close under my chin.

Loud talking was coming from the den area, I think. Dad was saying something to Martha I just couldn't make it out. I was sure it wasn't nice. Maybe he was going to leave me alone? A light went on, probably in the kitchen. Dad always got a bottle of water to take to his bedroom at night. Some time went by. The light went out. I closed my eyes. "Please God, pretty please, don't let him come in my room," I kept praying over and over.

Then all of a sudden he burst in screaming, "Get your lazy ass up this minute." I flew out of bed. I was scared. I stood there asking him what was wrong. He demanded, "Come with me missy." I followed

67

close behind. "This!" He screamed. I ask, "What"? My dad screamed again, even louder, "THIS"! "You left my "GD" dish towel on the floor! How many times have I told you before you leave *MY* kitchen it better be "D" "F" n spotless!" Trembling with fear, my shaky voice spoke, "I didn't leave it on the floor, I promise. "He yelled back, "Well I sure the "F" didn't. I've been at the spa, remember dummy." I kept telling the monster over and over that I didn't do it. He wouldn't believe me. I saw it in his evil eyes.

Dad's mom came flying into the kitchen. He turned to her and said that I left *his* kitchen in a mess! In a mess! The dish towel was on the spotless, sanitary floor. Martha timidly spoke, "Oh, I must have accidentally knocked it off when I carried the mop to your bathroom." My dad started screaming at her to quit covering up for my lying ass. She kept trying to get a word in. It wasn't going to happen. You can never talk over my dad, when he's in one of his rages. This was a 'doozy', one of the worst I had ever seen! He kept calling us liars. I tried holding back the tears, but it was too much to bear. Absolutely insane madness!

I pleaded and pleaded with my dad, "I promise, I didn't leave it on the floor, I promise." He wasn't even hearing me. I noticed in the corner a bucket of soapy water. There was an extra large yellow sponge lying right by it. My evil dad saw me looking at it, and hoarsely growled, "I knew you wouldn't tell me the truth about the dish towel, so you will scrubbed this floor until it shines, you got that missy!" All I timidly could say was, "Yes."

So, I immediately got down on my hands and knees and started scrubbing. Martha tried one more time to explain. She surprisingly was trying to stand up to her son. This was a first. I think she just felt sorry for me. The minute Martha opened her mouth, Dad told her to shut the Hell up. She didn't dare say another word. I guess she tried. I slightly tilted my head to the left and watched Martha and Mr. Evil leave the kitchen. Martha, I'm sure, went back to Dad's bedroom to finish her chores and Mr. Evil, to his office to play on his computer. Honestly, from the bottom of my heart, they both made me sick, but for different reasons.

I scrubbed away for two hours. My hands were hurting. My knees were scraped up pretty bad. I bumped into the cabinets a couple of times. I knew bruises would be showing up! I backed into the corner of the wood panel next to the refrigerator. That one hurt! I felt like

Cinderella. Only one difference, I had a wicked Dad instead of a wicked stepmother.

I finally finished the absurd chore. I dumped the barely dirty water into the kitchen sink and wiped it out until completely dry. Next, I dried the countertops and all the wood on the cabinets closest to the floor. I neatly folded the "dish towel", still sitting on the counter and hung it back in place. I put the bucket and sponge back in the kitchen closet, turned off the lights and walked out. This maddening night would permanently remain in my brain!

I painfully tiptoed down to the office. Mr. Insane was facing the computer. "I finished scrubbing the floor," I quietly spoke. He never turned around. He just said in a very hoarse voice, "Get your ass to bed before I get my belt out." I hurried sore body to my bedroom as fast as I could. My door hadn't completely closed, when tears showed up. I looked down at my favorite T-shirt and cried some more. It was filthy, soaking wet. I pulled it over my head and got out of my wet jean shorts. My underwear was even wet. I took a quick shower and then collapsed into bed. I didn't even brush my teeth or hair. I was wiped out. All I wanted to do was sleep and dream about Rain E.

I lay there looking up at my ceiling, listening to the rain. I had forgotten all about the thunderstorm. It was relaxing me. For some strange reason, I started thinking about my grandfather clock at home and wishing time would fly by fast! I wanted out of here. I was getting sleepy. Barely moving my lips, I breathed out the words "Rain E, my dear Rain E, are you nearby? Please help me get through this nightmare visit. My dad is getting meaner and meaner. I thought I was getting over being scared of him. I thought wrong!" I slowly rolled over on my left side to watch the storm. Tears filled my eyes then ended up on my pillowcase. I fell asleep on top of them.

*"Faith is taking the first step even
when you don't see the whole staircase."*

Martin Luther King, Jr.

Chapter 7

I woke up in the middle of the night, having to go to the bathroom. I hated when that happened. I thought maybe I could just hold it, but then I remembered my mom telling me to never do that. She said it wasn't good for the kidneys. Moms are always right! So, I rubbed my eyes and lifted my sore, aching body up to a standing position.

The carpet felt extra soft. It was much thicker than usual. I scooted my feet around. It felt wonderful. As I was looking down thinking I was standing on a rug, I noticed I had on my colorful pajama short set. When did I do that? My tired body made it to the bathroom. I washed my hands and headed back to bed. Carefully walking not to injure myself, I opened my eyes a little more and looked straight ahead.

Standing right smack in front of me was a humongous door. Slowly looking up, I leaned my head so far back, I almost tipped over. Wow! I was staring at a very tall building in the shape of a grandfather clock. Where was I? Was I dreaming? What was going on? Then I heard her. "I'm up here Rachel. You have to come to me," Rain E yelled down. I yelled up, "How?" Rain E loudly answered, "Go through the door and climb the stairs. I'm waiting at the top. I have been eagerly awaiting your arrival, so hurry as fast as your sore legs can go." I eagerly yelled back, "Okay, I'll be right up."

I stared directly at the huge door. It was going to take both hands to turn the extra large doorknob. I placed my hands on each side and grunted as I turned the knob to the left. To my surprise, it was easy. The door opened almost by itself. I stepped inside the clock. I couldn't believe it. I was standing inside a clock. This was definitely a first! I looked up and saw hundreds, maybe thousands of steps. Wow! This was going to take some time to reach the top. I held on to the rail and off I went.

I started out slow, then climbing a little faster. Within seconds, I was flying up the steps. Rain E called out again to hurry because there was no time to waste. I wondered what I would be doing this visit? It didn't really matter because I was with Rain E and away from my dad. There were so many steps. I stopped a couple of times to rest my *sore* legs! I could finally see the top. I took off running even faster than before. It didn't matter how bad I hurt. I could hardly wait to see Rain E again. How did Rain E know I had sore legs? Strange!

I was huffing and puffing with each step. I was climbing so fast that I realized I went too far. I was in such a hurry that I flew right past the exit door, on the left. So I turned back around. I was about to take my first step, when I lost my balance. I instantly grabbed the rail. The stairs had disappeared. I screamed out, "The stairs are gone! Rain E, THE STAIRS ARE GONE!!! What do I do? Rain E, are you there? Tell me what to do! What happened to the stairs?" Rain E yelled, "Rachel, you need to get out of the building clock!" "No kidding," I abruptly yelled back. I didn't mean to sound so sarcastic. I was just panicking. I screamed out again, "I'm trapped! I want to get out of this clock." "Rachel you can find the way out, I'm sure of it. You can do it!" Rain E called out with such confidence.

I looked up to God and prayed, "Thank you God for letting me see Rain E again. Now, *help* me get out of here! God, the closer I am to Rain E, the farther I am away from my dad. Please help me find a way out!" At that precise moment, I heard Rain E holler, "Rachel check all around you, there is a way out!"

I twisted my body to the left and saw a funny shaped latch about a foot away. The latch was on top of an opening in the shape of a rainbow. There was only one problem. I was going to have to lean across some boards in order to get to it. Even on my tiptoes, I would barely be able to reach it, without taking my feet off the *soon to be* disappearing step. I was in a pickle! I kept positive thoughts. I kept telling myself that I could do this. I came this far and cannot go backwards, so I had to go forward. All I had to do was keep at least one strong foot balanced on the step. I learned how strong feet were from my mom. She told me the feet have one fourth of all the bones in the body. This was a time I needed all those strong bones working diligently together, extra hard!

So, I balanced myself on my toes and stretched my arms to grab the latch. Got it! It easily opened. I stood there on both feet, staring at the hole. I was nervous and too scared to move. I started thinking I might not be able to do this. Then, I remembered one of my favorite Bible verses I memorized last year (Philippians 4:13). It says, "I can do all things through Christ which strengthens me". I took a deep breath and tilted my body towards the hole. My heels were now completely off the ground. I leaned in closer on my tiptoes. Still, the only way I could see out the opening was by lifting my left foot off the step, and keeping my big right toe still touching for safety. I had no other option.

Taking a deep breath, I lifted my left foot. My head was now sticking through the opening. My big right toe was still touching the step, but just barely. I could vaguely see the ground. I heard Rain E, "Rachel, I can see you! You are almost out of the clock." I grabbed the opening with both hands and lifted my body completely off the last step. I looked back through a small hole in the wall and sure enough the step was gone. I was now dangling, with my head outside the clock and the rest of me, inside the clock. I kept quietly chanting, "I can do this, I can do this, I can do this."

I pulled half of my body through the opening. I could see Rain E below. She yelled up, "Rachel, pull your body all the way through and balance yourself on the minute hand, right after it strikes on the three." I yelled down, "Okay." I only had to wait a couple of more minutes. It was already past the two. I held on tight. It finally struck on the three. I pulled the rest of my body all the way through the opening and lowered it down, until I was firmly sitting on the hand. I couldn't believe it. I was sitting outside on an enormous clock. Pretty cool! I looked down and all around and saw Rain E looking up. I kept a steady balance. I could see her proudly smiling at me. I was proudly smiling too!

Rain E hollered, "As soon as the hand is near the six, you will be close enough to the ground, to jump off." I sat patiently on the clock hand staying as still as possible. Each time the hand moved another minute I had to hang on a little tighter, because I was at an angle. I was almost to the five. It wouldn't be much longer. The minute hand moved again. I kept a tight grip. I patiently waited, counting to sixty seconds. The hand was now on the five. I had one more minute before the hand moved again. I was finally close enough to jump.

I slowly pulled both legs up into a squatted position. Carefully balancing, I cautiously lifted myself up. I was now standing on the minute hand, of the biggest clock I have ever seen. I could clearly see Rain E nearby. I counted 1 2 3 and let go. I hit the ground landing on my butt. "Ouch!" Thank goodness I landed on the thick plush grass. It only hurt a little, well, a little more than a little. I stood up. Rain E was about twenty feet right in front of me. I smiled at her and she smiled back saying, "You're finally back. Boy have I missed you kid." Like I said before, I love the way Rain E talks.

"Stay there Rachel, I'm going to cartwheel to you." I said, "Okay, ready when you are." As I stood there watching Rain E prepare to do her cartwheel. I couldn't help but notice how comfortable and cool looking she was dressed. She was wearing the most beautiful white blouse with big puffy short sleeves that looked just like clouds. Short sleeves showing her sparkling arms. At that moment, I sadly remembered the many times I have had to wear long sleeves to cover up my bruises, bites and scars caused by my abusive dad. I felt so ashamed. I quickly turned my attention to her shorts. I loved them! They were a crystal blue ocean color. She had on the coolest looking dark brown, gladiator sandals. I looked down. I forgot I was barefooted. Oh well!

My eyes focused on Rain E's face. She laughed out, "Here I come, ready or not!" Then unexpectedly, she kicked off her sandals, one at a time. I watched the left one fly high in the sky, then the right. They both went up into the clouds. I kept watching for the sandals. They never came back down. I began to realize this was a magical place, full of surprises. Rain E was magical and most definitely full of surprises.

Now barefooted, Rain E stood perfectly still. She smiled at me then took off. Her arms hit the ground, at the same time. Her legs came straight up and over her head, then finishing the most perfectly, straight cartwheel I have ever seen. She even seemed to be moving in slow motion, like they do in movies. Rain E came all the way around, landing right in front of me with both arms straight out. She grinned and glanced at the sky and back at me. I looked up and out of the sky came her sandals. I watched them gently land in the palm of her left hand. Rain E glanced up again. I looked up. Next, my eyes now wide open, saw another pair fall. These sandals landed in her right hand. I looked at Rain E. She smiled big. The extra pair was for me.

Holding both pairs of sandals, Rain E gave me a great big hug. She pulled back and saw the tears forming in my eyes and asked, "Has that dad of yours been treating you badly?" I was in shock! How did she know to ask me that? Did Rain E know about the dish towel? Maybe she figured something happened because of my sad face. Whatever Rain E knew, she never mentioned it. I didn't want to talk about, either. We finally connected. I was with my Rain E again.

She had a concerned look on her face and I knew why. I was wearing a nervous, guilty look on mine. Rain E kept patiently waiting, without words. I finally blurted out, "Rain E, I did something bad!" "What could you possibly do that was bad?" Rain E asked. "This is bad! I am deeply ashamed of myself. When I was trapped inside the clock, I screamed at God to help me. It just came out. I was scared and frustrated. Do you think He's mad at me?"

"Goodness me, my precious friend. Don't you know God is a rock," Rain E firmly stated. "He's like that wood headboard on your bed, strong and solid. When you cried out for help, He totally understood your motive. Rachel, God knows what's in your heart. You called on Him and that's all that mattered. I promise you're not the first Christian who has yelled at God. Cry and scream all you want. You are one of His children. God not only wants to hear from you, He can take it! He wants to be your headboard. So bang that frustration right out of you it. Your headboard, so to speak, will always be stronger than you." Do you understand what I'm saying to you Rachel?"

I bit my bottom lip and thought for a moment. "Sounds like God is with me all the time, even when I'm sleeping." Rain E giggled and said, "You are a special and delightful child, such a joy to be with. You make me smile. Always remember God wants you to call on Him. If it sometimes comes out loud, that's okay. He will absorb it!"

"Rachel, you became angry with God, through prayer. Your faith is definitely present! Uncertain times teach you how to move closer to God and God closer to you. God was teaching you something when you were in the clock. You were in the dark. You were trapped and very scared, and yet you still prayed for help, to the one who could help you. That's Everything!! Look around Rachel. You are now out of the darkness. There will be more dark times, but you know "Who" to call on. So do!"

I listened to everything Rain E said to me. She sure knew how to make me feel better. My eyes stared at her beautiful face. Rain E looked very contented. Not me! Confusing and curious thoughts entered my head. How did she know my headboard was made of wood? How did she know how God felt? How did she know I was scared? How did she know about my sore legs? I was studying Rain E's face for any kind of clue. I kept all this inside me, never uttering a word. Rain E spoke again, "Rachel, I love your curious mind. You're something else!" My eyebrows shot up. I think she was listening to my thoughts.

We plopped down on the thick green grass. While thanking Rain E for the footwear, I slipped on my magical sandals. I gratefully said, "They fit perfect!" Rain E smiled and said, "Imagine that!" I smiled too and said, "Imagine that! We just giggled. As we were getting up, I got a closer look at her white blouse. There were imprints of tiny white clouds all over the front. On top of each cloud was a sort of streak of light. It glimmered. What a different, but beautiful blouse! Boy, I wished I had one like it! I told Rain E how much I loved her blouse. She grinned from ear to ear.

I was staring at her face and clothes when she mysteriously announced, "Before we start having a grand old time, I need to do something very important. I almost forgot!" Rain E passed by me. I watched her briskly walk over to the face of the clock. She stopped and looked up at the hands. Then she turned to the left and around the side of the clock building. While Rain E was gone, I looked up at the clock. It was 12:27 am. That was freaky! The clock was still on the exact time, when I jumped off. A few minutes later, Rain E returned and shouted, "Okay it's now "No Time, Play Time"!

We took off walking up a medium size hill. Rain E firmly grabbed my hand. We started skipping. It didn't seem to bother my legs. They actually felt warm, like they were healing. Weird! I was full of such energy. I even started laughing and laughing. I couldn't stop. Skipping and laughing; two fun things I used to do in the past. It felt great bringing them back to the present.

Present is a wonderful word, with different meanings. Of course the obvious one is a 'gift'. The other one means 'today' or 'at the moment'. The last meaning reminded me of something Mom read to me. To this day, I have never forgotten it. It goes, "Yesterday is history, tomorrow is a mystery, today is God's gift, that's why we call it the present." A very clever saying! According to Mom, it was a famous quote by a man named Bill Keane. He drew cartoons for a living. What a neat job to have!

We were swinging our arms back and forth, skipping all the way to the top. Breathing became much harder while skipping. I was just about out of breath! Rain E admitted loudly, "This is most certainly a challenging task. I'm up to it. Are you my best bud?" She called me her best bud. Wow! Huffing and puffing some, but enjoying every minute, I answered, "I love doing anything with my best bud." At last, we made it! We conquered the hill! Going up, I noticed lots of new trees and bushes I didn't remember seeing on my first visit. This place was something else. Spectacular came to mind and of course amazing! Rain E's home WAS absolutely amazing!

Now standing on a flattened part of the hilltop, we decided to take a rest on the comfy grass. I leaned back on my elbows. Rain E did the same. She proclaimed, "I forgot to tell you I love what you are wearing. It looks so comfortable. I like the colorful pattern." I answered, "Thanks, it's called a psychedelic pattern from the 60's." Rain E touched the fabric, then the large bruise on my arm and leg. She reached for my scratched-up right hand and held it for a brief moment, gently caressing it. I saw such caring-concerned look in her compassionate eyes. She softly smiled at me, without saying a word. She knew what happened. I barely cracked a smile then looked away.

As we were relaxing, my eyes wandered in every direction. I was looking to my right when I asked what plants were near us. Rain E eagerly said, "Those closest to us are called Hyssop, also known as Ezov." I quickly interrupted, "Like in the Bible. I learned all about Hyssop, at school. Moses used Hyssop to sprinkle lamb's blood over both sides of the doorframe, so the angel of death would pass by (Exodus 12:22). I like that story. What's that by the Hyssop?" Rain E continued, "Those are Box Thorns. They are very thorny, hence the name. Behind them is a Chestnut tree."

"See over to your back right, off by itself, that is an Olive tree. You can always tell because it is short and squatty and has a very twisted trunk." I politely interrupted again. "I also know lots about the Olive tree from my Bible class. The "Mount of Olives" is mentioned in the New Testament. Olive roves once covered its slopes. It's near the city of Jerusalem. Jesus often sat there with his disciples telling about events yet to come. He was praying when the men came and arrested Him. Jesus ascended to Heaven from the "Mount of Olives" (Acts 1:9-12). That's a very important place, as far as I'm concerned. I also love black and green olives, so does my mom."

"Hey what's that tree on the other side of the Hyssop?" Rain E said, "That is a fig tree." I commented, "I've never seen one in person. I love figs too." Rain E continued, "The fig has been around a very long time. It was one of the first plants ever cultivated by humans." I remarked, "Wow, I didn't know that. Makes sense! Figs are mentioned in the Bible. Last year at school, I learned about Jesus cursing a fig tree. He was hungry and the tree had only leaves on it, not fruit. He got mad and after he cursed it, the tree withered." Matthew (21:19)

"Speaking of trees," Rain E shared, "Those magnificent species and the prophets of the Bible share an important characteristic; both are planted for the future. An example is Isaiah. He was to speak and write what God told him to and eventually some people would listen." Rain E was so smart, almost as smart as my mom. I enjoyed listening to her. She sure knew the Bible!

A slight breeze passed by. I instantly smelled mint. Rain E stood up and helped me up. She said it was time to go. I said that I wasn't ready to leave. She said we were just leaving the hill. We started walking on the backside. About half way down, I smelled mint, again. I looked over to my left and then on the other side of Rain E I saw it.

We stopped for a minute. I walked over to the mint. It was growing all around a bunch of huge rocks. It smelled heavenly. Rain E thought so too. We started walking again at a slower pace. I kept going on and on about all the plants and trees. Rain E just kept listening to me rambling on. I really enjoyed looking at everything. The sky was clear. Not a cloud insight. The whole place was incredible. I never even stepped on any leaves or twigs. It was as though I entered into a perfect painting.

I could see the pond to the left of me. "The Flowers of the Week Garden" was straight ahead. We passed right by the pond and to the garden. I finally stopped yapping. It never seemed to bother Rain E. She was a great listener! I liked that she listened to me. My dad never did. Nothing I ever said to him was important. I was important to Mom and now Rain E. Maybe I "WAS" important!

We stopped in front of the garden gate. Rain E finally spoke, "I need to finish my chores. Would you like to help?" "You have chores?" I surprisingly asked. Rain E proudly pointed out, "Sure do, chores build character, if they are not accompanied with humiliation." I didn't know exactly what that meant, so I just smiled and gladly responded, "I would love to help you!" Rain E took off past the gate.

A few feet away, I saw gently swaying an oversized clipboard hanging on the fence. It was gleaming from the sunlight. I curiously watched Rain E lift it off the hooks. I could see a gorgeous feather pen attached to the right side. Rain E immediately removed the pen and started writing something at the top. I couldn't make out what she was writing. Rain E lifted one piece of paper. It must have been important. She read for several minutes, then hung the clipboard back on the hooks and walked back to me.

We were standing right by the gate. I didn't see any flowers. Rain E spoke, "Hum! Let me see!" She spun around once, and then spun me around once. I looked past the gate. My eyes bugged out. I shouted, "Yellow Roses!" I flung open the gate and took off running down the winding paths.

In and out, stopping to gracefully touch and smell the roses. They were beautiful! Some of them were in full bloom and some were just about ready to bloom. There were no tiny buds like the red roses, I saw last time. That was oddly strange! I walked and even skipped throughout the garden. The paths were gravel with a few larger stones here and there. The rest of the ground was covered in short grass. After I inspected every path and all the roses, I went to find Rain E. I didn't see her.

When I got closer to the gate, she was bent over two medium size buckets, one red and the other orange. Rain E straightened back up. She handed me the orange bucket and kept the red one. Orange is one of my school colors. I looked in my bucket and saw something inside moving. I took a closer look. It was ladybugs! There must have been thousands. Rain E stated, "It is for the roses."

I immediately remembered that Mom always bought live ladybugs every spring. She would keep them in a cool place for a couple of days, so they could calm down from the shipping experience. On the third day, early in the evening, Mom would let me open the bags. I would carefully release them on top of the roses, making sure they all got out. I asked her why we did it just before dark. She told me that the ladybugs would have all night to settle in to their new home, "Our Garden". You know, I never saw Mom use chemicals on the roses, only ladybugs. She said that it was nature's way of protecting them.

Rain E's bucket contained plant food. She gave me the ladybugs on purpose. I just knew it! We slowly walked on every path. Rain E was in front of me. She fed the roses and I protected them. It was a peaceful place for these lucky ladybugs to live. After we finished, I asked Rain E if the roses needed to be watered. She said that the sky would take care of the rest. Rain E was my kind of gardener!

The chores were finished. Rain E took my bucket and both of us sat down next to the gate. "That is done!" Rain E announced, wiping the leftover rose food off her hands, then cleaning them with the back of her blue shorts. Never saw any smudges! Weird! "Thank you for helping me Rachel. You did a wonderful job! Time to move on to the next chore!" I wondered what the next chore was going to be? Again, it didn't matter. Anything I did with Rain E was fun! Chores with her never caused tears.

We walked out. I closed the gate and put the latch on. While standing, admiring the yellow roses, I said, "These are my Mom's favorite flowers. "Imagine that!" Rain E chuckled. I happily said, "I'm so glad I got to see them." Rain E answered, "It's what you wished for, when I spun you around." I gasp out loud! How did she know I wanted to see yellow roses? How did Rain E know so much about Mom and me? It was a mystery! A fun mystery! Rain E reached for my left hand. It was warmer than usual, maybe from the rose food. We turned and walked away from the gate.

Not far down the path, I turned my head to the right and took one last glimpse of the flowers. My feet were going one direction and my head was twisting all around. I was definitely stumbling in my steps. Rain E didn't seem to mind. We slowed down a bit. As I was enjoying my last look, I thought how much Mom would have loved seeing all these yellow roses together. She would have just died! I mean it. She literally would have dropped dead! It was so magnificent. The yellow roses would be in my drawing, for sure! I finally had my body going in one direction. We started walking at a normal pace. Rain E held my left hand the whole way.

I could see the pond up ahead. As we were getting closer, I eyed the back of the red bench. It was resting in the same spot. We were about ten feet behind the bench, when Rain E scared the 'dickens' out of me by abruptly yanking me towards her. I lost my balance. Rain E apologized. She wanted to be "directly" behind the bench.

Just as we reached it, Rain E went to the left of the bench and I went to the right. Our arms were stretched out as far as they could go, without releasing our hands. That's what she wanted to do, circle the bench at each end. I came around first. I looked down and saw another color added. It was orange. Rain E was now standing beside me. We let go of our hands. I immediately said, "Rain E, the bench is now two colors, red and orange just like the rose buckets." Rain E giggled and said, "Imagine that!" I loved that saying!

I sat on the orange part and Rain E sat right beside me.

"So what do you think about the new color?" Rain E asked? I said, "I like orange. It's one of my school colors and one of the colors in my bedspread. It's a warm color. You know, it's a combination of red and yellow. The only thing I don't like is it reminds me of Halloween. That's my dad's birthday and orange reminds me of mean and scary things, like him."

Rain E commented, "I'm sorry for that, Rachel. I truly am, but orange has a lot of good meanings. It can represent endurance, as well as control. It's a harvest color. A color associated with the fall, including Halloween. Orange is a vibrant, healthy color. I believe orange encourages self-respect and respect for others. There is though, another meaning. It also symbolizes separation. That is all I will say about that, for now. Just remember, I told you this." I told Rain E I would. I was learning so much from my new friend.

I was getting comfy on the bench, thinking we were going to sit awhile. Wrong! Rain E jumped up and shouted, "Come on. There is something else I want you to see!" Rain E took my right hand and pulled me up. Within seconds, my hand was oven warm. We walked towards the pond. Over to my right, was a "far-out" looking bridge (I learned that word from my mom).

From where I was standing, I could see the left railing. It was a rainbow shape. The curved wood boards were painted white. We strolled right up to the start of the bridge and stopped. Now with a closer look, I could now see the white boards were outlined in a dark green color. There were no scratches or nicks in the wood. Almost perfect looking and quite stunning! I was just about to share my opinion, when Rain E happily announced, "Let's go!" Still holding my hand, we stepped onto the bridge. It was wide enough to walk right beside one another.

About halfway across, we stopped. Rain E released my hand, and walked over to the right rail. I followed. A few minutes went by. I stayed quiet and just looked down and around the pond. The sunlight was beautifully reflecting on the water. Small ripples gently moved back and forth. It was soothing to the mind and soul.

Rain E softly spoke, "I love small, intimate bridges! They are a purposeful connection, providing a passage over a gap, allowing people to cross from one side to the other. A bridge connects things, sometime important things. Rachel, do you understand what I am saying?" I stated, "I think I do. You're talking about God, is that right?" A huge smile covered Rain E's face. She asked, "Have you ever heard the expression, "He bridges the gap"? I politely said, "No, I haven't lived that long on earth." Rain E chuckled, and explained differently, "What do you think a bridge means, or what does it mean to you?" I said, "To me, a bridge can connect you with God, if you let it, but you have make sure you're on the right bridge that God's already on." "Rachel, I am astonished at your level of thinking at such a young age!" I lit up inside. Rain E always knew how to make me feel great.

I reached out with my right hand, and touched her rainbow pigtails. Then, out-of-nowhere, a shining beam of light shot down from the sky. Rain E's hair was glowing. Her face and freckles sparkled. She was breathtaking! I couldn't take my eyes off of her. Few more minutes pass by. We smiled at each other and started slowly walking, until we reached the other side of the bridge.

There was a small deck. It was solid white and in the shape of a donut. I mean like a real donut, with a hole cut out in the middle. We sat down, crisscross applesauce. While sitting, I realized this bridge wasn't here on my last visit. I was sure of it. Hmmm! Strange! I looked all around the pond, twisting my head in both directions, to see if there was anything else I had missed. Nope, only the bridge as far as I could tell!

I looked straight up into the sky. It was almost too bright to look at. I put my hands over my eyes, like a visor. Without warning, another beam of light came flying down. It was coming towards me. I quickly scooted back. The light passed in front of my eyes and struck the water inside the cutout. The water splashed all over the deck and me. I couldn't believe what I just witnessed. The water finally settled to a gentle back and forth movement.

I reached into the hole. My right fingers felt the warmth of the water. I swished them around, making a circle. My head stayed near the water. All of a sudden, I yanked my fingers out and screamed, "Oh my goodness! Rain E, look at all the different colored little fish, there's gobs of them! Nearly scared the 'bajibbies' out of me. I can see everything under the water. It must have been the beam of light. It's so crystal clear. The water is as clear as the ocean water in the Cayman Islands. I went there on vacation, when I was very young."

"You had a blast, didn't you?" Rain E stated. I glared at my mysterious friend after that last remark. "Keep looking." Rain E said. "Do you see anything unusual?"

I looked back at the pond and watched the different small fish swim by, then some turtles and even frogs. There was lots of seaweed and rocks with moss on top. I kept my eyes glued on the water. Next, a saw a larger fish swim by and then even a larger one. The fish kept getting bigger and bigger. From behind some seaweed, out came another tiny fish. It swam right by one of the larger ones. This kept going on for some time. I was sure I would see the larger fish swallow the tiny fish, in one big gulp. It never happened. I continued watching. Fascinating!

Looking down through the hole, the water reminded me of the aquariums at Sea World. The big fish were swimming right along with the smallest fish. They never bothered each other. Rain E whispered, "It's time to feed them." I watched as she lifted a red bucket over my head. Funny thing, it had been sitting behind me the whole time. At least, I think it had been sitting behind me. I was driving myself crazy, trying to figure this magical, mystery place I had been blessed to be a part of.

Anyway, Rain E opened the bucket. I curiously peeked in and saw lots of fish food. She used the scoop that was in the bucket and then handed it to me. "I would like for you to slowly pour it into the pond, walking all around the circle deck." Rain E said. I jumped to my feet. "Yeah! I get to feed the fish! I love feeding the fish and ducks at the lake!" I said with so much enthusiasm. I walked around the deck, slowly sifting the food into the water. After I finished, I cheerfully sat back down. I thought, "Chores with Rain E are so different than with my evil dad. Rain E's chores, like Mom's end with praise. Dad's chores end with pain!"

Rain E sat beside me and quietly said, "Watch what happens." I stared at the water. All at the same time, every size fish, plus the turtles and frogs came to the surface. I watched the food slowly trickle down. Different size fish grabbed it. I was in shock. "My gracious me! They're not only sharing, they're not bothering one other." I shouted. Rain E commented, "That is absolutely correct. They are showing total respect for one another and sharing because they know I'm the one who provides the food. I always come back, at the same time each day. They don't have to devour each other. They live in complete harmony. Do you understand what I'm saying?" "I do. I understand every word, including "devour." The different fish are showing me how to have respect for one another," I proudly answered.

"It's sad, because I *wasn't* learning this at my dad's. My dad is the one who devours everyone. He's the one who has no respect. He only cares about HIMSELF and his OWN needs! I will always remember to respect myself, and all those around me, especially my mom. I respect God and His word more than anything. When you used the word *devour*, it reminded me of the whale that swallowed Jonah."

"I would love to hear the story," Rain E quickly responded. I said, "I remember in kindergarten, my teacher read us the short, but good Bible story. It was all about how Jonah disobeyed God. He tried to run away from God. Jonah was on a ship and was tossed into the ocean. He was swallowed by a giant fish or whale, which God provided. While Jonah was sitting inside the belly of the whale, he cried out to God. He even praised Him. Jonah was inside the huge fish for three days. Then God commanded the whale to vomit him up onto dry land. Jonah now obeyed God, but later he got mad at Him for not destroying the wicked people. In the end, God was concerned even for the wicked."

Rain E said, "That was remarkable and very accurate, according to the book in the Old Testament. Rachel, you continue to amaze me with your sincere insight. What did you think about how the story ended?" I simply told Rain E, "God has compassion even for the wicked, hoping someday they will cross that bridge to get to Him." Then I added, "Maybe someday God will help my dad behave, and learn to respect others." I looked at Rain E. She was speechless. After feeding the fish, I put the scoop back up into the bucket and left it there for Rain E to use the next day.

We strolled back over the bridge and to our bench and sat down. We sat there in silence while relaxing. I love that we had quiet times together. I believe Rain E knew I desperately needed it. I was admiring the view, when this time I reached for Rain E's hand. It was warm, as usual. She squeezed it three times. I gasped! I then squeezed twice. I was in shock. How did she know about this?

This is one of my special secrets, with my mom. When Rain E squeezed my hand, it brought back another wonderful childhood memory, when I was around age five. Mom would lie down beside me on my bed, and was always teaching me something new. She would make learning fun and interesting.

One night, just before Mom got up, she grabbed my hand and kissed it. Then she squeezed it three times. I asked if that meant anything. Mom said it stood for "I Love You." I told Mom to squeeze my hand again. She did. This time I immediately squeeze back, twice. I smiled and said that mine meant "Me Too". This became a tradition like our nightly prayers. I will pass it on to my kids. Rain E is now a part of our traditions. I wonder if other people know about this? You can show love in many ways. Mom and I show our love through saying the words, hugging, signing, or hand squeezing.

I got up and moved to Rain E's other side. I held her other hand. I wanted both my hands warm. Rain E gave me so much warmth and love, just like Mom. I never got loving warmth from Dad. I was only exposed to his heated temperament.

My mind drifted back to the dish towel and even before that, to the triangle brownies. I was going to really try to stay out of Dad's way, during the last week of my final and stressful summer visit. I could hardly wait until it ended. Dad made me so nervous. I had been eating more because I was so stressed, which was causing me to gain weight. I could see it, but Rain E hadn't noticed yet. I think my mom had, but she never brought it up. She knew why I was gaining weight. She hated that I have to spend time with my dad. One more week, that was all! Thank goodness he worked and would be gone during the day.

I felt a tug on my arm. "Rachel, are you okay'? I've been trying to get your attention for several minutes," Rain E panicked. "Oh, I'm sorry," I must have drifted off," I replied. "You must have been in really deep thought. Anything you want to share, I'm a great listener!" I quietly responded, "Thank you, but no thank you. I was just daydreaming." I didn't bring up anything. I just wanted to enjoy my time with Rain E.

Without warning, Rain E jumped up and shouted, "Let's go for a swim. We're through with all the chores. It will be a blast! We can swim in our clothes." I was thrilled, but a bit scared and had to ask, "Are there any snakes in the pond?" Rain E chuckled, "Of course not silly. There are no serpents here." That was an odd response. I guess she meant there were no snakes, since snakes and serpents were the same thing.

We got up from the bench, hand in hand and dashed barefoot straight into the pond, in our clothes. I couldn't believe it! The pond water was as warm as Rain E's hand, maybe a smidgen more. It was like being in a giant bathtub. Rain E was splashing her arms in and out of the water. She looked at me and said, "I love to swim in my clothes. It is so adventurous. Don't you think so Rachel?" I shouted to the sky, "Me toooo!" We laughed and laughed and splashed and splashed. Time seem to fly by. I didn't want to leave. I wish I could stay here the entire time while I was staying at my dad's. It felt so good to laugh. I mean truly laugh!

I swam all over the pond. I practiced my backstroke that Mom taught me. I swam underwater and even did flips. I climbed up onto a huge rock and practiced on my cannonballs. Rain E even did one. I was floating on my back, when I lifted my head to see where she was. Rain E rolled onto her back and paddled over to me. We were side by side. She took my hand. I closed my eyes and pretended we were sea otters, because they like to hold each other's paw when sleeping, so they don't drift apart. I learned that in science and from my mom. I opened my eyes. Looking up at the sky, I called out, "Heaven can't be far away!"

Rain E asked, "What makes you think that?" I said, "Because it's so beautiful and so peaceful here. And you are so beautiful. You make me feel so beautiful." Rain E squeezed my hand three times. I squeezed back twice.

I was getting tired, so I swam close to the edge and waded out of the pond. Rain E followed. I stretched my wet body on top of the thick plush grass. I was face down. In quiet thoughts, I thanked God for Rain E being a part of my life. I rolled over on my back and just looked up to the heavens. I could see Rain E about five feet away.

She was in a seated position, knees bent and both palms perched on the grass. As I was watching her, she spoke, "I am so glad you are a part of my life!" Okay, now that was weird. We both stayed quiet, after that remark. I kept thinking about MY mysterious friend. How did she know everything I was thinking, everything that went on in my life, my likes and dislikes, my ups and downs, and my fears? How? I guess I would figure it out someday.

I turned my head and thanked Rain E for rescuing me once again, from the insanity at the condo. She just smiled back. Rain E has such a lovely face. It was sparkling even more, after the swim. Her freckles were so shiny they looked wet. Different colors were surfacing underneath the freckles. Rain E had the greenest eyes like my mom. Those rainbow pigtails! I never noticed before, but her hair came out rainbow colors, from the scalp to the very tip. Wow! Rain E realized I had been studying her face and hair. She didn't seem to mind. I closed my eyes again.

I was almost asleep, when all of a sudden, Rain E burst out, "Pardon me Rachel, but my mind needs to speak!" She was so serious. "Remember when you told me your dad said you were fat." I said, "Yeah." "That has been bothering me for some time now. I want to say something to you and I do not want you to ever forget it! Okay?" I timidly answered "Okay." "Rachel you are beautiful inside and out. You are NOT fat, or chubby. Your dad is just mean and hateful and that is the truth! That is all I have to say!" I was speechless. I thought to myself that Rain E was some kind of wonderful friend. She remembered what I told her the first time we met. With a lump in my throat, I said, "Thank you, Rain E, you are as kind as my mother." I looked up at the sky and closed my eyes my once more.

I tried reaching for Rain E's hand, but I couldn't move my arm. I slightly opened my eyes. I was back under my comforter. There was an extremely heavy pressure right on top of me. I could hardly breathe, but was too scared to move or even peek. Then just like that, the pressure was gone. I stayed still. My stuffed black and white kitty had been on top of me the whole time.

I slowly peeked over the comforter, to see my dad walk out of my room. He only had on his underwear. Was my dad on top of me while I was sleeping? That really gave me the creeps! I was going to have to tell Mom about this. I stayed under my comforter, just in case "Mr. Evil" decided to come back. I felt my clothes. They were dry. Were they dry when I was lying on the grass? I didn't remember. I did remember how much fun I had and how much better I felt about myself. Rain E was making that happen. I felt a little happier and stronger inside. I peeked over the comforter again.

I got up and tiptoed to the hallway. Ex-grandma was still asleep on the den sofa. I tiptoed to Dad's bedroom. I could hear his sleep machine going. Good, he was back in bed. I tiptoed back to the kitchen and poured myself a bowl of cereal. I quietly and quickly ate. As usual, I washed the bowl and spoon, dried them, and carefully put everything away, without making a sound. I wiped the countertop and sink with my shirt. I wasn't about to touch *the dishtowel*. It represented evil. I got back to my bedroom, without disturbing the "Prison Warden."

I climbed into bed and under my comforter. I rested thinking about Rain E, the yellow roses, feeding the fish, swimming and of course, climbing all the way to the top of the building clock and then out through the face. That was something! What an accomplishment! I didn't think I had it in me. God and Rain E proved me wrong. I wish I could tell Mom. She would be so proud of me.

Listening to the storm, I could hear Mom's calming voice saying, "God hears your prayers and He WILL answer them." Mom was absolutely right, about everything. I knew God had to be the reason I met Rain E. I was sure of it. What a terrific, adventurous night! I fell asleep. It was almost noon, when I woke up. The storm outside was over. No more rain pounding against the window.

I heard someone coming down the hallway. I stayed under my comforter. My door opened. I could smell it was my dad. I silently prayed "Please, pretty please, don't get on top of me. Oh God make him go away, please." I heard, "I'm taking you home today. I got a call and have to be out of town again." Dad grabbed my toes on my right foot. He started popping them, one at a time. I kicked at him and screamed, "Stop it!" He let go and yelled, "Get your worthless ass ready, we're leaving in an hour. I called your "F" n mother and asked the rotten "B" to give me one of her weeks since I'm losing one, plus some days. She said flat out "No!" Dad stormed out.

I stayed under my comforter, grinning ear to ear. I looked up to God and thanked Him for another miracle and for giving me a tough mom. I flew out of bed, changed back into my jeans and favorite T-shirt. I shoved my pajama short set in my backpack. I will be wearing them again, after my scrapes heal. I walked out to the hallway with my backpack and kitty under my arm. My ex-grandma was still asleep. She also sleeps with a machine. Dad barked, "Let's go, get a move on."

We headed to the parking garage. The elevator wasn't working. Dad bitched about that. He bitched about everything that disrupted or inconvenienced his life. I kept my mouth shut. He was acting like a child, so someone needed to be the adult, ME! He wanted me to say something so badly, so he could yell at me. I refused to respond. I was becoming more aware of his problems and they were "PROBLEMS". Now that Mom was not around, I was seeing it for myself. He walked ahead of me, like he always did everyone, all the way to the car. He unlocked it and I crawled in the back. This was the car ride I have been looking forward to all summer. We pulled out of the garage. I was out of the wicked, "Damn Evil Tower". Rapunzel (ME) was going home!

The sky was blue. Not a cloud in sight. I was released from prison. Freedom! I rested my head back on the seat and closed my eyes, reliving all the nightmares I have endured at the "Damn Evil Tower" and wondering why it was all happening to me. I think forcing a child to be with an abusive parent is worse than wrong, IT'S SICK!!!! My dad was getting worse. He flipped out over everything during my stay. I will never forget the *dishtowel* and never forget you two judges who insisted I live in HELL half the summer. I hated what I was feeling. I knew it was wrong to hate, but I did. My life was a nightmare, all because of your dumb decisions.

I thought family judges cared about kids. Didn't they teach that in school? Were you two asleep in the classroom, because you were certainly asleep in the courtroom, each time my mom was there? Maybe that's why judges always wore long robes, so they could sleep. When my mom was asking for your help, were you even awake? You two being asleep was the only reason that made sense to me on why I had to be with my dad. Was there a reason you let a bad person win?

As I continued resting, I remembered this one particular day, earlier this summer. I walked into Mom's bedroom. She was reading from her cherished Bible, she's had a long, long time and wanted to show me a specific verse. It was in the book of Psalms, one of our favorites. Mom was always reading her Bible, a lot more since filing for divorce. She loved this specific Bible. I know for a fact, it got read more than any of her other Bibles. It was called *The Living Bible*.

When my mom was in high school, Bible was offered as an elective in the public schools. She took the class with the same teacher, for three years. *The Living Bible* was the textbook used in the classroom. My mouth literary dropped open the first time Mom showed it to me. Let me tell you, it looked like a school textbook. Just about every page was covered with written notes on the sides, across the top and bottom, and verses underlined in different colored markers. Exclamations punctuated Mom's favorite verses and books! I was more than impressed, I was proud! I told Mom I wanted the exact same Bible. We went to a Christian bookstore, but the nice lady said it was no longer in circulation. So, Mom lets me read hers, anytime I want.

We sat next to each other on the small sofa. Mom read the verse to me and then explained in detail what it meant. I want every judge and politician to read and even memorize it!! It's Psalms (58:1-5,9-11). For everyone reading my book, this is what *The Living Bible says,* "Justice? YOU HIGH and mighty politicians don't even know the meaning of the word! Fairness? Which of you had any left? Not one! All your dealings are crooked: you give "justice" in exchange for bribes. These men are born sinners, lying from their earliest words! They are poisonous as deadly snakes, cobras that close their ears to the most expert of charmers. God will destroy them. The godly will rejoice in the triumph of right. Then at last everyone will know that good is rewarded, and that there is a God who judges justly here on earth." I hope this wakes up all people in powerful positions. To the judges my mom stood before, remember this; I now know your names, thanks to my dad's big mouth, and I will never forget them!!

The car hit a big bump in the road, causing my head to hit the ceiling. I came out of my daydreaming. We were in my neighborhood. I was almost to "my" home! Yeah!! The stinky, perfumed car pulled into the driveway. Dad pitched my phone to me. It almost hit me in the eye. No apology. What a jerk! I knew it wasn't a nice word, but it was the nicest of the bad words. The phone fell on the floorboard. When I bent over to retrieve it, I could smell the perfume. Gross!! This would be getting sanitized tonight.

I tucked my phone into my backpack and said nothing. My evil dad impatiently waited for me to get out. I opened the car door and slowly took my time, on purpose. I wouldn't be seeing Dad for a while, so I wanted to leave him with something to stew over. What he did to me this summer was worse than awful. Someone needed to do the same to him. As I was almost out of the cat, I gave him a look to remember. This time my evil dad didn't even say goodbye. Big deal! I slammed the door and walked straight to "MY" home, my loving, happy, safe, and VERY quiet home. I had survived another miserable summer at the "Damn Evil Tower".

The moment I reached the front door, Mom immediately opened it and hugged me along with my stuff. We walked into the house. Grandma was standing there. I gave her a big hug. She said, "I am so glad to see you. Goodness gracious me! You must have grown a foot this summer! Are you sure you're just ten years old?" Grandma is always funny.

Sugar was on the stairs. I excused myself and headed up to unpack and change out of my dirty, stinky perfumed clothes, and to sanitize my phone. Sugar followed me. Mom surprised me saying we were going to brunch. I screamed out, "Yeah! My favorite place." Mom and Grandma were already dressed. I think they planned this, since I came home early. What a wonderful pair they are!

I changed into my leggings and long sleeved sparkly shirt. I was brushing my hair, when I noticed a glare on the bathroom mirror. I quickly turned around and looked out my window. I saw the image of a rainbow disappear. I smiled. I knew it was Rain E. I bet she just wanted to make sure I was home safe. I love her. I hollered, "Almost ready. Be right down!" I sanitized my phone, looked around my beautiful room and flew down the stairs with my dirty, stinky clothes. I dumped 'um in the utility. We were out the door. It was brunch time!

The restaurant was gorgeous as usual. Mom had reserved a table by the window. It was self-serve. I got some meat and vegetables before the desserts. Mom's rule! The food is always d*elish*. While we were eating, Mom asked me if everything went okay at Dad's. She and Grandma were staring at me, waiting for an answer. I leaned over and whispered, "Can we talk about it later?" Mom, with a compassionate, but concerned look on her face said, "Sure. We'll talk tonight." With relief I answered, "Thank you." Dad screaming at his mother would be the topic of conversation tonight. I hadn't decided if I would mention the other stuff.

We all finished eating and went to the car. Mom asked if I wanted to stop by the sports store and get my tennis shoes for school. "Yes, yes, yes," I said. "I love the sports store!" Mom bought me two pairs of tennis shoes, one for school, and one for home. She always buys what I need and like. Something Dad has yet to grasp. When we got home, I called my best friend. We played games on the computer the whole time we were talking. We talked about everything. Her parents are divorce too, so she knows what I'm going through. She has to spend time with her dad, but he's not as bad as mine.

It was getting dark outside. Mom came in and said it was bedtime. I said goodbye to my best friend and headed upstairs. I took a quick bath and got ready for bed. I put on my long-sleeved red, blue and white plaid pajama set. Mom knew how much I love them. It was a Christmas gift from Mom. I usually only wear them during the winter, but I had to hide some scrapes on my arms and legs, from scrubbing Dad's floor, and I didn't want her to see them. I was so ashamed of myself. I knew I shouldn't be, but I was. So sad! I was covering up something I hated with something I loved, my pajamas!

I leaped into bed, and covered up with my comforter and blankets. I reached under the left side of my bed. Yep, the drawing pad and pencils were still hiding. Mom walked in. I abruptly sat up. Thank goodness she didn't ask what I was doing. She sat on the bed beside me. We said our prayer. Mom asked, "Aren't those pajamas hot?" I said," No, they're so comfy I wanted to wear them." Mom continued, "What did you want to tell me?"

I told her, "Dad screamed at his mother worse than ever. I don't get her. Why doesn't she just walk out?" Mom explained, "I've known that woman for over twenty years. She will never stand up to her precious baby, no matter what he does or says to her. I know this firsthand." "What's firsthand mean?" I asked. Mom said, "It means, I have knowledge of something very bad that happened to that woman. Funny thing is she told me herself. I recorded the conversation because I knew someday it would come in handy. That day hasn't arrived yet, but it will. She probably doesn't even remember being recorded." "Wow!" I remarked and asked, "Can I hear the tape?" "No my dear. You are too young to concern yourself with this matter." I then asked, "What about when I'm an adult?" When I asked Mom that, she paused for a moment, and firmly answered, "Yes. You need to hear the truth."

"I have the tape, plus others, in a safe place. Rachel, with all you have gone through, you have earned the right to know the whole truth." I smiled at Mom and said, "I love you." Mom leaned over and gave me a long kiss on the forehead and squeezed my left hand twice. "Sleep well my love," Mom said as she left my room and turned the lights out. I threw my comforter over my head and closed my eyes. I lay there thinking about the tapes and wondering what was on them? It must be pretty bad for Mom to secretly keep them hidden. I decided not to tell her about the dish towel, someday, just not now. I crashed.

The next morning, I woke up when my body woke up. That NEVER happens at Dad's. I was rested and happy. I heard Mom coming up the stairs. She walked in and asked if I wanted to go to lunch. I asked what time it was. She said it was 1:00 pm. Wow Wee! I got to really sleep in. I told her I would love to eat lunch. Mom said, "You pick the restaurant." "How about Spaghetti?" I eagerly asked. "Sounds good to me," Mom happily responded. She was already dressed. I flew out of bed. I asked if Grandma wanted to go. Mom said she wanted to stay in and do her puzzles. She left and went downstairs to wait.

I was putting on jeans, when I noticed the scrapes and bruises were gone. They disappeared, after only two days. I looked at my hands and arms. They were also healed. I was sitting on the edge of my bed, staring at my hands, with such amazement. Two warm tears landed on them. Rain E's warm pond! It healed my body. I stayed seated for a few more minutes, trying to make sense of it all. I wiped my eyes dry. My wonderful Rain E! She never said a thing about my cuts and bruises. She only touched them.

I got up and hurried to the stairs. I slid down on the banister the rest of the way down. "I'm ready when you are." I said with a glow. We left. In the car Mom and I talked about school starting in a few weeks. Mom said that after lunch, we needed to get some new school uniforms and anything else I might need. We didn't get home until after dark. It was a fun-filled day. I loved shopping with Mom. The rest of the night Mom and I watched movies and I fell asleep on the sofa.

I woke up with my comforter on top of me. I looked over at the window to see a sunny morning. Mom was still asleep. I got up and poured myself a bowl of Lucky Charms and went back to the den to watch cartoons. As I was eating, I couldn't help but think about how different my home and Dad's home is. I was eating cereal in the den, watching TV in peace and quiet, and no worries on how the kitchen looks. I left the empty bowl on the coffee table and cuddled up on the sofa. When Mom came in, she grabbed my bowl and took it into the kitchen, never saying a word about me leaving it there.

After cartoons, I went upstairs and changed into sweat shorts and another T-shirt. I had just come out of the bathroom, when Mom walked in asking if I wanted to run some errands with her. I politely declined. I wanted to stay to work on my drawing. I went to check on Grandma. She was fine.

Back in my room, I reached under my bed and pulled out my pad and pencils. Comfy on my bed, I began drawing the building clock. I spent some time on it. Then I added yellow roses to the garden. I put a number "2" right above them, since it was the second flower I saw and a "1" above the red roses. I had just started on the bridge, when I heard Mom come in. I quickly put everything away and headed downstairs. Mom was unloading the car. I helped. After groceries were put up, she made lunch. It was my favorite sandwich, tuna fish.

After eating, I went back up to my room to watch TV. I must have watched cartoons and movies for some time, because night showed up the same time Mom did. We said our prayer. Mom left and I got ready for bed. Leaving the bathroom, I walked over to my bay window and thought about Rain E. I was gazing out, night dreaming about her. The sky was shining beautifully, because of all the stars.

It was at that moment I realized, I only saw Rain E when I was at my dad's. It only occurred after something horrible happened to me. There was never a need to see her when I was with Mom. Nothing bad ever happened here. I jumped into bed. I lay there wondering what would happen to me next time at Dad's. Sad final thought to have at the end of the day! I finally fell asleep.

School was starting in a week and a half. I had to go back to Mr. Evil the first weekend, right after school started. Yuck!! Mom let my best friend spend the night. One more summer time together before hitting the books! We stayed up all night watching movies and eating. I had popcorn. My best friend Jenna ate Mom's homegrown cherry tomatoes with salt. I've never seen one person consume so many tomatoes at one time. I'm surprised her skin's not red.

We were helping ourselves to some Kisses in the candy dish when Mom walked into the kitchen. Jenna commented, "I wonder who came up with the idea of a swirly candy like this? I asked, "Mom, were Kisses around when you were young?" Mom sat down at the table with us and said, "Hershey Kisses were around when your grandmother was young."

Jenna and I looked at each other and at the same time and went, "Wooowww!" Mom continued, "William Hershey first made caramels, but became fascinated with chocolate when he got a close-up look at the art of chocolate-making at an Exposition. He sold his caramel company and started working on making the best milk chocolate bar for all to enjoy. Back then chocolate was a luxury only the wealthy could afford. Mr. Hershey changed that! His first chocolate bar was simply known as the Hershey Bar. He later created the Hershey Kisses."

"One very interesting fact, Mr. Hershey and his wife Catherine had booked a passage on the Titanic, while vacationing in Europe. Supposedly he got word from an employee on an urgent business matter. So they gave up their luxury stateroom and came back three days earlier on the German ship Amerika. In a strange coincidence while the Amerika was making its way back across the ocean, word was sent to Titanic warning of the icebergs in the area where the ship eventually went down."

"Word spread of all the people who also gave up their booked passage due to different circumstances. They became known as the "Just Missed It" club. At the famous Hershey museum, in Hershey, Pennsylvania, is the $300 deposit ticket Mr. Hershey paid for a 1st class passage aboard Titanic. I often wonder how the candy industry would have turned out if he had been on that fatal voyage."

"It was years after the sinking of the Titanic that other candy bars were invented including one of my favorites, Almond Joy. Henry Reese, a family friend of Milton Hershey also lived in Hershey, Pennsylvania. Mr. Hershey's company supplied the chocolate coating for his Reese's peanut butter cups." After that good true story, Jenna and I could only say again, "Wooowww!" I added, "I'm glad Mr. Hershey and his wife came home early. I bet God had something to do with it."

Mom left and went to bed. We finished filling our tummies with Kisses. Jenna and I decided to watch Titanic. The movie was just getting started when Jenna said, "Your mom sure can tell true stories in a clever way that you end up learning something. She should be a teacher, even at our school." I stated, "She's already a teacher, my teacher. You should hear her true story about a tornado!" Jenna was bug-eyed. I told her I would get Mom to tell it, if I remembered. We fell asleep after the movie ended. It was a fun and educational sleepover.

Tuesday arrived. I was back in school. It was great seeing everyone. I met a couple of new girls. They are very nice. One in particular liked everything I did. Mom picked me up and we went to eat. I told her about my new friends. I know she was happy that I loved my school so much. The rest of the week flew by.

It was the dreaded Friday. Back to the "Damn Evil Tower". After school, Mom and I grabbed a sandwich. We didn't talk much. Not much to say. I had to go and that was that! We got home around 5:30 pm. I carried all my stuff to my room. I had just enough time to change. I grabbed my secret box and everything I needed. I got my drawing pad and pencils out from under my bed and wrapped them in my school jacket. I didn't want Mom to see the drawing until it's finished! I know I was being sneaky, but I wanted to work on it at Dad's. Sugar was at the top of the stairs. I leaned over and gave her a big kiss on the head. Mom was sitting at the bottom. I joined her. It was close to leaving time. Mom took my hands and prayed to God to watch over me.

Here came *the honks*. I hugged her, and dragged my body all the way to the car. I turned back and waved. We signed "I Love You". I hated getting in *that* car. I had no choice. Just like the song lyrics, *"For in this world they have no voice, they have no choice."* Those heartbreaking words came from the song *Bless the Beasts and Children* sung by The Carpenters (written by Barry De Vorzon and Perry L Botkin). Mom used to sing it to me when I was little. I always thought it was a pretty song, still do, but now I sadly grasped the meaning of the lyrics. I climbed in the back and we drove away. At the end of the street, Dad abruptly stopped. Here came the hand. I gave the monster my phone, along with a dirty look. My mouth stayed shut, but not for long.

The Lord is close to the brokenhearted;
he rescues those whose spirits are crushed.

Psalm 34:18 (NLT)

Chapter 8

On the way to the condo, I was thinking about school, Rain E and my evil dad. Even though it was hot and humid, I was glad school started. Now, I only had to be with him every other weekend, until Christmas Break. Boy, do I remember last year! Those Fridays that I had to go with Dad were worse than depressing they were frightening! I would wake up and immediately ask Mom if it was *"his"* Friday. When she said yes, my insides would start churning and my head would start aching. Mom saw the nervousness on my face. I saw the helplessness on hers. Our drive to school was a quiet one. She always told me to have a wonderful day. I tried, but I just couldn't, all because of my dad. Now starts a new school year, but this time I had Rain E.

I had been in the car for about ten minutes when Mr. Evil snapped at me, "What the "F" is wrong with you missy?" I just looked out the window. He growled again, "I asked you a "GD" "F" n question." I turned my head and firmly said, "Mom said I was allowed to have a phone. The judge said so! I am supposed to be able to talk to her when I'm away!" He yelled, "I don't give a "GD" what the judges say, especially that "F" n "B" judge. Like I'm gonna do what some woman tells me. So shut your "F" n" mouth!" My dad liked thinking he had power and control over everyone. He didn't control my mom and he knew it.

We were almost to the condo, when Dad's phone rang. It was Ronny, his teenage boyfriend. He said he was stopping by. Big Whoop Tee Do! Why does he always have to be there hen I'm there? There are other weekends when I'm not around. Why couldn't my hateful dad keep him away from me? I had told him over and over I didn't want to be around him or his brother. They both give me the creeps. Dad keeps shoving them on me thinking I would eventually like them. Fat chance! Because of that scumbag judge, I was forced to be around Ronny and his brother Blake. I knew this upset Mom more than anything. She tried for two years to keep those teenage boys away from me. She was so troubled when she lost that battle in court. I think she was more upset that I heard the news first.

It happened on the following required two-hour weekly dinner visit, after the final trial. I was crying my eyes out, when I walked in the house. Mom asked me what was wrong. "Dad said the judge is making me be around "The Boys!" Mom, I don't want to be around them," I screamed out! I was hysterically crying and sobbing so much I couldn't catch my breath. Mom was furious.

She walked into her bedroom and immediately called her attorney. "You gutless chicken," she screamed. "Why didn't you call me when you received the judge's ruling? My daughter just delivered the news to me that she has to be around the teenage boys. She's hysterical. A child did your dirty work. You are the sorriest excuse of a family attorney!!" There was silence, followed by loud cries. Mom stayed in her room for several minutes. When the door finally opened, she looked straight at me, "I'm so sorry, so very, very sorry." I ran to her and held on tight. I told Mom, "It's not your fault. You did everything possible to protect me. It's the judge. I thought I was going get to speak with him."

With frustration and anger, Mom exploded, "That deadbeat attorney said he filed a motion for you to speak privately with the judge. It never happened. He did nothing he said he would. He was also lousy in court! I don't think I will ever forgive him and the main lady attorney for lying to me and dragging this case out so they could bleed me dry. All they did was take my money, not to mention my respect. They crushed my spirit and I hope someday it backfires on them. God will get them for their deceitful ways. I'm sure of that! Again, I am so sorry, my sweet Rachel. We'll get through this. God will help." Mom paused for a moment and pondered, "I still can't believe the judge ruled in your Dad's favor, after all the incriminating evidence my attorneys had on "The Boys" and him. I just don't get it."

I told Mom, "Dad gave me this smug, almost devilish look and said that I would get used to them. They're my new family. He even wants me to call them Uncle Ronny and Uncle Blake. Can you believe that?" I screamed at him, "NO WAY". Mom lifted my chin and said, "Rachel they are not your family and never will be. You do not have to call them uncles." I told mom that Dad said I was just being mean and hateful. Creepy! My dad running around with teenage boys! Just creepy! Mom eased my mind by telling me that the judge never said he was making me see "The Boys". She said that all came from Dad's sick head and that the judge only ruled that I could be around them.

I was calming down some. We sat next to each other on the den sofa. As I was drying my eyes, I glanced at a photo of Mom and me on the fireplace mantel. It was taken at Disney World. It reminded me of when Dad still lived at home. It was after that trip, things drastically changed. I looked at Mom and asked if she remembered the trip to Disney World. Boy did she ever!

Mom clearly vocalized, "It was only a couple of weeks later, when your dad showed up at the house with the teenage boys. I thought he had lost his marbles, literally gone crazy. Who were they? Where did they come from? Anyway, it was a Sunday. We were going to the lake and he invited them. Your dad looked at me and asked if we wanted to join them. It was our plans and we were shoved aside. I remember getting in his face and saying, "No thanks!" I watched a grown man (your dad) drive off with the younger one in the front and the other boy in the back."

"From that point on, he was spending every waking moment with his "New Boyfriends". He spent more time with them than he did with us." I commented, "I still remember the day you were crushed more than ever. It was Thanksgiving. You told me it was you and Dad's twentieth anniversary. That's a lot of years. Dad not only forgot, he called and said he was taking "The Boys" to dinner. The hurt in your eyes! You were so quiet the rest of the night. We played the game Sorry. Dad came home really late. He passed by us and didn't say a word. You never said a word either." Mom also shared that she would always remember that night. She told me that was the final hurt. Mom finally filed for divorce. I didn't blame her at all.

A loud noise came from outside. It startled me. I must have been in deep thought. I turned around to see out the back window. A storm was near. I turned back around. Just as we were pulling into the condo Dad's phone rang again. Of course it was Ronny. Dad had it on speaker. Ronny said he would be there shortly. He was icky! We parked and I gathered up all my stuff. We weren't in the condo five minutes, when Ronny called from the lobby. My dad was so thrilled. I rolled my eyes and went straight to my room. I dumped my homework stuff on the bed and placed my box under it. I quickly went back to the door and closed it 'almost' all the way. I could see my grown-up dad looking through the front door peephole. He was standing there, like a small kid waiting for Santa. How sickening! My dad was acting like a goofy teenager.

Ronny walked in and gave creepy Dad a big hug. They went straight to the office to look at "Who Knows What"! I kept my door slightly open so I could hear if they came down the hall. The condo was smaller than a house. There were only two bedrooms, (mine and the monster), a den, dining and a kitchen area. Oh yeah, and an office. I did like that there was a big balcony in the den and in my room.

I unwrapped my drawing pad and hid it on the top shelf of my closet. I changed into some sweat shorts and a long sleeve T-shirt, and played games on my Nintendo. I wished I could call my mom, but Mr. Evil had my phone. He thought he was some kind of king, always in charge. He made me sick!

Some time went by. I got up went to the bathroom and then to the den, to watch some TV. As I came out of my room, I took a quick peek in the office. They were still in there. Ronny was standing behind Dad, who was sitting in the chair, facing the computer. I was about to turn and go to the den, when Ronny stepped to Dad's left side. I could see the computer screen, but not real clear. What I did see were naked boys playing leapfrog. I think it was leapfrog. Why were they naked? I have NEVER played leapfrog naked. Gross! Gross!! Gross!!! I rushed to the den and quickly turned on the TV. I watched my cartoons until I fell asleep.

I was abruptly awakened with a pillow hitting my face. I looked up. Dad was standing there, laughing. He was always doing mean things to me and I never knew why. It was not funny! It was mean! He barked, "Ronny's spending the night and he's sleeping in your room. Your ass is on the sofa." Before I could even say another word after "But" my dad shut me up fast. "You're sleeping on the sofa and that's final!" I couldn't believe him? I was sleeping on the sofa and that creep was in my bed. My dad was sick!! Everything about my dad and these teenage boyfriends made me sick. He cared more about them than he did me. I knew why Ronny hung out with my dad. He bought him lots of expensive gifts, including a motorcycle and cowboy boots.

Dad wouldn't even buy me a five-dollar Beanie Boo. What was with this teenager? Why was he looking at naked boys with my dad? Mom was going to know about this!

I went to my bedroom and grabbed my pillow and comforter. I didn't even change clothes. I curled up on the den sofa. At first it was hard to sleep, the two of them were laughing, talking, and cussing so loud. They were saying words I have never heard before, like fag-it and queer. What did those words even mean? Mom would know about this too. Finally I was able to fall asleep.

My stomach woke me up in the middle of the night. It was growling! I had forgotten to eat dinner. The condo was pitch black. I quietly tiptoed, like a burglar, to the kitchen. I had just stepped inside, when I heard a noise from the hall. I quickly squatted and remained quiet. I put my hand over my mouth and nose for extra assurance. I leaned into the hallway and saw my bedroom door open. Someone walked out. I pulled my body back and stayed perfectly still and extra quiet. Another door opened then closed. I slowly raised myself and waited a few minutes to make sure the coast was clear, before grabbing some food.

I knew exactly where the green apples were. I felt around on the counter, until I touched the bowl, grabbed one and dashed back to the sofa. I got under the comforter, cleaned the apple with the bottom of my shirt, and started eating. With every bite, I kept thinking how scary that was, not knowing who was moving around in the night. I felt like I was in some kind of horror movie.

After eating, I tiptoed back to the kitchen. Cracking open the refrigerator, I blindly reached in and grabbed a bottle of water. As the refrigerator door shut I saw the paper towel holder, sitting on the left counter. I pulled off only one tiny sheet, and headed back to my "second class citizen" bed. I carefully wrapped the apple core and stuck it under the sofa. I kept the bottle under my comforter, so Dad wouldn't see it. Finally, I fell back to sleep. What a night!

The next morning, I was cruelly awakened to a stuffed animal being shoved in my face. I couldn't breathe. With both hands, I kept trying to remove it. I could tell see that it was my dad. I screamed out, "Stop it!!" My dad just kept doing it. He didn't care what I was saying. He continued pushing the fur so deep in my eyes and nose, until I couldn't see anything at all. I was getting madder and madder. So mad, because he woke me up in such a cruel way! Dad wouldn't stop. He kept twisting and turning the stuff animal, pressing it even harder into my face. I kept swinging my arms in every direction, gasping for air. That's when I struck him in the face with my fist. All I could do was fight with my arms. He just happened to be in the line of fire. He backed away and yelled, "Son of a "B" that hurt you brat!" "Too bad," I thought to myself, "He deserved it. I'm getting sick and tired of him bothering me." After Mr. Evil stormed off, I was able to fall back to sleep. It didn't last long.

Once again, I was awakened by surprise, with my butt landing on the ground. My evil dad yanked me off the sofa, by my ankles. I hit the ground HARD. I got up crying and asked, "Why did you do that?" With the devil behind his eyes, he got right up to my face and said, "You deserved it for hitting me!" "You pulled me off the sofa," I cried. Dad ignored me. He left the den, only wearing his underwear. I realized he dressed like that in front of Ronny. Disgustingly Gross!

I went out on the balcony for some alone time, because Ronny was still sleeping in my bed. As I stood there looking up to the sky, I cried out in prayer, "Why does my life have to be like this? What did I do to deserve this? What? Why do I have to be with my mean dad? Why God, Why? Rain E, if you can hear me, I need to see you. I'm so sad. My dad is so cruel! I can't call my mom, so I'm calling you." I dropped my head into my hands. Tears were filling them. With my warm breath I whispered, "Please, someone up there, help me, please!" I sat on one of the balcony chairs. Ouch! My rear end was already sore and hurting bad. I wasn't about to tell my dad. He would just say he was glad it was hurting and then laugh about it.

Mr. Evil came out on the balcony and said Ronny was leaving. He ordered me to get my lazy ass up and go pull all of the sheets off my bed. He reminded me that his mother was coming over to clean, as usual. I glanced into the condo to see Ronny leaving my room. I went back inside. Dad was at the front door saying goodbye to him. I walked slowly to my room, watching the two of them. They hugged for a long time. Dad opened the door and as Ronny left, he popped him on his hinny, and squeezed it. Why? It grossed me out big time!! Dad closed the door. I quickly hurried and made it to my room, before he saw me. He was still just wearing his underwear.

I walked up to my bed, to remove the sheets. I smelled a bad odor, a nasty odor! I guess Ronny didn't bathe before getting into MY bed. After I pulled the top sheet off, I saw a large stain near the foot of the bed. "Just Great! Ronny spilt a drink in my bed." I immediately contemplated. I leaned over. It smelled awful. "What kind of drink was that?" I thought and gagged at the same time. I took the bottom sheet off and took both to the utility. I never want to sleep in that bed again, but I knew I would l have to. As I walked out, "Meany" was coming down the hallway. He screamed for me to get my ass on the homework. I hated the way he talked to me. I asked if I could first get something to eat. He yelled back to just make sure I cleaned up my mess.

In the *hospital* kitchen, I got out my cereal, milk, bowl and a spoon and ate over the sink, like always. I cleaned and put everything back in its proper place. I routinely dried out the sink, with my shirt. I was NEVER touching the dish towel, EVER again. I headed back to my room, changed shirts and placed my wet one over the shower rod. I would be taking it home to wash. The detergent Dad used stunk. I noticed he bought the cheapest stuff for Martha and me to use, yet he spent all the money he wanted on himself and "The Boys." Why was that? Did that mean Martha and me are cheap and the boys are worth more?

I gathered up my first weekend of homework and went to the kitchen table. I got out the dull math. It was my least favorite subject. Mr. Half-Naked walked into the kitchen, to refill his coffee cup. He always prepared his coffee overnight and set the timer to come on in the morning. I never knew why he drank coffee, by the time he added twelve small packs of the artificial sweetener (I've counted them before), he might as well been drinking syrup. I guess, 'to each his own'.

Just as Dad was leaving the kitchen, his mother arrived. He was about to say something to me, when the conversation turned to her. Here came the list of chores along with some unkind, humiliating choice words. "Get your "F" n" worthless, lazy ass cleaning this place spotless! Start with the laundry. The sheets need to be washed twice. If you think you can hold that information in your pea-sized brain."

I kept my face down and my hands over my ears to try to drown out the cussing. He continued humiliating her with more unkind words, "Don't forget I bought you a brand new washer and dryer last week. I expect some work out of you." That was my dad. A price came with gifts, unlike Santa Claus. Santa Claus gifts were free giving you joy, happiness, and a feeling of love. Mr. Evil gave you nothing but guilt, sadness, and a feeling of worthlessness. After the drill Sergeant finished yelling, he left the room and went back to his office.

Martha walked over to me and in her sad and mousy voice said, "Hi". Not even "Hi Tweetie". I could tell she was embarrassed. She should be. Martha was the reason her son treated her and everybody else like dirt. It was 100% her fault. She never taught him how to behave and now she is so beaten down, it was now too late. I think this was one of the main reasons my mom divorced Mr. Evil. I knew it was so disrespectful to call my dad ugly names and complain about my ex-grandma. I couldn't help the way I felt. Dads are supposed to protect and take care of you and so should grandmas. Dad and his mom did neither.

When I would call him Mr. Evil to myself, I pretended he was not my dad and it would help some. I learned to just block him out of my mind. This was the only way I could survive my time with him. I have other names I call my dad, but only under my breath. God, and now Rain E exclusively hear those names. They know how evil my dad is! He will always be mean and hateful to me, because he enjoys it. Someday if Mr. Evil even tries to be nice to me, it will be too late. The damage will have been done!

Martha stayed busy cleaning the entire condo. I finally finished my homework, of course without any help from Dad. The drill Sergeant came out of his bedroom and said he was going to steam. I guess he finally decided to clothe himself. Thank goodness he would be gone for a while! After my room was cleaned, I thanked my ex-grandma and politely told her I wanted to be alone. I closed my door and went straight to my closet. I reach up and got my drawing. Sitting next to it was one of my boot shoeboxes. It was the perfect place to hide my pad. Dad would never look in there. I don't think so. I hope not!

I climbed up on my bed and got out my colored pencils, from my backpack to add the finishing touches to both roses. I drew the bridge over the pond, coloring it white and green. It was fun drawing lots of different size and colored fish. I added orange to the red bench. After adding all the plants and trees I could remember, I rested my hand. I glanced over at my window and thought about Rain E. Oh my goodness! My rainbow pajamas! I almost forgot. I reached under my bed and pulled out the secret box I snuck them out in, without Mom noticing. They were still neatly wrapped in the tissue paper from the store. I unwrapped the pajamas and held them in front me. "I do believe Rain E will love them. Rainbow colors all over, and a rainbow on the back," I proudly said to myself.

Several hours went by. I heard the monster open the front door. With no time to spare, I quickly gathered up all my colored pencils and drawing and shoved them under my bed, along with my pajamas. Whew! I got it done before the door opened. I nervously sat up on my bed. I grabbed a book I always kept under one of my pillows and opened it up. That was close!!

The door violently flew open, bouncing off the wall. "Get dressed. I'm hungry," he barked. He never apologized for yanking me off the sofa and not an "I'm sorry" for shoving a stuffed animal in my face. He was ready to eat. It was always about him, where he wanted to eat, where he wanted to travel, where he wanted to shop. He always has the final word. My dad thinks the world was put here just for him. I got up and put some long jeans on with my T- shirt. The three of us went to eat at *HIS* favorite restaurant. Nothing was said at dinner.

The second we stepped into the condo, Dad growled, "Get your ass to bed, fast." I hurried to my room and closed the door. To this day I have never understood why he always started every sentence "mean". He was mean to me, mean to his mom and mean to everyone he came in contact with. Mean and Insane! Another pertinent reason Mom kicked Dad out of the house!

I got my stuff and headed straight to my bathroom. Thinking about my drawing and Rain E's beautiful pond, I decided to create a small one in the shower. I stepped in and put a towel over the drain. The water filled up fast. I sat there enjoying my pond, not realizing the water was pouring out all over the bathroom floor. When I got out, I panicked! Oh My Gosh! The water was everywhere! My heart started beating so fast. I knew I had to get this cleaned up, before *He* comes in. I quickly put on a nightshirt and gym shorts.

Then it happened! Mr. Evil was at the door banging and pounding so hard I thought it was going to break loose from the hinges. "You've been in there long enough. Get your "F' n" fat ass to bed, NOW!!" I cleaned the water up the best I could. All the towels were soaking wet. I hid them in the shower and opened the door.

Dad spotted some of the water on the floor. He rudely brushed passed me and over to the shower door. He saw the pile of towels in the corner and lost it. I tried to explain the small pond was just for fun and it was just an accident. Over and over I kept telling him how sorry I was for making a mess. He couldn't hear me over his loud, screaming voice. He was in a rage. Then, he got right in my face and screamed, "Just look at this "F" mess! Do I need to get my "GD" belt out and beat the liv'in "S" out of you?" I was terrified. My dad was out of control. His mother ran in asking, "What is going? What is all the screaming?" She saw the wet towels in the shower, and me back on the floor still trying to mop up the water. Dad left, yelling that he would be right back.

His mother got down on the floor and started helping me clean up. I whispered in her ear that he was getting his belt and I was scared. I saw in her face, that she was scared for me. She was scared for herself too. She had seen that look in her son's eyes before. Mr. Evil came back in carrying his thick belt. He began swinging it near me, hitting the door, the walls, the floor and almost his mother. She tried to get him to stop, but that was a losing battle. He was in such a rage there was no stopping him.

My dad would flip out over anything, but this was the worst I had ever seen. I knew he was a neat freak. Everything in the house had to be perfect. He would go absolutely insane, if there is a crumb of food on the floor, a towel not folded perfect, (remember), food cans have to be lined up straight with the names showing, same with the drinks in the refrigerator, and the list goes on.

His own mother had to vacuum the carpet in the same direction. If she did it wrong Dad made her do it over. Mom said it was like walking on pins and needles, living with Dad. Now I understood what that meant. If you barely did something my dad didn't like, that pin went right up into your foot. It would hurt and take a while to feel better. Then another pin or needle would shoot through you. That pain was constant, living with my dad!

Dad kept screaming and swinging his belt. He told his mom to finish cleaning the "F" n mess. Then he glared at me, like the devil, and told me to get my ass to my room, NOW! I was almost by him when I stumbled, bumping his leg. I looked up. Dad raised a hand above his head. I cried out, "No dad, no don't hit me, please!! I'm sorry for making the mess, it will never happen again." I think he was just trying to scare me some more and to remind me of who was in charge. I was trying to get past him as fast as I could. My hands were covering my face. I glanced up to see where his swinging belt was, when it struck my right eye hard. I screamed out and ran to my room.

Mr. Evil followed me. I was crying and crying, asking him why he hit me in the face. In his evil, devil voice he said, "If you tell your mother what happened, you will live to regret it. You got that!" I didn't know what he meant. He continued screaming, "I will tell the therapist, you hurt yourself on purpose to make me look bad and that you are a "GD" liar just like your mother. Doesn't matter what you tell the therapist. He doesn't believe you anyway. Trust me, he's on my side." I was more scared than ever. Then he barked, "I will kill your mother and you will be living with me! How would you like that missy?" Before he left my bedroom, he gave me the most chilling, evilest look. He turned the lights off as he left. I quickly got up to shut the door and to see where he was going. Of course it was the office. He lived on his computer.

His mother finished cleaning up the bathroom mess. She said it was late and decided to spend the night. I think she wanted to make sure I was going to be okay. I did feel a little safer having her here, after what happened tonight. I got into bed. The front of my shirt was wet from the water on the bathroom floor, along with my tears. My eye was stinging so badly! Finally, all was quiet. I stayed very still, thinking about what had happened.

The last light went off in the condo. The monster went to bed. I reached under my bed and grabbed the new pajamas. I carefully pulled my wet T-shirt over my head, and then took my shorts off. I set them by the bed and hurried to put the rainbow pajamas on. I'm now glad I brought them with me. After the horrible night I just had, I know they will help me feel better. I can hardly wait to show them to Rain E. I know it was so sneaky, bringing them from home, especially without asking Mom. I don't think she would have minded at all. I just wasn't ready to tell her about Rain E and I didn't want to have to lie.

With the lights off and wearing my new rainbow pajamas, maybe now I could sleep. My eyes were closed. The right one was slightly throbbing. My fingers were touching the soft flannel pajamas as my mind wandered back to last weekend, shopping with Mom. I could still see it so clearly. I was walking into my favorite clothing store, when I immediately spotted the beautiful rainbow pajamas, hanging on the back wall. Mom also thought they were lovely. She bought them for me. She saw how happy it made me. Mom also added that I needed some new pajamas, because I was growing fast. I think deep down inside she knew how much I loved them. That was a happy memory.

A few tears fell from my eyes. I tried to dry them, but it hurt when I wiped my right eye. I quietly cried out to God, "Please help me. I want to see Rain E. I need to see Rain E. I miss her. Help me God, Please!" I finally fell asleep, but not for long.

I woke up to a scary thunderstorm and instantly threw my white, comfy comforter over my head. Why is it that you always feel safe if you have something warm over you? That comforter protected me from danger. While I was under there, it reminded me of the fluffy clouds at Rain E's home. I wanted so much to be there. The storm was getting louder and I was getting scared. I wasn't scared enough to wake evil dad. Instead, I decided to make a fort with my comforter.

While I was on my back I raised my knees, so the bottom of my feet could be flat on the bed. Then, I kept my hands above my head. My elbows, along with my hands and knees, held the fort up pretty good. Sometimes the middle of the comforter would gently float down and land on my face. My hands would just push it back up. Sometimes blowing with my nose and mouth would make it go back up. The air that came out made my fort warm. It helped relax me. I continued blowing a few more times, painstakingly trying to keep the comforter up. My arms tired and fell to my side. I dozed off.

*"Joy descends gently upon us like the evening dew,
and does not patter down like a hailstorm."*

Jean Paul

Chapter 9

My eyes barely opened to my white fort comfortably resting on my nose. Out of habit, I blew on it with my warm breath. I opened my eyes a little wider and noticed it had vanished. Still in my "Sleep Mode", I casually looked around and realized it wasn't my comforter I blew on. It was a fluffy white cloud. A fluffy white cloud!!! Yikes! Was I dreaming? Surely I was dreaming. I closed my eyes, stayed completely still and just waited for my dream to end.

Then I heard a boy's voice. Carefully lifting my head, I looked around. The voice was moving closer to me. A large cloud moved out of the way. I saw him. He was riding on top of another fluffy white cloud. As the boy came closer, he yelled out, "Do not be afraid. I'm Bolt." Rachel, I'm a close friend of R A IN. She asked me to come and get you." Wow! This wasn't a dream! Bolt IS real! He even pronounced her name correctly. I need to practice saying R A IN, her name!

I lifted my body and saw Bolt getting closer. I called out, "You have a much easier name to pronounce." Bolt said, "Easy for you Rachel. You deserve to have at least one easy name to say, since the hardest one is yet to come. Oops, I shouldn't have said that." Bolt looked up as though he was in trouble. I was too confused to ask what he was talking about. I was thinking about my face. I kept my bruised right eye slightly covered so Bolt wouldn't see it. I felt ashamed and embarrassed. I don't know why, I just did. Here I thought I was getting stronger and my dad beat me down once again.

Bolt drove his cloud, and parked it right beside me. I got a real good look at him. He was a nice looking boy, with curly blonde hair and crystal blue eyes. Still had a little baby fat around the stomach. He was cute! Beautiful fair-colored skin! He was wearing some sort of a bodysuit. It was gray with black splotches here and there. I told him I liked it. He said it was easy to wear when he was in the clouds. He added that the splotches change color according to the weather. The color gray represented rain, with black thunderclouds. You know, the black splotches did look like thunderstorm clouds. Bolt was definitely entertaining and what a sense of humor, just like Rain E!

We kept talking a bit, sitting comfortably on our individual clouds. He was chattier than Rain E, kind of like me. Bolt told me R A IN was finishing up her work at the flower garden. He came to meet me and then to take me to her. "We have to hurry," Bolt frantically stated. "She will be waiting. I sometimes ramble on and waste time, that's my biggest problem, wasting time." I said, "I don't think you are wasting time when getting to know someone. That's what I call "Special" time."

Bolt looked right at my face and said, "R A IN said you were special, I agree. I also think you are very nice and have a good eye for fashion." I removed my hand covering my right eye, smiled and said, "Thanks." Bolt saw my eye. Was that why he said I had a good eye for fashion? I knew he wasn't making fun of it. He was too nice and considerate. "Hey, Rachel I like what you're wearing. You like mine and I like yours," Bolt announced.

Oh my! Bolt wasn't talking about my black eye. He really was talking about fashion. Bolt looked at my eye, as though the bruise wasn't even there. I felt so loved. We smiled at each other. Bolt stated, "Okay, my new friend, I'm ready go, if you are," I cautiously spoke, "Excuse me for asking, but for goodness sakes how are we going to get down to the ground?" "That's easy. Rachel, look above your head." I cautiously tilted my head and gasped!

Magically the clouds were now all the colors of the rainbow. It was unbelievable! As I was looking at all of them, I realized Bolt knew my name. I never told him in our conversation. Can he read my thoughts like Rain E? Wow! I felt special. Bolt said, "Reach out and grab a favorite colored cloud." I asked, "Won't I fall?" Bolt assured me that wouldn't happen and to trust him. I did. I trusted everything about Rain E's Rainbow.

I reached out and grabbed a blue cloud and all of a sudden it turned into a blue umbrella. The umbrella floated straight down and landed right smack in front of the entrance gate to "The Flowers of the Week

Garden". I hollered, "Bye Bolt! I enjoyed our time together!" I heard him say just two wonderful words, "Me Too!"

Rain E was standing tall, grin and all, waiting for ME! "Hi there pal," Rain E said with a smile. "Want to help me finish pruning the daisies?" "Daisies," I shouted, "I love daisies! I would love to help." Rain E declared, "I truly believe daisies are the happiest of flowers. They are shaped like the sun. That is how the sun is always drawn." She was absolutely right.

Rain E added, "These flowers will make you feel happy again, Rachel. I know you have been extremely sad." I asked her, "How did you know I was sad?" "You chose a blue cloud. Like when you are feeling blue," Rain E commented. Rain E always knew how I was feeling inside. I was surprised she never mentioned my eye. Somehow I felt she already knew what had happened to me, but didn't pry. I loved that about her.

We finished all the garden chores. I strolled up and down all the garden paths like before. The daisies were happy looking. They were standing tall, perky and proud, showing so much confidence. The way I should be. We washed and dried our hands and walked out the main gate. I said, "Thank you Rain E that was so enjoyable. I'm glad I got to see the flower garden again." Rain E genuinely answered, "I know how much you love flowers Rachel, and they really love you. They seem to smile, every time you visit. You ready?" I naturally responded, "Ready for what?" "I want to show you something at the bottom of a specific hill." "Okay." I happily added.

We climbed to the top of the hill. I looked down to see several kites resting on the plush green grass. "We are going to fly today," Rain E announced. I corrected her, "You mean we're going to fly kites." "No, the kites are going to fly us," Rain E giggled. "You need to feel free and far away from your dad. Let's start by racing down the hill!" So we grabbed each other's hand and tore off running, laughing the whole way down the hill.

Rain E let me choose first. I chose the beautiful butterfly kite. Always wondered what it would be like to ride on the back of a butterfly! I was about to find out. Rain E climbed on the back of a dove kite. I had to gently climb on my kite, because my rear end hurt. I also wanted to make sure not to damage the delicate wings. This was going to be quite an adventure. I hope I live to tell about it!

With his love, he will calm all your fears.

Zephaniah 3:17 (NLT)

Chapter 10

I was a bit nervous. Anybody would be. I looked to my left. Rain E was on her dove. She looked at me, then at her kite. I watched her lean forward and whisper in the dove's ears. Where are the ears?? It was obvious these two knew each other. Rain E's dove kite glanced at my butterfly kite and gave a slight nod. I gasped out loud. Rain E's kite moved! My kite looked back at me and nodded, then at Rain E and her dove kite. The kites came alive!! There was movement under me. My kite was soft, which helped cushion my sore butt. I was adjusting my position, when I saw the kites look at each other one more time, as though they knew what was expected of them.

Dove kite took off. Rain E screamed out, "Ya Whooooo!" I hugged my kite's lower neck. Off we went. Leaving the ground, I glanced down and saw only a few clouds. I was moving through the air. I screamed, "Ya Whooooo!" It was the perfect phrase. My butterfly kept right up with Rain E's dove. All four of us were gliding smoothly across the incredible sky. I looked over at Rain E's kite. Her dove had unusual, but interesting colors. The head was a dark gray brown. The neck was the same as the head, except for the speckled areas of bright fluorescent green color. It was uniquely beautiful. The wings were white and gray. Those dove wings could spread out farther than you can imagine.

My butterfly kite's wings could do the same. As I was riding, I could see the top wings were mostly black and outlined in a bright blue. I glanced back and noticed the bottom wings were the same bright blue, but with black dots near the back. The two colors were magnificent together. Funny, black and blue looks spectacular on a butterfly, not so much on a child's face! Maybe that's why I choose the butterfly. Two colors perfectly placed on something of beauty!

These two living kites were so incredible they needed to be honored with a name. I named them Butterfly and Dove, names well deserving and yet practical. I leaned in close to Butterfly and whispered her name and added, "You can't hear me, because butterflies can't hear, but I wanted to tell you anyway. Maybe you can understand through the vibrations of my voice. I lifted my body up, then forward, to see where Rain E was. Butterfly looked back at me. I gasped, "You can hear me?" If so, nod twice. Butterfly nodded once. I waited and waited. Here came the second nod. I yelled out with so much zest and overwhelming joy, "Butterfly can hear! My Butterfly can hear!!!!"

We continued going through cloud after cloud, climbing higher and higher into the sky. The ride was amazing. Dove and Butterfly seem to know every part of the sky. They stayed right together. I looked around as much as possible, without falling off. I saw some very unique shaped clouds. Some were even in the form of angels. As a matter of fact, I thought I saw actual angels amongst the rather thick white clouds. Butterfly was staring at them too. She glanced to the right. Her eyes stayed focused on the clouds. Then she glanced to her left. I watched her expression the whole time. She knew something about these clouds. Butterfly then looked straight ahead.

We were close to Rain E and Dove. I watched them as they passed through the clouds. I almost fell off, so I held on tighter. Dove and Rain E slowly nodded their heads to each side of the clouds. Butterfly also nodded. I joined in. They knew something. It was a privilege to be among these three. We were nodding to royalty, just like people bowing and lowering their heads to a king and queen, but our nods were to a higher authority. I felt honored and blessed to be a part of Rain E's life. Butterfly kept her eyes on the clouds and on Dove. I believe the angel clouds were guiding us on our jourr ey. It was peaceful and so surreal up here high in the sky. Such a smooth ride!

Then all of a sudden, Rain E took a turn abruptly to the left. We followed close behind. Up ahead the clouds were thicker and darker. I didn't panic, well, maybe a little. Butterfly stayed right behind Dove, as though they knew this route. I watched Rain E press on. She went straight into the dark clouds, on purpose. Why? The situation was getting a little scary. The sky was now completely black. The clouds started making a lot of noise. The rain began, a lot of rain! In no time at all this became a vicious, vicious storm. These were the darkest, blackest clouds I had ever seen and I was up inside of them! I kept telling myself to stay calm, because I was with Rain E. She would get us through.

At first it was hard to make out anything. Then, I looked closely to my right, squinting my eyes. I could have sworn I saw hands coming out of the dark clouds, or was I just seeing things? I held on tighter than ever to Butterfly. "Butterfly, get me out of here!" I frightfully leaned in and shrieked. I looked up again and couldn't see Dove. This time I screamed out, "Rain E where are you?" Rain E yelled back, "I'm still here, we are almost out. Hang on!" I yelled back, "Okay!"

Butterfly pressed on. I bet she had flown through many storms. Rain was coming down hard. The tornado-like wind was fierce. Butterfly was going up, then down, as the winds kept shifting. My body was being thrown in every direction. Sometimes my hinny lifted up, then down, causing shooting pain. I tried my best to stay snug tight to her neck, but was having a difficult time holding on. I must have looked like one of those cowboys at the rodeo, riding a bronco bull. I even had to tuck both arms and legs around Butterfly's body. She didn't seem to mind at all.

The rain kept pouring and pouring. We were soaking wet. This was one violent storm! I was scared!! "God Help Us!!!" I cried out. At that very moment, I saw the clear sky below me. We made it out. I thanked God immediately. I hugged Butterfly, and lifted my head. I loosened up my grip and politely said to her, "I hope I didn't choke you!" Butterfly leaned her head back as far as she could. I think she was showing me that she could breathe just fine.

I looked up. Wow, the sky was beautiful. The clouds were so white and fluffy, just like when I first arrived. I was looking ahead, watching Rain E and Dove, when the clouds parted. Sitting on top of the last cloud was Bolt. He waved to me and I waved back. As we passed by, I heard him shout, "See you at Christmas!" I quickly responded, "Okay!" After he said that, I realized I was going to be back at Christmas. A warm feeling of love filled my insides. My heart didn't feel as empty. I now had four pals; Rain E, Bolt, Dove and Butterfly. Christmas was only a few months away. I would be seeing my Rainbow friends during the holidays.

We kept moving towards a mountain up ahead. Our kites smoothly landed near the top, as if they knew that this was the final destination.

Rain E climbed off first. She hurried over to help me. I think she knew my butt was sore, now even worse from the ride. She must have heard me moaning, when I first climbed on Butterfly. Dove and Butterfly stayed on the ground. I think they were taking a break. They certainly deserved one.

Rain E took my hand and we walked a short distance to get to the very top of the mountain. The walk took a little out of me, having a sore hinny and all. As we were getting closer, I could see the back of the red bench. We finally reached the top. It was incredible! Absolutely the most amazing view! Dove and Butterfly flew right by. Rain E waved goodbye. I waved goodbye to Butterfly hollering, "Thank you for the ride." They were gone, just like that, disappearing into the heavens.

I turned to go sit on the bench. As I approached, I saw three colors, red, orange and now yellow. I wondered why, but didn't ask. It was lovely looking. I gently sat down on the yellow color. I was exhausted! Rain E sat down next to me on my right side. She was close enough to get a good look at my bruised eye, but still never mentioned it. We sat there in complete silence. I started thinking why Rain E turned and went straight into the dark clouds, when the rest of the sky was mostly clear. Maybe I would find out! Even though I got scared, the ride was a blast!!!!

Our surroundings were as quiet as the inside of a library. I thought about my horrible weekend and the storm I just went through. This was the perfect place to think. I felt so close to God. Heaven surely must have been on the other side of the clouds. I think Rain E was teaching me the importance of quiet time and listening to one's inner self. She always seemed to know there was a time to talk and a time listen. This was definitely a time to listen.

Calmness came over me. It took traveling through a scary storm to make me realize something important. God was with me the whole time and has always been there during all my other storms. You know, God has been there during a lot of storms involving people; like a big ark, a bad city, a huge fish, a stormy sea, a lion's den, a jail, a sea that opened up so the people could get to safety and now a storm riding on a butterfly!! Isn't GOD GREAT! It took this storm to help me start feeling better about ME!!

This third time with Rain E was an amazing time! Still quiet as a mouse, I looked back up at the amazing sky. It was filled with more fluffy, white clouds. No more black ones. Rain E got me through them.

Oh goodness me! I just realized the dark clouds represented my dad and the white clouds represented my safety. I put all my trust in God and Rain E to get me through and they did! This happened for a reason. Mom has always told me to trust in God and He will get you through the storm. Boy, He did!

It was like the story in Matthew (9-14:31-33) when Peter was in the high waves of the water. He screamed out to The Lord for help. Jesus rescued him. Peter had little faith. I will not have little faith. I will keep my faith strong no matter what happens. A smile, with peacefulness, covered my face. Rain E was quietly smiling too. I know she could hear my thoughts. Maybe she knows about the story of Peter in the water.

After a lot of time passed by, Rain E gently took my hand in hers. It warmed in seconds. Tears came rolling down my cheeks. All it took was her gentle touch. At that moment I realized she knew the horrible things that happened to me. I quietly cried for several minutes. Rain E softly spoke, "Rachel, I apologize if I scared you when we going through the dark clouds and frightening storm. Sometimes we have to go through them. How else can we get to the beautiful white clouds and peaceful sky?" Rain E always knew how to word things so I could understand, just like my mom.

"This is what your life has been like, a bad storm," Rain E added. "You will still go through more bad ones, I'm sure of it. Just remember who is waiting on the calmer side of the storm. There WILL be peace and calm in your life. There will be a silver lining; something better awaiting you! I will help you find that silver lining, I promise. We will get through this together. I'm always here. I will never leave your heart." Wow! Rain E said she would never leave my heart. I wondered what she meant?

Everything Rain E said made my eyes tear up. I tried to hold them back, but one huge tear dropped out of my bruised right eye. I was reaching up to wipe it off my cheek when out of the corner of that eye I could see Rain E turning her head. She took her left hand and wiped it away, before I did, then said, "Rachel, your face is now dry and your ears are calm." I smiled, never tuning my head. We just quietly sat there, staring at the magnificent view. In the distance, I saw a streak of silver clouds drift by. That must be my silver lining Rain E was talking about!

Rain E softly spoke again, "Rachel, I really love your rainbow pajamas. You looked so terrific and fashionable riding Butterfly. What a fun partner to ride with! You rode like a pro." I smiled and giggled, "I love your rainbow shirt and rainbow leggings. They look like a bodysuit." Rain E chuckled, "It is. I like to wear it when I'm riding. So you enjoyed the ride, minus the storm?" I quickly answered, "Are you kidding? It was a blast! A little frightening at times, but I got to talk to a butterfly. Maybe there will be a time I can ride Dove."

Rain E stated, "Actually, Dove is a pigeon. They are similar. She is a Racing Homing pigeon, like the one Noah sent out to look for dry land. Have you ever heard of them?" I politely answered, "I know what a pigeon is. I just didn't know they had special names. Makes sense! There are different kinds of butterflies. I'm going to look pigeons up when I get home."

Rain E added, "When you look up Racing Homing pigeons, look up Cher Ami, a very famous pigeon." "Tell me. Tell me!" I said excitedly. Rain E looked up into the sky. A bolt of light came out from behind a cloud. I watched as Rain E smiled. She turned facing me, lifting her left leg up on the bench and stretched her left arm across the top. I turned and did the same, only opposite.

Rain E started, "A long time ago, way before you were born, there was a war going on between your country and Germany. I interrupted, "I know. It was WW2." Rain E continued. "Yes, that is true, but this one occurred before WW2. It was called WW1. There was a battle intensely going on in the country of France. The US army soldiers were trapped behind enemy lines. The Germans were firing in all directions. The only hope for a rescue would have to come from a message carried by a special bird, a pigeon."

"Pigeons were used as messengers, in different situations. They are very smart and can fly very fast! These trapped US soldiers had three pigeons with them. The first two they sent, were shot down. The third and last one was their final hope. This pigeon was carrying a message that read "Our enemy artillery is dropping a barrage on US. For Heaven's sake, stop it!" So Cher Ami, the pigeon's name, was released. The men watched as he was shot down. All were in despair."

"Then all of a sudden, Cher Ami started flying again. This pigeon was dodging all the bullets. Pigeons can go 92 mph. He made it to a division 25 miles away, in 25 minutes. That is super-fast! When Cher Ami arrived, he collapsed. The Army medic immediately operated on him for a long time. This brave pigeon had been shot in the breast, blinding one eye and had severe damage to one leg. Cher Ami lived that day and saved the lives of 194 U.S. soldiers of the 77th Division known as the "Men of the Lost Battalion", October 4, 1908. That wonderful, compassionate doctor even carved a small wooden leg for him. He flew a total of 12 missions and received many medals. Cher Ami died six months later, due to the wounds he suffered."

"One final part of the story, during the army examination, the doctor discovered Cher Ami was a female! So a female "WAS" in combat in WW1! Word spread fast about this courageous bird, touching the hearts of millions. After she died the army wanted her to be remembered. She is now at the Smithsonian in your State Capital, Washington D.C. (her final resting place). God created Cher Ami and look what she accomplished in her life. Cher Ami means "dear friend". She was some kind of extraordinary bird!"

"How did you like that true story?" I was mesmerized. I told Rain E, "You tell stories as good as my mom! Thank you. I never realized you knew so much about my country. Wow! Can you tell me something about a butterfly? Please!" Rain E looked up. Once again, a bright light appeared. She smiled and said, "Okay. First let me point out, the butterfly has many interesting facts. Some of them are: they can see red, green and yellow; they taste with their feet and butterflies have 3 pair of legs. This specific one I am going to tell you about is a butterfly from the country New Guinea."

"There lives the largest butterfly in the world. It is call the Queen Alexandria. When she expands her wings, they are almost a foot long. The most interesting fact about this butterfly is that she lays her eggs on a poisonous leave of a pine-vine. Throughout all the stages of this butterfly's life, it continues feeding on these poisonous leaves. The leaves do not affect the butterfly. It provides protection. Red hair is present, warning predators the butterfly is highly toxic. Another interesting fact, butterflies cannot fly if their body temperature is less than 86 degrees. So if you see a butterfly flying, it's warm."

Rain E continued, "Okay my sweet Rachel, now you tell me something." I asked, "What would you like to know?" "The new color yellow added to the bench. Tell me what you think about *Yellow*." I remarked, "Yellow is a happy color. It's warm like the sun. It's the brightest color the human eye can see. The sun makes you feel good. My mom told me that yellow represents life." Rain E smiled and said,

"You and your mother are so smart. Remember yellow can also represent self-confidence." I commented, "I never knew that."

We sat there and continued enjoying our time together. I thought about Cher Ami. I bet Mom knew about her life, if not, it will still be fun to tell her the incredible story. I closed my eyes. I could hear Rain E fiddling with something. I peeked with one eye. She had her special clipboard, marking on the top sheet. I never saw the clipboard around the bench. Strange! Very strange! I closed my eye again and just rested.

Some time went by and when I opened both eyes, I was staring at my bedroom ceiling. My time had ended with Rain E. I quickly got up and changed back into my wet clothes. They had dried some. The pajamas were back in their box ready to go back home. I got under my comforter. I was feeling better. I was just about to close my eyes and relive my wonderful time with Rain E, when I heard footsteps in the hallway. My door slung open. "Is your homework done?" Evil Dad growled. I stuck my head out and fearfully responded, "Yes." He hatefully added, "It better be!"

Dad started moving towards me. Oh no! Was he going to hit me again? I didn't see the belt. Was he going to use his fist, like he did on Martha? He stopped right by my bed and leaned forward very close to me. I guess he was admiring his work. In his scary voice, he asked "What's that on your face? Have you been making another "F" mess?" I immediately answered, "No! What are you talking about?" Grumpy Dad added, "You have paint on your face!" I reached up and touched around my eyes and cheeks. It didn't feel anything different. Mr. Evil walked all around my room and then into my closet. I kept my eyes glued to him. I quietly moved my lips, whispering, "I hope he doesn't look up?" He walked out and growled, "Clean that "F" n "S" off your face." Mr. Evil stormed out, never looking under the bed. That was a close call!

I jumped out of bed and ran to my desk. I pulled out my small hand mirror. I gasped! I brought the mirror closer to my bruised eye. There were rainbow colors in the corner, all around the bruise. I studied it for several minutes. Then I remembered Rain E wiped my tear away, with her left hand. She left her mark on me. My Rain E is now a part of me. I reached up to see if it came off. I looked down at my right hand. The rainbow colors were now in my hand. I looked back at my face. The

126

rainbow colors were gone. The bruise was still there but it didn't seem to hurt anymore. It was Rain E's touch.

I got dressed, packed my pajamas and drawing in my backpack so my dad wouldn't see them. I was going home in a few hours. Mr. Evil yelled from the hallway to get some breakfast. I firmly stated that I wasn't hungry and I wasn't. I was full of happiness! I just wanted to get home and add to my drawing. Dad yelled again that he was taking me home shortly, because he had get ready for another trial. Remember, I mentioned my dad was an attorney. I told him I was all ready to go. He always seemed to take me home early. Who cared? Another prayer was answered. We quickly left the condo. I jumped into the backseat.

On our way, evil dad yapped about how I deserved my black eye. I kept my head down, ignoring him. He demanded, "You better have a believable story to tell your mother about what happened this weekend." I briefly glared at him and dropped my head again. "I see you got the "S" off your face." I never looked back up. Instead I looked at my right hand and the rainbow colors were gone. Wow! They must be inside me now because I never washed them off.

A few minutes later, my cell phone struck my head. He actually threw it at me. I picked it up and kept it in my hand, never looking up. Mean, vulgar, rude, unkind, loud, and hurtful, all rolled in to one human, my dad. "Manners" live outside his body! I never spoke. Dad was not going to get a rise out of me no matter how hard he tried. I had feelings of anger and fear inside me. I know it was a dumb mistake clogging up the drain, but like my mom always says "The punishment should fit the crime". If stopping up the drain is a crime, it probably is, at least at Dad's.

We pulled in my driveway. Dad kept the doors locked, so he could scare me some more. He threatened, "You better behave next time you are with me! You got that missy!" He unlocked the car. As I was getting out, I heard, "I Wov Ou!" My mouth dropped. After everything that happened to me, that was the last thing he said in baby talk! I wanted to throw up. I slammed the door, never responding. The sad truth was, I had already thought of a good story about my black eye. It was a given, Mom would be asking. She was my mom and worried every time I was with the monster. Walking to the front door I asked God, "Help my Mom understand my fear!"

Juggling everything high in my arms, I made it to the porch. I blindly leaned into the front door and rang the doorbell with my left middle finger tip. Mom was there in an instant. She immediately asked, "Are you in there? Can I help carry something?" I giggled and politely answered, "I've got it!" "Are you sure I can't help?" "No thank you," I added. I quickly dashed by Mom, holding my backpack and stuff next to my face, to hide my black eye and carefully headed upstairs. I slightly turned my head to the left and told mom, "Just want to get everything put up before dinner." "Okay silly," Mom said. "Something sure smells good!" I knew it was her chili.

I made it to my room dumping everything on the bed. It was a heavy load! I pulled out the drawing pad and placed it on my pillows. Next, came my pajamas. I straddled them across the back of my chair and cracked open the window a couple of inches. The breeze would greatly help remove some of the smelly perfume. I hurried fast, just in case Mom surprised me, wanting to help. After completely cleaning out my backpack, I neatly put everything up in its place. Oh no! I forgot the apple core under the den sofa. I would have to slyly retrieve it on my next visit, hoping Mr. Evil didn't discover it first!

I went into the bathroom and changed clothes. They stunk worse than usual. Mom will have to add extra detergent. There have been times I've had to sit my stuffed animals on the back porch overnight to get rid of the gross smell! As I walked by my bed, I saw my spy glasses and had a brilliant idea. The glasses would hide my black eye! Maybe Mom would let me wear them during dinner?

I tiptoed out of my room and stood at the top of the stairs to see where she was. Mom was in the den, waiting for me. I hollered that I would be right down. She called out, "Hurry my sweet. I've missed you! Hope you're hungry?" I said a loud, "Yes!" Give me one more minute." I watched her walk from the den to the kitchen. I went back to my bedroom, picked up my stinky clothes and put my spy glasses on. I turned the lights out and closed the door behind me.

The entire house smelled of wonderful, happy memories. All those fun memories cooking with Mom! I even chuckled to myself remembering my first cooking experience. From the time I could look over the kitchen counter, Mom was always letting me help her in anyway I could. I felt so grown-up. I was only around five, yet somehow I can still remember walking into the kitchen.

Mom was cooking spaghetti. I watched as she reached into the large pot and pulled out one very long strand. Out of the corner of her eye, she smiled and winked at me. Then, all of a sudden, the strand went flying through the air. It hit the wall, next to the stove and stuck! Wow! Mom was throwing food. How much fun!! I watched her remove it from the wall. She turned and announced, "The spaghetti is ready!" I had a puzzling, but amusing look on my face. "That's how the Italians know," she said. I asked, "Know what?" Mom explained, "It's an old tradition, that if the pasta sticks to the wall, it is perfectly cooked and ready to eat!" She added, "Would you like to try it?" I said a big, "Yes!!"

So Mom carefully took out one strand and handed it to me. It was still hot. I walked a little closer to the wall and flung it. Wow! The spaghetti was part of the wall. That was fun. Mom let me throw one more, actually three. I pretended we were doing a cooking show. I told Mom it was called, "Cooking Cousins." I didn't know why. It just came to me. We laughed and laughed. What a happy memory!

I made my way down to the kitchen, first dropping my clothes in the utility hamper. Mom had her back to me, dishing up the chili. She was wearing black knee-length leggings and a T-shirt from my school. She just had on thick socks, no shoes. Without even looking at me, she said, "You need to remove your spy glasses." "Holy Moly!" I said to myself. When did she see them? Moms really DO have eyes in back of their heads! I stood there stunned and just said, "Okay." Mom had just sat the bowls on the table when I remembered I had left the drawing out on my bed.

In a panic voice, "I forgot to do something! I'll be right back." "Can't it wait?" Mom asked. "No!" I took off my spy glasses and raced upstairs. When I reached my room, I quickly flipped the lights on. There it was. My drawing pad, resting on the bed pillows. I sat my spy glasses on the skirted table and placed the drawing pad under my mattress for safekeeping. Easy to access when I was in bed! I turned the lights back off, shut my door and rushed downstairs, in no time at all. Boy, that was a close call. I wasn't ready for Mom to see the drawing.

Back in the kitchen, we sat down. My chili was cooled and ready to enjoy. We bowed our heads and thanked God for our meal. Mom also thanked God for my safe return home. We sat and ate in silence. The chili was awesome! Mom raised her head. Oh no, here it came. "Are you enjoying school this year in the new building? You are growing up way too fast!" I sat there in shock. She didn't mention my black eye. With relief I said, "I love the new building. It's awesome!" Mom continued, "That was some storm we had this weekend. Did you hide under your comforter?" I smiled and said, "Yeah, but I wasn't as scared this time. I built a fort with it. I love when it rains on Dad's weekends." Mom had a puzzled look on her face.

We continued talking about other things. I hoped so much that I wouldn't have to lie about my eye. I was feeling scared and ashamed at the same time. Ashamed of having to lie to my mom and scared of what my dad would do to me if I didn't lie. That was a lot for a kid my age to have to deal with. Mom was strangely calm. The dreaded question came next. "Are you going to tell me about your black eye?" Mom quietly asked. The hurt in her eyes was almost too much to bear. I dropped my head feeling such shame. I didn't deserve being hit, but I still felt ashamed. I honestly believe Mom stayed calm for me. She hates every time I have to go to Dad's, because no matter what happens, no one helps us.

So here came, *The Lie*. I kept my head down and explained, "I was walking down the hallway, outside the door to Dad's condo, when I dropped his laptop. I bent over the same time Dad did. He grabbed it first and while coming up, the laptop hit my right eye. He said he was sorry (boy that was the biggest lie)". I lifted my head up to see Mom's face. I could see tears filling her eyes. I knew she didn't believe me. Dad never says the words "I'm sorry". She asked if that was the truth. I answered, "Yes, Mom, yes I promise. Please don't call Dad, please, please, pretty please!!!!!!"

I kept begging and begging, over and over for her not to even call the attorney or the police. I was hysterically crying and crying. Tears were flooding my face. I scooted my chair out and went to Mom, grabbing onto her arms. Mom got up from the table and hugged me. We were both crying. She took her hand and dried my tears, then hers and said, "I'm so very, very sorry bad things happen to you when you are with your dad." "I know Mom. I'll be okay, just please don't call anyone," I pleaded. Mom sadly stated, "You're not okay. I feel so helpless. Are you sure you don't want me to call the police? They can at least make a report." I begged and pleaded to do nothing. She could see that I was terrified.

Mom walked over to the counter, got her phone and took a photo of my black eye. I guess some day it might help. We sat back down and finished our chili. The whole time we were talking and crying, I realized Grandma wasn't around. I asked Mom if she was in her room. Mom told me that Grandma went to dinner with some close lady, church friends. I was glad she wasn't here to see my eye. After I finished my chili, I put my bowl and spoon in the kitchen sink. I didn't have to scour them, in this home.

Mom continued eating. I kissed her on the cheek and excused myself to go get ready for bed. As I walked away, I turned and looked back. Mom's hands were together and her head down. I knew she was praying to God to help me. I felt even more ashamed than ever. She has tried over and over to protect me from my crazy, evil dad. No one else, just Mom!

When I reached the stairs, Mom call out, "I'll be up later to say goodnight." Her voice sounded so beaten down. I headed on up to take a much needed long bath. The moment I got in, the hot water felt great! I placed the washcloth over my bad eye. The heat helped. It was a wonderful and very soothing bath. After drying off, I gently slipped on my favorite plaid nightgown, protecting my eye and climbed into bed.

Some time went by. Mom walked in. She sat on the side of the bed and we said our prayer, alternating the verses. We have been doing it that way, since I could talk. Mom leaned over and gave me a long kiss on my forehead. At the exact time, we said, "I love you". She was staring at me. I stared back for a few minutes then said, "Mom, I want to tell you a true story I heard about a famous pigeon." (I wanted to change the subject away from the black eye.) Mom looked right into my eyes and to my astonishment said, "You wouldn't be talking about Cher Ami, would you?" "You know about her?" I surprisingly asked. "How do you know? Tell me."

Mom shared, "I learned about her when I was a little girl, younger than you. Grandma's dad, my grandfather and your great, grandfather told me. His only brother John was a soldier during WW1. The war department never sent both sons of one family, so "Papa", my grandfather stayed home taking care of his family."

"After the war ended, Great Uncle John came home. He told the whole family all about the remarkable pigeon named Cher Ami. Word spread fast how it saved the lives of many soldiers. Cher Ami flew many missions and after she died, she was placed in the Smithsonian for everyone to learn about her." I blurted, "Wow! Mom, you know everything in the whole wild world. Did you also know the soldiers thought Cher Ami was a boy pigeon?" Mom quickly answered, "I DID! So you see, there was a female in combat during WW1."

Wow! Those are the same words Rain E used. Freaky! Mom got up. She was about to flip the light switch, when she turned, suspiciously asking, "How did you know about Cher Ami? Did you learn it at school?" I said, "A little bird whispered it in my ear." We laughed a little. Mom added, "Get some rest silly. I love you!" "I love you, MORE," I yelled out! The lights went out. Mom yelled outside my door, "MOST!" I smiled and yelled, "MOSTER!"

Just as I closed my eyes, Sugar jumped on top of me and started preparing her bed, on ME! I hadn't seen her all night. I knew she was glad I was home. I was equally glad. She curled up so close to me, her tail was tickling my side. I leaned over and gave her a kiss on the head. She licked my face, near my black eye. I touched the bruise one last time, wiping off the slobber.

Looking at my hand, I was so ashamed with the made-up story I had to tell. I know Mom didn't believe me. I thought, "My first black eye at the hands of a parent! I wonder how many other kids remember their first?" I rolled over onto the good side of my face and gently felt my bad eye one last time. My hand fell down, past my waist. I fell asleep holding Sugar's paw and hoping the eye would never be mentioned again!

*Let the heads of those who surround me be covered
with the trouble their lips have caused.*

Psalm 140:9 (NIV)

Chapter 11

Two wonderful weeks with Mom! I always cherish my time with her! School is much harder this year. Three hours of homework every night. It was okay. I got use to it. Regardless of the learning part, I will always love my school, mainly because of all my Christian friends. Most of us have been there since kindergarten.

It was once again the *dreaded* Friday. I woke up feeling nervous, as usual. Mom made my favorite breakfast. She knows how much I love her scramble eggs with grated cheese. They were yummy! I finished breakfast and got dressed. Mom was waiting in the car. I got in and we were off. On the way to school, Mom took my left hand and squeezed it tight. She told me to have a wonderful day. I know what she was trying to do. She didn't want me thinking about going to Dad's this evening. She could see it on my sad face.

We pulled up to Logic Building. Mom said, "Have a fun day." I walked in front of our car and took one last look at her. We both smiled. As I walked to my homeroom, I decided I was going at least try and have a fun day. My school is fun and I have fun friends. A few bully girls, actually one, but she leaves me alone. I wish she would leave the other girls alone! She thinks she is hot stuff, but she's not to most of the girls. Guess there's one at every school. Wonder if the other school's bullies are as snotty as ours? I guess she's snotty because her mom is.

The school day came to an end. Darn it! Excuse my language. Walking out of the building, I could see Mom was first in line. She always arrives early on the Fridays I go to the "Damn Evil Tower". Mom always wants to spend as much time together, before *the honks*. We got home and I finished my homework, because Dad never helps me. Oh, what a surprise! I finished just in time for Mom and I to say our "Stair Prayers". That's what I named them. I just never told Mom until today. Mom told me I was very clever. She looked at my face and asked if everything was okay. I told her I wasn't sure, that I just felt a little different this time. She asked if I was getting sick. I told her I just felt funny inside, not sick.

For some odd reason, I wasn't emotionally prepared for this visit. We talked a bit. "Mom, can I ask you something? Mom said, "Absolutely! Did something else happen to you? Please tell me!" I said, "I just want to ask you what the meaning of some words I heard Dad use, last time I was there." Mom answered with sort of a question, "Okay?" "What does "fag-it" and "queer" mean?" Mom was silent, but not for long. "Excuse me!" Mom exploded. "Where and when did you hear those disgraceful words?" I told her, "Dad called Ronny those names. What do they mean?"

Mom forcefully explained, "Those two unkind words are used by people who are unkind. They describe a certain group of men in a very bad way. Do you understand?" "Why did Dad say it to Ronny?" I asked. Mom said she would she would explain more when I was older. I was okay with the answer. I thought they sounded like bad words. I heard one of them once on the school playground. People can be so cruel, like my Dad. I was going to ask about the naked boys playing leapfrog, but ran out of time. I will though!

Here came *the honks,* one right after another. I thanked Mom for telling me the truth. We hugged. I stepped outside and turned to walk backwards. Mom and I signed "I Love You," like always. When I turned around, I glanced at the front of the car. Someone was sitting by Dad. The windows are so tinted, I couldn't tell who it was. I climbed into the back and to my stunned surprise it was a really old-looking lady. She immediately turned and said, "Hi. I'm Sissy. You can call me 'Mama Sissy' or just 'Mom', which ever you like or which ever suits you best."

I was in shock. I mean the kind of shock when the mouth stays open for some time. This old lady, whom I've never met before, wanted me to call her 'Mom'. "Is she nuts?" I asked myself. I know my dad put her up to this. He's been trying for two years to make me hate my mom. From the moment Mom filed for divorce, my evil dad had said mean and hateful things about her. Lies, lies, lies! He would even call her an "F" n "B" to my face, trying to get me to hate her. My mom, who I love more than him! That bugs my dad the most. She's my mom. Why shouldn't I love her? She NEVER hurts me. Dad actually told me she didn't really love me. Why would my dad or any dad, say such a mean thing? Didn't he realize how deeply that hurt me?

This old lady was waiting for me to answer her. So I did. I deliberately looked out my window, and firmly said, "No thank you, I already have a mom. Don't need another one!" I didn't even look to see her reaction. I was so mad. You know, I didn't even remember if she mentioned her last name. All I could think about was her wanting to push my mom out of my life. I was repulsed!

This stranger was trying to replace my mom and that was NEVER going to happen. She was a monster as far as I was concerned. Most monsters only have a first name. So I didn't care what her last name was. To me she was "Monster Sissy", not "Mama Sissy". This old lady wanted to be my mom! UH!! FAT CHANCE!! What was even worse, my parents weren't even divorced. I remained quiet the rest of the trip.

The front-seat monsters kept whispering. This went on the whole way back to the condo. I just glared out the window. When we pulled into the garage, I got out and slammed my door. Funny, my dad didn't even make a comment, not even in the elevator. It made me wonder what he was up to. When we reached the front door, I pushed my way past them and walked straight to my room. I turned to shut my door and saw Sissy go into my dad's bedroom. Why was she going in there? Dad walked in behind her and shut the door. I had to hear what was going on, so I quietly tiptoed down there.

My dad talks so loud, I could hear him saying, "Well "S"! That didn't go over so well. Just keep working on her, you can break her in." I thought, "You can break her in? What am I, an animal! Break me in! I know where the toilet is! I don't pee on the floor!" Then I heard, "I'm working on getting the "B" ex out of the picture." Oh my goodness. I hurried back to my room and closed my door. I was shaking inside. My dad was talking to his new girlfriend about getting rid of my mom. That means she's in on it!

I was in my room for some time, when there was a soft knocked on my door. "Rachel, it's Sissy Mom, can I come in?" I answered, "No, I'm studying and want to be left alone." She left. A few minutes later, Mr. Evil barged in. He started screaming about why I was being such an "F" n brat to Sissy. He actually said, "I order you to treat her nice, because she is here to stay!" I looked at him and asked, "What do you mean, here?" He said that Sissy moved in last week. I glared at him and said with confidence, "You're not even divorced and now you have a woman living with you. That's a sin!"

He stormed out of my room. Every time I talked Bible stuff, he had nothing to say. I should bring the subject up more often. As Dad was walking down the hallway, I got up and yelled, "You need to go to the library and check out a Bible. Look in Exodus. That's where you will find the Ten Commandments, if you've ever even heard of them!" I shut my door and plopped down on my bed. I looked up at my ceiling. You know, that felt good talking about the Bible. I must be getting stronger, because Dad walked away completely ignoring me. Who he is really ignoring is God. Wonder when God will let him know this? At least I have one Christian parent.

While on my bed, I started thinking about my parents. I had a wonderful relationship with my mom. My relationship with my dad was like a ladder. I was supposed to be near the top. You always put God first, or at least you better and then your wife or husband, followed by your kids. I had been taught this. On my Dad's ladder, HE was at the top (guess cause he thinks he's God), next came his work, then his car and stuff, then his teenage boyfriends and now the "new" live-in girlfriend. I didn't know exactly where the ex-grandma fitted in. Didn't matter, I was below all of them. I was so close to the bottom, the day would come when I could finally step off this sad ladder.

I gave up a long time ago, fighting for the appropriate spot on *his* ladder. All I ever wanted was Dad's love and attention. Even just a crumb of affection! Was that too much to ask for? I knew would never happen. Sadly, I didn't care anymore. My dad was incapable of loving anyone else. My mom had been trying to help me see and understand this.

It wasn't until I was away from my mom and was spending time alone with my dad, to really see what she was talking about. In school, I had been studying Medieval Times. One day, the teacher was going over the Roman and Greek period. I heard her say the word "Narcissus". My eyes bugged out. Mom had called my dad that name. I paid extra attention, when the teacher started talking. She said, "There was a man named Narcissus. One day, he saw his reflection in a pond and he fell in love with himself. He thought he was the greatest and everyone around him was to serve just him." "Oh my goodness sakes! That's my dad! I mean, that's my dad!! He can only love himself. No room for anyone else." I said to myself.

That same day, after school, I got in the car and immediately told Mom, "I get it now, I know why Dad is the way he is. We learned about Narcissus in my Latin class." Mom didn't say much. I think she was sad and glad I discovered this on my own. I'm glad I now know! My dad is sick, mentally sick. Now I would have to be stronger than ever, to cope with him and a new girlfriend.

I had been taught at my Christian school, that to become a stronger Christian you needed strong branches of faith. Like a tree, your branches would grow and shoot up and out in every direction. You just needed to make sure your branches were growing in the right direction. My branches were going to reach up and hold on to what was important.

So far, my strong tree branches were my mom, my Christian school, my church, my Rain E and most important God. God, Rain E and Mom have helped my tree (ME) grow branches of strength, healing and courage. My branches WILL continue growing and growing and growing, for the rest of my life. Maybe my tree will become as big as the Giant Sequoia, believed to be the largest living organism in the world! I learned that in my science class.

Even though my tree would be huge, there will still be no place for my dad, not for somebody mean and cruel like him. He had hurt me and Martha most of all, and he wanted to kill my mom. Now why would I want someone like him on my "faith" tree?

There was a time, long, long ago, I wanted him to love me, but now I know that was impossible. Just that tiny crumb of caring affection would have made all the difference in the world. Now with a new girlfriend, there was no room for me at all! A new girlfriend! I couldn't believe it! Now I was going to be around TWO sinners, Sissy and Mr. Evil. Yuk!!

I wondered what she saw in him? I guess it was the money. She looked so much older than my dad, like a mother. I thought to myself, "Hey! Maybe that's why he found her. He said he wanted a younger maid. Maybe she's the new maid. I bet Martha won't be coming to clean anymore."

The funny thing is Sissy reminded me of Martha. She was also very mousy quiet. I could tell immediately she did everything Mr. Evil says. She was shorter than him and that was short! She had dull reddish-brown hair and very pale skin. Sissy also wore pale clothes like Martha. She almost looked sick. She had to be sick to be with my dad. One puzzling thought, "Maybe, just maybe, Sissy 'might' protect me."

Fearing people is a dangerous trap,
but trusting the Lord means safety.

Proverbs 29:25 (NLT)

Chapter 12

I stayed in my room studying for my weekly tests. Studying at the condo always helped keep my mind off being with evil dad. I was going over my Latin words, when the doorbell rang. It was "The Boys". The two teenage boys over again on my weekend! They gave me the creeps, mostly Ronny. Blake wasn't so bad. I heard one of them call Sissy, Aunt "Sissy Mom". Sissy was their aunt. So that was how my dad met her. I see one big happy, creepy family and now they were trying to make me a part of it and push my wonderful, devoted mom out of the picture! I thought I was going to puke on my pillow. That's why she wanted me to call her "Sissy Mom". That was what "The Boys" call her. I could hear all of them laughing and talking loud.

Mr. Evil burst into my room and told me to say "Hi" to Uncle Ronny and Uncle Blake. I looked at him and said, "They're NOT my uncles like I told you before. Mom said so!" He growled, "Quit being such a "F" n "B" and do what I say!" I couldn't believe what I heard. My mean and evil dad just called me a "B" for the first time. I was crushed. I guess he would call me that from now on. He called his mother that and my mom. He continued, "Sissy and "The Boys" are going to the store. You wanna go?" I firmly stated, "No thank you, I don't even know them. I'm not supposed to go off with strangers. Aren't you going?" Dad said, "No, I have to take care of some business." He stomped out slamming the door. Sissy and "The Boys" left.

My Latin homework was almost finished, when I started getting thirsty. I headed to the kitchen for a bottle of water. My eyes spotted Dad on the den balcony. I walked over to let him know I was getting something to drink. That was the rule! The sliding glass door was a few inches open. He had his back to me, leaning over the balcony rail.

As I got closer, I could hear him talking on his cell phone. Just as I was about to slide the glass door completely open I heard Dad angrily yelling to the person on the phone, the chilling words, "I want her dead, NOW! How much?" I froze. For a moment, I absolutely couldn't move. My ears kept listening. My evil dad was talking so violently loud that he was scaring me with the words he was using. It had to be about Mom!

I started breathing faster. So fast, you could hear it. I took my left hand and covered my mouth. My plotting dad kept talking louder and louder. Somehow I was going to have to get to my room, as fast as possible, without him knowing. I kept my eyes glued on Mr. Evil. I slowly and quietly tiptoed backwards. My forehead started sweating. The sweat made it to my left fingers and began dripping between them and into my eyes. They started burning. I didn't care. I just wanted to escape the den.

I took one big backwards step at a time. My hateful dad kept talking to whomever. I stayed focused. I was halfway through the den. The hallway was just a few feet away. My eyes were now burning worse, from the salty, sweaty tears. I never removed my left hand from my mouth. Too afraid I might make a loud noise! My badly, burning eyes stayed locked on my dad's back. I used my right hand to guide me backwards.

I touched the cabinet holding the huge TV. Next, I glided my hand across the TV screen. I was between the coffee table and TV. As I was moving slowing, my right calf bumped into the corner of the coffee table. A silent "Ouch"! That really hurt! The flower arrangement started to fall. I quickly bent over and grabbed it with both hands, then took a quick look. Dad still had his back to me. Boy, that was close! This was one time where his loud talking paid off.

I stood straight up. I took a couple of smaller steps backwards and looked down at the coffee table to make sure everything was in place. Oh no, I saw drops of liquid by the arrangement. It must have been my sweat. I panicked some more. My heart was pounding so loud it was traveling through my ears. For now, the drops would have to stay. Hoped they wouldn't get noticed!

I passed by the TV cabinet. I was getting close to the hallway. Just a few more small steps and I would able to dash to my bedroom. My eyes were still fixed on my wicked dad. He started to turn. I stopped. I stayed perfectly still. I squeezed my hand over my mouth even tighter.

I was trembling with fear. Then for some odd reason, I remembered my "Spy Handbook" and what it says to do in a dangerous situation. This was very much a dangerous situation. It said to remain calm, think clear and use your surroundings.

I took a deep breath and stayed focused. My evil dad turned towards the left of the balcony. The balcony rail was "L" shaped. It was longer across the front, with just a smaller rail on the left side. He now had his side to me. I took another step back and could now feel the wall. I watched as he started to turn towards me. If he sees me, it would be bad news. He stopped. Then he turned back around to the longer part of the rail. His back was to me again. Whew!

My right hand stayed on the wall until I felt the corner. "Almost there! Just stay calm, Rachel," I told myself. As I was watching my wicked dad, a bright beam of light came down from the sky. It blinded me, and the balcony. I quickly turned to the right and raced to my room. I made it!

I closed my door and stood there shaking and sweating. My heart was pounding louder than ever! I have never been this scared in my life. I was just a young kid dealing with all of this. I was more scared of my dad than ever before. "Thank you God for getting me to my room unnoticed," I prayed in silence. Then I gasped! I realized God or Rain E sent the beam of light. Someone did, because it was completely dark outside. Wow! They "WERE" watching over me!!!!

I was safe in my room for now, even though I didn't feel safe anymore. After my heart and body calmed down, I went to my bathroom and washed the sweat off my face. I cupped my hands and drank the faucet water. There was no way I was getting a bottle of water, not now!! I placed a hot washcloth over my face and went to lie on my bed. That was the scariest situation! I felt like I was in some kind of spy movie. Wow! That was the second time I remembered my spy kit. I was so glad I got it for Christmas last year. It more than came in handy, at the insane prison!

As I was resting, everything that just had happened replayed in mind. Who was my dad talking too? Was he going to get someone to kill my mom? Was he going to pay somebody money, like you see on TV? Did he hate my mom that much? Did my mom know something bad about my dad, so he has to kill her? The questions kept filling my stressed-out brain. Surely my dad wouldn't go through with it. He would go to jail, or would he? He was after all, an attorney. I removed my towel, looked at my reflection in the desk mirror and started thinking maybe he wanted me dead too. What am I going to do? How was I going to get through this weekend, knowing all this? I had to warn Mom, *IF*, I get back home.

I decided to take a quick shower. I locked the door behind me, just in case my dad was going to kill me first. I was out before Sissy and "The Boys" returned. I dried off and put on some comfortable shorts and a sports T-shirt from my dresser. I was already for bed, when I heard everyone come in. Quickly, I leaped into bed with my Bible homework and immediately turned to my Bible verse. I had to memorize it by Wednesday. "Low and behold" like Mom says, I couldn't believe my eyes. The Bible verse was "Put on the Armor of God." Boy did that come at the right time!!

Mr. Evil casually walked into my room, because every room is his room. He barked that Blake went home, but Ronny was spending the night and to get my ass to the sofa all in one breath, then left. Why couldn't Ronny stay with his brother? Here I go again, Miss "Not Important At All"! I gathered up my pillow, comforter and stuffed kitty and headed to the den. I didn't say a word, because I was too scared to speak. Besides, it wouldn't make any difference.

It was about an hour, before all the lights were finally off. Now, I could go to sleep. I was so tired and wanted to sleep, but it was hard. My mind couldn't stop thinking about what my dad said on the phone, the new girlfriend, and of course Ronny sleeping in my bed, again. Why couldn't "HE" sleep on the sofa? It was MY room, not his! Ronny smelled something awful. Like I've said before, "It's so weird and very creepy." I guess Sissy didn't mind him staying. Oh yeah, like her opinion counted!

I scrunched up my pillow, then got as cozy as I could with my comforter. I held on tight to my kitty and stared at the moon. A creepy full moon at that! This moon caused goose bumps to surface on my skin. The kind of moon I've seen on a scary *Scooby-Doo* cartoon. The sky was full of stars. There were definitely no signs of a storm tonight. I guess I wouldn't be seeing Rain E, even though I felt like she was nearby. The beam of light that showed up on the balcony tonight was most definitely, heavenly sent! After praying, I crashed!

The next morning I woke up shivering, half of my body was uncovered. Creepy strange! I always stayed completely under my comforter. I guess I kicked it off in the middle of the night. As I reached

144

down to grab it, I remembered the apple core. I felt under the sofa and then got down and looked. It was gone. Martha must have found it. Thank goodness!

I was the first one up, so I went to the kitchen for some breakfast. There was a box of donuts on the counter. I guess Sissy bought them last night. I lifted the lid and some were already missing. Good! I wouldn't get balled out for eating something first. I was hungry. I didn't eat any dinner last night. Toooo scared to leave my room (the den)! I grabbed a chocolate glazed and a chocolate cake donut. I carefully carried both over to the kitchen sink. I gobbled them up fast and drank some milk straight from the carton. I know that's not right, but I was too tired to clean dishes. I wiped the counter with my shirt, picked up a few crumbs that fell on the floor and wash them down the drain then wiped the sink dry. Everything looked good.

I was about to go lay back down, when I saw the light on in Dad's office. I walked over there to see what he was doing. Nobody was in there, but the computer was on. As I got closer, I saw a bunch of photos. A bunch of photos of me, asleep! My mouth dropped open. There were several photos of me, sleeping on the sofa and even some when I was in my bed. Who took these photos and why? I clicked on one of them and kept clicking photo after photo, all of me. There were a few of me asleep on the sofa with over half of my body exposed. There was one with part of my butt showing.

Did Ronny and/ or my dad take photos of me last night while I was sleeping or was it just Ronny? Did Ronny touch me while I was sleeping? Next important question: When were the photos taken of me, in my bed? I was feeling sick to my stomach. I wanted to go home. I didn't want to stay another night, especially if Ronny was still here. Then it came to me. My "Spy Handbook"! It always says to get what is called "Hard Evidence". Hard evidence I could show Mom! This was hard evidence!

On my hands and knees, I secretly snuck into my dad's bedroom to rescue my cell phone, charging on the table on his side of bed. I crawled back to the hallway and ran to the office. I took several disturbing photos of me from the computer and emailed them to Mom's phone. I quickly removed them from my phone into 'trash'. Mom was going to flip out. Then, I quietly crawled back into the bedroom and placed my phone back on the table. I glanced at the bed. My dad and Sissy never woke up. My dad's loud sleep machine helped cover up any sound I might have made. I still couldn't believe that woman was sleeping in bed with my dad. Gross!!

I scurried back to the sofa and hid under my comforter. Boy, that was a little risky, but a successful, sneaky job well performed! I felt like a real detective, even though a bit scared. I wondered if real detectives ever felt scared? I tucked my legs and arms tightly around the comforter, in case I fell back to sleep. This way no one could take another photo of my body without waking me. It was too nerve-racking to sleep, so I just closed my eyes.

A few hours later everyone was up. I heard my dad go into his office, He screamed, "Ronny, get your lazy ass in here NOW!" I peeked over my comforter to see him head to the office. I heard the door close. When Dad and creepy Ronny finally came out, I peeked again. They were both suspiciously quiet, as though they had been caught. Dad was only wearing his underwear. Ronny had on navy sweat pants, no top. Nothing was said to me and I never brought up the photos.

I saw Ronny head into the kitchen. I rushed to my bedroom to get ready for the day. While I was getting dressed, I heard him leave. Thank goodness he was gone. I peeked out the door. Dad said, "Let's go." I said, "Go where?" He said, "To steam at a new spa. Sissy and I go there a lot. It will now be a family time together. I'm ready, so get a move on!" I didn't want to go, but I didn't have a choice in the matter. Family time! Get real! I knew what Mr. Evil was up to.

When we arrived, Sissy and I went to the women's side and Dad went to the men's side. I felt very awkward going with a person I had only met yesterday. The minute we walked into the locker room, my mouth dropped open. (That seems to happen to me a lot these days). I was in total shock and beyond embarrassed. Everyone was naked. Totally naked, from top to bottom!

This Asian-looking lady handed me an orange jumpsuit. It looked like what people wore in hospitals and doctors offices. Thank goodness, I didn't have to be naked. I think it would have been against the law. This place was disgusting! I saw women's body parts I shouldn't have seen. I wanted to leave so bad. Sissy even got naked. Gross! Before Sissy went into the spa area, she asked me if I wanted to get a foot massage. I yelled out, "Are you kidding me! NO! I don't want a grown man touching my body. That's sick!" Sissy said, "It will be fun, something we can do together." I rolled my eyes in disgust.

Sissy went into the water with other naked women. I sat on a wood bench and played on my Nintendo. I didn't want to look up. A few minutes later that same Asian lady came over and asked me if I wanted to watch the movie that was playing in the next room. I asked her what it was. She said it was, *Silence of the Lambs*. I quickly responded, "No thank you, my mom told me never to watch that movie." After that, the lady left me alone.

Finally, Sissy was through doing whatever. I changed back into my clothes and left the nasty orange suit in the locker room. Sissy dressed and we headed out. Dad was waiting for us. I looked at him and asked him why he brought me here. He didn't even answer me. He knew I would be telling Mom about this sinful place. We ate and got back around 9 pm. I went straight to bed. Dad and Sissy did the same.

The next morning, Dad rudely came in my room and said he was sorry that he had to take me home in an hour because he and Sissy had plans. Sorry? Was he kidding me? Yeah! I was going home early again, with lots to tell mom. I flew out of bed. Like Speedy Gonzales, I quickly changed and packed all my stuff in record time. After this weekend, I was more than ready to go. Within five minutes, we were out the door. I climbed into the backseat. I could hardly wait to tell Mom about my creepy, nasty and very nerve-wracking scary weekend!

"The bond that links your true family is not one of blood, but one of respect and joy in each other's life."

Richard Bach

Chapter 13

Nothing much was said during the drive home. Oh, the two of them chitchatted, but never with me. I stayed quiet on purpose. There was not one thing nice I wanted to say to those two. I looked out the window and occasionally at the front seat. I glanced just in time to see my dad bite Sissy's fingers. She screamed out, "Oh baby that hurts!" Oh brother! Sissy sure can't deny Dad bites! Maybe now he won't bite me anymore since he has someone new to nibble on!

Just before we reached my street, Dad pulled the car over onto the side of the road. He put it in park and turned to me, "I want you to give Sissy a hug, NOW!" I said a big fat, "NO"! He sat there, for several minutes, trying to force me to hug a woman I met two days ago. Sissy spoke up and said to just forget it. So Dad tore out down the street to *MY* home.

He pulled in the driveway. I wasn't even completely out of his car, when he called me a mean "F" n brat. Sissy said nothing in my defense. I just glared at her and slammed the door. Mr. Evil sped off, fast. His tires were screeching. I shook my head and mumbled, "Who cares about them and wherever they're going! I can think of one place, that's very hot!"

I was home. I raced to the front door and rang the doorbell. Grandma was already waiting for me. I hugged her and asked where Mom was. Grandma said that she ran to the store to get everything to make her homemade soup. I hurried upstairs and crashed on my bed. I had a lot to tell Mom. I just needed to figure out the right time. For right now, all I wanted to do was rest! I didn't sleep enough at Dad's. Like Rain E always says, "Imagine that"! I giggled. I whispered her words one more time and fell asleep.

The smell of Mom's homemade soup pleasantly awakened me. I rolled over to my left side to find Sugar curled up on my leopard pillow. That's funny, a cat on a leopard pillow! Maybe she thinks it's her mom? I stretched my arms as far as they could go, sending tingles throughout my body. I was refreshed. I looked out my window and it was dark outside. I wondered how long I had been sleeping! It didn't matter. Mom always let me rest. She knew I came home from Dad's extremely exhausted. Mom always said that I had to play 'catch up sleep' every other weekend.

I was just getting out of bed, when my door cracked open. It was my beautiful mom. She softly spoke, "I was just checking to see if you were up." I smiled and ran to her. We hugged for a long time. I said, "I feel safe now!" Mom pushed me back and asked, "What do you mean NOW?" "I'll tell you later. I'm just glad to be home!" "Are you sure you don't want to talk about it right now?" Mom asked. I answered, "No." "Well, okay my love. Soup will be ready in about an hour. Do you want to go over your Latin and your Bible verse?" I said, "Yes, I'll be right down". Mom left. I rinsed my face, grabbed my homework, and hurried down to join her.

I sat down at the table and got out my Bible verse and Latin vocab words. Mom was stirring the big pot of soup. I looked up and noticed what she was wearing. She dresses so cool for a mom. She had on black leggings and a two layer long, lacy top. It was white and had some black in it. She had on her black UGG slippers. Her long dark brown hair was all scrunched up into a bun. She walked over to the table and I showed her my Bible verse. She immediately said it was one of her favorites. We went over it for about 20 minutes and then the Latin vocab words. Mom made up Latin quizzes for me to practice. I finished them all.

Mom got up to stir the soup again. She took a bite of the meat and said it was ready. I called for Grandma to come down. Mom dished up three bowls for the table. We all sat down and gave thanks to God. The soup was *delish*! We laughed and talked about different stuff. In the back of my mind, I was going to have to tell Mom about the phone call and photos of me, just not tonight. I would tell her tomorrow. This night was too perfect to be ruined. I was full of soup and love.

After a yummy dinner, I hugged the both of them. My homework stayed piled on the table. Something you NEVER did at the prison condo. I dragged my still tired body upstairs. I reached the top and

150

yelled out, "The soup was yummy! Thank you for making it!" Mom yelled back, "Your welcome! I'll be up later to tuck you in!"

I walked in my room to find Sugar, now curled up on my pillow. She always moved from pillow to pillow to blanket to blanket, throughout the house, except Grandma's room. That room was off limits. I didn't know who won that battle more often, Grandma or Sugar, but I had a strong feeling it was Grandma. Honestly, I think Sugar was fine having the rest of the house. Sugar thought the whole house was hers, anyway. That was just the way cats think. I leaned over and gave her a peck on the head. She never budged. I guess I would be fighting her for my pillow after bathing!

Have you ever fallen asleep in the tub? I did! It was beyond relaxing. When I woke up, I got out, brushed my teeth and then my hair. I put on my favorite rainbow pajamas. Coming out of the bathroom, I noticed Sugar was back on the leopard pillow. Thank goodness! I was too tired to fight tonight. I climbed into bed and covered completely up with my thick comforter. I fell fast asleep. I didn't know what time Mom came in to kiss me good night and say our nightly prayer of "Now I Lay Me Down To Sleep", all I know is she did.

The morning light awakened me. It was shooting through the blinds brighter than ever. I jumped out of bed to look. When I turned the cord, the brightness blinded me for a moment. I stumbled backwards onto Sugar. She quickly got out of the way. I lifted just my head. I couldn't see anything but brightness. I remembered my spy glasses on the table.

I stretched my right arm and was able to grab them. I slipped them over my head to get a better look. I walked back over to the window and raised the blinds all the way up. The sky was so bright, almost too bright even with my spy glasses on. This was now the second brightest sky I had ever seen. "Was Rain E in this one too?" I hopefully asked myself.

As I kept trying to stare at the sky without damaging my eyes, I saw it. Sunbeams were swirling around a cloud. It looked like that specific cloud was coming towards me. It was beautiful. "Is this for me to see?" I wondered to myself, "Does it have some special meaning?" Rain E only came during storms. Was there someone new I was going to meet? Was there something new in my life? I stood there for several minutes watching the bright swirling cloud. It was moving closer and closer to my window. Then all of a sudden, it hit my window hard! I fell backwards on my bed. Then, just like that, it was gone. I sat there staring out the window thinking, "Wow, what was that all about?"

Mom called out, "Rachel Dear, get dressed, I need to talk to you." I yelled back, "Okay, be right down." Then I pondered, "I wonder what Mom wants to talk to me about?" The moment I left my room, I passed Sugar at the top of the stairs basking in the sun. She was getting her vitamin D for the day. Mom told me that when the sun warmed her fur, she licked it and the vitamin went into her body. I looked at the window above the front door. The sky was back to normal. I wondered if Sugar got another glimpse of the bright light after leaving my room? Maybe it was coming through all the windows? I leaned over to pet her. I immediately thought, "Wow! Warmer fur!! Wish she could tell me if she saw the bright light? I will never know!"

Mom was sitting in the den. I joined her. She said, "I just got off the phone with your dad and we are going to the library to meet with him." I asked Mom, "Is everything alright?" She assured me it was. Mom said there was something she and Dad were to tell me together. I simply said, "Okay." It couldn't be bad news. Mom was calm. I went to the kitchen. Mom had homemade biscuits keeping warm in the microwave. I got a couple along with some red plum jam. I kept looking at Mom sipping her coffee. She was acting so mysterious. I wondered what was so important that they have to tell me together? It must be extremely important, because Mom would never go anywhere to meet with Mr. Evil.

I finished my biscuits and glass of milk. Mom said we would be leaving in about 15 minutes. I went back upstairs and quickly dressed. I came back down, passing Sugar, now sleeping in the den chair. Like I said before, she moves from room to room. She just shows up out of nowhere. That silly cat of mine was now on a thick soft animal print blanket. She blended right in, almost camouflage. Mom kept the blanket in the chair, for Sugar and her loose hair. I knew lots of families who do the same. I scratched her ears and headed out. Mom was already in the car. I jumped in and we were on our way.

We pulled into the parking lot. Dad was already there, sitting in his car. We parked and all got out at the same time. The three of us walked in, not saying a word. We went through the library working our way to the back and outside on the porch. We sat down at a round table.

Mom started talking first. "Rachel, how far back can you remember?" I asked, "Why?" Mom said, "I'd like to know, just curious." I thought for a moment and said, "I remember you pushing me on my pink and white tricycle, up and down the driveway." "Do you remember Dad's brother?" Mom asked. I answered, "Yes. He was nice to me." Dad still hadn't said a word. Mom continued, "Dad's brother, your Uncle Ben, loved you very much. He wanted you to have a better life." I asked, "What do you mean?" "Dad's brother, who you call your uncle, is your biological father. Do you understand?" With a little confusion I asked, "So, my real dad is Ben and he gave me away so I could have a better life?" I was silent for a moment. Those words: "A better life". Dad jumped in and said, "Yes, we adopted you!"

Mom and Dad stared at me, I guess to see how I was going to react. I was okay with it. Then I asked about my birth mom. Mom told me that she was a kind lady, but mentally ill and couldn't take care of me. My real dad also had a lot of health problems. I knew he used to drink and do drugs. I overheard Dad screaming at Martha about it.

Mom said, "Because of your real dad's poor choice of lifestyle, he knew he wouldn't live long. He did a lot of damage to his body from drugs and drinking. Most important, Ben never wanted Martha to get her hands on you, because she didn't know how to be a parent. That was his greatest fear and concern. He came to me and asked if I would raise you. I said I would." Wow! Mom loves me more than I ever realized. She stayed with Mr. Evil just to protect me.

We all stayed quiet. Then, I said, "I remember being with my real dad when I was very young. He had a red truck. I remember riding in it. He was always smoking. It must have been hard for him to give me up." Mom answered, "It was! He loved you so much. He didn't want you to go down his "same" road." I thought to myself that if he had kept me, I wouldn't have a mean and horrible dad, but I also wouldn't have a wonderful mother. Too bad, my real dad wasn't married to my mom. We would all be happy. I wonder what he would do, if he knew his brother was hurting me? I would ask Mom later.

Mom then told me she couldn't have children and I was meant to be her daughter. Boy, I really felt even more special! I didn't want to talk about it anymore and asked Mom if we could leave. She said that we could. We all got up and went to our cars. Dad tried to hug me. I backed away. He got in his car and sped off. We got in ours. Before Mom started the car I asked, "Then, I have an older sister, right?" Mom said, "Yes, but, you are never to be around her, without your dad present, court ordered." I said, "It's because of the way she's living."

Mom simply answered, "Yes." She didn't go into any details about my sister's life. I did know she drank a lot and also did drugs. I saw it with my own eyes, at my ex-grandma's house. I told Mom and she put a stop to it.

Also, my blood sister lived with a man the judge said I was never to be around because he did something really bad. If my sister's boyfriend is so bad that I couldn't be around him, then why did the judge force me to be around Dad? I just didn't get it. Who could worse than my dad? That judge must be mixed-up in the head. I wondered what my sister's boyfriend did that was so bad? I didn't talk about them anymore. Mom would eventually tell me when the time was right. On the way home, I was feeling happy and sad inside. I was happy I had my mom and you know why I was sad.

When we arrived home, I went straight to my room. Mom knew I wanted to be by myself, after the library meeting. She always understood when I wanted to be alone. This was one of those times. That's why she's the best! I stayed in my room until dark took over the sky. I studied some and secretly worked on my drawing. I started thinking about the library meeting. I was okay with everything. I still had one more question. I knew Mom would be up later to tuck me in and say our prayer. I would ask her then.

I got up to take a shower and wash my hair. School was tomorrow. I hurried. After I finished getting ready for bed, I put my rainbow pajamas back on. They were still at the end of the bed. I wear them to feel closer to Rain E. I let my hair dry naturally to be curly. I just got under my comforter, when there was a knock on the door. I jokingly laughed, "Who is it?" Mom answered, "Who's in my Rachel's room?" Mom is so silly! She came in and sat on the bed. She asked if I was okay with today's news. I told her I was fine. I asked if Grandma was in her room. She said she was. Mom said that Grandma was extra tired and just wanted to rest all day. Mom and I said our prayer and she kissed me goodnight.

She got up to leave, when I had to ask what had been on my mind since leaving the library, "Mom, if my real dad was still alive, do you think he would kill Dad?" Mom quickly came back and sat down on my side of the bed. She took my right hand in hers and said only one sobering word, "Yes!" Mom paused then added, "He would have never allowed your dad to hurt you, He loved you that much and more. It was his main concern. That was why he only wanted me to adopt you, but that couldn't happen, because I was married. Never forget how much he loved you! Get some rest, my love, we will talk some more later." She kissed my hand, then both cheeks.

As Mom was walking out, she glanced at my drawing pad and asked, "What are you drawing?" "Oh, just mountains, trees and flowers. Stuff like that," I fibbed. "I would love to see it when it's finished," Mom proudly said. I smiled saying, "You will!" She turned out lights and shut my door. I quickly thought, "That was a close call. I'll have to be more careful next time." I reached for the drawing and slid it under the bed. I threw my comforter back over my entire body. I closed my eyes and smiled. I whispered softly, "I wish my real dad was alive. Dad, if you're listening, this is your daughter Rachel. I love you and miss you!" I closed my eyes and was almost asleep when I shot up in bed.

"Oh my! WOOO!" I said out loud. "The swirling bright light around the cloud! It must have been from God. God knows everything! He knew I was going to find out about my adoption. I wonder if Rain E knows? If God didn't tell her, I will, when I see her again. I hope it's SOON!" I closed my eyes again. This time just whispering, "What a day!"

"Where words fail, music speaks."

Hans Christian Andersen

Chapter 14

The rest of the week flew by. I kept my adoption a secret, along with all that happened last weekend. I wasn't ready to tell my friends I was adopted, at least not yet. The school tests this week were extra challenging, especially math and Latin. By Friday evening, I was pooped. Mom ordered pizza. I got ready for bed early. We ate and watched movies 'til midnight. When I climbed in bed, I easily fell asleep.

Saturday morning I woke up to Christmas music. Mom always started listening to it every October. I believe she knew every word to every Christmas song ever sung. She loved, not only the songs about Jesus, she loved all the fun songs too. I asked her once why she listens to Christmas music so much. She told me that it gave her an inner peace and she felt closer to God. She always did get emotional over specific songs. Some of my fondest memories involved Christmas music. They still would make me smile, just thinking about them!

When I was very, very young, barely speaking, Mom would sit me on her lap and sing fun Christmas songs to me. I still remember one in particular. It began, "A Christmas bell was crying, then Santa heard it say, I just can't seem to jingle and I can't go on the sleigh." There was another one called *Must be Santa* (written by Hal Moore and Bill Frederick and recorded by Mitch Miller in 1960). I loved that one too! I also loved the song *Jingle Bells*. Most kids do. Actually, I bet ALL kids do!

There's this wonderful lady singer, who just happens to be my Mom's favorite actress in the whole wide world, who would sing the song *Jingle Bells* really fast. I loved trying to keep up with her. Every time the song would end I would make Mommy play it again. I would just say, "Again." It was wonderful calling her "Mommy". I still do from time to time. I remembered asking her if the song *Jingle Bells* was around when she was a kid.

Mom said that *Jingle Bells* had been around since the 1800's. She said it was originally called *One Horse Open Sleigh*. I actually looked it up on the computer. Mom was right! James Pierpont wrote it in 1850! He was inspired by the annual one-horse open-sleigh races, held in his hometown of Medford, Massachusetts. Years later, when they could record the song, many people sang it, but it was Bing Crosby with the Andrew sisters, who made the song the most popular. He was in the movie *White Christmas*. We watch it every Christmas. I like the different ways people sing the song *Jingle Bells*, but the fast way is still the best!

Then, there was the beautiful Christmas piano music. One of my Mom's dearest and closest friends is a well-known and talented piano composer. According to her, he played all over the world. He has even played in our home. Mom listens to his music year round. She has his CD in the car right now. He performed all different kinds of music, but Mom really loved his Christmas music the best. Anyway, Mom has always loved Christmas music and well, I do too.

The music was playing throughout the entire house, not too loud, just right. I took my time getting out of bed. I was so relaxed. Isn't it sad I have to go to an awful "house" then return to a wonderful "home"! That was the difference right there. One is just a "House" and the other is a "Home". I know I'm lucky to have at least one happy home. Many kids don't even have that.

The day arrived. It was time to tell Mom about the phone call and photos. I've been thinking about it all week. I know I should have told her sooner, but I was confused. My dad wants to kill Mom then he's with her telling me I'm adopted. All of this nearly drove me crazy. Then there were all the hard tests at school. My brain was fried! So much on it, but now I absolutely have to tell her what I overheard. If I don't tell Mom to protect herself and something happens, it would be my fault. I think this is much more important than the photos.

I put on my favorite leggings and a short sleeve T-shirt and headed downstairs. Mom was just pulling cinnamon rolls out of the oven. I grabbed two, while still warm! Mom poured me some milk and herself some coffee. We sat down at the kitchen table. She could see something was wrong.

Mom took one long sip of coffee and asked, "Rachel, is there something you need to tell me? I noticed you were quieter than usual last night." "Mom, I have to tell you something really bad," my voice quivered. "What is it dear? Did your dad hurt you again?" Mom asked. I blurted out, "No, it's about you! I'm scared Dad is going to kill you! I overheard him talking on his cell phone. He told someone he wanted you dead. He even asked how much it would cost!"

Mom looked at me with almost no reaction. She didn't look scared at all and I asked her why. What she said to me next, will stay with me forever. Mom calmly stated, "Rachel, your dad has wanted to kill me ever since I found out what he was doing behind my back. It was very bad, actually disgusting. I can't stop him or anyone else who wants to kill me. They will find a way."

Mom paused, then continued, "I will not waste anymore of my precious time worrying about what your dad is or is not going to do to me. I will be fine, because God is watching over me. That's all the comfort and real protection I need. Thank you so much for the warning. I'm so sorry you overheard that. You must have been frightened to death. I'll keep my guard up. One last thing, your dad will NEVER know we talked."

I was stunned and relieved at the same time. My mom is something else! She's so much stronger, since leaving my evil dad. I think God made her stronger. Maybe that's why she fought with *Him* so much. I have secretly heard her loudly crying out to God, night after night. If God is like a headboard like Rain E said, that's good news, because Mom's headboard is iron. God IS stronger than Mom. She has handed so much to God! He has NEVER left her side. He is strong like iron.

You know what, I believe God can always handle Mom's worries and problems. He's God. Enough said! I knew how much God loved my mom, but more important, I knew how much my mom loved God. Everything that she was going through and still never walked away from our Father. I did feel sorry for God when He was listening to my Mom's loud voice. I always wondered if God ever got a headache from the loud talks? I even wondered if God ever had to take Advil? Mom would take it when she had a really bad headache.

I have been taught to take all my problems and worries to God, because He is our Heavenly Father. Kids have had fights with their parents, so I guess it was okay to have fights with God. God wants us to come to Him, just like we go to our parents. Like Rain E said, "God can take it, because He's God". Hummm, for some strange reason, I was beginning to think she has known God for quite some time. It had been weeks and I was missing Rain E badly! Mom would get help from God and now I was getting help from my Rain E. I also know Mom got a lot of help from reading her Bible and listening to all her Christmas music. Maybe I should to listen to more Christmas music?

I was relieved after I told Mom what Dad wanted to do. I still can't get over her reaction! I don't think she will be feeling the same way about the photos of me. She always becomes extremely upset over the bad things that happen to me, that involve Dad. I don't blame her at all. I would probably feel the same way if I was a mom and my daughter was getting hurt. I decided not to tell her about the photos, for a while. Soon though!

For now, I wanted to enjoy my time listening to Christmas music and remembering the past. Mom used to and still does sing out loud and twirl me around the living room every time the music is playing. I love being silly with her. I have always joined in on the singing. It's corny I know, but I like corny. Tomorrow, I would find all the songs she sang to me at my happy young age and make a Christmas CD to listen to when I'm in the car and at bedtime!

You have collected all my tears in your bottle.

Psalms 56:8 (NLT)

Chapter 15

How time flies, when it's corny fun time! Thanksgiving was two weeks away. Dad and his new girlfriend were going out of town. His mother Martha was going too. I had to go with them, even though I didn't want to. I dread every time I had travel with those two. Mom hadn't feeling very good. She said she was just tired from dealing with everything and not to worry. I know she has been upset for a long time, constantly losing in court and me having to being around "The Boys".

I hated being around them. They grossed me out. My dad, a grown man running around with teenage boys! I've said it before, "It's just sick and very creepy." Mom knew more about "The Boys" than she was letting on. She said she would tell me when I'm older. "I wonder what it is?" I thought.

The week before Thanksgiving, one of our dogs, well Mom's dog, got up from napping on the kitchen floor. I watched as he started walking crooked towards her. Mom was sitting at the end of the sofa. I was at the kitchen table doing homework and Grandma was upstairs. Our other dog stayed on the floor near me. Mom turned just as he, "her baby" was getting closer. He was stumbling around. He fell down right by Mom's feet. She quickly got on the floor by him.

I got up from the table and ran to the bottom of the stairs and screamed for Grandma. Mom's best friend was now on his side. I watched as Mom scooped him up in her arms and held him tightly. Grandma was now downstairs. I told her what had happened. I was standing by Mom, when she screamed at me to leave the room, "NOW!" Grandma firmly said, "GO!" I ran to the end of the hallway and stopped. I could hear Mom yelling out to Grandma, "Something's wrong. I think he's dying." I turned and tiptoed back. I had to see what was going on. I just had to! I could see Mom on the floor. She and our dog were in front of the fireplace. Grandma was standing next to Mom's right. I stood there facing them.

Mom gently, but carefully, cuddled our male dog in her arms, with so much tenderness and compassion. I tearfully watched as this loving, precious dog jerked his back leg, twice. Mom held him tighter. I tried to stay quiet as possible, but it was so hard. I didn't think she could hear me, over her loud cries. Mom leaned over and whispered in his left ear. He struggled lifting his head. I couldn't take my heart-breaking eyes off of him as he lovingly stared at his mom.

Then it happened! He kicked out, jerking his leg a third time, and final time! I watched his head collapse on Mom's arms. She screamed out, "NO, dear God, NO", and began crying louder than I had ever heard her in my entire life. Her best friend was gone. Tears fell down my cheeks. I stood there in shock. Just like that, our dog was gone. I watched as Mom kept her head in his fur for several minutes. Her cries were filled with so much agonizing pain. She couldn't move.

I finally walked in. Grandma looked right at my face and said two words that I will never forget, "He's gone." More tears came out of my eyes. They kept coming, covering my entire face and neck. I bent down next to Mom and kissed our beautiful male dog on the head and softly said, "I hope you had fun, living with us! I will miss you!" Grandma gently took my arm and told me, "Let your mother cry over him, until she stops, if that's possible." She and I went to the kitchen. Mom needed to be alone.

Some time went by. I quietly walked back into the den, tears still flowing down my cheeks, all the way to my T-shirt. Mom struggled to stand. She left to go get his favorite blanket. A few minutes later, Mom returned and respectfully wrapped our dog up and carried him to the hall bathroom. I stood outside the door and watched Mom hug him one last time. As she stood up, one tear fell on his nose. I cried even harder. I couldn't stop. I cried for Mom. Her broken heart and unbearable suffering was too much to bear! How would she get through this?

Mom walked out and we hugged. She looked at me and said, "He's at peace now." She closed the bathroom door and walked straight to her bedroom, closing the door behind her. I knew Mom would be taking him to the vet tomorrow to be cremated and put in a beautiful box. Her beloved furry best friend would be joining the other best friends in the master bedroom closet. I stood there by the bathroom door and softly whispered, "I love you sweet angel. Tell the others I love them too."

I went upstairs and got ready for bed. Grandma came in to check on me. She told me that this was a complete shock to Mom and she would need a lot of time to heal. I just nodded back at Grandma trying to make sense of all of it. There were no words I could say without tears joining them.

I got into bed and said "our" prayer. I then asked God, "Why did this happen? Why? Why now? Everything my mom has been through, I don't understand? Why God? Why? She doesn't deserve this! This incredible dog was so young. He gave her so much love and attention. She has loved all our pets, but he was her most loyal companion. So much has been taken from my mom and now this! Forgive me for being so full of anger and hurt. I can't help it. Please help me under-stand. Please God comfort my mom. She is hurting worse than I have ever seen. I'm scared something is going to happen to her. Please, help her get through this." I cried and cried, until the crying put me to sleep.

The next morning I got up, without Mom having to call me. I dressed and went downstairs. I walked over to the hall bathroom. Mom had already put our dog in the trunk. I walked into the kitchen to find her. She was in there, still crying. Her eyes were so red. I bet the tears kept coming all night.

This male dog was closer to her than all the others. I mean he never left her side. At a very young age, Mom and I would play hide-n-go seek in the house. I never had any problem finding her. All I had to look for was her dog. He was always standing right beside his mom and my mom too. I will always remember that.

Mom asked if I was ready to leave for school. I was. We stopped on the way and got a breakfast burrito and OJ. Mom stayed quiet. When we pulled into the school. I looked at her and she looked back. I told her I was so sad she was hurting and that I loved her so much! She told me that she loved me too.

While we were waiting in the car, I softly spoke, "Mom, can I asked you something? I know it may be a bad time but I really want to know. Please tell me, if you want to." Mom looked at me and said, "Of course, honey, what would you like to ask me?" I stated, "First, I'm sorry I disobeyed you. I walked back to the end of the hall and watched everything. I saw our dog die in your arms. Mom, what did you whisper in his ear?"

165

Mom dropped her head. Tears ran down her face landing on her legs. She raised her head, looked ahead and said, "I told him, "It's okay to leave me. I'll be all right. Not to worry. I don't want you to suffer. You can go. I love you so much! I will miss you." I started crying and reached for Mom's hand. She kept looking straight ahead.

When we pulled forward, Mom turned to me and sadly spoke, "Thank you for loving him, he will miss you too!" I dried my face with my leftover napkin from breakfast. As I got out of the car, I watched Mom and her best friend drive away. I would never see him again. One more tear fell out of my eye. I watched until they were completely out of sight. I wished I could have gone with Mom to the vet.

Mom picked me up that afternoon. She was quiet. I asked her if there was anything I could do for her. She told me she just needed time. It was hard going to our home, without one of our family members there. When we arrived, Mom asked if I wanted a sandwich. I said I would make it myself. I watched her head to the master bedroom. Mom had to check on one of our female cats resting in the bathroom. She had not been feeling well.

I headed upstairs and got ready for bed early. I was so sad and just wanted to go to bed. Grandma checked on me. She and I were both very worried about Mom. Grandma said, "This just about destroyed your mother. The two of them were inseparable." I agreed. I gave Grandma a hug and climbed into bed. She said goodnight and turned the light off, on her way out. I turned my lamp on and did my homework. After it was all completed, I just lay there in the dark thinking about our dog. Some time went by. I rolled over on my side and called out to God again to please comfort my mom. I told Him that she needed it badly! This sad day finally came to an end!

The next morning I woke up earlier than usual. The first thing I thought of was how empty our home felt. The last two days were some of the worse I have had to live through. Seeing our dog dying will haunt me for a long time. Now I understand why Mom asked me to leave the room. I also think she needed that last moment alone with him. I dragged myself out of bed and got dressed for school. I picked up my backpack and headed downstairs. If you thought things couldn't get any worse, well they did.

For the last couple of weeks, our sweet and smallest cat had been sick. Mom had taken her twice to the vet. They said it was a bladder infection. She wasn't getting better. Mom took her back to the vet the day before our dog died. The vet said her vital signs were fine, whatever that meant. Mom told them she wasn't eating much and was losing a lot of weight. Mom tried to get her to eat. She was even forcing water down her. Nothing helped. Mom had put her in the hall bathroom to rest and so the other cats wouldn't bother her.

That morning Mom checked on her, and she was dead, two days after our beloved dog died. Mom was hysterically crying, again. In two days we lost two pets. I didn't think she was going to survive this. So once again, Mom wrapped her up in her favorite blanket and put her in the trunk of the car. She would be heading to the vet again, after dropping me off at school. This time I didn't have anything to say. I was in total shock.

It was Friday. We got out at noon because it was the beginning of our Thanksgiving break. Mom picked me up. She asked how our school party was. I told her it was fun. I asked her how she was. She said she would eventually get better. Mom told me that everyone at the vet's office were shocked beyond belief and very worried about her. I was too; she had been crying now for two days, almost non-stop.

When we got home it was extra quiet now with two pets gone. Grandma was in the kitchen. I stood by her and watched Mom in a daze, walk to her bedroom and gently close the door. Grandma quietly said to me, "I'm very worried about your mother. I have never seen her so emotionally broken. She has had these pets a long time. They were her life, before you came into her life." Grandma was right. All our pets, except Sugar, had been a part of Mom's life, before I was born. Wow! I felt so sorry for her losses. She has already said goodbye to her first two loving dogs a few years ago. Now, two in two days! Heartbreaking and devastating!

I stayed quiet as a mouse not disturbing Mom at all. Grandma helped me with my homework. Yes, there is homework during Thanksgiving break. What a sad holiday! Mom tried to be happy, since it was Thanksgiving. I had to go to with Dad on Wednesday. It was his year to have me on Thanksgiving Day, so Mom, Grandma and I celebrated ours on Sunday. It was awesome, as usual. Mom is an incredible cook! With all the sadness in her heart, she still took the time to cook a wonderful turkey meal.

Wednesday unfortunately arrived. I had to leave at noon. Mom and I sat on the stairs around 11:30 am. We prayed and then just talked about our pets. We shared funny stories about them. It felt good to laugh a little. We both needed it. Here came *the honks*. We got up and hugged. Mom kissed me on the forehead. As I walked out, I turned like always, and we both signed, "I LOVE YOU". This time we did it twice! First one for us, and the other for our pets who have died! After I signed, it dawned on me Mom and I have a lot of traditions, like our nightly prayer, Sign language, our "Stair Prayers", our talks, hand squeezing and Saturday eating out. Good traditions that I will carry on!

I climbed in the backseat. I hated leaving Mom at such a rough time. My ex-grandma was sitting there. I said nothing. She could tell I didn't want to talk to her or the other two. I was too worried about Mom and could care less about their worthless, petty lives. Dad pulled out, and I waved to Mom one last time. She looked deeply depressed. I would miss her and pray for her every night. At the end of the block, here came the hand. I had my cell phone ready. I glared at them with such hatred. No one said a thing. We were off to the airport. I hadn't been in the car very long, when the cussing started.

Martha was frantically going through her purse. She was pulling everything out, one at a time. She said to Mr. Evil in her meek, pathetic voice, "I can't find my boarding pass you gave me at the house. I think I left it on the kitchen counter, because you were in such a hurry." Here it came, "You stupid, dumb mother "F" r. If you had a brain, you would be dangerous." I still didn't understand what that meant! Then Mr. Evil added, "We are not turning around. You'll have to get another one at the counter. We're going on through security! If you miss the plane, you and your stupid "A" can pay for a cab home. I swear Martha you are the queen of the brain dead!"

Sissy jumped in, "Stop yelling at your mother, your daughter is in the car." Wow! I couldn't believe she back talked my dad. Big mistake. Here it came again, now directed at her, "Shut the "F" up, you got that, or you can keep your "A" at home too." Sissy never said another word. I wasn't about to talk because I was next in the line of fire. We parked and went straight to the security line. I watched Martha go to the counter. It didn't take long and she was back in the security line. We were only a few people ahead of her. All that cussing and screaming in the car for nothing! Everyone made it through security and headed to our specific gate.

When we got there, I started feeling bad. I told Mr. Evil that my throat hurt. He snapped, "That's just great!" I think he would have cussed at me for being sick, but there were too many people around and someone might call the police or security. He told Martha to go buy me some cough drops, before getting on the plane. He told her, because I wasn't important enough for him to go. My dad, Mr. Evil was upset that I didn't feel good and I might ruin *his* trip. You know, he is "Narcissus", just like the original one from long ago. HE only matters, no one else does!

We boarded the plane. By this time, I was feeling crummy. My body started aching. I didn't tell dad. Why bother. I sat by the window, then Martha, then Sissy on the aisle. Mr. Narcissus was across from Sissy. Good! Far away from me as possible! We were flying to Miami. I tried to sleep on the plane, but I couldn't get comfortable. Martha could see I didn't feel good. She even touched my forehead. I heard her whisper to Sissy that I felt hot. Sissy said she would get me something for a fever when the plane landed. I guess she cared a little. Maybe she didn't want my Mom screaming at her for not taking care of me, and Mom would!!

By the time we landed, I was burning up with fever. "Mr. You Know Who", (pick any name), went to get the rental car. We all got in and headed to the hotel. I felt worse than worse! I just wanted to go to bed. My throat was killing me so bad, it hurt to swallow. We checked in and guess what, all four of us had to share one room. My dad is too cheap to get two rooms. He makes a lot of money, but only spends it on himself.

Martha was to sleep in one bed, next to Sissy and the "King" in the other. I got the roll away. Martha, "Miss Christian", that she claimed to be, had to sleep next to her evil son. She had to be a part of the sick and sinful sleeping arrangements, because she doesn't have enough guts to stand up to her son. Martha never even asked him if she and I could get our own room.

So, the four of us were crammed into one room for four nights. Four in four! It didn't matter much to me, because I felt awful. I went straight to bed. Martha was ordered by Dad to stay in the room with me, while he and Sissy went sightseeing. Maybe God is punishing Martha for all the times she didn't protect me and for lying in court? I slept all day and all night. I never even heard my rotten dad and Sissy come in.

The next morning was Thanksgiving. I didn't want to get out of bed, but I had to. Dad forced me to go eat at the big buffet. We all got dressed and headed down to the dining room. Dad was wearing a pair of black pants and a tan colored long sleeve shirt and black shoes. Sissy had on a black dress and high heels. Martha was wearing a beige long sleeve top with matching pants (like I said before, she only wore three different colors). Her shoes were also beige. She looked like a walking Band-Aid. I had on my black pants and a gray and black long sleeve top. It had sequins on it. I love it. Mom bought it for me to take on the trip.

We all walked around helping ourselves to the food. I dished up only a few green beans, a small slice of turkey and some cheese. I drank hot tea. I barely ate what was on my plate. The hot tea felt good on my throat, so I ordered another one, then a third. I was too weak to eat. I felt crummy all over. While everyone was eating, I placed my head down on my right arm. Mr. Evil kept screaming at me to sit up. I just ignored him.

Martha touched my forehead. She finally told her son that I was burning up. I told Dad I had to go lay down. Martha took me upstairs. I changed into my pajamas and got on the roll away. I told Martha to go finish her meal. I said I would be okay. She said she would eat fast and be right back up. I finally could go to sleep.

I was just barely awake when everyone came back to the room. All I remember was Martha and Sissy standing over me. Martha looked at me and saw I was sweating all over. Dad finally decided to call his doctor friend, from back home. The doctor called in some medicine for me. Mr. Narcissus had to take time out of his busy vacation schedule to go get it.

I had two different medicines to take. One was a pill and the other was liquid. Martha gave both of them to me. I just rested. While I was trying to go back to sleep, I could hear the three of them yapping. I actually heard my uncaring dad say, "I'm not letting 'this' ruin my vacation. Let's go she'll be fine. It serves her right for getting sick. Her "GD" "B" mother probably did this on purpose." Can you believe him? He is blaming my mom, miles away, for me being sick. I'm a "this" to him. He can't even say that "I" ruined his vacation. I'm a thing!

The next thing I heard was the door open and close. They were all gone. I was glad to be alone. I can't stand any of them, especially my evil dad. The other two are way too scared to ever stand up to him, even when I am sick. They are really messed up, pathetic people. I would call Mom, but my phone was taken away from me. So here I was alone in a hotel room. I softly cried out, because my throat was hurting, "Rain E, where are you? I wish I could see you. I hate being on this trip. I miss you and my mom. Rain E, are you near?" I closed my eyes and fell asleep.

I woke up hours later, still by myself. It was dark outside. My throat was now burning. I got up and went to the bathroom. My medicine was sitting on the counter. I read the back of the liquid bottle. It said take one teaspoon every four hours. Surely it had been four hours! It was nighttime. I rinsed out the spoon lying next to the bottle and poured the medicine in it. I took it and then drank some water from the sink faucet. I went back to my rollaway bed.

I hadn't been there for very long, when they all walked in. Martha asked? "How are you feeling Tweetie?" I rolled my eyes and thought, "Good grief!" I simply answered, "Awful, my throat and now my left ear hurts." Dad griped, "Great! I guess YOU ruined this trip!" That was it! I quickly snapped back with my raspy voice, "I can't help getting sick, it just happened." That felt good talking back to him. I felt so bad I didn't care what I said to him. He stopped griping, for the moment.

The rest of the trip went by dreadfully slow. I wasn't getting any better. Sissy even said that maybe I should see a doctor. Dad flat-out said, "We're leaving for the airport in one hour. Her mother can take her when we get home." Martha started to say something, when my dad barked, "Not another word from either of you. Shut your "GD" mouths and finish packing." I lifted myself out of my horrible bed and dressed.

I went to the bathroom and took another spoonful of medicine. Martha walked in and gathered up everything to pack. I whispered, "I can't talk. My voice is hoarse." She looked worried, not for me, for what would happen to her letting a child suffer, her own grandchild! Martha knew she was in trouble. I could see it in her baggy eyes. She was worried about herself. Trouble was coming in the form of an angry, caring, loving woman; my mom.

I walked out of the bathroom and waited until it was time to leave. I saw Martha walk over and whisper in Sissy's ear. I bet it was about me!! Still, neither one had the guts to say anything to my evil dad. They were more scared of him, than me being deathly sick. Boy, wait until I get home. Mom IS going to let them have it, I promise you. This is one time I couldn't hide my injuries from her. She will see how miserable I feel, and of course, all the medicines I still had to take.

We made it to the airport, just in time to board the plane. I sat by the window again. I pulled my legs up to my chest and curled up in a ball. I went to sleep thinking about Mom. The next thing I remember was Martha nudging me to wake up. She said that we were home. Finally back to MY home. We got all our stuff from the plane and headed to Dad's car in the parking garage. I got in the backseat and curled up with my blanket I had left there. Everyone was quiet. There was no talking all the way to Mom's. We pulled up in the driveway and I quickly climbed out. Dad got my bag from he trunk. He tried to hug me, but I push him away. I loudly said, "Don't touch me!" He got in his car. I never said goodbye to any of them. That was the worst trip I had ever been on!

"That which does not kill us makes us stronger."

Friedrich Nietzsche

Chapter 16

I was within feet of the front door, when I noticed Grandma standing there. She greeted me, "Rachel," she quietly spoke, "I need to talk to you." Grandma sounded so serious, not funny at all. I immediately asked, "Where's Mom?" Grandma said, "That's what I need to talk to you about." I panicked, "Is Mom okay, tell me, please, is she dead? Where is she? Is she dead?" I tried to run to her room, but Grandma grabbed my arm. "Rachel, your mother is not dead. She's resting in bed. Sit down, I need to talk to you," she firmly stated.

We moved to the stairs. Grandma was helping me with my bags and stuff. She reached for one the same time I did. She had that motherly concerned look. Grandma applied her hand on my forehead. "Oh my goodness child, you are burning up!" I told her how sick I was the whole time in Miami. Grandma wanted to take my temperature. I told her to tell me about Mom. I needed to know if she was okay.

Grandma said, "This past Wednesday, the day you left, your mother had a mild heart attack." I screamed out, "No!!" As the tears began, I started to run to her room. Grandma stopped me again. I quieted down some. She calmly continued, "Your mother woke me up at midnight complaining of pain shooting down her left arm. She was drenched in sweat! She said that her heart was racing so fast and she couldn't stop it and it was causing a great amount of tightness in her chest. I quickly got dressed."

"Your brave mother drove herself to the emergency room, with me in the car praying the whole way. When we arrived, a nurse immediately took your mother to a room. I waited in the lobby, still praying and panicking at the same time." Grandma took a deep breath then continued, "About twenty minutes went by when finally a nurse came and escorted me to her private room. She said your mother was in stable condition."

"I walked in to find your mother hooked up to several machines. The doctor came in a little later. He ran lots of tests, and said the arteries were clear, but the heart muscle took a beating." I was in shock. I don't know if I could have handled seeing Mom like that. How did Grandma? Grandma added, "The doctor spent a lot of time talking to the both of us. Your mother had to stay at the hospital until her heartbeat returned to a normal rate. We were there until the next morning. The doctor said your mother suffered a mild heart attack brought on by stress and needed to rest for a couple of weeks."

I wiped my tears off my face and asked if I could see her. Grandma said that Mom would love that. I got up and dashed to her bedroom. I quietly opened the door. Mom opened her eyes and smiled. I ran to her. I started crying again. Mom looked at me and said, "My sweet love, I'll be okay, I promise. I just have to take it easy for a while." Mom kissed my forehead and then abruptly pushed me back. "Rachel, you are burning up! Go get the thermometer in the cabinet above the toilet. Hurry!"

I brought it back in record time. Mom immediately turned it on and placed it under my tongue. I watched her eyes bug out. The thermometer wasn't in my mouth for very long when it beeped! Mom took it out. She reached for her reading glasses on the skirted table and screamed out, "We're going to the night clinic. Go get Grandma, she'll have to drive!"

While Mom carefully got out of bed and dressed, I ran and got Grandma. Mom was putting on her UGGS when we walked in. She looked at Grandma and said I had a temperature of 104. I thought Grandma was going to pass out. She told Mom that I felt hot. The three of us jumped into Grandma's car and headed to the late night clinic. Here was Mom, recovering from heart problems and I was burning up with fever. Thank goodness Grandma moved in with us.

We arrived at the clinic just before it closed. I was the only patient there. The nurse took all of us to a room in the back. She took my temperature and blood pressure. That blood pressure wrap always squeezes my arm too tight. I guess that's what it's supposed to do. It still uncomfortably hurts. Then the nurse looked at my throat and listened to my breathing. She poked on my neck and back. She left, saying the doctor would be right in. I was on the table curled up. I felt awful. It was about five minutes, when the doctor walked in with the nurse. He looked at my throat and listened to my breathing. He then told the nurse to swab my throat. They also took some of my blood. The doctor and nurse left the room.

A few minutes later, another medical person came in. She was told to take an X-Ray of my chest. Mom walked back with me to the X-Ray room. The lady took several pictures. When she finished, Mom and I went back to my waiting room, where Grandma was. Mom looked so tired and very weak. No one said a word. We just sat there waiting and waiting for a long time.

Finally the doctor came in. He didn't look happy. He looked right at my mom and stated, "Not only does your daughter have strep throat and an ear infection, she has pneumonia." I thought Mom was going to fall out of her chair. The doctor said that one of my lungs was in bad shape. He told her I would be out of school for several days. Then, he harshly asked, "Why didn't you bring her in earlier? This could have all been prevented."

Mom looked at me. I begged, "Let me tell the doctor Mom. Please!" She said, "Go right ahead." I began, "I was with my uncaring dad the last four days. I didn't feel good on the plane and was sick the whole trip. My dad refused to take me to the doctor, because he wanted to sightsee. He stated that I was NOT going to ruin HIS vacation!" The doctor whipped his head around to Mom and firmly said, "I would like his phone number!" She gladly gave it to him. We left. I looked at Grandma. She was so mad I saw anger coming out of her sweet face.

Grandma drove us to the all-night pharmacy, to pick up my medicine. When we got home I went straight to bed and so did Mom. Poor Grandma had to take care of both of us all because of my self-centered dad. That night in bed, I thanked God over and over for my mom not dying. I wouldn't want to live without her and God knew that. I was sick, but happy to be back home. I knew I would be well-taken care of by two amazing women. I covered up with my comforter and was asleep in no time at all!

177

*"There is nothing like staying
at home for real comfort."*

Jane Austen

Chapter 17

I woke up the next day to find my wonderful Mom by my bed. My mom who was recovering from heart problems! I softly asked, "Mom, Mom are you awake?" She opened her eyes and smiled, "Yes, my sweet. How are you feeling?" I said, "No, how are you feeling?" We both softly giggled. "When did you come to my room?" Mom yawned, "In the middle of the night. Do you remember me waking you up to give you your medicine and take your temperature?" I answered, "No." "Thank goodness it dropped to 100 F, which is a lot safer!" What a mom I have!

She got up and asked me if I wanted some chicken noodle soup. I answered with a big YES! So, Mom went downstairs. Next thing I heard was Grandma getting on to her. She loudly ordered her back to bed. I was still in bed when Grandma came in, carrying the bowl of soup. She handed me a bell to ring, if I needed anything. Then she ordered me to stay in bed, unless I had to use the bathroom. I always minded her when "strict" orders came out of her mouth. She could be tough when she wanted to be. So, I rested in my room and Mom rested in hers for a whole week.

At the end of the week, it dawned on me that it was already December. Christmas would soon be here! I was dreading it this year, because I had to be with evil dad and the "girlfriend" for 17 days. I would only be with Mom for five days up until noon on Christmas Day. After that, I had to be with Mr. Scrooge, (his holiday name), until school started back. Who came up with such a crazy schedule? I called him *Mr. Scrooge*, only under my breath. He was a Scrooge! He was mean and hateful to everyone around him and even mean and hateful to people he had never met. Dad told me at Thanksgiving the three of us were going to California. Oh boy, I could hardly wait. (Of course I was being sarcastic).

Another vacation! Thinking about the trip at Thanksgiving, I completely forgot to ask Mom something. I was so sick it just slipped my mind. We were leaving the airport. I was in the backseat with Martha when I witnessed a man pull out in front of Dad, strictly by accident. He was in the wrong lane. No big deal! My mean and evil dad yelled, "You "GD" "F" n "N", watch where you're going!"

I couldn't believe my ears. Here I was already sick, and now sicker listening to his filthy mouth. His bad language was getting worse! No one said a word. I felt bad and Sissy and ex-grandma were too scared to speak. I just wanted to get home to Mom. As we drove past the man, I got a closer look at him. He was an older, black man and he kind of looked like a grandpa. He looked nice. What was that "N" word Dad said to him?

It was now Sunday and I had missed a whole week of school because of my uncaring dad. All the homework! Mom would help me catch up. I climbed out of bed and went downstairs to check on my resilient Mom. I walked into her bedroom and she was still asleep. Just as I was quietly leaving she called out, "Hey stranger, how are you feeling?" I said, "That's funny, I was coming to ask you the same question."

Mom said, "Come crawl in bed with me." I did. All the wonderful childhood memories instantly came back! Mom would tell me stories to help me fall asleep and of course during bad storms. We would take turns making up fun games at bedtime. All these special memories would stay with me forever! I was snuggled up to her, when Grandma walked in. She asked how both of us were feeling and if we needed anything. We were fine. Mom had the TV on low. She said it always 'lulled' her to sleep. I think 'lull' meant, "talking quiet". I rested my head on a big fluffy pillow and peacefully fell asleep.

It was late afternoon when I woke up. Mom was still watching TV. I went to the bathroom and then jumped back in bed. It was freezing cold in her room, just the way she liked it. I didn't know how Mom slept in an icebox. She kept a heating pad under the sheets. It was a permanent part of the bed. It kept us toasty! Mom was watching an old movie. I'm sure it was one of her favorites! I started watching it too.

It was at a scene where a black man was being treated mean by a bunch of white policemen. I heard that "N" word and yelled out, "Mom, that's the word!! I forgot to ask you!" Mom jerked in bed and said, "Oh my goodness Rachel, you startled me!" "I'm sorry. The movie you're watching, that white man said a word I heard Dad yell out at the airport." Mom turned the TV sound all the way down and asked, "What word?" I just blurted it out. Mom was in shock! She scolded me, "Rachel, don't ever use that word again, you understand young lady!" I innocently asked, "What did I say that was bad. Is it that word? What does it mean?"

Mom explained to me it was a horrible, disgraceful word describing another human being who had darker skin. I told Mom that I was so glad she told me, because two of my closest friends at school were dark-skinned. I would have been kicked out of my Christian school, if I had said it to them, all because of my dad. I told Mom, "Thank you for telling me. Figures! It came out of Dad's mouth. I will never use it and I will tell Dad to never say it. I doubt that he will stop, but at least I can tell him I don't want to hear it."

Mom told me to always ask her about anything I saw or heard that bothered me, when I was with Dad. I said I would, even though I still hadn't mentioned the photos of me sleeping. No way was I bringing it up now! Mom needed her rest. She told me that she was sorry I had to hear that awful, awful word. Boy, I was really glad I remembered to ask Mom before I went back to school tomorrow.

I then asked, "Why are you watching a movie with that word in it?" Mom said, "Good point! Well, it's a powerful and very good movie. I love the actors playing their roles. Rachel it wasn't that long ago that people of different races were treated horribly in this country. Some parts of the country they still are. I think they make these movies to remind us how people hurt others, just because of the color of their skin. It's a sad shame." I agreed. Mom told me to never forget that we were all equal in the eyes of God, but there were still people who didn't see this and they would have to account it to Him someday. I immediately thought of my filthy-mouthed dad. He would be doing a lot of explaining to God for the way he chose to live his life.

Mom and I stayed in bed all day watching movies. One of my most favorite ones came on. It was *Meet Me In St Louis*. I would have never heard of that movie, much less ever seen it, if it hadn't been for my mom. She watched all the oldies. Some were pretty good. I loved this one so much I bought it. Then Mom's favorite Alfred Hitchcock movie came on, *To Catch A Thief*. It WAS good! I had seen several of Alfred Hitchcock's movies. He made good movies! The only one I was not allowed to watch until I was older was *Psycho*. Mom shared with me an interesting fact about Mr. Hitchcock. He was briefly seen in all his movies. Mom said it was called a *cameo* appearance.

We must have watched four or so movies, before the stars came out. Grandma brought us snacks and checked on us all day. I finally said I was going to bed, to another bed! We said our prayer and good nights. I hugged and kissed Mom and said, "I'm so glad you're my mom. You know EVERYTHING, including the best old movies! I enjoyed *To Catch A Thief.* I'm going to carefully watch for Mr. Hitchcock the next time one of his movies comes on." Mom softly smiled.

I headed upstairs and took a quick shower, then finished getting ready for bed. I got out my school clothes, turned the lights out and jumped into bed. It was wonderful spending the day watching old movies with someone you love. I wondered how many other kids my age watch old movies! I got under my comforter and I thanked God again for saving my Mom's life. I asked Him to watch over all the kids who didn't have good parents, then fell asleep.

It was Monday and finally I was back at school. I was thrilled to see all my friends especially my best friend. I had a lot of homework to do. Mom worked with me each night for several days until I was completely caught up. The next three weeks went by fast, way too fast! It was Friday before Christmas. We got out of school at noon.

Mom picked me up and we went straight home and packed for a weekend stay at a very fancy hotel in a town nearby. There was an art auction all weekend. The hotel room was free. The art company provided meals for all the art collectors. I could go because I was just old enough. I was going to spend three wonderful days in a fancy hotel, with just my mom. Yea!!

We were getting the car packed when my nasty dad called. He wanted to come get me to do some last minute Christmas shopping. Mom very loudly told him, "No! You have had plenty of time to shop before now!" I loved it when she told him to stop bugging her and just follow the schedule. Mom was fuming! He was going to have me for 17 days and still wanted to cut into my 5 measly days with Mom. Unbelievable! It was all about him! It will always be about him!

We said our goodbyes to Grandma and headed out the door. My evil dad sent Mom a text. She was driving, so I looked at it. Dad said Mom was selfish and a worthless "B". Mom told me to just ignore it and not read anymore. She was sorry I read that one. A few minutes later, the same message showed up on my phone. Dad even spelled out the word "B". I showed Mom and she immediately called him. She ripped him apart for his choice words on a minor's phone. She abruptly hung up on him. Mom said that he was trying to ruin what few days we had together at Christmas. Mom was right! I turned my phone off. He was not going to ruin our short vacation!

The hotel stay was a blast! The meals were wonderful. Mom and I looked at a lot of art, but didn't buy anything. The last two days flew by way too fast. On the third day, we got up, ate the final meal, packed and drove home. We were both quiet in the car. Mom was playing her piano friend's new Christmas CD. It was beautiful.

We pulled into the garage and Grandma came out to greet us. She asked how everything was and if we had a good time. She said it had been raining all weekend. Grandma told us that last night was one of the worst storms she has ever lived through. She said that there was a lot of rain, severe wind and even hail. Grandma added that the electricity was off for several hours. She said that our female dog barked off and on until the storm finally passed through early in the morning. We all walked in and saw Fluff Ball, our only living dog, sound asleep by the fireplace. Now exhausted, Grandma just wanted to go back to bed. She was glad we had a great time.

Mom unpacked and just relaxed. She said we would make the Christmas cookies later on this afternoon. I went upstairs and watched TV, until it was time to bake. Several hours passed. Mom called for me. She was ready to start the cookies. We baked all night into the wee hours. It took forever to decorate the sugar cookies, but it was a blast. They turned out beautifully with all the different colored icings and sprinkles. This had been a family tradition that goes all the way back to when Mom was a little girl. It was a mess to clean up, but a fun mess. Grandma showed up just as we finished the clean up. That was very clever and timely of her!

I bathed and climbed into bed. Mom came up with my last pill. I had to take this medicine for a month, because I was having a hard time recovering from pneumonia. Mom took my temperature. It was finally normal. I just started learning about temperatures in math. Very interesting! We talked about the fun art auction, and said our prayer. Mom kissed me goodnight. As she was walking out, I asked, "How many more days before I have to go with Dad?" Mom sadly answered, "Two." She turned off the lights. Two days! I would be gone from Mom for so long. I hoped Rain E would show it!

*"The best thing one can do
when it's raining is to let it rain."*

Henry Wadsworth Longfellow

Chapter 18

For two days straight, all I could think about was going with my evil dad for 17 days. It was Christmas Eve and tomorrow I would be leaving. Mom, Grandma and I went to our church. It was a wonderful service. When we got home, we all watched Christmas movies, including White Christmas. Mom let me open a couple of my regular presents in between movies. It had been fun opening my "12 Days of Christmas" presents leading up to Christmas Day.

It was midnight when the last movie ended. Grandma went to bed and I sat with Mom a little longer. She was extra quiet. I knew why. Too many days having to spend with Dad! There was nothing Mom could do about it. Thanks again worthless judges! I told her that I would be okay and not to worry. The sad truth was that I didn't know if I would be okay, especially now after the conversation I heard on the balcony. I hugged and kissed Mom. We said our prayer and I went to bed.

It was Christmas morning! I grabbed my robe and dashed downstairs. Mom and Grandma were already up. How is it that Mom is always up before me every Christmas morning? Does that happen in other families? I went straight to the tree. There were lots of unwrapped presents. Those were from Santa. I know Mom was really Santa, I think? Mom said I could start opening. I ripped them apart as fast as I could. I got lots of what I asked for, including a new Razor scooter. Mom said I could take it with me to Dad's. I didn't want to. He wouldn't take me anywhere to ride it. I asked Mom if I could ride my new scooter before Dad showed up. She said I could.

I changed clothes and went to the front yard. I rode up and down the sidewalks for a long time. Mom came out and told me I needed to get ready to go with my dad. I was going in when Mr. Scrooge pulled up. I was already dressed for the dreaded visit. I went in and told Mom that Dad was here. I didn't want to go! I didn't want to go! Mom could see it in my face. She whispered in my right ear, "I love you sooooo much!" I got choked up. "I didn't want to go! I didn't want to go!" I kept saying it to myself, over and over.

I hugged Mom long and whispered, "I love you sooooo much! Thank Santa for the scooter." I let go and headed to the car door. I turned and signed "I Love You", and then said it out loud. Mom signed and yelled back, "I Love You Too!"

I got in and Dad drove away. I kept watching Mom until we were out of sight. I turned around to a hand in my face. This time it was Sissy's hand. She demanded, "Give it to me!" Oh my goodness gracious me!! She had become him. Now I was dealing with double, evil trouble! Dad glanced over at Sissy, as though they planned this. As evil dad was driving, he stated, "We're opening presents at Martha's, then straight to the airport." I abruptly interrupted, "I haven't packed yet." "Sissy packed for you." Dad smugly said. "I don't want HER packing for me ever again! She's NOT my mom and never will be!!"

Dad slammed on his brakes. My body bashed into the back of Sissy's seat. He whipped his head around and said, "None of your "F" n sassy lip today, you got that! Stop acting like a brat!" Hey, there was a change he didn't call me the "B" word. We were back to "brat"! It didn't matter what he called me, because it didn't matter to him, as long as it came out cruel and degrading. Bad words were showing up more frequently since the divorce was dragging on! With his less than sunny position, he thought he was hurting Mom, but he was really hurting me!

We pulled up to Martha's house. I opened the car door and just glared at my dad. Martha was standing at the door. She greeted me with, "Merry Christmas Tweetie! I'm so glad you are spending Christmas with your real blood family." "I'm not!" I spouted off. "I've already spent Christmas with my real family. Blood doesn't make you a family!" Martha was stunned. She said back to me, "That's not very nice to say to your family!" I came in closer to her and said, "Your son's not very nice and he's not what I call *family.*" This time she was speechless. Can you believe what that witch said that to me? Can you believe what came out of my mouth?

My dad deliberately brushed up against me as he passed by, going into the house. Martha and Sissy strolled on in. I added even louder,

"I'm only here because I have to be!" I walked all the way in and sat down by the fireplace. I just stared at the three of them. I knew it was rude to speak that way to my grandmother, but there was nothing 'grand' about her.

Every time I looked at her face, I remembered Mom telling me how she lied in court and didn't help protect me from her 'precious' son. Mr. Scrooge glared back with a hateful, devil look, but he never said a word. Everyone moved to the living room to open presents. I sat in the corner, farthest from the tree and THEM!!! As Martha was handing out the gifts, I glanced over at *The Girlfriend*. My dad handed her two boxes, one small and one medium size.

The first one she opened was a huge sapphire and diamond necklace. I heard her tell Dad, "It's the one you picked out. Oh Baby! I knew you would buy it for me." Right as Sissy was saying that, she looked at me. She had the necklace in between her fingers, as though she was telling me, she could get my dad to buy her anything. Big deal! She put the necklace back into a blue velvet case and opened box number two.

Sissy pulled out a pair of black UGGS. My heart sank. Mom had told Mr. Scrooge and her a month ago that I wanted some black UGGS. I kept opening my presents, but no UGGS. Instead, I got a bunch of 'crystal rocks'. Rocks from my dad! He looked at me and said, "You better like them! They cost me 200 dollars!" I hurtfully spouted off, (along with anger in my voice), "You wasted your money. You keep'um!" I couldn't believe it! Sissy got my boots, along with an expensive necklace. I got rocks!

Another memorable event that would NEVER leave my brain! My dad had done plenty of hateful and hurtful things to me, but this was the worst. I never dreamed he could be so inhuman. It was on THIS day, I finally realized, my dad was the devil. No one could be that cruel on Christmas Day, no one but the devil!

I left all my gifts in the corner. I didn't care if I ever saw any of that stuff again. We all piled in the car. Martha rode with us, so she could drive Dad's car back to her house. When we got to the airport, our plane was delayed for two hours because of a thunderstorm. I firmly told Dad to let me have his or my phone so I could call Mom. He handed me my phone and growled, "Make it quick missy!" I said back, "Why? We're not going anywhere, anytime soon." He just gave me a nasty look. That felt good, being mean to a mean person.

I went to the bathroom, of course Sissy tagged along. I called Mom from the stall. I knew Sissy was standing outside the door. They never let me talk to my mom in private. I didn't care anymore about *Their Rules*. I was going to talk to my mom, whether Sissy listened in on or not. I told Mom the plane was delayed. She asked how Christmas was at Martha's. I loudly answered, "Sissy got my UGGS and I got ROCKS!" Mom said, "Excuse me!" I repeated it, even louder, "I GOT ROCKS!!! NO UGGS!!!!"

Mom was beyond mad. She firmly said, "I will deal with those two when you return home." It sounded like she was grinding her teeth, the way she was talking. She got even madder when I told her I had to hang up, because Sissy was standing outside my stall. We said our goodbyes, and I walked out. I pitched my phone to Sissy and said, "I didn't need to go to the bathroom after all." I strolled back to our gate and plopped down in an uncomfortable airport chair. I got out my earplugs and hand-held Nintendo. I played my games, with a smirk on my face.

Finally on the plane! I sat by the window. Sissy sat next to me, and mean Dad was on the aisle. I took a quick glance at both of them and closed my eyes. All I wanted to do was sleep. (When I'm asleep, they're not around). Sissy woke me up, when we landed. It was pouring down rain. Dad made a nasty remark about it. Heaven forbid, *his* trip would be ruined. I smirked again. I think this happened for a reason. I believe God was most certainly mad at those two. Sissy got *MY* UGGS because Dad loved hurting me. I could see it now!

After we stepped off the plane, Dad took off ahead of Sissy and me. So rude! We followed him straight to the rental car and loaded everything. The moment we pulled out of the parking garage, it started raining harder. I thought it was very funny, even though I was the only one that felt that way. The hotel we were staying at was right on the ocean. I did like that. When we pulled up to the entrance, Dad finally stopped griping. He griped and complained all the way to the hotel. He gripes and bitches about everything, but this was worse than usual.

There were only two beds in our hotel room. They were sleeping in one and I was in the other. It grossed me out that I had to sleep next to them. They neatly unpacked. I went to the balcony and just watched the rain join the ocean. We stayed at the hotel the whole day. It rained all day and night. I kept wondering if I would see Rain E during this trip. The next morning it was still raining, actually pouring. The two of them got up first. Looked like they didn't get any beauty sleep! I slowly crawled out of bed and got ready. We ate at the breakfast buffet then shopped at the hotel stores. Sissy bought me an umbrella. Maybe NOW she felt bad about the UGGS. Who knows? Who cares?

I walked outside and headed to the ocean. The rain was coming down pretty hard. The lightning lit up the sky, followed by the loud thunder. The umbrella wasn't helping much, so I quickly raced back up and inside to where Sissy was standing. I asked where Dad went. She said, "He went to steam, where else." You know, the way Sissy answered, I think she was getting tired of his steaming. Everyday, whether at the condo or on a trip, Dad was always steaming, in more ways than one. He steamed for hours at a time. I thought it was abnormal, but that's just me!

A couple of more days went by when Mr. Scrooge decided to drive to the nearby local city. All the way in the car, it showered. When we got there, we tried to walk around and see stuff, but it was too wet. We ate and drove back in the pouring rain. You couldn't see anything, but rain. I think the whole state must have been raining. I couldn't help but feel pleased. It was sweet revenge!

I watched the sky the whole way, hoping to see Rain E like before, but never did. By the time we reached our hotel, it was raining so hard, it sounded like hail. We all got out at the valet. Sissy and I headed to the room. Dad went straight to the spa to steam, *again*. I crashed on my bed. All the rain was making me sleepy. I closed my eyes and rested. Sissy did the same.

We were rudely awakened when "You Know Who" barged in. He wanted to go eat. Sissy changed her clothes. I begged Dad to let me stay in the room. I kept begging and pleading, until Sissy finally told him to let me stay. Wow! They left. I took a quick shower and changed into my rainbow pajamas. My bed was closest to the balcony, so I watched the rain until I was asleep. I never heard them come in.

The next morning, I woke up first. I went straight to the balcony and sat in one of the damp chairs. I stared into the sky. All I saw was dark rain clouds. It was lightly raining and very peaceful. My ears were getting a rest from all the loud, bad words Dad had been vomiting from his mouth the whole trip. He NEVER gave it a rest!! Tomorrow we were going home. You know, there was only one fun thing I did in the last four days. That was when I attempted to head down the many steps to the ocean while it was raining. Wished I had made it to the sand and ocean water! I wanted to go to the beach. I didn't care it was raining.

While I was still on the balcony, Sissy opened the door. She said for me to come in and change clothes. I walked back in, wet butt and all. Dad was already dressed. He told me to quickly change so *he* could go eat. It was always about him. I asked if I could go down to the ocean. He said we were going somewhere else and it would have to be later. That meant "No". So we all left the room, and went to eat at the buffet and then headed to the valet.

We didn't drive far. The violent rain started attacking the car. Dad gave up and came back to the hotel. He went to steam and Sissy and I went up to the room. I climbed into bed and watched TV. Mr. Scrooge came in a few hours later, and of course wanted to go eat. So he and Sissy left again. They knew I didn't want to go. I had my snacks and water I brought on the trip. I just wanted to sleep and did just that.

The last day of this miserable vacation finally arrived. Dad and Sissy must have packed last night when they came in. I woke up and looked over at a chair in the corner. Everything was neatly folded and perfectly placed in my bag. I immediately snickered, "Dad must be training Sissy." I changed into my navy and bright green sweat pants and matching top. I put on my favorite tennis shoes. Dad and Sissy were already casually dressed. I finished getting ready in the bathroom. We went downstairs for breakfast. It was the buffet again, but this time there was even more food. Sissy said it was the Sunday Brunch buffet. I was very hungry! I walked around and loaded up my plate. I was sitting down at our table, when I looked out the window and, guess what? It had stopped raining! That was the funniest and sweetest thing to witness. This happened for a reason. I really believed it in my heart and soul.

We finished eating and went back to get our stuff. I got to the valet first. They were a few steps behind me. This nice black man put all the bags in the trunk, except my backpack. I kept it with me. I kept watching Dad. Wow! He never called the man that bad word probably because we were at a fancy hotel where Dad enjoyed steaming. I climbed into the backseat with my backpack. They piled in the front. Dad was fiddling with the radio for some time.

There was a knocked on my window. It was the nice black man. I rolled it down and he handed me a red rose bud. I looked at his lovely face and said, "Thank you." He said back, "I bet red roses are your favorite flowers, and of course, the *rain,* another favorite." Then he winked. My voice gasped. I just looked at him, and answered, "Yes, red roses are my favorite." He smiled and then winked again and said, "Imagine that!" My eyes bugged out, and at the same time my eyebrows shot up to the top of my forehead. I was at a loss of words. As we pulled away from the hotel, I turned and got on my knees so that I could continue watching the nice man from the rear window. He waved at me. I waved back.

As we pulled further away, we kept waving at each other. While I was watching the nice man wave, the strangest thing happened next. His hand folded into a fist. I kept watching. He took his index finger and pointed it up to the sky. I gasped again. I waved back with my index finger. Dad told me to turn around and sit back down. I did. I didn't want to get thrown into Sissy's seat again. I tried to see the man, by turning my head as far as I could to the right, but he was gone. Just like that, he was gone. I put my red rose bud in the zipper pocket of my backpack.

The second strangest thing happened. I mean spooky strange! In a civil way, I said to those two heathens in the front seat, "That black man was so nice to me!" Sissy sharply replied, "What black man?" I said, "The one who put the bags in the trunk." She spouted off, "He wasn't black he was white." My hateful dad jumped in, "You must be seeing things." I tried to talk, but they both shut me up. I wasn't seeing things. I knew exactly what I saw. I saw what God and Rain E wanted me to see. I looked up to God and whispered, "Thank you for "Rain" E and the red rose!

An incredible feeling, like none other, took over my body. I felt it throughout. The nice man was Rain E. She gave me the rose. She came in the disguise of a black man; a person my dad always talked bad about. I remembered that the Bible said you should always be kind to a stranger because, you never know if you are talking to an angel (Hebrews 13:2). This time Rain E came to ME in a thunderstorm, as usual. I truly felt it! I knew at that moment I would make it through the next 13 days. This trip happened for a reason.

When we got on the plane, I opened the zipper to look at my red rose. I had to make sure it was real. I touched the soft petals with my fingertips, smiled and closed my eyes until the plane landed. I woke up refreshed. That was one of the best sleeps I have ever had. "Imagine that"!

Martha picked us up. She was there when we walked out. I guess if she arrived late, evil Dad would cuss her out. We put everything in the trunk. Martha got in the backseat and we drove to her house, then to the condo. As soon as the front opened, I ran straight to my room. I took the red rose bud out of the zipper pocket and placed it in middle of one of my books, so it would dry flat. I sat two more books on top and moved all three to my wooden headboard shelf. I learned this crafty book trick from Mom. I wanted the flower to be near me while I was sleeping.

I unpacked all my dirty clothes for Sissy to wash. I took a bath and then got ready for bed. I was so tired from the whole day. I climbed into bed and began saying 'our' prayer, pretending Mom was beside me. I was half way through when my door opened. I quickly closed both eyes. I heard Sissy say, "She's asleep." She turned out my light and closed the door. I opened my eyes and continued 'our' prayer. Then I prayed, "God, please make the next 13 days go by fast. Please speed up the clock, Amen. Oops! I'm sorry God, I forgot to say, in Jesus' name, Amen." I rolled over to my left side and stared out the balcony window. I thanked Rain E for coming to California. I crashed!

The next morning, I was abruptly awakened to screaming going on outside my door. Guess who was doing the screaming? Yep! You guessed it. I quietly snuck to my door to listen. Mr. Evil was yelling at Sissy. I cracked it open enough to hear the noise coming from the kitchen. 99% of the noise was coming out of Dad's mouth! I kept listening and watching with one eye. I heard him scream at Sissy for making the coffee wrong. He yelled, "Earth to Sissy, Earth to Sissy! Is there a brain in there?" Sissy answered, "I made it the same way, like you showed me." Grumpy said, "Wrong, Meathead! Forget it! I'll grab some real coffee on the way to the spa."

The flash of Dad's body blew by. I quickly yanked my head back. Thank goodness he didn't come through my door. He would have knocked me to the floor. He must have already been dressed, because the door slammed fast. I went back to bed. I stayed there trying to make sense of my crazy dad. He was getting crazier, as the days went by. Most people come back relaxed after a vacation. Not him! He comes back more crazy. How was I going to make it through this long visit?

I covered up with my comforter and thought about the nice black man who gave me the rose. Was it Rain E? I glanced at my balcony. Then I heard a soft knock at my door. I said, "Come in." It was Sissy,

who else. She said that my dad went to steam. I answered, "I heard."
I said nothing else. If Sissy couldn't stop that mouth, she would either
have to learn how to live with it or leave.

Mom tried until she was worn out. Sissy left saying she was going
to do some cleaning. She closed my door and never mentioned the fight.
What could she say without sounding like a pathetic fool? My cruel
dad humiliated her. The only reason she took his abuse was because of
the money. I had a creepy suspicion that someday she would turn on
him and get even. Maybe? Maybe not! I just sensed it!

Oh, that I might have my request,
that God would grant what I hope for.

Job 6:8 (NIV)

Chapter 19

C hristmas Break was finally over! I don't mean to sound so negative, but Christmas is supposed to be a wondrous, uplifting time. Christmas should be happy, kind, peaceful, enjoyable and maybe snowy, like it always is with my mom! Not this Christmas! Not for me! Not with my dad! Mine was sad, cruel, loud, vulgar, and wet! As devastating as my Christmas started out with Mr. Scrooge (Dad), it became almost bearable.

The constant rain that kept annoying my dad and the uplifting, unexpected surprise visit (both taking place in California), made all the difference. The nice black man with the red rose was the main highlight of my drawn out, dreadful stay. The rain made me smile. It was an amusing, yet gratifying "revengeful" plus!

I was more than glad to be back at school and "HOME". Always great, seeing all my friends after a long break! I missed my best friend the most. I wanted to see her during the break, but my dad NEVER lets me see any of my friends on his time. During my Christmas Break, I wondered many times if I would ever tell my best friend about Rain E!

The first week flew by. The following week was my 11th birthday, just three weeks after Christmas. "What a fun blast getting presents twice in one month! Three long and hurtful years have passed since Mom filed for divorce. Can you believe it? Three years of agonizing, forced visits with the monster! Would it ever change? I hoped.

Thank goodness for Rain E and now Bolt! They had become a part of my soul. Still praying to see Rain E and even Bolt again! I thought it would have been at Christmas. Maybe Bolt meant next Christmas? If so, Rain E and funny Bolt will still be in my life for at least another year. Yea!! New questions had entered my brain. Who was the nice black man in California and why months had gone by without being a part of Rain E Rainbow's home again? I prayed I would get my answers soon! For now, I keep Rain E tucked away in my heart and Bolt inside my funny bone.

My birthday finally arrived! I was required to spend 2 hours with my dad because of the miserable family law. I dressed for school and flew downstairs. The moment I left my room, the heavenly aroma of homemade biscuits filled the air. I knew they were for the birthday girl! Mom had made her famous, yummy but healthy shake, just for me. She created a long time ago. My plate of biscuits and drink were waiting for my arrival! Before I sat down, Mom gave me 11 long hugs. I ate and we took off for school. Mom was bringing a special cake during lunch.

At school, my class sang "Happy Birthday". Mom arrived right on time. Everybody loved the decorated "cookie" cake. The rest of the day was a blast, because of all the extra birthday attention! After Mom picked me, we drove straight home. I walked in finding a kitchen table decorated with many gifts and balloons. I think Mom always bought me extra gifts, because of my difficult life with Dad.

I ripped open the presents. Mom got me the coolest black leather jacket, plus extra fun clothes, and gift cards to two of my favorite stores! Grandma gave me a gift card, plus money. Mom lit my other birthday cookie cake that was just for us to enjoy. She and Grandma sang "Happy Birthday"! It was almost 6:00 pm. Grandma wished me a happy birthday one more time, before she retired to her bedroom.

Mom and I moved to the stairs. Before we started to pray, I told Mom how much these prayers had helped me. Praying with her had become very special for me. Our bond was stronger than ever and could never be broken, no matter how hard my evil dad tried. Mom prayed to God to watch over me. She thanked God that I was her daughter. I got choked up. Mom reached up and tenderly touched my cheek. One of my tears fell on her hand. She gently smiled. I smiled too. I started to speak when here came *the honks*.

We walked out together. Mom stayed on the front porch. I walked backwards all the way to the car. I signed "I Love You" and thanked her again for a wonderful birthday. Evil dad and Sissy were in the car, along with Martha. I got in the backseat with Martha and here it came; "Happy Birthday Tweetie". "I know I know," I said to myself. "Just ignore her." Couldn't she just once call me Rachel?" Was that too much to ask? I loved my name. It was a Bible name of an incredible woman.

Mom told me the whole story of Rachel in the book of Genesis. She said, "The meeting between Jacob and Rachel was of God. Jacob fell in love with Rachel from the moment he saw her, but had to work seven years for her father Laban, before he could marry her. He worked those seven years but Laban didn't keep his promise. He tricked him into marrying Rachel's sister Leah, because she was older and had to marry first. He worked another seven years for their father. Then, and only then, Jacob was able to marry his beloved Rachel (Genesis 29:25-30 NIV). Rachel was lucky in marriage!" I thought, "He must have loved her a lot! 14 years! Wow!"

I learned in my Bible class that Rachel was the mother of Joseph and Benjamin. Of all the children Jacob fathered, Joseph was the greatest and godliest and his favorite. He became the savior of Israel. One sad, but interesting fact about Rachel, she was the first of only two women mentioned in the Bible, to die while giving birth. She died giving birth to Benjamin. (Genesis 35:17-20 NIV) Rachel at least had a loving husband. I hope Mom finds that kind of love someday. She deserves it after the way my dad treated her.

As we were driving to the restaurant, Dad demanded that I say hello to "Sissy Mom" on *MY* birthday. I raised my voice, "She's not my mom, so stop forcing me to call her that." Mr. Evil stopped talking for the time being. We arrived at a Thai restaurant on my birthday, because it was Dad's favorite. When we reached our table, Dad handed me a baby stuffed animal. Can you believe that? I looked at all of them and snidely remarked, "Gee, thanks. Rocks for Christmas and a baby gift for my birthday!" No one said a word.

I could hardly eat anything. I went from the happy birthday party to this. Martha actually said she was the one who bought the baby stuffed animal. I looked at her, "Now it makes sense. You treat your son like a baby and now you want to treat me that way too. No thanks. I like being treated like a grown-up. You should call my mom and find out how you do this, if she will even speak to you." Martha said nothing. Dad on the other hand, started yelling at me to quit being a mean and hateful brat.

Dad demanded again for me to call his live-in, "Sissy Mom". Once again I loudly said, "No"! Stop trying to push her on me. I have a mom." Then I screamed, "Stop it! Stop it! Stop it!" at the top of my lungs. I couldn't believe what I said. It just came out. The waiters were staring at me with worried looks on their faces. I knew my dad could hurt me in many ways but he was never going to hurt me this way. Mom was never going to be pushed out of my life, ever! That was the main thing I would never abide by. Why couldn't my evil dad get that through his conniving brain? Then he barked the same old "Better get use to it. This is your new family, whether you like it or not. Sissy is here to stay."

That last comment sent me through the roof! (Not really, I was still sitting at the table, even though, I wished I was outside) I glared at the three of them and firmly said, "Everyone at this table, listen up! I have an announcement. I have to be here because the court says so, but I don't have to when I'm older and I won't!" The discussion came to an end. I looked at Dad and said that I wanted to go home. He was through eating. We got in the car. No one said a word the whole way back to *my* home. It felt good to tell them off. I was sure I would be punished this weekend at Dad's.

I tried to leave the baby stuffed animal in the car. Meany dad told me to take it. I showed it to Mom the minute I walked in the door. She was in shock. She jokingly asked if they even knew how old I was. I told her I said the same thing. She put it in the closet to keep it out of sight! I got ready for bed. I was just getting under my comforter, when Mom walked in and sat beside me.

She was about to say our prayer, when I interrupted, "Mom, while I was at dinner, I started thinking about the song *Happy Birthday*. Do you know who was the first person to have *Happy Birthday* sung to them?" Mom said, "I have no idea, but I do know who wrote it. It was two sisters with the last name Hill."

"They were born in the mid 1800's. One sister wrote the music and the other the 'lyrics', (that meant the words.) Their first names were Patty and Mildred. Patty was a schoolteacher. She came up with the idea to sing to the class each morning, as they arrived. Originally the song was called *Good Morning to All*. The children loved it so much. It was the children who supposedly changed the lyrics to suit their needs."

"No one knows for sure who wrote the *Happy Birthday* words, but speculation says it was Patty Hill. Anyway, that was how the song came about. Rachel my love, did you know it is the most recognized song in the English language?" I had my eyes still closed and answered,

"No, I didn't know that. Makes sense! It's sung everyday in the world. Did people in the Bible celebrate birthdays? The birth of Jesus is in the Bible." Mom stated, "You are absolutely correct. An interesting fact about Jesus, yes, it mentions His birth, but God did not record the exact day, only when His Son died. That's in Matthew 26:2. John also wrote of the event."

"I do remember from my high school Bible class, birthdays are mentioned three times in the Bible all resulting in deaths. That's why some religions do not celebrate birthdays. The first one mentioned in the Bible was when the King of Egypt became enraged with his wine tastier and his baker. He threw them in prison where Joseph (Rachel's son) was. They both had dreams, which they did not understand. "Interpreting dreams is God's business," Joseph replied (Genesis 40:8) (The Living Bible)."

"Joseph asked the two men to tell him what they saw. The wine taster's dream had a successful outcome, not the same result for the baker. In his dream, the baker saw three baskets of pastries on his head. The top basket contained all kinds of bakery goods for the Pharaoh, but the birds showed up and ate the goods. Joseph told the baker that the three baskets represented three days. He told him, "Three days from now the King will cut off your head and hang your body from a tree." Pharaoh's birthday came three days later and had the baker killed (Genesis 40)."

"The next birthday occurred in the book of Job. One of Job's sons was celebrating his birthday. God allowed Satan to kill all of Job's sons and daughters, while they were feasting in the oldest brother's home. In the Bible, it describes a mighty wind that destroyed the house. I think it was a tornado (Job 1:18-19). King Herod's birthday was the last one mentioned." I slightly opened my eyes and proudly spoke, "I know about this birthday. I remember it from my Bible class. Herod was king when John the Baptist lived. John preached about the sinful life the king and his queen Herodias were living."

"On King Herod's birthday, the queen's daughter was asked to dance. Before the dance started, she asked what the king would give her. Herod said, "Anything you want". She danced, and asked for John the Baptist's head on a tray. King Herod didn't want to, but he didn't want to back down in front of all his guests. The head was delivered (Matthew 14:1-12) (The Living Bible)." As soon as I finished the story, I was asleep. "Wow! When did you become a Bible scholar?"

Mom asked. "Rachel, Rachel, Are you awake? Goodnight my love, sweet dreams."

It wasn't until the next morning that I realized I fell asleep before saying our prayer. The last words I remember were "Bible scholar". I must have conked out. I sure did sleep well! I always do after Mom's interesting stories. She says they "lull" me to sleep, just like the TV does her. Anyway, Mom sure knows how to take my mind off Dad!

Last night Mom told me that because my birthday fell on a school night, she and Grandma were taking me to eat at the wonderful resort this weekend. Sunday arrived! After church, we celebrated in style. Mom surprised me with my very own Bible. She even had my name engraved on the front. Now I could look up all the stories Mom shared with me, whenever I wanted to. This was the best extra gift. MOM ROCKED!

As the weeks marched on, I noticed Mom was feeling much better. She finally recovered from her heart attack. Her body and spirit was getting stronger each day. I was so glad she was her tough self, again! Spring Break arrived. Dad was supposed to keep me the whole week, but he brought me home early. Once again, he only kept me when he wanted to.

The next two weeks, I studied for the required school Nova tests; I took them every year. They lasted a whole week. Mom helped me take a lot of practice tests in all the subjects. It was now the end of March. Last time at Dad's, I was informed that he bought a house. He and Sissy would be moving out of the condo after Easter. I was thrilled to be leaving the high-rise prison.

Easter was upon us. It happened again! For three years in a row, I had spent Easter with my dad because it fell on his weekends. That stunk! The judges STUNK! The whole court system STUNK! I hadn't been to church on the last two Easters and now this would be number "3". My dad NEVER went to church, not even on Christmas. I thought, "If I can't visit my church, maybe I can visit Rain E." I couldn't believe it had been six months since I last saw her. I had been missing her, more than ever. Would I ever see her again? I did hope so. She was the reason I was stronger. I wanted to tell her just that! I missed her so much. I prayed to God over and over. I just tried holding on to my faith.

Mom always told me to trust in The Lord. I'm sorry to say, it was hard at times, but I kept trying. My mom was so amazing! After her heart attack, she completely changed her outlook on life. She told me that my evil dad and those two judges were NEVER going to kill her! Mom never puts up with my dad's crap, pardon my language, but that was what it was! Just because he won in court last year, he thought he could get away with anything concerning me. He was never going to get away with anything, as long as Mom was around.

The next week, school let out on Thursday at noon and because of Easter and Good Friday, I had to go to my Dad's Thursday night. Mom and I went to lunch after school. She wanted to spend some alone time with me and do something special for Easter. We ate at one of my favorite restaurants. We talked and laughed all through lunch. We finished lunch and went to my favorite stores. Mom bought me a new outfit. Too bad I couldn't wear it to church on Easter!

We got home an hour or so before I had to go with Dad. I packed all my stuff. Mom and I sat at the kitchen table and talked for about an hour. We then moved to the stairs. Since I wasn't going to be in church, Mom kind of acted like a pastor and we had our own private service. I hadn't notice, but one of her Bible's was sitting on the stairs. She picked it up and read (Matthew 27, 28 NIV). It was all about the trial of Jesus, and the horrific crucifixion, when He was on the cross and finally cried out to God. Mom went into detail about Jesus dying, rising up and leaving the tomb.

Then she flipped over to John (20:10-16 NIV) and it said that after Jesus rose from the dead, the first person he spoke to was a woman. It was Mary Magdalene. She had been crying because Jesus was taken from the tomb. Mary glanced over her shoulder and saw someone standing behind her. It was Jesus, but Mary thought he was the gardener. Then Jesus spoke, "Mary!" She turned around and said the most heavenly word, "Master!" I loved that story! It was a woman story! Mom was such a vivid storyteller! It didn't matter if she was telling a true story from the Bible, real life people or just make-believe. She could make you feel like you are actually there. I know she learned it from her dad.

After the short sermon, we prayed and thanked God for sending His son to Earth. I hugged Mom. She kissed me on the face. We started talking again, when I heard *the honks*. We helped each other up. I got all my homework and put it into my backpack and we both walked out the front door. She stayed on the porch. I was halfway to the car and like always, I turned and signed "I Love You!" I thought, "All these years, and we still never forget."

I got in the backseat and said nothing. We drove straight to Martha's. She had dinner ready for us. (My evil dad always makes her cook dinner, at least once a week, I guess so he can get in his weekly scream). While we were eating, the doorbell rang. Martha went to see who was there. I could hear it was James, my blood sister's nasty boyfriend. He wanted to come in.

Dad instantly jumped up from the table and rushed to the front door. Sissy stayed with me. Dad and Martha were telling James that I was in the other room and he had to leave. They knew I was NEVER to be around him! Mom would find out from me! He finally left. I thought to myself, "At least the court protected me from him."

He must have done something really bad for the law to keep him away from me. I mean REALLY bad, worse than bad. Worse than what my dad did to me, because court was making me be around him. I still didn't get it. Mom told me a little more about James. She said that he went to jail for a long time. I wonder what he did that was so bad? He has a good Bible name. He should read all about James, the half-brother of Jesus.

We finished eating, got in the car and drove to the condo. When we got there, I went straight to my room, with all my stuffed piled high in my arms. Dad nor Sissy lent a helping hand. I guess those heavy car keys were all DAD could handle! I dumped everything on the floor by my bed. I was tired and just wanted to go to bed, without being bothered. I took a quick shower, put my nightgown on and climbed into bed with wet hair. I had zero energy. No one bothered me all night. That was a first.

The next morning, "Good Friday", I woke up and went straight to the kitchen. I grabbed a bottle of water and an apple and went back to my room. I quickly ate the apple and wrapped the core in a Kleenex and zipped it up in my backpack. I heard them! Sissy came in and said we were going to eat later on tonight. I rudely answered, "Whatever!" I would apologize for my behavior, but they treat me worse!

I stayed in my room all day and secretly worked on my drawing. I played on my Nintendo and just rested on my bed. A couple of hours went by. Mr. Evil opened the door. He told me to put on something halfway decent, (whatever that meant). He was acting like a messenger or a delivery service, passing on the info. I put on my black pants, white top and short black boots. I was brushing my hair, when I heard him scream that it was time to go. I could smell my stinky dad from the hallway.

From the moment I left my room, all the way to the car, I had to put my hand over my nose, because of the amount of perfume Dad, including Sissy, were wearing. This time Dad had more on than usual. It made me gag! We got in the car and it stunk even worse than normal. Did he come down here and spray perfume in the car?

As we were leaving, stinky Dad told me that we were picking up "The Boys". I got nauseous thinking about riding in the backseat with the two *Pigpens*. They had as much dirt on them as the character in Charlie Brown. They both stunk so BAD! Maybe that was why more perfume smell was in the car? I stayed quiet all the way to "The Boys" house. Dad pulled up and honked. They both came right out. (I guess they jump when my dad says jump)!

So the five of us drove to a *Fancy Nancy* restaurant in another town nearby. I tried to stay silent during the meal, but Ronny kept poking me in the side. I told him over and over to leave me alone. I even asked Dad to make him stop. He ignored me. I finally got up and went and sat in the lobby.

My evil dad came out and started cussing me out. He called me a mean and hateful "F' n "B" and said I was just like my mother. When Mr. Evil said that, I yelled, "Good! I love that I am just like my mom. Thank you for noticing." He got even angrier because I stood up to him. You know, I couldn't even believe it came out of my mouth. In the last few months, colorful, choice words have rolled off my tongue. Maybe I was getting stronger?

I was still sitting, when Mr. Evil grabbed my right arm. He yanked it so hard, my shoulder popped. A man standing near the front door saw everything. He yelled out to my dad to let me go. Wow, he told my dad what to do. I had never seen anyone, besides Mom, standing up to my dad. A perfect stranger cared more about me than those 26 worthless adults, who didn't help me in court. Wished he could have been my judge!

Dad turned to the man and told him to mind his own "GD" "F' n business. I thought he was going to get into a fistfight with the nice man. Sissy showed up. She yelled for "The Boys". They pulled Dad away from the man. I watched the kind man go for help. A new man, who worked there, showed up and politely told my dad to leave and never come back. Dad stormed out. I strolled out, gloating.

We all piled back in the car. Dad immediately started screaming at me. He blamed everything on me. He even cruelly added that because of me, he was never allowed to go back to one of his favorite restaurants, ever again. I didn't say anything back. He hurt my arm. He hurt my feelings. Another bruise on the outside to match the bruise growing on the inside! This time Mom would know he truth about how the bruising happened. She will see my bruised arm. She will hear my bruised heart. Sadness in the voice always gives it away! I told Dad I wouldn't lie to Mom, not this time. He shut up. That felt good, but he was still going to do something mean to me. I just didn't know what.

We dropped off "The Boys" and drove to the condo. We pulled in the garage. The moment the car doors opened, it thundered big time! The noise was terrifying. We dashed to the elevator and up to the condo. As Dad was opening the front door, violent thunder erupted again. He dropped his keys and, of course, loudly cussed. Finally the door was unlocked. The instant it was pushed back, I raced to my bedroom and slid open my balcony door. For some strange reason, I needed to be a part of it.

The sky was as scary looking as my dad. The thunderstorm had now taken control of the town. It was definitely a violent, very angry storm. Strange, I didn't feel afraid, for the most part. I looked up and prayed, "Dear God, please, I need to see Rain E, please, pretty please. I know this is going to be a very bad weekend. Please protect me and let me see her again. In Jesus name, Amen."

I stayed there awhile thinking about the nice man at the restaurant. I felt my arm. It was already extremely sore. I was sure it would turn black and blue by tomorrow. The storm was getting louder and louder and louder. I bet it was unusually louder, because my dad was so mean to me. My mean dad was loud, so God had to be louder. God wanted me to know who was in charge.

I went in and took a quick shower. I had no idea what Dad and Sissy were doing. I only cared about sleeping and hopefully seeing Rain E. I changed into my new golden- colored nightgown and jumped into bed. All the lights went out. My room was as dark as a haunted house. I rolled over on my side to watch and wait for the sky to light up, in hopes of spotting Rain E.

All of a sudden, the thunder loudly rumbled sending lightning shooting across the sky. I abruptly sat up it was so loud! As I was staring at the storm I remembered one interesting fact I learned in science class; Thunder is a direct result of lightning. You can never have thunder without lightning, but you can have lightning without thunder. Sometimes in certain storms, the thunder is just too far away to hear. I had no idea what made me think of that. It had to be Rain E! She and storms just went together!

A light came on in the hallway. I fell back on my pillow and barely closed my eyes. Sissy peeked her head in then quietly closed the door. I pretended to be asleep. Dad never came to check on me. That was not only weird, but also a miracle. Maybe Sissy calmed him down? I rolled back over on my left side and watched the sky. I jerked every time the lightning showed itself. I kept watching for any sign of Rain E. My eyes were getting sleepy. I tried my best to keep them open, but I was way too tired! I fell asleep listening to the storm.

*A mirror reflects a man's face, but what he is
really like is shown by the kind of friends he chooses.*

Proverbs 27:19 (The Living Bible)

Chapter 20

I t was early, early in the morning. My ears woke up first. Rain was hitting my balcony rail. Rain but no Rain E! I thought for sure, I would see her this weekend, especially after what happened last night. I didn't understand. I was with Rain E three times in four months, now six months later and still no visit.

While still lying on my left side watching the rain, I could feel the pain in my bruised arm. It started throbbing. Suddenly, the surprise of loud thunder and lightning caused me to fall out of bed. I did a complete roll, landing on my bruised arm. Ouch! I stayed still waiting for the pain to go down. Barely lifting my head, I could see puddles of rain covering the balcony. I looked up at the storm clouds, thinking just maybe I would get a glimpse at Rain E moving towards me, like before. All I saw was rain, lots of rain. It hadn't stopped since I arrived yesterday. Tomorrow was Easter. In a flash, I wondered if it would still be raining?

Another Easter with my disgusting dad! Didn't seem fair. I had already been here for two nights, but it seemed like two months. Easter with the Non-Christian people! My dad could care less about church. I still can't believe 3 years have gone by without an Easter church service. I 100% believe Easter will always be the most important day of the year. I deeply thought, "I wonder how many people also believe this? I wonder how many don't believe this? I wish everyone believed! Maybe someday my wish will come true. Tonight I will have my own private Easter and read about Jesus. I hope I'm not too tired. I love reading from my very own Bible. It helps a lot when I'm with Mr. Evil."

Earlier in the book I mentioned my mom had my name engraved on my Bible. What I didn't mention was I only wanted my first and middle name 'Rachel Rene'. I never wanted my last name on a sacred book. Now when I open my Bible, I never have to see my dad's name. My Bible is holy. My dad is not! Mom didn't have his last name anymore. I didn't want it either. Someday, I hope I can change it to my mom's last name. I knew I had to wait until I turned 18. For now, I was stuck with it and him.

I stretched out on the floor and stared at the ceiling. I was dreading for Mr. Evil to wake up. I closed my eyes. Some time went by. I heard someone in the hallway. It was probably Sissy going to the kitchen. It was her job to make the master's coffee, no matter how it turned out. My bruised arm really hurt. I decided to take a look and headed to the bathroom.

Standing close to the mirror, I examined the bruise. Oh my gracious! It was green and purple. I moved in closer and saw a red dot right in the middle. My evil dad must have broken a blood vessel! I went back to my bed, put a pillow over my head and cried and cried! I asked God, "Why does my dad want to hurt me? Does he enjoy hurting me? Why doesn't Sissy stop him? Will he kill my mom? Will he kill me? Will he always win in court?" Questions and more questions kept filling my head. I worried every time I had to be with him. I was so scared Dad would come in and kill me, while I was sleeping. That was a lot for a kid to worry about. Too young and worrying about being killed! So many thoughts stayed on my mind all the time! I wished I could stop thinking about them, but I just couldn't!

I heard some more noises from the hallway. There was a knock on my door. "Rachel, are you hungry?" Sissy asked? I yelled back, "A little." Sissy said, "I made some eggs. Would you like some? Your dad's still asleep." I jumped out of bed and yelled that I would be right out. I grabbed my robe and slippers and dashed to the kitchen. Sissy already had a plate of scrambled eggs ready.

I walked over to the sink and quickly ate them. I wanted to finish before Mr. Evil stormed in. I started to clean my plate, when Sissy politely said, "Just put it in the sink. I will clean up." "That's okay, I'll clean it," I said with confusion. I washed my plate and fork and put them back up. I wiped out the sink and grabbed a bottle of water and went back to my room. While I was lying on my bed, I kept pondering over Sissy. Why was she being so nice to me? Something was up! Sissy never went out of her way to be nice to me, ever!

Some time went by. The monster was finally up. I could hear him talking with Sissy. I couldn't make out what they were saying, which was strange, because my dad always talks so loud. I closed my eyes and pretended to be asleep, but it was hard. I couldn't stop thinking about this morning and why Sissy was acting so "human". It hit me! Oh my goodness! I was to be baptized tonight at my church. How did I forget that? Mom even forgot, I think. I wondered if Mr. Evil would let me call her? I doubt it. I wondered if Mom has called him. I wanted to be baptized tonight! Some of my school friends were also being baptized. That's why I chose this day.

An hour went by. Finally, Mr. Evil barged into my room. He said he was going to steam. He would be back in a couple of hours. He added that we had plans tonight. I quietly asked, "Is it at my church?" Evil dad said, "No ma'am. We have other plans and you are going!" I raised my voice, "I'm supposed to be baptized tonight! Does Mom know you're not taking me?" I couldn't believe what came out of his mouth. Mr. Evil said, "Screw her. You're on my weekend. I decide what we do, not your "B" mother." I was in total shock. My evil, evil dad was refusing to let me be baptized. All I could say was, "God forgive him!" He stormed out, slamming the door. Now I knew why Sissy was trying to be so nice to me. She already knew about this. She disgusted me even more! I heard the front door slam. Mr. Evil must have left to go steam. He steamed so much I wished he would just evaporate. I learned that word in science. It means, "to disappear or vanish into thin air".

With all the commotion going on, I didn't notice that the thunderstorm was getting worse. I went out on my balcony. I'm telling you, this was one bad storm!! The sky was dark and gloomy. There was so much non-stop heavy rain falling, I couldn't even see the building across the street. The wind started throwing the rain in all directions. I quickly dashed inside.

The powerful storm was pressing up against my glass door so hard it took extra muscle to slide it shut. My face and part of clothes were soaked. My right arm started throbbing again. I dried off and walked out to the hallway to find Sissy. She was in the kitchen eating something over the sink. (I guess she also had to eat at the same location

209

as me). I saw her coffee cup on the counter next to the dishtowel. Her back was slightly to me.

I quietly tiptoed by her and dashed to their bedroom. My cell phone was sitting on the end table being charged. I grabbed it and took two photos of my arm in record time. I immediately sent them to Mom's phone. I erased the photos, just in case Mr. Evil looked in my phone. I put it back on the charger and slowly walked to the end of the hallway. I peeked in the kitchen. Sissy was gone. My heart started pounding. I was panicking. I got close to the den. I saw her sitting on one of the chairs on the balcony. Thank goodness! I crossed over to the other side of the hallway. I leaned my head out just far enough to see her. She was still sitting. Whew!!! She never saw me.

I rushed into my bedroom and collapsed on my bed. My heart was still pounding. I stayed there for a few minutes. I was proud of myself for taking the photos. That was sneaky scary getting my phone. I wished now I had called or text Mom about not being baptized. I was so upset. I bet Mom was more upset. I would have to be baptized on one of Mom's weekends. One thing for sure, Dad would never be told.

Dad was gone most of the day. Several hours went by. Hunger pains were filling my tummy. I went to the kitchen and got an apple and some cheese slices. Sissy walked in, making me nervous. I immediately said I would clean up my mess. I saw her staring at my bruised arm. She said nothing. I put the cheese package back in the refrigerator, perfectly in place. The label was facing forward, with a smaller wrapped cheese package next to it. I grabbed a bottle of water, passed right by her in silence and went back to my room. After eating my apple, I wrapped the core in Kleenex, as usual, and zipped it up in my backpack with the other one. I got out my IPad to watch a movie. I wanted to work on my drawing, but my arm hurt too much. The rain started beating against the window. It was now hailing. Funny, it was kind of calming. I was at the end of my movie, when I fell asleep.

It didn't last long, because of the loud noise coming from the hall. Dad was back and growling at Sissy to get her ass ready. Then he barged into my room and told me to get my ass dressed. So rude! I asked where we were going. Mr. Evil said, "To a country western concert." I exploded asking, "In this pouring down rain?" We're going to drive in this storm?" "Yes ma'am! Now get your butt dressed before I get my belt out," Mr. Evil smarted off.

I just glared at his evil face, as I walked to my closet. He slammed the door shut. I changed into my jeans and a long sleeved blue shirt then put my tennis shoes on. There was no way I was going to ruin the red cowboy boots Mom gave me. After I was completely dressed and ready, I walked over to my balcony window. Standing and moving my head side to side, I was thinking out loud, "We're going out in this weather! My dad is nuts! I mean he's cuckoo!!"

The three of us left the condo. When we got to the elevator, there was a note saying it was not working, probably from the storm! Dad cussed about that. We had to walk down several flights. I snickered to myself, "Ha! Ha! Things not working out for Mr. Evil!" I think God was trying to get his wicked attention. Finally, we made it to the car. The minute we left the parking garage, I noticed several trees uprooted across the street in the park. The wind was blowing the rain in a circle like a water tornado. Branches and debris were flying everywhere!

We turned the corner to get on the freeway. It was now flash flooding. I asked how far it was to the concert. Sissy said it was about an hour away. An hour away! I lay down on the backseat and covered up with my jacket I was carrying. The storm was scaring me. If Mom knew I was out in this, she would rip Dad's head off. I stayed under the jacket until we got there, besides I didn't want to watch my crazy dad driving. He drives reckless enough in good weather.

The whole way, I kept thinking about rain and Rain E. Surely, this would be the weekend I would see her. I quietly prayed to God to get me to the concert safe and sound and to please let me see Rain E. You know, after I finished praying, I felt better, as though God was telling me something. Some time went by. The traffic was extra slow. I couldn't believe there were other people out in this storm! I felt the car park and sat up. If this was the concert, it didn't look very crowded. The water was everywhere! The rain slowed to a shower.

Mr. Evil waded through the water to the main entrance. I gladly watched as the wonderful rainwater was obviously ruining his brand new boots. I saw him talking to a couple of policemen. When he got back in the car, the cussing and yelling started. Sissy asked what was wrong. "The band couldn't make it, due to the weather, sorry Sons of "B" s," evil Dad cussed. On and on he cussed about the concert, his expensive boots getting ruined and of course the weather. He was cussing out nature! That said it ALL!! Now I was really glad I didn't wear my red leather boots. Ha! Ha! And another Ha! I thought it was

211

funny about his boots. Maybe God *was* punishing him for hurting me and for not letting me be baptized.

We headed back to the condo. I lay back down and covered up with my jacket. That wonderful piece of clothing kept my satisfying smile hidden from those two. We were near downtown, when Dad said to Sissy, "Let's just go to the bar." Did he say a bar? I was too young to go in a bar. Sissy spoke up, "Rachel is too young. You will get in trouble. Do you want "your" ex finding out?" Dad snapped at her, "Shut up! This isn't your business. I'm NEVER going to get in trouble and that's all I will say. Besides, Blake will be working. He'll let her in."

Blake was standing at the front door when we arrived. In a low voice he whispered, "Go to the back and I'll be back later to check on you shortly." As we walked in, I heard him tell Sissy to keep a close eye on me. I guess because I wasn't supposed to be there. It was so noisy and crowded inside. We worked our way to the back corner. There was a small bar nearby.

We were just sitting down, when this teenage-looking girl and boy walked up. "Hi guys," the girl shouted. She looked at me and said, "You must be Rachel. I'm Delilah, your future sexy, big sis. Hang with me and I'll show you how to land a guy." I looked at her and blurted out, "What???" Sissy butted in, "Delilah, Shhhh. Not now." I asked Delilah, "How old are you?" She proudly answered, "Almost 22!"

The boy walked up behind her. He grabbed her around the waist. She added, "And this is my almost husband Tray." Tray just gave me a goofy wave. Hanging all over him, she slurred, "Hands off, he's mine!" Again I said, "What???" With confusion I asked, "What do you mean 'almost' husband?" This goofy boyfriend stupidly stated, "Well ya see here, I'm still married to my first "B" wife and she's been giving me a lot of trouble since she found out about my new "B"." Sissy jumped in again and told both of them to shut their mouths. She was glaring right at Tray when she said it. Sissy told me to just ignore his drunken ass.

I was in total shock. Who were these people? They were the most lowlife filthy-mouthed losers I had ever met. Were these the kind of people my dad liked to be around? I guess because my sick dad always cusses and acts idiotic just like them. No wonder Mom divorced him! Boy, I wish I could! Sissy and crazy Dad got up to go dance. Sissy told

Delilah and Tray to watch me. Wait a minute! Those two were going to watch ME? This I had to see!

The second Dad and Sissy left the table, the two of them started kissing and kissing all over each other's face. How were they breathing? It was nasty! Now, how were THEY watching ME? Tray couldn't even stay in his seat. He fell on the floor, twice. The second time, he got up and staggered to the bar. I could clearly see him from my seat. "Hey my sexy "B", want another beer?" Tray loudly slurred. Delilah hollered back, "You bet, sexy hunk!" What's a hunk? They were slurring their words and burping at the same time.

I was still seated next to "Burping Beer" Delilah, when this pretty girl walked by. You could smell her perfume ten feet away. She smelled worse than my dad. Delilah abruptly screamed out, "You smell like a French whore!" The girl just gave her a mean look along with a wave of just the middle finger and kept walking. What kind of wave was that?

I asked Delilah, "What's a French whore?" She said, "A nasty, cheap woman who sleeps with men without being married to them." I quickly responded, "Oh, like Sissy." Delilah tried to say her mother wasn't a whore, but she was having a hard time explaining, while burping. I would check with Mom when I got home. She always told me the truth in a way I could understand, whether the explanation was detailed or not. Either way was okay by me.

Delilah stood up and started swaying back and forth. I was getting dizzy just watching her. She burped beer in my face and told me to stay put. It was funny watching her stumble all the way to the bar, where she joined that harebrained boyfriend. The two of them continued each downing a beer then alternating with some kind of brown liquid in a tiny glass. I heard the bartender asked if they wanted another 'boilermaker', (whatever that was!) Tray loudly burped, "You bet! Keep um comin'!"

I was repulsed and embarrassed watching those two shout obscenities to everyone who walked by. These people (and this place) were something else! I felt like I had crossed over into an abnormal version of the movie *The Time Machine* and landed on the "Planet of Idiots"! Oh brother, I thought Blake and Ronny were disgusting. These two definitely won the award. They were worse than just disgusting, they were vulgar, sickening and obnoxious! I had watched enough of this show!

As I was turning my chair in the opposite direction, I spotted Sissy's purse. It was slightly opened. I saw my cell phone, quickly grabbed it and discreetly took a few photos. One photo was of two ladies breasts and butts hanging out of their clothes. They had on the shortest skirts and tightest tops. All the guys walking by were staring and sticking their tongues out. Gross! I wanted to throw up! I took another photo of Tray and Delilah at the bar, and one more of the name of the bar.

I kept my eyes on evil Dad, Sissy, Tray and Delilah the whole time. I secretly sent the photos to Mom's email, then erased them and put the phone back in Sissy's purse. I got it all done before the dance was over. I was getting to be a great detective! It was an easy task to complete especially when dealing with degenerates and knuckleheads like these! I knew degenerates meant "Losers" and that's what they were. "Knuckleheads"! Self-explanatory!

Tray and Delilah made their way back to the table. Delilah sat on top on Tray's legs, facing him. The kissing started up again. I turned and looked the other way. While I was watching all the people, this old man came up to the table. He politely asked me, "Hey, little lady, where's your mom?" I firmly said, "I'm not supposed to talk to strangers." Tray and Delilah stopped kissing and looked at the man.

Delilah slurred, "She's my little slisterrrrrr." Tray added, "Get lost old man!" The man seemed genuinely concerned. He asked me, "Is that true? Is she your big sister? You can tell me the truth." With pleasure I said, "No sir. She's not my big sister!" Delilah gave me a dirty look. I looked right back at her and stated, "I DON'T LIE! Neither should YOU!" The caring old man said he would be right back.

While he was gone, Dad and Sissy showed up. Delilah told them about the old man. Dad hurried his words, "Quickly, let's get our stuff and get out of here." We all rushed outside. We were in the parking lot when I heard the old man scream, "There they are!" He was standing with another man, in a uniform. I think he was a policeman. I saw Blake walk over to them. He must have calmed them down.

As the old man walked away he yelled out, "You two need to get a room, take it inside!" I asked Sissy what that meant. She ignored me. Instead, she gave Delilah a mean look. I would ask Mom about this too. The man then yelled, "What the hell are you other two doing bringing a child to a bar? Get some parent counseling!" Dad said nothing. He didn't want to bring attention to himself.

We all piled in the car and headed back to the condo. Ronny got on his motorcycle. I heard him say he would see us tomorrow. Thank goodness he wasn't spending the night! When we got back, Mr. Evil said I had to finish my homework. I told him I was so tired. He didn't care. I went to my room and got out of my stinky clothes. They smelled of smoke, beer and burps! I rinsed off and put on a pair of shorts and a T-shirt. I quickly headed back to the kitchen table, so I wouldn't get hit with the belt. I had to stay up late because all of us were going to a brunch on Easter. Mr. Evil checked on me a couple of times.

It was 3:00 am when I finally finished. I know, because I looked at the kitchen clock. The condo was quiet. Mr. Evil must have gone to bed. I put all my homework and books in my backpack and left it on the table. I didn't even know if my math problems were right or wrong. Who cared at 3:00 am in the morning! I was now allowed to go to bed. I dragged my tired body to my bedroom and closed the door. I went into the bathroom just to wash my face and brushed my teeth. I wanted to take a long hot shower, but I was too exhausted. I changed into my golden-colored nightgown. The moment my head hit the pillow, I was out. That was the last thing I remembered.

And be sure to put into practice what you hear.

Mark 4:24 (The Living Bible)

Chapter 21

Thump!!! Ouch!! I mean, a big Ouch!! Oh, my bruised arm. The pain was throbbing and hurting worse than ever. My goodness! What happened? I instantly thought, "I must have fallen out of bed. Wow! I haven't done that since I was little!" As I lay there on the floor, my eyes looked side to side. The room felt strange. It was still slightly dark. The floor was extra soft. I mean extra, extra soft! I slowly turned my head to the right. About a foot away, I noticed a pair of feet. It wasn't my dad's feet. They were too small. It had to be Sissy. She must have heard me fall out of bed. Sometimes she sleeps in the den chair, because of her injured back. Whatever reason, Sissy sleeps in the den from time to time.

I lay there completely still. I was trying to stay quiet, but my body wasn't cooperating. My breathing was getting louder and my heart was pounding. I kept staring at the mysterious feet. They never moved. There was just enough space between them to see my bedroom door. I kept my eyes locked on it. Something looked different. The door was black. "Wait a minute, my door's not black! I must be dreaming," I confusedly thought. I slowly raised my head and looked straight up. I saw them. It was those pigtails, those beautiful, colorful pigtails! They were dangling so close to me, that my fingers could touch the ends of the braids.

I pushed myself back and sat on my knees. As I was looking up, I heard the most wonderful words. "Howdy friend, long time no see!" It was my Rain E. My long lost Rain E! I was back!! She stuck her hand out and once again said, "I have a hand for your hand!" Rain E helped me to my feet. I smiled saying, "Howdy to you, friend. Long time no see!" We giggled and looked straight into each other's eyes. Tears were filling all four. A big hug followed.

As I was wiping away my tears, Rain E wrapped her hands completely around mine. I watched a reddish warm glow surround them. They were dry from the tears and toasty, in seconds. Rain E held on to them a bit longer. The warm love traveled throughout my body. I never took my eyes off this miracle. She was healing the sadness in me.

This time, there was something different about Rain E. I just couldn't figure it out. I felt closer to her than ever, as though I was supposed to. "Thank you for warming my hands and my heart," I politely spoke. Rain E kindly smiled at me. I kept staring at my glowing hands, when Rain E's pigtails brushed up against my legs. They brushed up against my legs? That's what was different! Her pigtails had grown, a lot! They hung clear down to her knees. They even sparkled more, if you can "imagine that". Rain E sparkled more.

I couldn't take my eyes off my friend. Rain E was also staring at me. She spoke, "You have grown, in more ways than one! I can see it in your eyes, my friend." There was a pause. Rain E then said, "I love your bright-colored gown. Gold is one of my favorite colors." I smiled and said, "Thank you very much. I love what your wearing too." It was a long sundress, white with small green poke-a-dots all over. It was sleeveless like mine. There were tiny white feathers covering the very bottom of the dress, all the way around. Rain E was barefoot like me.

I saw her brown sandals lying on the grass. Then I glanced over Rain E's shoulder and saw mine leaning up against her door. A smile covered my face. I said to myself her famous two words "Imagine that!" Rain E giggled and said out loud, "Yes, Imagine that!" I forgot she could hear my inner thoughts. It was wonderful being back after all these months. This was my fourth visit. I wondered why it took so long to come back? Maybe Rain E will tell me. I had so much to tell her. So much had happened in the last six months, but I had a suspicion she already knew. Still, I wanted Rain E to hear it from my mouth.

We sat down on the thick grass. I lay back for just a moment. It was more comfortable than my bed. I moved my arms back and forth. It was incredibly soft grass! Rain E stayed seated with her legs crossed. She was close enough to see my bruised arm, but never mentioned it and neither did I. I finally sat up.

We slipped our sandals on and helped each other stand. I dusted off my gown. To my surprise, there was no grass or dirt on me. As a matter of fact, there were no grass stains anywhere on my gown or skin. Wow, the WARM, plush green grass didn't leave stains! It must have been magical grass, because the whole time I was on the ground I felt EXTRA warm and relaxed.

Standing there, Rain E said, "I want you to see "The Flowers of the Week Garden". I think you will like the new flower. I excitedly responded, "Yeah! I get to see the garden again. I've seen it every visit. Thank you, thank you!" Rain E smiled and said, "You're very welcome, but first, there is someone I want you to meet." "There are more people here?" I curiously asked. Rain E answered, "Sort of." That was an odd response. She took my left hand and whispered in my ear "It's time!" I softly whispered back, "Time for what?" "You will see," she answered.

We headed out in the opposite direction of the garden and pond. I saw a small hill in the distance. The interesting trees and bushes were everywhere. The sky was a soft blue color with streaks of clouds going across. The sun stayed covered up. We were walking slowly enough allowing me to gaze at the beautiful sky. Then I slowed down, almost stopping. I was staring at a specific group of clouds, when I saw what looked to be white-winged angels mixed in with them. I kept trying to stare at them, but there were too many distractions.

The sky would go from extremely bright to a little bright. The clouds kept shifting in all directions, making it almost impossible to stay focused. I even held my right hand up over my forehead to get a better look. At that moment, we started walking faster, I think on purpose. Rain E had never really hurried me, not until now. She always let me enjoy her magical surroundings! Wonder what was up? We finally reached the top of the hill. I looked up at the sky again and whatever celestial beings I thought I spotted were gone.

Standing at the top, I looked down. The other side of the hill was a little steeper. My hands were now down by my side for balance. I needed to make sure I watched my every step. Before we started going down, I did a quick turn. I saw Rain E's home, the pond and flower garden to my left and the mysterious cave was on my right. I knew Rain E was watching me, but she didn't comment. I was taking it all in for my drawing. I turned back around and said I was ready to go. We slowly headed down. This side of the hill was also covered in carpet- looking grass, but there were no trees or bushes on it. Weird!

One side thick with trees and plants, the other side bare! I'm sure there was a reason why!

In the distance, I could just see some kind of archway. That was it! I was intended to notice "just" the "archway". As we got closer to the bottom, I saw a lady standing with her back to us. She was near the extremely tall archway. We kept walking towards her. I wanted to go faster, but Rain E kept me at a slower pace. I think she was teaching me patience. She wanted me to take it all in and appreciate where I was. I had been learning that on each visit.

We finally arrived at the archway. It was covered with green leaves and vines with tiny white flowers. I could smell a heavenly scent coming from them. The mysterious lady was just a few feet away. She was taller than the both of us. Her beautiful black hair hung clear down to her waist. She was wearing the most exquisite dress. It was a soft blue-gray sparkling color that hugged her very curvy body, all the way down past her behind. Then, from the top of her legs to the ground, the dress was gracefully flowing.

Now closer, I observed the sleeves had slits in the fabric from the shoulder to the wrist. Under the arms were different lengths of sparkling white fringe. There were hundreds of tiny, tiny white feathers all over the fabric. Politely moving in closer, I could see the sparkle was coming from 'dazzling' diamonds outlining the entire dress. There must have been hundreds! The fabric looked like velvet. This dress was not only exquisite, it was stunning, absolutely stunning! I mean it took my breath away. The colors reminded me of the heavenly sky!

While I was checking out her dress, the lady turned around and looked directly at me. I took a sudden step back. She was as stunning looking as her dress, maybe more. She kept staring at me, as though I was late for an appointment. Then, she smiled. What a smile! She had the whitest teeth. Her eyes were brown like mine. Her skin was the color of mocha. It was beautiful! Her face was lovely. She sparkled like Rain E. I instantly felt very comfortable around her. I looked straight at her face and smiled back.

The lady spoke, "Hello my dear. My name is S TOR MY, and you are?" I quickly answered, "I'm Rachel Rene. I'm sorry, what did you say your name was?" My name is S TOR MY." I asked again, I'm sorry, I'm not clear what you are saying." She paused for a moment. She didn't seem upset. I was the one upset. Now, another distinctive name of another amazing individual, and I couldn't pronounce it! How embarrassing! So, I just looked at her incredible dress. I was admiring her sleeves, when the lady raised her right hand and brushed a lock of hair away from her eye. As she was lifting her arm, I spotted a silver and gold bracelet on her wrist. I asked if I could take a closer look. She graciously replied, "Yes."

Like a jewelry appraiser, I leaned over and closely examined the bracelet. It was unique and looked very old. Etched in the bracelet were the letters, S T O R M Y. With a puzzled look on my face, I asked, "Is that your name?" She replied, "Why yes dear, S TOR MY is my name." "So that's what you're saying," I commented with relief. Then, I asked, "Did someone in your family give you the bracelet? Was it a family 'heirloom' (a word I learned from my mom, meaning an object that has been in a family for generations)?" Mom had old jewelry from her great grandmother. The nice lady politely answered, "You might say that. The bracelet IS very special."

I looked at the bracelet and letters again. Then I remarked, "Hey, did you know your name spells, stormy?" S TOR MY gracefully lifted the bracelet close to her face and studied it. Then she declared, "You know, you are absolutely correct!" In a very quiet and polite voice I asked, "Can I call you Stormy? I'm having a most difficult time pronouncing your real name." S TOR MY smiled and simply said, "Yes, my sweet, you may. Stormy it is!"

As I kept staring at her face, I noticed she was older and refined looking, like a mother. I liked Stormy very much. I wondered how DID Rain E know her? Hopefully I would find out. A few minutes passed by. This time, Stormy turned to Rain E and said, "It's time! Time to go on the "Dove Walk"!" Stormy took a step forward exposing her left bare foot. Wow! An elegant lady barefooted!

On her left big toe was a silver and gold ring. It matched the bracelet. I didn't say anything. What could I have said without sounding goofy? She was wearing a toe ring. It was something extra to add to her uniqueness. Stormy was unique. Rain E was unique, even Bolt was unique. Everyone was unique. They should call their place here, "Unique"!

A few minutes later, Rain E reached into her left pocket and pulled out a solid white handkerchief. Stormy said, "Rachel, my dear child, we need to blindfold you for reasons you are not to know, just yet." I said, "Okay, but can I first take a closer look at the archway entrance? I have my own reasons." We all laughed. Stormy said, "That would be fine. We have a few minutes to spare." I took a couple of steps forward and looked up and all away around the arch. I was trying to look deeper into the walkway but it was too dark to see anything.

The entire entrance had a familiar fragrance. I walked up to one of the tiny white flowered vines gently swaying in the light breeze. I grabbed on to it and discovered the inviting smell was coming from the white flowers. I glanced back at Stormy and Rain E to ask about them, when I noticed how nervous they were acting. Before I could ask about the flowers, Rain E announced, "They are Honeysuckle." Once again, she knew what I was thinking.

Stormy stepped towards me. She said, "It's time to enter the archway and begin the "Dove Walk"." I stated, "Sure is dark in there. Do we need a flashlight?" They giggled at the same time. Rain E commented on how humorous I was and said that a handheld light would not be necessary. That was an odd response! I guess it meant "No"!

Stormy asked if I was ready. I simple answered, "I am." Rain E carefully placed the blindfold over my eyes. It was warm from her holding it. She tied it in the back of my head. "Does that feel okay Rachel?" Rain E asked. I replied, "It's nice and warm and just fine!" These two kind, but mysterious individuals were going to guide me to 'who knows where'. I didn't feel scared, a bit anxious maybe, because knew I was in good hands.

Stormy took my right hand and Rain E took my left. We stepped forward. Stormy immediately let go of my hand and clapped 7 times, because I counted them. She took my hand again. You know, as soon as Stormy stopped clapping, my "In the Dark" surroundings seemed brighter. I wondered if she used one of those "clap on clap off" gadgets that you see on TV? Stormy said, "Let us begin." My body started tingling all over. Butterflies were filling my stomach. I felt safe though. This was to be the most incredible journey of my life and I couldn't see it. My other senses would have to take over. Rain E said, "Rachel, hold on tightly to our hands. We will not let go, until we get completely through the walkway." We took our first step together, then another. We were on our way!

My life is so Bad its so Bad I could
Die and its all my Daps falt
Because he Bits me and pinches
me and yells at my mom some one
help me my Dad tells my mom that
he will Kill her and me and
Curses! Very Bad words
like the B word and the s word
and the F word and the D word
and the GD word he doesn't
go to church and doesn't pray
omeosh I hate my Dad my mom
and Dets Dertect me from him.
One time my Dad went crazy
he yelled lowder then ever
Befor my mom has a
mira on a Dour to her closet

"The best and most beautiful things in the world
cannot be seen or even touched-they
must be felt with the heart."

Helen Keller

Chapter 22

The fragrant Honeysuckle was an enjoyable comfort during my impaired, but exciting adventure. We had been walking for only a short while, when I accidentally stumbled over some kind of rock. I went down "hard" on my knees, along with Rain E. She apologized for not watching me more carefully. I told her that I was okay and not to worry. As I was coming up, I grabbed hold of some kind of wooden handrail.

I was almost to my feet when I felt something extremely soft with my other hand. It was right above the handrail. It was as soft as feathers. It fact, it felt just like feathers! Odd! Standing again, I tried feeling around for the mysterious feathers, but Rain E quickly guided me back to Stormy. They each took one of my hands and we continued on.

We walked just a few more steps when Stormy announced, "We have reached the end of the archway. Rachel before your blindfold is removed, it is of the utmost importance not to look back." I said to both of them, "I promise, because I remember in the Bible what happened to Lot's curious wife when she turned around to look back at the sinful cities!" I took a deep breath and added, "I don't want to turn into a pillar of salt." Stormy and Rain E both squeezed my hands at the same time. I think they were assuring me that would not happen. I wasn't going to take a chance, because who wants to be salt?

Rain E removed my blindfold. I opened my eyes to the most magnificent sight. It was snow! Beautiful white snow in front of me, covering just the ground! The funny thing was, it didn't feel cold at all. How was the snow not melting? Only one answer I can think of! Anything was possible in a magical place! I looked straight ahead, never behind me! Not even a sneak peek. I asked Stormy, who was a few steps in front of me, "Can I taste the snow? I love snow and snow cones." Stormy looked straight at Rain E who was also a few steps ahead of me. As a matter of fact, they were standing almost next to each other.

Stormy spoke, "It's time!" That was third time those words had been spoken. I asked, "Time for what?" They both stepped aside and I stepped forward. I was now nestled between them. Rain E said, "Go ahead Rachel, reach down and taste the snow." I slowly bent over and the moment I touched the snow, it moved! I fell back on my butt. As Rain E and Stormy were helping me up, I took a closer look. It wasn't snow at all. It was "DOVES", thousands, maybe millions of doves cuddled together.

The doves started moving about, then took off flying at the same time. I was stunned and amazed at what I was witnessing. I apologized to my friends, sincerely saying, "I'm terribly sorry I disturbed the doves resting." Stormy said, "They were not resting, they were waiting. Waiting just for you, Rachel!" "For me, why?" I asked. Stormy explained, "We began the "Dove Walk". Now we must complete the "Dove Walk". To do so, you will be selecting your own personal dove. See how they are flying in the sky! One of the doves will come straight to you. When that happens, you are to name her. Now keep watching."

They were all flying in a big circle, going to the left. Then all of a sudden one of the doves swooped down from the circle. This particular dove was coming straight towards me, like Stormy said. It circled around me once and stopped right in front of my face. The dove was consciously flapping its wings to stay in the same spot. I think she wanted me to hurry up and name her.

I gazed right into the dove's eyes. She winked at me. I gasped. She winked again. The name "Olive" just popped into my head. I said to the dove, "Hello Olive and winked back." Olive winked one more time and waved one of her wings, up and down. I waved back and expressed, "Hope to see you again real soon!" She circled once more around me before rejoining the rest of her companions. As I kept watching, the doves sailed straight up into the sky. I guess God was calling them home. I kept my eyes peeled until they were completely out of sight. That was something to witness!

I looked all around and then down. Where the doves had been resting was a path leading to "who knows where". We all started walking on it until we reached a cliff overlooking Rain E's home. The three of us sat down to rest. Stormy stated, "Rachel, you have now completed the "Dove Walk". "What did you think of this experience?" I told both of them, "This was by far the most amazing thing that had ever happened to me! Thank you for taking me on such an incredible journey." Rain E and Stormy said thank you at the same time. We all started laughing. I loved being with my extraordinary friends. If it were not for my mom, and school friends, I would never want to go back home. I kept this thought to myself.

We sat there and admired the beautiful surroundings. Stormy spoke again, "Rachel, how much do you know about the dove and its significance in the Bible?" I asked, "What does significance mean?" Stormy said, "I apologize, my dear. I mean, what do you know about the dove relating to the Bible?" A light bulb went off in my head. "Oh, I get it now!" I exclaimed. "Well, I think the dove is God's favorite bird. It must be! It's mentioned in the Bible more than any other bird, according to my mom." This time Rain E spoke, "Your mother is absolutely correct. What else do you know about the dove?" I continued, "I know there's a verse in the New Testament that describes Jesus and a dove descending from Heaven, when John the Baptist was baptizing Him." Stormy said I was correct adding that it was the apostles who wrote about it. She stated, "The dove IS mentioned in the Bible over 50 times."

Stormy asked me if I knew any Bible verses about the dove. I just said that I knew the dove was mentioned a lot in the Bible. She then asked me, "Do you have any favorite books of the Bible?" I proudly answered, "I love Psalms, Genesis, and reading about Jesus in the New Testament. My Mom's favorite books of the Bible are Romans, Isaiah and Psalms. She also loves Genesis and Exodus because of all the interesting facts. Her favorite verses are in these books."

"Just this past year, my classroom studied the book of Genesis. I learned about a woman named Rachel. A few months ago, I found out I was adopted. Mom told me she always loved the name Rachel and the story of Rachel in the Old Testament. She knew "everything" about her! Mom even shared that biblical story with me on the night of my 11th birthday. Two specifics stuck in my brain. Rachel was a strong woman. She cried out to God in times of sorrow. My mom is also strong. She too cried out to God in times of sorrow. She said that

God blessed her with me. That's why she named me Rachel. I hope I grow up to be just like my mom."

Stormy passionately replied, "God indeed blessed you and your mother. He brought the two of you together for a reason." I asked, "What is the reason God gave me a mean and evil dad?" Stormy and Rain E were silent. I guess it wasn't their place to say, so I didn't bring it up again. My last question must have upset them because they both looked sad. I only asked because I thought they might know the answer. We all stayed very quiet and enjoyed the view. It was some view!

A few minutes went by. Stormy spoke again. She never brought up my last question. Instead, she continued talking about the dove. Stormy turned to me and said, "Rachel, in the Bible, the dove was chosen for a specific, important task. This highly intelligent and reliable dove was one of two birds Noah sent to look for dry land, and found it. There are many wonderful verses throughout the Bible mentioning the dove. Like you pointed out the dove has even been linked with Jesus. The dove not only stands for peace, it mostly stands for purity. So from now on Rachel, when you see a dove, always remember what you have learned and how special this creature is." I said to Stormy, "I will always remember the dove and now my pet dove, Olive!"

We got up and I looked around to see if Olive was nearby. I turned to Rain E and then back to Stormy. She now had a very motherly, concerned look on her face. "Rachel, listen to what I have to say. My child, never think of harming yourself ever again. Let God take care of those who harm you. You and your mother have been through many storms and battles the last few years, and that truly saddens my heart. My sweet, sweet child, your biggest battle is yet to come. Hold on tighter to your faith and trust in God more than ever before. Let God get you through it. He will never leave your side."

"Remember the Bible verse you learned at school, Ephesians (6:11 NIV) "Put on the full armor of God, so that you can take your stand against the devil's schemes". Please continue repeating it to yourself for strength and comfort. It will serve your needs well. Your mother will handle the rest!" I was speechless! I turned to Rain E to ask what battle Stormy was talking about, and when I turned back around, she was gone. I whipped my head back around, and asked, "Where'd she go? She was just here. How'd she know about me wanting to hurt myself? How'd she know I learned that verse at school?"

Rain E humbly said, "All I can say is her time with you had come to an end. Take to heart she is never truly gone, just out of sight for the naked eyes." The way these two talk, it was sometimes hard to follow. I think Rain E was trying to tell me that Stormy was close by, in my soul, I think. Anyway, Stormy was gone, but I was still with Rain E. She looked at me and said, "Time to go see "The Flowers of the Week", I need to do something there." I grinned and said, "I'm ready, when you are!" We turned and headed back towards the garden and the pond. Even when I turned around, I never looked back at the archway. I kept my solemn promise!

"You've got to be an observer. And you've got to take time to listen to people talk, to watch what they do."

Jonathan Winters

Chapter 23

It was a nice walk with Rain E side by side, as usual. Speaking of walks, I would NEVER forget the "Dove Walk"! I would NEVER forget Stormy! She was so smart, amazing, caring and of course very beautiful. I loved my time with her, but being with Rain E was the best! I guess because I had been with her the most.

We came back down on a different hill that was even more beautiful. Everywhere my eyes roamed, there were new plants and trees. We stopped a couple of times to enjoy the scenery. When we reached the bottom of the hill, I could see the cave. I still wondered if I would ever go in it. Rain E saw me staring, but never brought it up. I didn't ask. I looked in the other direction and could see the garden was close by. I always loved seeing everything at Rain E's home, but the flower garden was my favorite.

We arrived there in no time at all. I opened the gate and walked right up to the new flowers. I definitely didn't know this one! There were many different colors of this flower, unlike before. I turned to ask the name of it, when Rain E instantly spoke, "They are called Camphires, also known as the Henna Flower." "Did you say Campfire," I asked? Rain E said, "No, Camp 'Hire', like you hire someone for a job, not a campfire, like you sit around." I uttered, "Oh! Camp "Hire" Got it!" I had that puzzling look on my face again. Rain E once again knew what I was thinking! She "must" be a mind reader, like God. I gasped! Rain E asked, "Rachel, is everything okay?" I quietly said, "I'm fine. I'll be just fine." Rain E just smiled at me. I stared at the flowers and thought, "Camphires! Interesting name and new to my brain!"

I started twirling around, with my arms straight out. Turning and turning feeling as free as my pet Olive! Then I took off briskly walking throughout the garden. I must have gone up and down all the paths at least five times, twirling and twirling and twirling on each one before finally stopping. Looking across the tops of the flowers, I spotted a group of pale red and pink ones bunched together. The colors blended beautifully, very pleasing to the eyes! I twirled across the path to where some white camphires were. I stopped for a brief moment because was a little dizzy from twirling.

"Twirling"! A marvelous word! "Marvelous"! A marvelous word! Marvelous was used in my Bible class, because it can mean 'miraculous supernatural', "The Lord's doing". Everything The Lord did and is still doing is marvelous! Twirling was one of my vocabulary words in reading class this past year. I remembered that twirling could be a combination of the words thrill or twist and whirl. Anyway combined, I loved twirling!

After catching my breath, I strolled up closer to one of the white flowers. There were lots of individual stems, poking straight up, that looked like tiny lollipops. The sizes of the flowers were small, medium and large. I immediately thought how much Mom would love this flower. I wondered if she even knew about the camphire flower? Her knowledge of flowers was quite impressive! When I get back home to her, I'll search the camphire on our computer.

The plan would go like this: I would be sitting at the computer; then call for Mom to come take a look; I would watch her facial expression to see if she knew about this flower. Sounds sneaky, but it was the only way of getting my answer, without me *spilling the beans* about Rain E and her home. "Spilling the beans" meant, "The Secret was Out"! I learned that in my Language Arts class. Someday Mom would know about Rain E, and then I could tell her the truth about the camphires. For right now I had to keep my secret and hope Mom never asked why I was looking up this particular flower.

I continued walking and sometimes running up and down the paths, smelling and touching the flowers. These flowers were very delicate and thin. My mind was in a daze taking it all in. There must have been a thousand camphires here! The different colors were exquisite! I especially liked the red with white edging. I loved the way the white outlined them, just like a marker. I took a long, deep breath. I started thinking about Mom, the camphire flowers, and the little white lie I might have to tell her. One time, Mom told me that a lie is a lie and coloring it doesn't make it any better. She has always been funny and painfully honest. I deeply thought, "I hope I don't have to lie? I hope God understands if I do?"

I must have been staring into space, when I realized Rain E was nowhere in sight. I walked back to the entrance and spotted her. She was standing outside the gate, to my far left, with her back was to me. I could see her arms and elbows poking out. As I got closer, Rain E slightly turned to her left. She was holding that sparkly clipboard in one hand and the feather pen in the other. I could see her hand moving across it.

I was just outside the gate, when Rain E put the clipboard back on the large hook. She must have heard me approaching, because she jerked around so quickly, before I reached her. She was now standing facing me, hiding the hanging clipboard and feather pen with her body. Rain E looked at me and said, "Okay, my dear, are you ready to go?" I begged, "NO! I don't want to go, not yet. I haven't seen you in months." "No silly! Not home! To the pond!" Rain E assured me. "Yeah! I love the pond." I exclaimed. So off we went, hand in hand.

As we were walking away from the garden I took a quick peek over my right shoulder, at the clipboard. All I could see were a lot of check marks and I think my name. "That clipboard must be about me," I whispered to myself. Rain E spoke, "Rachel, I'll tell you about the clipboard all in good time!" Once again, I forgot, Rain E could hear my thoughts and whispers.

Rain E softly spoke, "Be patient and just trust me." She squeezed my hand seven times. I know, because I counted them, just like when I counted the seven claps Stormy did at the archway entrance. Why seven? Rain E and Stormy were full of such interesting secrets. Secrets I hoped Rain E would eventually share with me.

It was a short and interesting walk to the pond. I kept noticing new and different plants. As a matter of fact, there were lots of new plants this time, I hadn't seen before. I abruptly stopped. Rain E had to stop too. Right beside the path was a strange-looking plant. My eyes bugged out. "Hey lookey there, it's a vegetable! It's cucumbers!" I remarked. I let go of Rain E's hand and bent over for a closer inspection. I glanced back at my friend and asked, "Can I eat one?" Rain E quickly answered, "Oh no, no, no! They can be potentially dangerous and they squirt." "They squirt?" I asked.

Rain E continued, "Yes, these are Squirting Cucumbers. When the cucumber ripens it expels its seeds containing a viscous liquid.

233

These seeds shoot out going 60 mph. They are potentially dangerous because if eaten before expulsion, a person or animal will painfully find out what happens when the seeds erupt inside them. So you see, the Squirting Cucumber can be fatal." "Wow! That's a wicked plant!" I commented. "It even looks wicked, with the hairy stems and scary, ugly yellow-color flowers. I can honestly say that I have never heard of this plant." I then had an evil thought, "I wish I could take one home and squirt my evil dad."

We walked a little further. I saw several tall tree-like bushes, with bright red-orange color, bell-shaped fruit. Rain E said, "Those are pomegranates." I said, "I know that fruit. Actually, I've enjoyed eating them, even though they're messy and the juice can leave stains. They're in the Bible. I bet Jesus ate them." Rain E softly laughed, "Rachel, you amaze me with your Biblical knowledge. I am so impressed." I told her I had good teachers: my mom and my school. "Rachel, you see over there to your right. Can you tell me what that tree is again? I looked and immediately announced, "It's an Olive tree, with that unusual squatty, twisted trunk."

We started walking again. Rain E pointed out the fig tree, the walnut tree, and the pistachio tree, along with mint, myrrh, and aloe vera plants. I knew the mint and aloe vera because Mom planted them in our garden. Then we passed by several flowering bushes. A slight breeze came across all the plants and trees, carrying a wonderful smell right into my nose. The smell stayed with me all the way to the pond. I enjoyed the walk so much. It was very educational and beautiful.

We were finally standing in front of the picturesque pond. I told Rain E, "I love ponds and so does my mom. My mom has always loved nature and art. She told me that the two blended perfectly together. She especially admired the French artists and their paintings of nature, one in particular who painted ponds, "many" paintings of ponds. Last year in my history class, I did a book report on him. Our class was studying Europe and we had to choose someone who was born in France. I chose Claude Monet. My mom has at least a dozen books on his life. I learned from her books and computer research that Monet must have loved painting water scenes, because his best-known works were of lily ponds." Rain E just quietly listened while I shared my story.

The water was perfectly still and silent, until a medium size fish came leaping out of it. Two more followed, as though they were playing. I watched for a few more seconds until they were gone. Rain

234

E asked if I wanted to rest a bit. I did. I was a little tired. I did more walking this trip. We turned completely around and headed to the bench. I was only a few feet away, when I spotted a new color. It was green. The bench was now red, orange, yellow and green. Wow! I mean, Wow! This time I was on Rain E's right side, because I wanted to sit on the green color.

We sat there in silence. I WAS tired and I think Rain E was too, but I wasn't quite sure. I took in several deep breaths. The air smelled clean and fresh! I started talking first, "I love the new color. Green is one of my mom's favorite colors because she loves working in the yard which, of course, is part of nature." There was a long pause in my voice. Then I said it, "I've missed you so much! Why has it been so long between visits? So much has happened!"

My voice started cracking as I told Rain E about evil dad, Sissy, the black UGGS, school, our pets dying and most of all, Mom's heart attack. I must have talked forever. Rain E quietly listened to every word I had to say. I stopped to catch my breath. Then I started telling her about the trip to California. Rain E interrupted, "Did anything unusual happen in California?" I suspiciously answered, "Yes." Then I added, "By any chance, did you show up at the hotel?" Rain E spoke, "Why do you ask?" I looked straight at her and stated, "That was you! You handed me the red rose bud, didn't you?"

Rain E never really admitted it, but I still think it was her in disguise. I contently smiled looking out over the pond. Rain E then said, "I am so sorry your mother suffered a heart attack. I truly am. Try to not worry. Your mother is strong in every aspect of her life. Strong as the color green you are sitting on. Your mother's green eyes show strength. Green also represents great healing powers and endurance. She has the endurance to get through these hard times. I believe your mother is stronger than you think. I believe you are just as strong. Always remember the color green for these reasons alone." "I will, Rain E. I promise I will," I answered all choked up. Rain E was something else! She knew the color of my mom's eyes and all about her inner strength. She also believed I possessed inner strength too!

Rain E continued, "Awhile ago we watched as the fish leaped out of the water. The fish knew to quickly return to its safe environment. It couldn't survive for very long a place it wasn't supposed to be. Rachel, there's an old saying, "Like a fish out of water". You are that fish! This is how your life has been at your Dad's. Just like that fish,

235

if left out in the wrong place something bad would eventually happen. It would take someone to come along and help the fish (You) get back to safety. You have your mother, her family, many, many wonderful friends and myself to help you stay in the water, so to speak."

"Tough times and tough choices will come along, but I know your heart and soul will keep you safe and you will make the right decisions. Your beliefs are intact. You will always go back to your Godly roots, because that is where you belong. Do you understand what I am saying to you?" I answered, "I know right from wrong and that my strong faith and beliefs will get me through the wrongs. I will stay strong and remember all those who are helping me." Rain E remarked that I was wise beyond my years. I faintly smiled.

Rain E stared deep into my eyes and asked, "Rachel, is there something else weighing on your heart?" I couldn't hold it in. I cried out, "Yes, I didn't get baptized! My mean and evil dad wouldn't take me." I burst into tears. Rain E, in her comforting voice said, "I am so sorry Rachel, truly sorry." I tightly embraced Rain E's arm with both hands and continued, "He's going to kill my mom. He's going to kill me. I just know he wants us dead. I'm scared Rain E, I'm scared!" Rain E gently took both my trembling hands in hers and said, "God will protect you and your mom. I promise you. I am watching over you too!"

It started sprinkling. I hadn't even noticed the dark, black cloud over us. When did that happen? Oh no, it was beginning to rain. I was leaving Rain E. I didn't want let go of her hands. I held on tight. I didn't want to go, not yet. I was scared of going back. Rain E kept holding my hands. They were so warm. It was making my body warm. I felt safe with her. She turned to me and spoke, "Be strong and remember Stormy's advice. Take a deep breath and breathe, just breathe."

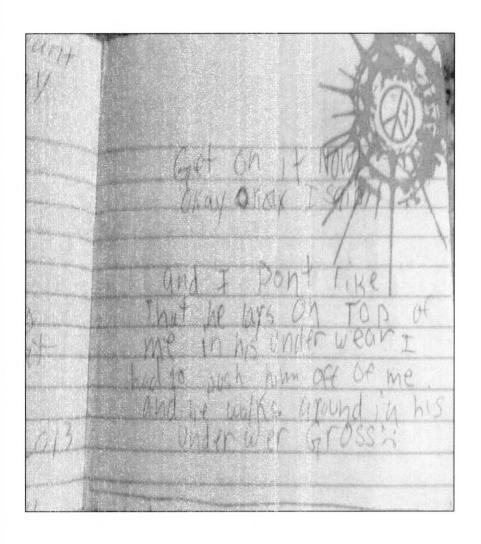

Stand firm then, with the belt of truth buckled
around your waist, with the breastplate
of righteousness in place.

Ephesians 6:14 (NIV)

Chapter 24

I kept breathing like Rain E said, but it was hard! I mean I was struggling just to catch my breath. There was a heavy pressure on top of
me. I opened my eyes. My evil dad was asleep on top of me. I tried to
push him off. He wouldn't budge. I was able to roll over onto my right
side, enough to make him fall on the floor. I looked down and there
was a scratchy towel laying on me. It stunk! I quickly flung it off to the
side. Now, for the second time, I smelled that bad, nasty odor.

Mr. Evil woke up and started screaming at me. Screaming at me
because I knocked him on the floor! I yelled back at him that I couldn't
breathe. He got up and stormed out of my room. He had on only his
white underwear. Why was my dad on top of me with just his underwear on? Where was Sissy all night? Why is this happening to me?

Once again, questions were racing through my frustrated brain. I
knew I was going to have to tell someone about this. I wouldn't see
Mom until after school tomorrow. I will have to tell my teacher. Mom
told me to tell others beside her, about anything bad that happens to
me while I'm at Dad's. She told me the more people I tell, the more it
would help us. We hoped!

It was Easter morning. My evil dad was asleep on top of me on
Easter morning! I will NEVER forget this Easter EVER! I closed my
eyes trying to go back to sleep. I wanted to go back to Rain E, Bolt and
now Stormy. Then it dawned on me what Stormy told me. This WAS
my worst battle! Stormy knew this was going to happen and that's
why she told me to put on "The Armor of God". That was exactly what
I would have to do!

Just when I was about to fall back to sleep, Dad slung the door
open. He screamed, "Get your lazy, "F" n ass out of bed and finish

your homework, NOW!" I yawned saying, "I'm still tired. I was up too late last night, besides I finished!" Then I saw it. He had that thick belt in his right hand. He started whipping it down on my mattress, inches from my leg.

I flew out of bed, fast! He was insanely swinging the belt in every direction. I kept crying out for him to stop. I said that I would get on my homework. I pleaded, "Stop, please stop, you're scaring me. I don't want another black eye, not on Easter Sunday." Sissy strolled in. I screamed at her to make him stop. She looked at me with her fingers in her mouth, and mumbled, "Sorry, can't help you," then turned and walked out. She left me in my room with a madman. I couldn't believe it. She was now on my, "I Could Care Less About" list, along with my ex-grandma and blood sister.

I grabbed both my pillows for protection and made it to my bedroom door. Then, I ran straight to the kitchen table. I quickly sat down and started checking my math. My crazy dad followed me. He hit the other end of the table with his belt and screamed "Don't leave this table until your homework is completed. I don't want that "B" mother of yours turning me into the school again, you got that!" With tears falling into my mouth, I swallowed and answered with a 'gaspy', "Yes."

I never left the kitchen table. I sat there shaking and crying, tried to compose myself. I wiped my running nose, dried my eyes and began flipping through my "completed" math and Latin homework. While I was looking at my Latin vocabulary list, two words stuck in my brain. The first one was "Dominus". It meant "Master or owner of slaves". That was definitely my dad. The other word was "Ancilla" (slave girl) and that was definitely, ME! The names fit perfectly!

I waited a bit then put all my homework neatly in the folders and stacked them all in one pile. My backpack was still in my bedroom. I wasn't about to leave the table, until I got permission from Mr. "Dominus". Sitting there, all I could think about was how insanely crazy my dad was. First he made me stay up late last night to do my homework, then Easter morning wanted me to do it again, even though it was already completed. When I tried to explain, he went berserk! Beyond crazy!

About ten minutes later, Dad stormed into the room and viciously asked if all my homework was done. Dropping my head, I fearfully answered again, "Yes." I kept my head down just in case he tried to strike me across the face. He growled, "Get your worthless ass dressed for Easter brunch." I flew to my room and closed the door. The tears showed up again. I stood there taking deep breaths, like Stormy and Rain E said. What a horrible, disgraceful way to start Easter. I whispered, "My dad could care less how he treats me. All he cares about is brunch. "Food", not "Faith"! Wonder if he cares about his "Final" home? His hot temper will fit right in!"

I went to the bathroom and got ready. I changed into my lovely sundress and sandals Mom had bought me. I stared at myself in the dresser mirror and didn't like what I was seeing. Such a sad face, a bruised body and a crushed spirit! At that precise, heart-wrenching moment, I decided I wasn't going to take any more crap from my dad. Stormy told me to put on the "Armor of God" so I confidently said to the mirror, "I WILL! I know my dad will still hurt me. That's a given, but I will NEVER become like his mother or Sissy! I WILL NOT!!! I will be strong like Mom!!"

A beam of light came through my balcony window and lit up the mirror. I smiled and cried at the same time. I knew it was Rain E. She heard my thoughts. I turned and marched to my balcony. Holding on to the rail, I glanced at my bruised arm. The bruise was gone!! I ran to the bathroom and sat on my counter to examine my entire arm. Then I remembered the warm grass. It must have healed my arm. I went back to the balcony and yelled, "Thank you Rain E. Thank you Stormy. Thank you Bolt." Then even louder, I tearfully yelled, "Thank you GOD"!!!! I stood there for several minutes drying my eyes. I took a deep breath then another, before going back inside.

When I reached the bedroom door, I turned and stared at my balcony. This was the balcony that connected me to Rain E! I would never see it again, after this dreadful weekend. My next forced visit with my evil dad will be at his new house. "Visit"! I liked that word, because it meant to come and go. It was not permanent. I may have had to "VISIT" Dad, but I always got to "GO" back home to Mom. "VISITS" with Rain E were also not permanent, but the big difference was, I didn't want to "GO" back home to Dad. I was happy and sad leaving the condo. Happy leaving all the horrible memories behind! Sad, because it was on my balcony where I first connected with Rain E! I paused for a moment, looked up and spoke, "Rain E, if you're listening. I'm moving. I hope you have the new address!"

I opened the door and left my bedroom. Mr. Evil and Sissy were sitting in the den. I quietly walked in. Sissy was trying to be nice by remarking that she really liked my new dress. So fake! I looked right at her face and said, "Thanks, my mom has great taste!" She said nothing else. Mr. Evil asked, "Are you two brain-deads ready to go. I'm hungry! We have to pick up number three brain-dead, so get a move on."

I watched Sissy to see if she would say anything. All she did was roll her eyes. She looked annoyed. Interesting! Maybe she was getting tired of Mr. Evil? It didn't really matter. She was never going to stand up to him, because she wanted all his money. Sissy was NEVER going to "Rock the Boat". That was as another funny saying I heard from Mom. It meant that Sissy would never make my dad mad. She didn't want to get her "A" booted out of the house! Excuse my language!

We headed to the car. In the elevator, I stood as far away from my dad as possible. He smelt awful. This time the perfume was gagging me so much I thought I was going to heave. We got in the car. I kept my hand over my mouth and nose. It was that bad. This time, Mom will have to wash my dress three times to get the stink out. She will probably put my sandals on the porch to let them air out.

Off we went to pick up Martha! We pulled into her driveway and of course here came *the honks*. Stinky dad was honking and honking until Martha appeared. When she got in the backseat, her son barked at her why it took so long. It didn't take long for Martha, just too long for him. Dad is "Mr. Impatient" and it was Martha's fault! I looked at Martha and she said nothing to her precious baby. She was scared of him just like Sissy. I THOUGHT Sissy was scared of Dad, but now I wasn't sure! "Wonder what was going on in that conniving brain of hers?" I pondered. Still those two made me sick.

All the way to the restaurant I thought about Mom. I wished I could have been there with her and the "fun" family. I bet they were all eating together. Seemed so unfair! Easter with Mom's family was a blast! She had the funniest brothers (my uncles). Nothing was fun about dad's family. All though I did think they were a big joke!

We arrived at the restaurant. Pulling into the parking area, I saw Ronny and Blake eagerly waiting by the entrance door. We all got out and the five of us went in. It was a buffet. I was glad of that. I could get just what I wanted to eat, not what Dad wanted me to eat! I kept quiet and just listened to all of their vulgar mouths. Everyone made an unkind remark about Mom and her family. The worst one of them all came out of my dad's filthy mouth. Right before we started eating,

Mr. Evil loudly said at the table, "Oh, do we need to pray or did the ex-bitch pray enough for us?" All the people around us were stunned. Dad devilishly laughed. I glared at him. He was not only mocking my mom, he was mocking Jesus. I wondered what God thought!

After we ate, Mr. Evil said we were going to the lake for an Easter egg hunt. I looked at him and said, "I'm not a baby. I don't want to hunt with babies!" Mr. Evil said, "Tough, you're hunting." Then he hit my arm. Hit me in the arm and no one said a word! We all left the restaurant together and headed to the lake. When we got there, I was by far the oldest kid. It WAS for babies! How embarrassing and humiliating!

This old man came out of an office and shouted to the kids to start hunting. I casually walked around and picked up a few. At one point, Mr. Evil told me not to grab so many. He said I needed to leave most of them for the younger kids. So I ask you, "Why did we even come at all?" First he wanted me to hunt! Then I was not supposed to pick up the eggs! So insane!

After the 'baby' egg hunt, we all sat around a picnic table until dark. Dad barked it was time to go. We all piled into the car. I sat between Martha and Blake. What was weird, Ronny sat next to Dad instead of Sissy. We dropped off "The Boys" at the restaurant to get their truck then headed to Martha's house. When Martha got out of the car, she said goodbye to me in that baby voice. This time I completely ignored her. By the time we reached the "Damn Evil Tower" I was worn out from the horrible day. I soaked in a hot bath. My arm was hurting where Dad hit me. After I got out, I put on my golden night-gown on so I could think about Rain E. I placed my school uniform across the chair and got all my stuffed packed. I turned the lights off and jumped in bed.

A few minutes later, Mr. Evil stuck his head in. He firmly said, "I know you're still awake, so listen up "Miss Piggy". You better not tell your mother about this weekend or I WILL kill her, you got that!" My mouth stayed shut and my eyes stayed closed. He said nothing else as he slammed the door. I opened my eyes and whispered, "I will tell! I will tell! I will tell my teacher tomorrow, everything from my dad sleeping on top of me, cussing at me and taking me to a bar. I will tell!"

This WAS the battle Stormy was talking about. I prayed to God in silence, asking Him to please be the sword in Mom's hand, because she was going to need that sword along with His divine help. I also asked

God to give me lots of extra courage. I was going to need it in order to discuss this miserable, "unholy" Easter weekend with my teacher. A few minutes passed then a comforting and reassuring feeling eased my worries. A tear fell out of my left eye. I rolled over on my left side. One more tear fell on my pillow. I placed my hand on top of the wet spot, closed my eyes and finally fell asleep.

The LORD is good, a stronghold in the day of trouble;
and He knows those who trust In Him.

Nahum 1:7 (NKJV)

Chapter 25

My eyes struggled to open. It was pitch dark outside. I yawned and yawned and yawned. Boy, last night wasn't as restful as I hoped it would be! I didn't sleep a darn bit! How could I? I had nightmares all night long about my disgusting dad lying on top of me. Praying to God and listening to Him did help some, but I woke up still thinking and worrying, "Why did he do that? Why? I don't understand." Thank goodness I woke up alone! Thank goodness no more scratchy towels! I would NEVER forget this Easter!

The smell of coffee entered my room. Sissy was up. She knocked on my door and said, "Time to get ready for school." I said nothing. At least she doesn't just barge in, like "you-know-who". I stayed in bed a few more minutes and thought about when I would talk to my teacher. Finally, I got up and headed to the bathroom, grabbing my uniform on the way.

I never really minded wearing uniforms. Mom reminded me, "It's not what you look like on the outside that counts it's what's on the inside that matters. Clothes can never cover up who you really are." She was right! I finished getting ready, then left *this* bathroom for the last time. I packed up all my stuff, including my drawing, which would soon include my new friends Stormy and Olive, and even the Squirting Cucumbers!

Before leaving, I took one final look around. So many horrible memories that will stay with me forever! Because of God, Rain E helped me survive this rotten, rotten place. I flipped the lights off and walked out never looking back. I strolled down the hallway looking for my dad. I peeked into his room to find him still asleep. I walked down to the kitchen. Sissy said she was driving me to school. I looked at her and firmly stated, "My mom told me to never get in the car with you, if you are the driver!" Sissy gave me a 'go to hell' look and said, "Let's go!" Again I said, "No!"

I stormed into Dad's bedroom and screamed, "I'm not getting in the car with Sissy!" I walked out and waited. I wasn't getting in the car with her. No way! She was legally blind in one eye and didn't even have a driver's license. Plus, a lot of other health issues, including no feeling in her feet. I was thinking about my safety.

Dad came stumbling out. He started in on me. "What's your problem? Get your ass in the car NOW!!" I said again, "No, I'm calling the police and then Mom." He shut up. He stormed back to his room and then returned with shorts, a T-shirt and his slippers on. He threw my cell phone at me and screamed, "Come on, Now!" I gathered up my stuff and glared at Sissy as I walked out. Nothing was said from the elevator to the school.

When Dad pulled into the car line, I immediately got out, slamming the door extra hard. I didn't even wait until we reached the main entrance. I just wanted out! I never turned to say goodbye. I walked straight into my building. Boy, did I have a lot on my mind! When I reached my classroom I had decided to talk to my teacher after school let out. My mind wandered all day. It was hard to stay focused. A couple of times my teacher (Mrs. D) asked if I was okay. She actually asked me if there was anything I wanted to share with her. "Wow! She MUST be a mind reader!" I surprisingly thought.

My teacher was so nice. She worried about me. She especially worried about me this past weekend. Mrs. D knew I had to be with my dad over the long Easter Break because Mom told her at our Easter program. That same day, a parent even talked with my mom about my abusive dad. The mother said her daughter came home all upset about what I had told her. I had confided in her about my dad hitting me with his thick belt. I guess she needed to tell her parents. The mother was shocked when Mom informed her it was true. Everyone at my school worried about me. They worried about all the kids. I was glad this was my school!

The day went by faster than I thought. When it was time to go, I walked up to my teacher's desk and whispered I needed to talk to her. She told me to just stay in the room and as soon as the kids were all outside, she would spend some time with me. I waited for about 20 minutes. Mrs. D walked back in and closed the door. She sat down right next to me. "Rachel, is everything alright?" My caring teacher asked. I paused for a moment to get up the nerve and courage to tell her everything.

I took a deep breath and softly spoke, "Not really Mrs. D. My mom told me to tell you if anything bad happened to me, while at my Dad's. She made it very clear to me that you know before she does. She has tried to tell the court what's happening to me, but they don't believe her. They only believe my Dad's lies." Mrs. D looked straight into my sad and scared eyes. I couldn't hold it in. I burst into tears. Mrs. D gently took both of my arms. I instantly reacted, "Ouch!" She wanted to see my arm. I said, "It's better." She asked, "What do you mean better?" I told her, "I accidently bumped it." I don't think she believed me the way she was looking at me.

Then Mrs. D said, "Tell me what happened." I cried for a few more minutes, and blurted out, "I woke up yesterday morning with my dad on top of me, asleep. It was difficult to breathe. I kept trying to wake him up. I pushed on his shoulders, with both my hands, but he didn't budge. Finally I was able to roll my body to the side and he fell on the floor. I looked down at my dad. He was only wearing underwear."

"I then looked down at my legs and there was an old scratchy towel on me. It smelled awful. I threw it on the floor. It reminded me of the time when one of Dad's young boyfriends spent the night. He slept in my room. I had to sleep on the sofa. The next morning I was ordered to strip my bed, because his mother was coming over to clean. I saw a large stain on the bottom sheet. I leaned over to smell it. It stunk! Mrs. D the scratchy towel smelled just like the sheet!" I stopped to take another deep breath.

Then I continued, "After my dad left the room, I tried to go back to sleep. A few minutes later he came in with his thick belt, screaming at me to finish my homework. He kept screaming and screaming, cussing and cussing. He called me bad words. I was so scared. I tried to tell him I just wanted to sleep a little more. I even tried to tell him all my homework was done. He was screaming so loud, he didn't hear me."

"Then my crazy dad took his belt and slung it against the wall and then on my bed. His live-in girlfriend walked in. I begged her to make him stop. She said she couldn't help me and just turned around and left! I grabbed both of my pillows, holding one on my back and one on my front. I hurried to the kitchen table. My dad followed me with his belt. I quickly sat down. I tried to tell him again I had finished all my homework last night. He didn't care. I was worse than scared I was terrified! I didn't want another black eye, not on Easter, and yes, my dad hurt my arm!"

Mrs. D interrupted, "Excuse me! Your dad gave you a black eye? Does your mother know this?" I answered, "Yes. She saw it the next day when I came home from Dad's. I wouldn't let her call the police. My dad threatened he would kill her if I told what really happened. Please, don't blame my mom. She has gone to court so many times. They may take me away from her. That's what my dad told me. He said that she was a liar. My mom's not a liar. My dad is. I wanted to call the police when it happened, but I didn't have my phone. My dad always takes it away from me when I'm with him."

After I finished talking, I wiped my tears from my face and neck. I looked at Mrs. D's face. She was in total shock. She got up and said she would be right back. A few minutes later Mrs. C and the school nurse walked in. Mrs. D told me to tell them what happened. She said it was important that they also know. So I did. They were in total shock! Mrs. C held my hands and told me, "Everything is going to be alright." I think she was just trying to calm me down. I yelled out, "Things are not alright!" Then I said to all of them that I was taken to a bar Saturday night, instead of getting baptized. I got up to get a Kleenex to blow my nose. When I sat back down, Mrs. D thanked me for being brave enough to share what had happened to me.

She said a prayer, asking God to watch over me. Mrs. D got up and said she would be right back and for me to stay put. The school nurse and Mrs. C walked out with her. I heard them whispering in the hall. Several minutes went by. Mom walked in. I could see that she had been crying. Mrs. D must have told her what I said. Mom walked over and hugged me. She brushed my hair back and kissed me on the forehead.

We gathered up all my stuff and went to the car. As I was getting in, I heard Mrs. C holler, "Call her tomorrow." Mom yelled back, "I will." Mom got in and just before we pulled out, I asked what Mrs. C was talking about. Mom took my left hand and said, "I am so sorry, my love, I am so very, very sorry. I feel like I've let you down." I tried to tell her I was okay, but I wasn't. I was a mess too.

Mom added, "Mrs. C gave me the name of an excellent lady attorney. She personally knows her and said she is tough. The school highly recommends her. Rachel, you do know the school has to report this. CPS will be talking to you again. I am so proud of you for having the strength to talk with your teacher. It took a lot of guts. I WILL be going back to court. This will be the biggest battle yet, but we will get through it. I promise! We will need to put on our "Armor of God", won't we?" Mom looked at me and softly smiled.

As we were driving home, I told Mom, "I'm not as scared of Dad as I used to be." Mom said, "I know you're getting stronger. I have seen a change in you." I felt great inside. I stood up and told about my mean dad. I did it! I felt as strong as my mom! Well, almost as strong! The battle Stormy mentioned was about to begin!

We pulled in the driveway and into the garage. Mom parked and looked at me. She told me again how sorry she was. She powerfully stated, "I will NEVER stop fighting for you, not until your dad is permanently out of your life!" As we were walking in I told her I needed to tell her everything that happened this weekend. Mom softly spoke, "Just rest tonight and we'll talk tomorrow, after school."

Upstairs I unpacked the hidden leftover food from my backpack and carried it down with all the beer-stinking, perfumed clothes. I dumped the clothes in the laundry room. While I was throwing away the secret leftover food in the kitchen trash compacter, Mom walked in and just gave me a sad, knowing smile. I quietly left the room. I didn't have any homework, so I played on the computer.

An hour later, Mom called for me to come eat. She made some sandwiches. We ate and watched Wheel of Fortune. I asked where Grandma was. Mom said that she had left this morning to visit her best friend who lived out of town. They had known each other for most of their lives. I was glad to just be with Mom, after this horrible weekend. I took a long hot bath. When I got out, to my surprise, lying on my bed was a new pajama short set next to an Easter basket full of goodies. Mom was the best! I ate one large chocolate egg, even though I had already brushed my teeth (couldn't resist).

Mom came up to check on me. We said our prayer, like always. At the end she ask God to send extra help to watch over us. Little did she know! We hugged. Before Mom got up, she sweetly said, "Head on your pillow, so eyes can rest. Jesus will bring you, His loving best. The angels will fly, to be by your side. That's whom He calls on, and they always abide. So go to sleep my sweet little one, tomorrow we'll have lots of fun!" Mom made that up. She wrote all the time.

When Mom reached the door, I told her how beautiful the lullaby was. She smiled and said that she wrote it just for me. The lights went off and Mom headed downstairs. I rolled over to look out my window. It was so peaceful. I was just about asleep when I heard a soft voice whisper in my ear, "I'm here." Then I heard, "Me too!" I knew it was Rain E and Stormy. I whispered back, "I'm glad!" Maybe I was dreaming. Maybe I was hearing voices. Maybe God allowed me to hear them. Could be any one of these reasons! It didn't matter. I was allowed to hear them. I closed my eyes and I whispered to them and Bolt, "Night."

*"I am not afraid of storms for
I am learning how to sail my ship."*

Louisa May Alcott

Chapter 26

I woke up before Mom did. I slept all night with both eyes closed. Never a need to be a dolphin at my home with Mom! I got ready for school then slid down the banister for fun. I was first in the kitchen. Mom walked in. "You beat me," she laughed. "What would you like for breakfast?" I answered, "A breakfast burrito." "Sounds good to me," Mom added. We were off. I stayed quiet, until we were in the car line to get breakfast. Mom ordered.

We pulled up and got our food. I was still quiet. Mom was listening to her favorite radio DJ's, when I blurted out, "What's a 'whore'?" Mom slammed on her breaks and turned off the radio. "Excuse me!" Mom exclaimed. "Where did you hear that word? Oh, let me guess, from your dad!" I answered, "Not from Dad, from Delilah, Sissy's daughter."

I went into detail, about my trip to the bar. Mom was appalled to say the least. Actually she was furious with Dad. I still wanted to know what the word meant. I told Mom that I didn't understand Delilah's answer. Mom told me, "A whore is a woman who sleeps with men she's not married to, for money." I point blank asked Mom, "Is Sissy a whore?" Mom answered. "According to the Bible, Sissy's not a whore, she's just living in sin with a man she's not married to!" I was glad Mom clarified that for me. I remembered reading about those kinds of women in my Bible. Jesus helped some of them change their ways. Luke (7:36-50 NKJ). I thanked Mom for telling me the truth. She was sorry I was dragged to a bar and had to be a part of such vulgarity.

Then I asked, "Mom, what does it mean to land a guy?" Mom abruptly stopped the car again. "Rachel, all these sayings are intended for grown-ups. I'm sorry you heard this kind of cheap, low life conversation. I truly am. I will tell you when you're old enough to understand." After that question, Mom was beyond disgusted with Dad. I saw it in her red face. We were in the school line, when Mom instructed me to never to repeat those words or sayings again. I promised. I got out and we said our goodbyes. School was easier than yesterday, because I got everything off my chest.

After morning snack break, my teacher asked how I was doing. I told her that I was a lot better. She said there was a lady I had to speak with. I asked if she was from CPS. Mrs. D said she was. I knew a lot about CPS. Mainly that they didn't help at all. So I went down the hallway into a room. This lady was waiting, seated at a long desk. I sat across from her. First came the fake sweet questions; "How are you? How old are you? How is school going? Do you know why I'm here? And on and on!' Then came the harder questions. The lady asked, "Could you tell me what happened? Did your Dad touch any of your privates? Did he threaten you? Did he hurt you in any other way? Did anyone tell you to say these things?" That did it!! The last question made me boiling mad.

I rudely interrupted this woman, "Ma'am I don't want to talk to you, but I have to. I have talked to three other women just like you in the last two years. It doesn't matter what I say. No one listens to my mom or me. She has gone to court so many times. No one has helped us and neither will you! You'll bring my dad in and he will twist my words around and in the end you will believe him. I know what my dad is doing to me is morally wrong. He abuses me. That's it!"

"The judges don't care, the attorneys don't care, the therapist, I'm forced to talk to doesn't care and you don't care either. I told my teacher and she cares, but the worthless judge won't let her or my doctors even speak in court. Please tell me why? I'm sorry if I sound rude and angry, but I am. I will have to continue seeing my dad until I'm old enough to walk away or he drops dead or he kills me. I'm tired of talking to adults. You people don't HELP!"

I stopped and took a long deep breath, and finished saying, "Can I leave now?" She sat there dumbfounded. What could she say? I stood up. Before I walked out, I pushed back my long sleeve and showed her my bruised arm. I glared a hole through her and left on my own. It was near lunchtime and I wanted to be with friends, not enemies.

After school I got in the car and told Mom what I said. She was so proud of me. I was proud of me. The rest of the ride home I deliberately stayed quiet. I needed to rest my mouth. We pulled in the garage, parked and headed into the house. I piled my school stuff on the kitchen table and headed to my room. I changed clothes and played some games on the computer.

After about an hour, I went to the kitchen table and finished my math. Mom had ordered pizza. After I finished all my other home-work, Mom checked it over, like always. The pizza arrived. We sat in the den, ate and watched *Wheel of Fortune*. Like I'd mentioned, Mom and Grandma loved that show! I liked it too, even though I didn't let on. The pizza was *delish*!

I excused myself to get ready for bed. When I got to the top, Mom hollered that she would be up later. I went to my room and unpacked the rest of my stuff from the weekend, putting it up as best I could. Mom wasn't a neat freak like Dad. I made sure I put my drawing under the bed. I jumped in the shower. When I got out, I looked at my arm again. The bruise was almost gone. I still put on my long sleeve blue and white nightgown to hide it. I didn't want to upset Mom anymore. I climbed into my wonderful, soft bed. Mom came in and we said our prayer. She kissed me goodnight and told me how much she loved me. I told her the same. She got up and flipped the lights off.

I heard talking right outside my door. I quietly got up to check it out. The upstairs was lit up by the moonlight coming through the win-dows. I stayed just inside my bedroom. Mom was leaning up against the banister. I could see her holding her hands together. I knew she was praying. I knew I was being sneaky. I couldn't help it. I worried about her having another heart attack. I was close enough to I hear her say, "He won't get away with this, he won't. I need "Your" help. This has got to stop! My daughter can't keep going through this. Father, please help us. In Jesus name."

Mom headed downstairs. I went back to bed. I rolled over and looked at the sky. Not only was the moon out, thousands of stars were out too. The sky was sparkling. The storm from this past weekend was over. A different storm would be here tomorrow. God wouldn't start this one, Mom would. God would just be assisting her. I felt good about this storm, and even better about myself! I told what happened to me. It was easy to fall asleep.

The next morning I woke up to the bright sun, peeking through the shutters. It was so bright I had to put a pillow over my head. I was trying to go back to sleep, when my nose inhaled a wonderful, familiar smell. It was Mom's homemade biscuits. The smell was filling the house. I couldn't sleep anymore. I quickly got ready for school, hurried downstairs and went straight to the kitchen. Mom was standing behind the island, buttering the biscuits.

She smiled and said, "Morning my love, hungry?" "Yes, yes, yes!" I answered. "The jams are on the table. I poured you a glass of milk." Mom sat down with her coffee and said, "Today is the day!" I asked, "Day for what?" "Finish eating, we'll talk in the car." With food in my mouth, I mumbled, "Okay."

Mom went to pull the car out. I gathered up my stuff and headed out. The minute I got in, I asked again. "Day for what?" Mom said that she had an appointment with the new lady attorney and would tell me about it after school. We talked a little, but mostly listened to our favorite radio station. The DJ's were so funny!

When we reached the school, Mom grabbed my hand and told me to have a wonderful day. I told her how much I loved her and thanked her again for explaining the "bar" lingo. I got out. Walking to my friends, I looked back at Mom. She blew me a kiss. It was a good day at school.

Mom picked me up right on time. On the way home, she told me all about the new attorney. Mom said that she was a 'tiger' and was going to put a stop to me seeing Dad, until we had a court hearing. After we got home, I did my homework and played with my pets. I was outside, when I heard Mom scream. I quickly ran in.

Mom hugged me and said, "My new attorney just called. She did it! She put a stop to you going to your dad's, until there's a hearing. It is all because of what happened over the Easter weekend." I jumped up and down, twirling around. It was finally some long-over-due good news. It wouldn't last, but at least I didn't have to go back to Dad's this weekend. I was scared for Mom, because my dad was crazy. He would be coming after her, I feared!

That night in bed, I told Mom in more detail about the bar, the nasty looking women and the nice man who tried to help me. I never mentioned my bruised arm. She told me she was sorry I had to see that kind of nasty stuff. I spoke up, "Mom there's something else I need to tell you that I think the new attorney should know." Mom simply asked, "What is it?" She had an uneasy and concerned look on her face.

I started, "One weekend, when Ronny spent the night, he and Dad were in the office looking at the computer watching naked boys playing leapfrog. Mom, why were those boys naked?" I watched as Mom's expression changed. She was appalled! She said that it was wrong for Dad to being looking at something inappropriate while I was there. Then I told Mom, "I saw photos of me while I was sleeping. I don't know who took them. It gave me the creeps."

Mom's eyes bugged out more. This time her face was mad! She could hardly speak. Mom just said she would tell all of this to the new attorney tomorrow. Mom added that she would not be calling Dad because she wanted the attorney to handle it. We said our prayer and thanked God for the new lady attorney. Mom kissed me on my cheeks, one after another, several times. Mom turned the lights out with me smiling. She was smiling too. "Goodnight Mommy," I said. "Goodnight my love," Mom said walking away. I threw my comforter over my head. That felt good calling her "Mommy". I fell asleep feeling safe!

The next two weeks flew by. Grandma made it back home safe and sound. She had a wonderful time with her "old", but funny friend. I was happy for her. I was happy at school and happy at home. I was going to enjoy it as long as I could. I would be going back to Mr. Evil, I was sure of it, but maybe he wouldn't be so evil this time. I doubted it though. Mom's court date was the following Friday. She and the new lady attorney were ready.

That day had arrived! After school, I went home with my best friend. I finished all my homework while I was there. I knew Mom would be tired. It was close to 6:00 pm when she picked me up. Mom was extra quiet. She looked sad. I thought to myself, "Oh no, court went bad." I cautiously asked if everything went okay. Mom said that it kind of did. She told some of what happened, only what I needed to know. She did tell me the lady judge ordered a social study on the whole family. Mom said I would have to talk to another person, but it would be a lady. I was glad about that. She also told me that Dad and even Sissy lied in court, without going into details.

What Mom told me next, I would have fallen over if I had not been sitting in the car! She said, "You have to go back to your Dad's next weekend." I interrupted her, "Why! Why! What's wrong with that lady judge?" Mom said, "There's more." "What?" I interrupted again. "The crazy, and I do mean crazy, lady judge put Sissy in charge of protecting you from your dad." I yelled at the top of my lungs, "No way! Dad abuses her! She suffered abuse by her first husband! I never told you Mom, but I overheard Sissy telling Martha that her first husband tossed her through a closed window. She has scars all over her body from the broken glass. This lady judge IS crazy in the head!! Why would she do that to me? Sounds like she's on Dad's side!"

It seemed no matter what happened to me, I had to be with my evil dad. I didn't understand the law. Was that lady judge just waiting for me to die so she could say that she had made a bad decision? Got news for you lady judge! You already made many bad decisions where I was concerned. I was not physically dead yet, only emotionally dead on the inside! Mom said Sissy had to swear on a Bible to protect me. Sissy was going to protect ME! What a joke! Sissy had to lie. She was so scared of what my dad would do to her, that she forgot what God was going to do to her. My own personal thought, "I don't think she even cares."

Once we got home, Mom went directly upstairs to Grandma's room to tell her all about what happened in court. I went up to my room. I could hear them. Grandma was also upset. I heard her say that there was something seriously wrong with our court system and those two judges. She was right. Mom stayed in there for some time. I went back downstairs to the office.

I got on the computer and looked up camphire flowers. Wow! They did come in different colors! They were also called Henna, just like Rain E said. I kept reading about them, when Mom walked in. "What are you looking at?" Mom asked. I answered, "Oh, just different kinds of flowers I might want add to our garden." Mom took a closer look at the screen and shocked me by saying, "Oh my goodness! I haven't thought about camphires in a long time. You know they're in the Bible!"

I casually asked, "How did you know that?" Mom continued, "Because there are only three kinds of flowers mentioned in the Bible, the camphire, the rose and the lily. By the way, the only flower Jesus ever spoke of was the lily. The lily family is said to include the crown daisy, chamomile and irises. There are many other flowering plants mentioned in the Bible, like the mandrake, sage and broom, but they are considered bushes. Did you know there were even Squirting Cucumbers a long time ago?"

I was very impressed with Mom's knowledge of plants and flowers in the Bible. I was not at all surprised. She read all the time, from books on history to gardening magazines, and from her Bibles, especially The Living Bible. Mom left the office and hollered, "I'm going to make us a quick dinner." I hollered back, "Okay, I'll go take a bath, but first I want to pull up information on the flowers mentioned in the Bible." I pulled up the info and it said the only flowers mentioned are the camphire, the rose and the lily. Mom was right! I shut off the computer and headed up to my room.

I was halfway up the stairs, when it hit me. My knees buckled. I had to sit down. Oh goodness gracious me! Chills went through my body. It all made sense. Everything growing at Rain E's home was mentioned in the Bible! Rain E was part of the Bible. Oh my dear Lord! It had to be. Rain E was a part of Heaven. Rain E was an angel. My angel! I was sure of it.

My body was quivering. My hands were trembling. I tightly held them together. It was God. He sent Rain E to "help me". It was in my letter. I always thought angels were males, but then again we don't know everything about how God works. I looked up and just said, "Thank you!" I paused and added, "Please God, let me see Rain E again, please."

I took my bath. I was drying off when I heard Mom call out that dinner was ready. I put on my comfortable blue and white plaid, long-sleeved nightgown. It used to be one of my favorites. Now I wear it when I need to cover up bruises. I would always remember it that way. Grandma joined me on the stairs. We went down together side by side. I noticed that I was now almost as tall as Grandma. Mom made a big plate of cheese nachos and some iced tea. We all sat at the table and enjoyed them. We talked a little. I helped clean up and made sure all the pets were fed. Mom said she was exhausted from being in court all day. She said she would be up, after she took a hot shower. Grandma said she was going up to work on her puzzles for a while. She loved her puzzles! We all went to our own rooms.

When I got into bed Sugar was already there. She must have missed me. Mom came up to say goodnight. She had on her long-sleeved red nightgown. She always looked good in red, especially with her beautiful dark hair. She even had on red fluffy socks. Mom stretched out next to me. She took my hand and said, "I haven't told you another childhood story in a while. Would you like to hear one?"

"Yes, Mommy, it helps me fall to sleep. Tell me about the tornado again, or one about an animal." I called her Mommy again.

Mom said, "I know a good and scary TRUE animal story!" We stared at the ceiling. I turned on my side to listen better, because Mom was the best storyteller! Still looking up at the ceiling, Mom started, "It was the summer I was ten. My family drove all the way to California in our new station wagon. They didn't have SUV's back then. It was called a Rambler. We traveled through many states, before reaching California. It took a couple of days to get there. We stopped and saw the sights along the way, like Billy the Kid's grave in New Mexico, the Petrified Forest National Park and Grand Canyon in Arizona"

"When we finally reached California, we toured this very famous home, The "Hurst Castle" in San Simeon, located on the central coast of California between Los Angeles and San Francisco. It WAS a castle, like nothing I had ever seen! It was enormous! On the tour, I found out, it was a female architect, Julia Morgan, who designed it. She was the first licensed woman architect in California. Quite impressive in those days during the 1930's and 40's! You know, it took 28 years to build."

"Mr. Hearst also had his own private zoo on the property. After his death, the animals were donated to zoos, except the zebras. To this day the descendants of those original zebras still roam free on the mountainsides. It was Hearst's request. Very informative tour! Anyway my dad took lots of photos! After walking all through the castle, we piled back into our red Rambler, and drove on the highway, right by the ocean. When I was older, I found out it was Highway 1."

"Dad stopped at a small beach cove area, so we could go for a swim. Mom and my brothers played on the beach. Dad rented a surfboard. He and I slowly waded out into the water with our clothes on. I was on the left of the surfboard and Dad was on the right. We paddled out far enough for our legs to float freely. To this day, I can still remember the warm water on my hands, but from the waist down the water was much colder. It was a murky, dark blue almost black color. So intimidating-dark, I couldn't see past my waist. That was a little scary, being my first time in deep, salty water!"

"We went out a little further. I remember looking across the ocean. You could see forever. It was quite a sight! The water was fairly calm with little to no waves. Our surfboard gently moved up and down along with the ripples. I looked over to my right. There were other people in the water. A bunch of kids were splashing and kicking, having a blast! Smaller ones were playing near the shoreline."

"We kept floating along with the ocean; it was so relaxing. Every once in a while a tiny wave would come across our surfboard. You could smell the salt in the water. Even with the smallest of waves shifting back and forth, one splashed on my face, immediately causing my eyes to burn. Some of the salty ocean water found its way into my mouth. I gagged!"

"We had now drifted out about twenty yards from shore. On my dad's side of the surfboard, I noticed a few guys swim by. As I turned my head back in the other direction, something caught the corner of my left eye. For a brief moment, it was sticking out of the water and then it was gone. I thought it was some kind of driftwood or a branch. When out of nowhere, something brushed up against me. My dad calmly told me to be very, very still. At that exact moment, my legs stopped moving. I slowly glanced back to my left again, and saw it. It was a fin, now about five feet from us. Wood wasn't brushing up against me! It was a shark! I was terrified! I started crying. My body was trembling and not from the cold water. I looked straight at my dad. He told me again to remain still. He kept his eyes on the shark. Dad said it was circling us."

"A couple of minutes went by. I heard some people scream "Shark!" I didn't have to look. I could hear them frantically trying to get out of the water and fast! I kept watching Dad, as he kept watching the shark. I saw his eyes open wider. I could see fear in him. Then all of a sudden he quickly grabbed my arms, digging his fingernails into my skin. Just as Dad held on tight, the shark bumped me hard! The surfboard shifted far to the right, then back to the left. He held on to me even tighter. Don't ask me how, but I heard my oldest brother scream out the words, "Dad!! Shark!!!""

"Dad kept telling me to try to be perfectly still and very quiet. It was hard. He could see the sheer terror in my teary eyes. By now I wasn't only scared, I was shivering! I can still recall trying to keep my body still, but it was trembling so badly. In a whispering, but chattering voice, I asked Dad if we were going to be eaten up. He kept assuring me that everything was going to be okay. I believed him. Dad did his best to calm one hysterical kid, ME! He would tell me stories to make me laugh. My scared eyes stayed glued on his face the whole time. It helped some. Then suddenly, Dad jerked his head looking all around.

He looked back at me and pointedly noted that the shark must have gone completely under water."

"Without delay, Dad started paddling fast, towards shore. He told me that I needed to paddle as fast as I could. He said that we had to get to shore and now! I think he knew the shark was going to attack. To this day, I remember crying out to God for help. It was at that precise moment, a huge surfing wave came out of nowhere and carried us onto the wet sand. We hurried to get entirely out of the water. When we did, I collapsed on my back."

"My brothers came running to my rescue. Mom wasn't far behind. I was breathing fast! My heart must have been racing 90 mph. I took several deep breaths in and out. I glanced up to see where the shark was. It had surfaced again, about five feet from shore. That shark must have been right under us the whole time. If that wave hadn't shown up, I would have been his lunch. I'm sure of it. Mom was hysterical, as she should be. Dad finally calmed her down. She ran back to get me a beach towel, then thoroughly checked my body. She lifted my shirt. I had scrape marks from the shark and a few scratches on my left leg. Dad retuned the surfboard."

"When he got back, he took a photo of all of us. Then Dad took one of just me with the ocean in the background. I still have that photo to this day." I interrupted Mom and remarked, "You MUST have been more than just scared!" "Terrified! I even peed in the ocean," Mom added. I inquired, "Was it a Great White?" Mom said, "I'm not sure. All the years I have been watching *Shark Week* I do believe it was either a baby great white or a blue shark. Who knows? I didn't care at the time. It was a shark and that's all that mattered!" "That's why you love to watch programs on sharks," I stated. Mom answered, "Maybe so. All I know is it scared the 'dickens' out of me."

"To this day, I still have nightmare shark dreams. I even wrote a poem about that eventful day. I'll try to find it and read it to you. Now you know why I don't go in the water, very often. I do know God brought the wave. He must have known someday I would be your mom and you would get to hear this vivid, yet captivating story."

"You know my sweet, I can even recall what I was wearing that frightful day. It was a matching short set made of sear-sucker fabric. The colors were pink, orange and white. Funny the things we remember! How was that for an animal story?" "That was the best ever! Will you tell it to me again tomorrow night? Please!" I begged! Mom answered, "We'll see silly, if it doesn't give you nightmares tonight."

"You know Rachel, that same year started off with a car hitting me while I was riding my bike. I spent my 10th birthday in the hospital. That was one memorable year!" I was blown away! My mom was almost killed by a car then almost eaten up by a shark! This most certainly will out shine all the other school playground stories!

Mom announced, "Time to go to sleep." We said our prayer. Before Mom left my room, I told her, "Thanks for the story." She said back, "You're welcome. I know an even a scarier true story that I'll tell you soon." I screamed out, "Yea!" The lights went out. I stayed relaxed on my back, wondering what the next story would be about. I thanked God for blessing me with such a wonderful mom who told good and true scary stories. I also asked God to help Mom fight my evil dad in court. I fell asleep without dreaming about sharks.

Friday was here. Back to evil Dad's! I was scared, really scared. I knew he was going to rip me apart over Mom and court. All day at school, I kept telling myself to be strong. At lunch, I confided in two of my closest friends about my dad. I could tell they were worried about me. When school let out, one of my friends told me to call the police if I got scared. She must have worried about me all day. I got in the car, and my two closest friends waved at me with fear in their eyes. Mom asked, "Is everything okay with the girls? Rachel, are you okay? Did you get into a fight or something?" I said, "Everything is fine." Mom stared at me. I don't think she believed me, at all, so she dropped the subject.

We grabbed a hamburger on the way home. She knew how much I hated Sissy's cooking. We talked about school. When we got home, I got my stuff ready for the horrible weekend. I decided to leave my drawing. I didn't want Mr. Evil finding it, because he might throw it away. Every time he got extremely mad, he took it out on me. One time, I showed him a ring I got. He ripped it off my finger and threw it in the toilet. That was how mean he was to me. I couldn't take a chance on him ruining my drawing. I hid it under my mattress. It was much safer at home.

Before I went downstairs, I text my dad to please stop hurting me and to just be nice. I put my cell phone back in my backpack and carried everything downstairs. I didn't tell Mom I text Dad. It was between him and me. I wanted to give him a chance to be nice to me. Mom was sitting in the den. I dumped my stuff by the door. As I walked towards her, she commented on the clothes I had on. Mom said that I looked nice.

I was wearing my black leggings and my favorite long-sleeved red sweater top. It was lightweight and comfy. I had on my short black boots. I thought I looked pretty good too. That was a first. I hadn't felt good about myself in a long, long time. I sat down beside her. Mom put her arms around me. She told me to be strong and to call the police, if anything bad happened. She added that if I couldn't get to my phone to just run to a neighbor's house and they would call the police for me. I said that I would, I even promised. It was 6:00 pm sharp.

Here came *the honks*. Mom hugged me and whispered, "God is with you." She opened the door and walked me to the car. I think she wanted to show Dad she wasn't scared of him. It made me feel better. She knocked with her knuckles, on Sissy's window. Sissy rolled it down. Mom leaned over and told the two of them, "Don't you two dare take this child's phone away from her ever again. You got that. I'll have you back in court sooner than you want." Mom stood back up and kissed me on the forehead. She really told them off.

As we were driving away, Mom signed "I Love You". I rolled the window down and signed back. I watched her until we were out of sight. The drive to Dad's was awkwardly quiet! He said nothing to me. Sissy never even said hello. Whenever my crazy dad was extra quiet, something was definitely not right. I would always get a nervous, creepy-feeling inside all because of, HIM! Or, maybe just maybe, this time he was behaving and was going to be nice to me! It would be a first! It didn't matter, because I was still going to do what I told my friends at school. Then he would finally get into trouble. I just had to get through the night. "Just get through the night! Just get through the night!" I kept whispering to myself during the antsy, uncomfortable ride.

*"I wonder how much of what weighs
me down is not mine to carry?"*

Anne Frank

Chapter 27

Dad drove us to the same Chinese restaurant for dinner. We all got out. He still said nothing to me as we walked in. We sat in a curved booth. I had to sit between them. I hated feeling trapped. This guy waiter came over and took our order. Of course, Mr. Evil ordered for everyone. After he left, I looked around. The restaurant was packed. Then I looked at Dad. He had a very intimidating look on his face as he pulled out his cell phone. I saw him go to his texts. He turned to me and started screaming and cussing at the top of his lungs over what I text him earlier.

Dad screamed, "What is this "BS"?" "What?" I asked. "This!" He shoved the cell phone in my face. Then he started reading and screaming at the same time saying, "Your mother put you up to this. Is that right?" I said back, "No! I just want you to be nice to me and stop hurting me." I started crying. He threatened, "If you ever text me any of this "GD" "BS" again, I will take your mother back to court and you will be living with me. How would you like that, missy?"

I screamed out, "No, I love my mom. I want to live with just her!" He was so obnoxiously loud people were staring with concern. He didn't care. The humiliation continued, "I'm sick and tired of you and your "B" mother's lies! It stops now! You got that!" At this time the manager walked over to ask if everything was okay. Couldn't he tell? Mr. Evil said that everything was NOW under control. He then handed him a twenty. Oh my goodness! He gave that man some money, I guess so he wouldn't call the police. All I could think to myself was, "Wait until Mom finds out about this! I will thoroughly enjoy breaking the news to her!"

The food arrived. I didn't eat one thing. I was too sick to my stomach. Besides, I got food poisoning here twice in two months. I sat there in disbelief and disgust staring at all the people around us, including Miss Sissy, who did nothing to help me. They all allowed a child to be abused in public. Was that what our world had come to? Sad! Very sad!

I watched as my evil dad shoved the food into his mouth. He barked at me to eat something. I just glared at him. I had an apple in my backpack. I would eat it when we got to the new house. The "New" house! Wonder if it was going to be "Hell" there too!

Mr. Evil and Sissy finished eating. I never took my eyes off "The Girlfriend" during the entire meal. She could have told my dad to stop cussing at me. I thought to myself, "I wonder how she would feel if Dad called her daughter a "GD" "F" n brat. Knowing him, he probably already has." What a loser of a human being!

We left the restaurant and drove to the "New" house. It wasn't far from my Dad's office. I'm sure that was the main reason he bought it. Why would my dad ever want to live near my school and my friends? Answer; "Mr. Narcissist"! We pulled up to the gate. Sissy started explaining, "It's a gated community and you have a code to get in." I'm sorry but I looked at her and said, "Duh, no kidding!" She shut up.

I thought to myself, "Don't try to be nice to me. Not now! It's so fake!" Dad growled at me. I didn't remember exactly what hateful words he was using. I had learned the best way to deal with my dad was to tune him out. I got in trouble no matter what, so why not just tune him out. It became the only way I could survive. My dad always looked for some reason to punish me. Mister Control! Ugh! Now the restaurant scene joined the 'memorable' list!

We pulled into the garage. I got all my stuff, without any assistance. Dad and Sissy headed on in. I was right behind. I put my backpack down on the "homework" table. Dad escorted me to the kitchen and opened the pantry door. There was a piece of paper hanging up by a magnet. It said at the top, *The Rules*. Dad told me to memorize all of them and we would get along just fine. What was this, "Boot Camp," or just ""Hell" that moved with them from the condo!

The rules read; No shoes on carpet, Only eat over the kitchen sink, No food outside the kitchen, No touching the walls, Bedroom kept spotless, No playing on the computer unless Dad is in the room, No playing outside, No sleeping after Dad's up (when Dad's up, everyone is up), Talking to your mother only 5 minutes a day in front of Dad or Sissy, Wipe out shower, sink and bathtub immediately after use, and The photo of your 'real' mother is to stay by your bedside.

I didn't know what he meant by that last rule, so he took me upstairs to my room. There was a photo of me as a baby in my birth mother's arms and my birth father, Dad's brother, standing beside us. My hateful dad told me it was not to be removed. He said he wanted to remind me that my mom was not my real mom. Then he smarted off, "Any 'ole person can adopt a kid, but I'm your blood relative. Your mother is nothing!" I looked straight at his face and said, "So that means everyone who adopts kids are nothing? Is that what you are telling me? My mom is nothing?" He took one step back, stared at me and stormed out. I yelled at him, "She's my mom. She chose me! You're not my dad, your brother was! He loved me! You hurt me!"

I slammed my door and got on my bed. I started looking around my room. The furniture! Uuuggglyyy! It was all dark brown. It looked more like boy furniture, than girl furniture. Why did he buy me boy furniture and put mine in the guest room? I stayed on my bed, thought about the restaurant and the 'new rules'. I guess I was going to have to do what I told my friends, and do it tonight. I closed my eyes and took a nap. It was dark, when I woke up.

I looked at my phone, which by the way, I could keep now, since Mom went back to court. I noticed all the texts and missed calls from her. I opened my door. I could hear Dad and Sissy downstairs watching a movie. I'm sure it was an animated one. That was the only kind of movie my dad ever watched. What was up with that? A grown-up that only watched cartoons! I personally thought that it was very strange, but again that's just me! I quietly shut my door and went into the bathroom to call Mom. The heck with the "Insane Rules"!

Mom's phone rang only once. She started hysterically yelling, "Thank goodness you are okay." I asked, "What are you talking about?" Mom told me, "I got a call from your close friend and her father, a minister. The father and daughter told me about your plan. Your friend said you told her at school you were going to run away at 5:00 am and go somewhere and call me. Is that true?"

"Honey, do not leave that house! If you feel you are in danger, please call 911. Please, I beg you, please do not leave that house! You could be kidnapped or killed. Please! Listen to your mother! I have also been trying to call the police. They called me back and said they couldn't get through the gate. I started yelling at them about you wanting to run away, because of your dad's abuse. Please, stay put! I will take care of this when you get back. Just stay in your room and away from your dad! I will see you in two days. Promise me."

I cried, "Mom, I promise. It's just so bad with Dad. He now has all these ridiculous and impossible rules to live by." Mom told me to just go to bed and rest. She said that she would tell her attorney Monday. I felt so bad that I scared Mom. I was going to run away. I had decided several weeks ago. I was just waiting until my dad moved to the new house.

The rest of the weekend was calm. Mr. Evil said nothing to me. I wondered if the police had called him. I would ask when I got home. It was Sunday. We stopped off at Martha's to eat lunch. Yes, it was chicken! It was always chicken, awful chicken! I drank some tea. I would eat when I got home.

When Dad, Sissy and Martha finished eating, they moved to the den. They started talking rudely about Mom. I told all of them to shut up. I was sick and tired of hearing them bad mouthing her. I shouted, "My mom's a Christian! There's nothing Christian about any of you!" They stopped talking.

I walked out to the car. Sissy and Dad came out a few minutes later. Martha stood at the door and tried to say goodbye. I never turned around. I got in the backseat. We were off. There was total silence all the way to Mom's. I was so proud I stood up for her. The three of them made me sicker than the thought of eating Martha's cooked chicken.

We pulled into my driveway. I got out fast, slamming the door. My dad pulled away speeding. He didn't even wait to see if I got in okay. He was pouting! I wanted to yell at him to go watch his cartoons. I didn't get the chance. Rain E was going to be so proud of me for standing up to those heathens. I knew what heathens were.

I reached the door. Grandma let me in. She said mom would be right back. She was at the grocery store. Grandma said she was making spaghetti tonight. I went upstairs and changed out of my stinky perfumed clothes and put on some "normal-smelling" ones. I went around to the side of my bed and lifted the mattress. The drawing was still there. I heard Mom come in. She yelled up to me. I raced down, dropping off the stinky clothes in the laundry room. We hugged and hugged. She had gone to get dinner. It was spaghetti.

Mom said that she didn't want to cook tonight. She wanted to spend more time talking with me. She was so worried. I told her that I would never run away. I said that I would call 911. Mom called for Grandma. We sat down at the table and gave thanks to our Lord. Mom handed out the food. It was good to be home. I wished I could stay here all the time! Why didn't those judges understand this? Why?

After we finished, Grandma cleaned up. Mom and I went to the den. I told her what happened at the Chinese restaurant. Mom was beyond furious. She got up and called the restaurant. I heard her screaming at the manager on why they allowed a child to be abused in public. She even asked them why they didn't call the police. Mom slammed the phone down and said that she was sorry I was humiliated in public. She told me that new attorney would be hearing about the restaurant. I looked at her and said, "Thank you Mom for loving me so such."

I was tired and went up to bed. Mom said she would be up later. I took a long, hot shower, washing Dad's stinky perfume out of my hair. I mean there was already *his* perfume smell throughout the 'new' house. I put on my short set pajamas and climbed into bed. I conked out. I know Mom came in, I just didn't know when.

I woke up to Mom calling me. She said, "Get dressed for school. We're going to grab some breakfast burritos." I hurried and rushed downstairs. It was always a treat to get breakfast to go. We were out the door in no time. That day at school, I thanked my close friend for calling my mom. It was test week at school. That meant no homework all week! This coming weekend was going to be carefree, relaxing and loads of FUN!! Couldn't wait 'til Saturday!

"The art of healing comes from nature, not from the physician. Therefore the physician must start from nature, with an open mind."

Paracelsus

Chapter 28

Summer was just around the corner. Mom had already gone to court twice, in the last two months. She really liked her new attorney. She told me a final trial was in July. The social worker from the courthouse called to set up an appointment. She needed to speak to the both of us. Mom told her I would be out of school next week, then with Dad. She set it up for the first week I was back home. Mom said the lady sounded nice on the phone.

I was glad I didn't have to see that male therapist anymore. He was awful! He never cared about me. He only cared about 'dads', because he was one. This uncaring therapist had two young daughters. I often wondered how he would feel if his wife divorced him and remarried a man who abused his daughters? Something to ponder over you loser of a therapist! Hope the new lady social worker is an improvement over the last one! (Mr. C)

It was now the middle of May. School was out. Unfortunately, I had to go with my dad tomorrow for 15 days. Sissy was still supposed to be protecting me. When was the protection going to kick in? Two months had already passed and zero protection. Was she wearing earplugs during court and didn't hear the "Protective" court order or did she just lie under oath for Mr. Evil? I bet money on the second reason!

Fifteen days, twice in the summer, not to mention every other weekend, I had to be away from Mom. I dreaded every summer! Maybe it would rain during Dad's time and I would see Rain E again. I hoped so. It had been over two months. I didn't want to go another six months between visits. The first time we met was last summer. Gosh, that was a whole year ago!

The dreaded day arrived! Dad was picking me up in a few hours. Surely it wouldn't be as bad as last summer, because Mom was keeping him in line and I was getting stronger inside. Mom asked me to come into the kitchen. She told me to hold out my arms. I asked why. She held out her phone and took photos of my arms, legs, face, stomach and back, pretty much my entire body. She told me that when I came back she would recheck for bruises and markings. Smart Mom! I asked her if everything was all right. She said she was okay. She just wanted to remind me to not take any crap from Dad. She hugged me and told me to call her often. I promised I would.

Here came *the honks*. Mom hugged me as we walked to the door. She didn't want to let go, neither did I. Summer was the hardest. Too many days away from Mom! I told her to tell Grandma goodbye. I headed to the car with my stuff. When I reached the car door, I turned and we signed. I got in and we drove away. Those two in the front seat were quiet. I think Dad knew I hated leaving Mom. If he didn't by now, he was an idiot. It was just the "narcissus" in him. I had seen it more and more. It really was all about him! Sissy didn't speak either. Dad had her 'well trained'. It showed! The three of us went to eat at the same "Food Poisoning" "Non-Protecting Child" Chinese restaurant. I had tea. Too scared to eat! When we got to the house, I went straight to my bedroom. Dad popped his head in to tell me we weren't taking a vacation. I didn't ask why. I didn't care. When he left the room, I took my pillow, placed it over my mouth and screamed with joy right into it. Yea! Double Yea! No trips!!

The first week flew by. I talked to my friends all day. I called Mom every night. I played games on my IPad. I started reading one of my two required summer books. Also this summer Mom sent all the 'summer' math homework to be done on Dad's time. She told him, she had done it the last three years. It was his turn! It was 4000 math problems, 40 pages with 100 problems on each page. It kept me busy.

The second week seemed to just drag on! Dad yelled at me every night to get the math done. He screamed so much I stayed stressed out. No one can listen to him day in and day out, without getting stressed. His mother was in her late seventies, but she looked like she was a hundred years old. Sissy looked almost dead! I was sure it was because she was with my constant-irritating wacko dad 24/7.

Four days before coming home, my psoriasis broke out. I had been telling my dad for two days my skin was itching badly! I told him

I needed my medicine from home. He ignored me. The day before going home, I woke up and the psoriasis had spread all over my body and was especially bad on my face. I had been itching so much puss was oozing out. I showed it to Sissy. She went and got Dad. He finally took me to one of those walk-in clinics.

The lady doctor came in. She confirmed it was psoriasis. It was such a bad outbreak it had become infected. I was given three different antibiotics, plus a topical. Dad sent Mom a text and photo of my arm from the doctor's office. How stupid was he? Answer; Very! He sent my "Never-Backed-Down" Mom "hard" evidence! Maybe because he knew what was coming! I think he was scared! He needed to be. I sat on the table, while the nice doctor went over the medication with my worthless dad.

Then, she came over to me and took a closer look at my left eye. The doctor was worried because the infection had spread near the corner. She turned and asked my dad why he waited so long to seek medical help. By the look on her face I believed she really wanted to rephrase it to; "Why didn't you get your sorry "A" to the doctor sooner so your daughter wouldn't be in pain? You worthless piece of cow dooky!"

My insensitive dad actually told the doctor that it didn't look that bad. I watched her facial expression again. I knew what she was thinking, because I was thinking it too, "What a self-centered buf-foon!" She rolled her eyes at Dad then wrote something on my chart. Maybe the doctor wrote that my dad was a 'bad' dad, plus everything unladylike she was thinking? She WAS a to-the-point caring doctor. The last thing she firmly told me was to not rub my eyes because it could become dangerous.

We left and went to get my meds. I was going home tomorrow. Mom was going to let Dad have it and good! Back at the house, I packed. I was extra excited, because in three days I was going to the beach with Mom. I was embarrassed over my nasty skin infection. It was Dad's fault! I blamed him 100%! I would have to wear long sleeves this time, for another reason. I couldn't hide my injured skin from Mom this time especially when she had the photo nervous Dad had sent. I decided to take a nice, long, warm bath. After I got out, I applied the medicine on my infected areas. I put on a long-sleeved T-shirt and a pair of jogging shorts. I climbed in bed and text Mom goodnight.

Laying there staring at the ceiling, I was thinking about how every time I was with my dad, something really bad happened to me. Then I thought about Rain E and all she had made me aware of in my life. I had changed a lot in the last year. I was now speaking up for myself. I was learning to love myself again. Mom would always love me, but it was nice to know how much God loved me too. He must. He sent Rain E.

She just "had" to live up there with Him. I was not quite sure, not yet. I prayed to God and asked Him if I could see Rain E next month, during my second, long, forced visit with Dad. I closed my eyes, dreaming about the ocean. Mom and I hadn't been on a real trip in two years. I could hardly wait! I was smiling when I fell asleep.

"Our prime purpose in this life is to help others. And if you can't help them, at least don't hurt them."

Dalai Lama

Chapter 29

My ears woke up, without abruptly alarming my brain. That rarely happened at my Dad's. The house was completely silent. No screaming to get my ass out of bed. Mr. Evil must have been at work. I jumped out of bed and barely opened the door. It was quiet downstairs. It was time to move into action! I grabbed my phone and shoved it in my short's pocket. I quietly tiptoed out the bedroom door. Standing at the top stairs, I saw Sissy walk into the kitchen. I went on down. She politely asked if I was hungry. I just grunted and cleared my throat. I got a glass of milk and, of course drank it over the sink. I washed my glass, dried it and put it away. I made sure the milk was back in the correct position in the drill Sergeant's refrigerator. Sissy walked out. Good! The coast was clear.

I hurried over to the pantry and opened the door to look at "The Rules". I didn't get a chance until now to get a photo. I quickly pulled out my cell phone and took a snap shot. Mom had to see this! She told me to get evidence, lots of hard evidence for court. I didn't know if the list of "The Rules" was hard evidence, but it was crazy evidence. I put the phone back in my pocket and reached for a banana. I slipped it under my shirt and walked out. I passed Sissy in the den, turned the corner and rushed upstairs.

When I got to my room, I closed the door and went straight over to my window. I cracked it open about a foot and ate my banana in peace. The air would help keep the banana smell out of my room. Certainly didn't want to get caught breaking one of the military rules! Wouldn't want the drill Sergeant to throw me in the brig!

I wrapped the peel in toilet paper and zipped it up in my backpack. The things I had to do to protect myself. Pretty sad, pretty crazy! The rest of the day I just read. I heard Dad come in. He yelled at me to get my ass ready to go. Yea! I was going home! I made it through the first grueling fifteen-day boot camp! I changed out of my sleep clothes into jeans and a long sleeved T-shirt. There was puss still coming out of the sores. I was glad to be getting home. Now a "real" mom would be taking care of me. She was going to flip out seeing my infected skin. I hurried down. We got in the car. Not much said driving home! What could Dad say? He was a lousy dad, but would never see it. I would always see it, in my skin and soon to be scars. Thanks a lot Dad!

We pulled in the driveway. I got out without speaking. Dad said nothing either. I think he knew what was coming. I walked to the front door. Grandma let me in. She said Mom was in the study. I said to myself, "Well here it goes, might as well get it over with!" I sat my stuff by the stairs and went straight to the office. Mom's back was to me. I announced, "I'm home Mom." Mom swiveled around in the computer chair and said, "My sweet is home. . . . . . Oh dear Lord, that son of. . . . . ." She stopped herself and came right up to me. "Rachel your face." I jumped in, "I know Mom, I know, but I tried to get Dad to take me to the doctor when it first broke out."

She took her hand and turned my face gently back and forth. Then she saw my legs. Mom asked me if there were any marks on my arms. I rolled up my sleeves. Mom literally died. She said it again, "That son of a "B" deadbeat dad!" She put her hand over her mouth and then formed it into a shaking fist. Mom was beside herself. She rarely ever cussed only when it concerned the "deadbeat", as Mom referred to him. I stood there while she examined my entire body. "I'll be right back," Mom firmly stated. She stormed off to her room. I followed. I knew "WHOM" she was calling!

When Mom got to her bedroom, she slammed the door hard! I stayed right outside. I wanted to hear her rip Dad apart. She did! Even with the door closed, I could still hear some of what was being said. "Pick up the phone you sorry excuse for a dad. I need to speak to you immediately!" Mom screamed. "Pick up the phone!" There was silence. Then I heard her voice again. "You can't lie your way out of this one! Call me ASAP!!" There was silence again, but this time longer.

I went to the kitchen and got something to eat. A few minutes later Mom walked in. She looked at me, "I am so sorry if you heard that." I told her, "It's okay. I know you just care about me." Mom asked me why I didn't come by and get my medicated cream. I told her the truth that Dad wouldn't bring me. That WAS the honest truth. Mom knew I was telling the truth this time. Why would I want to be miserable for days? She said we needed to see my doctor, before leaving for Florida.

While I was still in the kitchen, Mom grabbed her cell phone and took several photos of my infection. I knew she wanted it for evidence. I asked if I would have scars. Mom painfully answered, "Probably." I sat back down and finished my tuna fish sandwich. It was my favorite and Mom knew it! She sat down by me and gently stroked my arm. She was sad for me, being a preteen, knowing there would be scars left from the infection.

Scars because of my uncaring, inconsiderate dad! I already had scars inside, because of him, now I had ones on the outside to match. Dad never truly wanted me around. After all this time, I was nothing but a bother to him. Over time, I would probably forget the details of the years I endured with my dad, but I would never forget this. I would have a constant reminder whenever I looked at my skin. My dad wouldn't be permanently in my life, but my scars would be! I now understood 100% why my mom fought for me for so long and would always. She didn't want me to be scarred, but now I am, in more ways than one!

We talked a bit more. I headed up to my room with all my stuff to unpack. I passed by Grandma coming down the stairs. She just smiled at me and walked on by. She was definitely going to talk with Mom. I knew she heard everything. Even though Grandma was hard of hearing, Mom was extra loud and rightfully so. I got to my room and closed my door.

I dropped everything on the floor and just cried. I looked at my arms and cried some more. How could my dad do this to me? Did he hate me that much? I told him not to hurt me anymore and he still did. Is he really that uncaring and evil? I plopped down on my bed. I was pooped! I always had to rest after returning from "Hell". I fell asleep.

When I woke up it, my phone read 9:00 pm. I got up to go get ready for bed. That was funny! I took a shower, not too hot, because of my blisters. I toweled dry, carefully patting the scars. I didn't want them to start bleeding. I finished up in the bathroom and put on my rainbow pajamas. I wanted to have good dreams tonight and the pajamas would help.

I was climbing into bed when Mom knocked on my door. "Come on in," I hollered. Mom said she wanted to make sure I was all right. We talked for a while, mostly about Florida. We said our prayer. This time at the end, Mom asked God to heal my skin, and leave no scars. I loved her! She said, "Now get some rest, my love. I called and we're seeing the doctor tomorrow." I perked up, "I will Mommy, night!" "Night," Mom whispered. She left and turned the lights out. Once again, it felt good calling her "Mommy".

I waited a bit then reached inside the mattress for my drawing. Yep, It was still there! I would work on it tomorrow. As I was climbing back into bed, I noticed the stars were out. A lot of stars! I kept looking at them, when out of nowhere, three shooting stars streaked by. Wow! I had seen one before, but never three at the same time. I kept staring at the sky. I bet it was Rain E, Stormy and Bolt just letting me know that they were nearby! I got under my comforter and said, "Goodnight Rain E, Stormy, Bolt. Miss you!" One last heavy breath and a big yawn, and I fell asleep.

The next morning, the bright sun decided it was time to wake me up. Mom called up to tell me to get ready for the doctor's appointment. I walked out to the top of the stairs and called out, "Be down in ten minutes." I went and changed clothes. I put on some jean shorts and a sleeveless T-shirt. It would be easier for the doctor to examine me. I finished getting ready then doctored my infection.

When I got to the stairs, I held on to the rail and I jumped down, two steps at a time, until reaching the floor. That was fun! I saw my thongs by the front door. "Better make sure I pack those for Florida!" I reminded myself. I went to the kitchen for some milk. I heard Mom yell out not to eat much. She said we would eat breakfast after the appointment. Yea! I knew that meant pancakes! Mom was ready and so was I. On the way, she just told me to tell the doctor exactly when the rash started, so the doctor could document it.

We were exactly on time. The regular nurse took us to a room. Within minutes, my wonderful lady doctor walked in. "How are you, Miss Rachel?" she politely asked. I stuck my arms out. She came closer to me. Dr. H said, "It's psoriasis and a nasty one at that! It's also infected." Mom thought it might have been poison oak because of the oozing puss. The doctor asked Mom why she had let it get so bad, because it could have been prevented. Mom glanced at me and Dr. H saw it. Mom nodded for me to tell her, and I did just that. Dr. H got an ear full. She was appalled and mad. I watched her do a lot of writing on her laptop, just like the other lady doctor.

She finished typing then took a closer look at my left eye. She was also concerned like the first lady doctor. Once again, I was given strict instructions not to touch my eyes until the infection cleared up. I told Dr. H we were going to the beach. She said, "The salt water will be good for your skin and help speed up the healing." She patted my hand and gave me an encouraging smile. I told her that Mom had said the same about the salt water. I asked, "Will I have scars?" Dr. H tenderly answered, "Yes, I'm sorry, but yes. I want you to see a dermatologist when you return."

Mom saw my expression after the doctor's grim news. I saw a sad, but angry look in Mom's eyes, and I knew why. I knew whom the anger was directed towards, because I was feeling the exact same way. This was it! I was feeling hate in my heart. I knew I was not supposed to hate, but I couldn't help it. Mom was sad for me. I bet Rain E was going be sad for me too. I missed my friend from above. We left the doctor's office. "Time for pancakes," Mom happily expressed. She was trying her best to raise my spirits.

After eating, we did some last minute shopping. When we got home, I packed and then played games on the computer. Mom packed as well. We were ready to go! Grandma was staying home. Her job was to work on her puzzles and occasionally watch our pets. I know deep down inside she liked them, but it was really deep down inside her. I think that was the main reason Mom called to check in. The first thing she would always asked was, "Are the pets still alive?" Mom would ask questions in a humorous, but concerned way just to make sure everyone was fine.

Grandma always responded, "I think they're still alive, I haven't seen them lately, but their food disappears." Grandma was funny too! She was old and sometimes forgetful. Mom always left specific instructions for her, when she was home alone. I mean the refrigerator and kitchen counter was covered with sticky notes about the pets, the house, the lawn and the pool service. Don't get me wrong. Grandma did just fine. I think she loved it when we were gone. She liked the quiet.

Mom sliced up some green apples and cheese for me, one of my favorites. I played a little longer on some specific computer games with my friends then got ready for bed. The lights went out at 9:00 pm, because our flight was very early in the morning. I mean still dark-outside early! I was so excited about going to the beach that it was going to be a difficult night for sleeping. Wednesday morning arrived too soon. After calling for me twice to get up, Mom finally came upstairs and urgently announced, "Rachel, get up now! The cab will be here in 15 minutes." Then she left.

I tried to hurry as fast as my sleepy body could go. I took off my rainbow pajamas and shoved them into my already overstuffed luggage. A light shined from outside. The cab was here. I headed downstairs and out the door with Mom. Grandma yawned, waved goodbye and closed the front door. She was now officially on pet and house sitter duty. On the way to the airport, Mom and I hoped Grandma would wake up enough to remember there were three other warm bodies in the house needing her attention.

We were on our way to Florida! I was tired, but excited! At the airport, Mom said it was about a three-hour flight. I would definitely be sleeping the whole way. The moment we got on the plane I did just that. "Rachel, wake up. We're about to land," Mom whispered in my ear. I opened my eyes to water. It was the ocean. My face had been pressed up against the window the whole time. I stared outside until the plane landed. That was a wonderful flight, because I slept whole the way. I was refreshed! With our stuff ready to go, we were soon off the plane and headed to our next transportation, the cab. The ride wasn't too long. As soon as Mom checked us in, we went straight to the room and changed into our bathing suits.

First we went to the beach, to soak my skin. I played in the sand and water for about an hour. This hotel was so awesome! They brought you fruit on a stick for free. Mom got a glass of wine and I got a Shirley Temple with extra cherries. Mom ordered two sandwiches along with a fruit tray. When the food arrived, I decided to eat lunch with both legs under a mountain of sand. Mom joined me.

We talked and laughed and talked some more. One thing I commented on, "You know Mom, on all our vacations, Dad never went to the beach or pool with us, ever. Not even once. Why was that?" Mom answered, "I don't know. All he ever wanted to do was eat and steam." I stated, "Yeah! He still does. That's all we ever do on *his* vacations, eat at five-star restaurants and then he goes to steam. That's it! I love traveling with just you. You're loads of fun! I'm glad you are away from Dad. Someday I will be too."

We finished eating. I wanted to get back in the ocean. Mom wanted me to wait a little. She said if I would just sit in the water, I could go in now. So I did! I giggled and asked, "You coming in too?" She said, "I'll sit by you and let the water splash on me, but that's it!" I wondered if Mom would ever again chance going back into the shark-infested ocean? We stayed at the beach until the sun left us then moved to the pool, which was beautifully lighted. Mom let me swim a couple of hours. I met two sisters from Washington. One was my age. When I finally had to get out, I told them that I hoped to see them later.

Back in the room, I bathed and crashed. Mom had ordered room service, but I never woke up. She didn't care. She knew I was happy and tired. I woke up to the start of three more days of fun in the sun! It rained only one day, but not for long. That day we decided to shop. It wasn't too bad, just a light shower. Mom told me that it rained off and on in Florida all the time. It was fun shopping in the rain. Before we had to fly home, I got to swim with the sisters two more times. During the entire trip, I felt like a queen, with room service, sleeping in, swimming, and sleeping in some more. Lots of restful sleep! I sure dreaded going back to "Boot Camp".

We made it home safe and sound. Grandma and our three pets were still breathing. All were thrilled to see us, especially our pets. Grandma always fed them when Mom and I were away, but that was where she drew the line. She absolutely refused to kiss and cuddle with them. She did care about them more than she let on. I still remember how upset she was when Mom's dog died in her arms. I actually saw Grandma tear up when Mom carried him to the hall bathroom.

For the next two weeks I just played computer games, saw my best friend and shopped with Mom. The start of my final 15 days summer visit with my uncaring dad had arrived. Three summers of court-ordered forced visits with him had come and gone! Wow! The first two years I almost didn't survive. My dad constantly pinched, poked, hit, cussed at, bit, and made fun of me every time I was with him. The biting hurt the most. I still have a few faded scars from his nasty teeth. What kind of mother allowed their child to bite others? I knew that answer. A pathetic, doting, scared, wimpy mother, in other words my ex-Grandma, Martha. I have blamed her for years. She never stopped it when Dad was young, now it was such a bad habit it was way too late for him to change.

Why would any grown man bite people and animals? Yes, I said animals! Dad used to bite our dogs! Mom would scream and scream at him to stop it, demanding Dad seek help for his bad habit, but he never did. She would even call the police, but Dad would always tell them he was just "playing". It got to a point that Mom was watching our pets like a hawk the moment Dad came home.

Mom never saw Dad bite me, only the remaining marks he left behind. He was that sneaky. Mom would leave the room and Dad would bite me for no reason. She called the police on Dad, time after time. When they finally arrived, the bite mark had faded, so only a report was made. Talk about pathetic! What was wrong with those police officers! So Mom knew something drastically had to change to protect me (and even our pets), because the law enforcement wasn't. She filed for divorce never realizing more law enforcement people weren't going to help me either.

It took Mom's new lady attorney to win something in court. Two years later and finally the judge court-ordered Dad to never place his teeth on me ever again. Big deal! He has tried numerous times to bite me, but now I aggressively fight back. Pretty sad! Sissy and her family were now his new prey. Thank goodness all our pets were finally safe from "human bites", ever since Mom kicked Dad out of the house. Dad didn't care about anything the judge said. He better care about what the main "JUDGE" would say. The way Dad has chosen to live his life, I think it will be a short and to the point talk. That was my victimized opinion!

Last summer improved some, only because I met Rain E. She came into my life for a reason. That reason was because my mean dad hurt me. I needed extra help because no one was helping my mom, at least no one on earth. The ones that wanted to help never got the chance. Mom told me the teachers and doctors wanted to testify, but these two judges, especially the lady judge wouldn't let them speak. "WOULDN'T LET THEM SPEAK, SO I'M SPEAKING NOW" (in my book).

No wonder Mom felt so helpless. She kept praying and praying to God. I on the other hand decided to write God. He answered my prayer and sent Rain E. She had to have come from above. I felt a part of some kind of divinely, loving intervention every time we were together. Rain E always heard my thoughts, so I knew she would hear this one: "I hated going back to "Boot Camp"!

288

I sat on the stairs with Mom. She asked if I had packed my medicated cream. I told her that I did. She said that it looked like the ocean water helped the healing of the psoriasis. I thought so too. I had scars but they weren't as bad as we thought. How amazing! Mom planned our trip to the beach long before the psoriasis outbreak. God does work in mysterious ways!

Mom and I held hands. She squeezed mine three times. I squeezed twice. I didn't want to go! I didn't want to go! I was dreading seeing those two. I kept hoping inside I would see Rain E again. She would make all the difference in helping me get through the last, long, summer visit. Four months since our last visit, and "WHAT" a visit! The "Dove Walk", Stormy and my pet Olive! Maybe, just maybe, I would be seeing Rain E during this stay. Oh, I hoped so!

Here came *the honks*. Mom and I stood up, arm and arm. I looked up. Grandma was at the top of the stairs. She hated to see me go. I could hear it in her voice when she said goodbye. Mom walked me out. She softly whispered, "Remember 'The Armor of God'." I said, "I will." One other thing, "Remember the sand in your bathing suit bottoms!" I smiled and giggled. I hugged Mom and whispered back, "Remember the pebbles in your shoes!" Mom giggled too.

We were still holding on to each other half way to the car. I finally had to let go. Once at the car, I looked back and we signed like always, "I Love You". I got in and kept my eyes focused on Mom as the car drove away. I turned my head back and chuckled to myself, "The sand in my bathing suit bottoms!" Mom made me smile on purpose. She always tried her best to make me feel better.

Mr. Evil asked how my trip was. I boldly stated, "The best. All my trips with Mom are the best, but this one I will never forget." Mr. Evil asked in a nasty way, "Why's that?" I firmly answered, "Because I had to heal my body with the salt water, thank you very much!" He shut up and remained silent for the time being. I looked up and thought, "Did you hear that Rain E? I let him have it, just like Mom!"

I was back at "Boot Camp". On the way to my room, Dad said to change into pants. WE were eating at a "Five Star" restaurant and then going to a concert. I put on my black pants and a silver gray long sleeve top and black sandals. I didn't care if I got hot. I was too embarrassed for anyone to see my scars. I came out of my room and Mr. Evil remarked, "You're gonna burn up in that!" I just gave him the evil eye. Sissy even told him to drop it. I couldn't believe it. She told him to leave me alone. Did she actually have human feelings inside her monster body?" Neh!

When we got in the car. I asked, "What kind of concert is it?" Dad said that it was this man, (I had never heard of), performing outdoors. Whoop-T-Do! We quickly ate and headed to the "Old-Person" concert. It was warm and very humid outside. I looked around and saw only old people. My dad always took me to stuff I could care less about. A year ago I didn't know why, but now I do. Narcissist!

When we got home, Dad remarked, "What a great concert that was." I said nothing. Out of nowhere, he started in on me, "You ungrateful "F" n brat. Nothing pleases you. You're just like that "B" you live with." "Stop calling my mom a "B" when you live with a whore!" I yelled back. I couldn't believe that came out of my mouth. I even put my hand over it right after those truthful words came flying off my tongue. Maybe my mouth just needed to vomit up all the poison inside my angry body? I was tired of being hurt, tired of being cussed at, and tired of being beaten down. Mom once told me, "A dog can only be beaten for so long, before he eventually bites back." Now I know what that meant. I was that dog and I was now fighting back!!

At first Dad said nothing. I think he was in shock. Sissy stood there stunned! What could she say? She was living in sin. I called it what it was. Then I saw that look in Dad's eyes. Boy, here it came. "Get your "GD" worthless ass to your room NOW!" He was so red in the face. Then it happened!

As I walked by, Dad swung at me with his fist. Sissy screamed, "NO, STOP!" Unfortunately it was too late. The fist struck my back. I fell hard to the floor. I got up and tried to crawl away, but he kicked me in the back of my leg. Evil, wicked Dad remarked, "I should have never removed that dog leash I put on you when you were younger." Sissy pulled him back. She told me to get to my room.

I got up and raced upstairs. I made it and quickly shut the door. I was crying hysterically. I ran to my bathroom and locked the door. I was too scared to come out. I sat down on the floor, shaking. What just happened? I wanted to call Mom, but I didn't want to leave the bathroom to get my phone. I tried to pray, but was having a hard time getting the words out. My voice was cracking and gasping at the same time. All I could get out was, "Helllllllp meeeeee!" I curled up into a ball to try to sleep.

290

All of a sudden, BOOM!!!! "What was that?" I thought. It scared the 'dickens' out of me. My body jerked! Oh! Ouch! Uh, I moaned and groaned, as I pulled my sore, aching body up to a seated position. I scooted over to the door. I didn't hear any voices in my room, so I cracked it open. I looked out and saw the most heavenly sight. It was a storm!!! A loud, violent, wonderful thunderstorm!

I stuck my head out a little further. The sky was dark black except when lightning appeared. The crackling noises came again and again. The house was completely dark. I shut the bathroom door and curled back up with my towel. I called out with my tearful voice, "Rain EEE. Helllp meee, pleaseee!" The thunder came again. It was even louder than before. I reached for my hand towel and covered my ears. I closed my eyes. Thinking of Rain E, instead of loud thunder, helped me fall asleep!

*Now we see but a poor reflection as in a mirror, then
we shall see face to face. Now I know in part; then I
shall know fully even as I am fully known.*

1st Corinthians 13:12 (NIV)

Chapter 30

  "Ooh! Ouch!" I moaned. The most excruciating pain shot down my back. I woke up, still in a curled, cramped position. I desperately needed to stretch my legs. My once neatly pressed pants and top were now all twisted up. This bathroom was not the ideal place to sleep. I was able to sit on my knees. I remembered I had a pair of sweats and a school T- shirt lying over the tub. I felt around and found them and changed clothes in the dark. Next I located my sandals and put them back on. I pulled myself up, holding on to the door-knob. Weird! The doorknob felt different. It was extra-large. I didn't remember it being that big. I couldn't see because of being in the dark.

Now standing, I flipped the light switch on. Nothing! I felt around for the small lamp on the counter. It was also not working. Great! No electricity! Without making too much noise, I slowly opened the door. My creepy-feeling, dark room was a little frightening. I stepped out and blindly guided my way to the bedroom window to take a peek at the storm. I was just about there when a light went on in the hallway. I quickly squatted down behind my bed. The electricity was back on. I heard footsteps. They were getting closer. I froze. I didn't even want to look. I just wanted who ever it was to go away. The footsteps stopped. My heart started pounding. Beads of sweat were forming on my forehead. I put my hands over my mouth, because I was breathing loudly. I silently prayed, "Please, don't be Dad, Please don't be Dad, Please, don't be Dad"! I kept repeating it over and over in my head. It sounded more like a monk chant than a prayer.

The door slightly opened making an eerie, squeaking noise, then stopped. I could hear someone moving around, but no one spoke. There was a pause. Then the door suddenly closed. Whew! That was close. I wondered who it was? They didn't even turn on the light. "Ghostly" strange! I waited a few more minutes to make sure no one returned. I stretched out on the floor and closed my eyes. My pounding heart finally slowed down. As I lay there, I started thinking about the doorknob and why it was so big. Magically weird! I was still so tired. The storm was actually helping me relax. I didn't mind being on the floor. At least I was hidden.

I was almost asleep when another loud noise exploded right outside my window. I jerked it was so loud. I glanced up. Lightning lit up my room enough to see something swaying near my window. I curiously got up to check it out. It looked like a tree branch. Lightning struck again. For a brief moment I saw the big tree in the backyard. I didn't remember it being so close to the house. I decided to investigate further. I carefully opened the window. Rain was coming down. The tree branch was scratching the screen. I tried pushing it back but when I did, the screen fell off. Oh no, guess who was gonna get in trouble? ME!! I leaned out to see where it fell. No luck! Oh well I would find it tomorrow and try to put it back in place. If I couldn't, I would have to hide it under my bed. Anything, that kept Dad from screaming at me!

As I raised my head, the branch somehow managed to lodge itself in the window grooves, making it impossible to close. I tried pulling it out. It wouldn't budge. I used both hands and yanked on it. I was getting soaking wet. I yanked some more. I had to get that darn branch lose, because the rain would had eventually soaked Dad's carpet. I grabbed tighter and tried to push it away. It still wouldn't budge. As I lifted my body up trying to loosen it from another angle, I was violently slung out onto the branch. Now hanging on for dear life, I screamed, "Help me! Rain E, help me!"

My fingertips were slipping off the wet branch, one at a time. Finally the last one let go. I was free falling to my death. On the way down, I grabbed a smaller branch and was able to pull myself up. My clothes were soaked. My whole body was soaked. I sat there in the rain, thanking God that I didn't fall to my death. As I looked up to see how in heaven's name I was going to get back to my room, I saw something. I saw "her" in the distance. It was my Rain E. She yelled for me to walk on the branch towards her. I did just that. I took off, wet clothes and all. One Interesting aspect, the branch was longer than it looked. I kept slowly and carefully walking, balancing every step. I felt like an Olympic gymnast on a balance beam, minus the fancy flips. When I skillfully reached the end, the rain stopped. The sky was a clear blue. I was with Rain E again!

Standing there I recalled all my unique, even a bit dangerous, ways that connected us. I first arrived falling off my balcony, then going through a huge building clock, waking up on a fluffy cloud, falling out of bed and now carefully treading on a thick branch in my soaked clothes. It didn't matter how I reached Rain E. I REACHED Rain E. That was all that mattered!

The branch lowered me down, like an escalator to the roof of her home. I stepped off. I looked around for Rain E. She yelled out, "I'm down here." This time she didn't tell me how to get to the ground. I had to figure it out for myself. I walked to the very front of the roof and looked around. I saw an opening at the back right corner. Once again, carefully balancing, I walked across the tile roof. I made in one piece. It wasn't an opening. It was a slide. The same slide I slid down on my first visit. I called out, "Be right down." Rain E shouted, "Okay, I'm waiting." I positioned myself in the middle and with both hands I pushed off and started going fast. The slide curved to the left and then to the right. It was perfectly straight when I landed on my butt. "Plop! Ouch!" I was okay. There was a large puffy pillow waiting for me.

While I was still sitting there a pair of legs walked up. Then two hands were in my face. I grabbed them. It was Rain E's hands! Her warm hands! As she was helping me to my feet, I painfully grunted. My back and injured leg were sore. We were now face to face. I smiled big. Rain E smiled, but not as big. I could tell she was looking at my scars, but never said a word.

"Hey kiddo, I have missed your beautiful face something awful," Rain E said. A complement using the words "awful" and" beautiful" in the same sentence. That was my Rain E! "Come on my sweet, no time to waste," she added. I immediately answered, "I'm ready when you are." Then like always. I asked, "Where are we going?" Rain E simply answered, "You will see. Race you!"

Off she ran. I chased after her. We were laughing more than we were running. Finally, we ended up at the top of a familiar hill. I rested my hands on my thighs to catch my breath. "Goodness me!' I thought. "My clothes were completely dry." Rain E was right beside me. She bent over and smiled. I shook my head. Somehow Rain E dried my clothes. I guess it was when her warm hands helped me up. I was still bent over when I asked again, "Where are we headed?" "Look up," Rain E announced. I slowly raised my head and saw it. THE CAVE!! "We're going to the cave?" I asked. "Yes. It is time," Rain E mysteriously answered.

I immediately added, "You sound frightened. Any vampire bats in there?" "No bats, but there will be things of a different fear," Rain E said so seriously. I was even more confused and a bit nervous. I asked "What kind of FEAR?" Rain E only said, "I will be with you the whole time. Shall we go?" I was ready and scared at the same time. Rain E took my left hand. We cautiously walked down the hill, holding on to each other. I looked all around. We kept walking at a steady pace. What a sight! There was brand new landscape to see.

Along the way we passed by lot of small shrubs and boulder sized rocks. There were many other different sized rocks scattered about. Many were near the cave entrance. I bet they used to be part of it! I walked up to a group of rocks to really study them. They were a dingy brown color. I got my face even closer and saw unusual looking plants with clumps of flowers growing straight out of them. I knew Rain E saw me gazing at them. She had been silent going down the hill. Finally she spoke, "Those are Zamzumit Hamidbar plants. They are something else! Unique plants growing right out of the rock, requiring little to almost no space for the roots. Somehow they manage to survive. I always wondered if they would survive better, if given the chance to leave. There is not much space where they are now. Lots of time, but such limited space to flourish. Oh how they could grow if removed from the "rock"." I straighten up at looked at Rain E. She gave me an encouraging smile.

She was talking about me. I was the plant trapped inside the rock. Just like the movie *The Rock*, I was living in my own prison. I hadn't seen that movie, but I did remember seeing a movie about the prison. It was a good one. I wondered if Rain E ever saw it? I went to see "*The Rock*" on a trip to San Francisco. I was very young. I remembered riding on a ferry to get to it. It wasn't a prison anymore, just a tourist attraction since those guys escaped. Someday I will be able to escape my prison. Then someone could make a movie about my life. Rain E sure knew how to stir up my brain. Maybe that was why we met. It only took about ten minutes to reach the cave entrance.

Just before we stepped inside the cave, Rain E stopped me. She remarked that my T-shirt was on backwards. I looked down and realized she was right. At least my sweats were put on correctly. I told her

I had to change in the dark. I was too ashamed to tell her why I was in the bathroom. Rain E stunned me when she said, "You were really cramped in the bathroom, were you not?" I started to ask her how she knew that. Then I remembered she knew everything.

My clothes were dark and drab compared to what she had on. It was a red, yellow, orange, green and blue sundress. The colors were all mixed together like a tie-dyed T-shirt. It had short sleeves. There were small colored jewels, at the very bottom. I squatted to get a closer look. They were all different sizes and shapes. They sparkled! Her dress was beautiful. I wished I had a dress like that! I also wished I had changed into my rainbow pajamas. Oh well, at least I was back. Rain E also had on her sandals.

"Let's go," Rain E said. She took my hand again. The cave had a low entrance. We had to duck down and stay down for about five feet into the cave. Finally we were able to stand up straight. It was a dark and dreary usual-looking cave, not at all fitting in with Rain E's home. I asked again if there were any bats. I even told Rain E that bats were the only mammals that could fly. I learned that in my science class.

I could barely see anything. Rain E held on to my hand and guided me deeper into the cave. We stopped for a moment. Rain E looked all around. I did the same. I could sort of tell that there were black, slick looking walls. The ground was a hard-packed dirt and felt very dry. I saw a brighter part of the cave at the other end. I asked Rain E if we would be going there later. She said that we would.

We took a few more steps forward. I tripped and fell to the ground. Rain E asked, "Are you okay?" I said, "I think so." I felt around. Something was sticking up from the dirt. I told Rain E, "I think I found what I tripped over." "What is it?" She asked. "I'm not sure. The edges feel smooth." "Can you pull it out?" Rain E inquired. "I don't know, it's stuck." Rain E told me to try lifting it out. Maybe it was a treasure? Maybe that was why Rain E brought me here?

I sat down on my knees and started digging with both hands. I dug my fingers into the hard ground working all around the object. I was getting frustrated, almost angry. I started sweating. I didn't understand why Rain E wasn't helping. Kind of like the time I was stuck in the clock! She wanted me to figure it out all by myself. So I kept digging.

Finally, it was loose enough to lift out. I shouted, "Rain E, I got it!" The edges felt round and smooth. I brought it closer to my face. It was a mirror! I could kind of see the smooth edges were polished

297

quartz stones all around the outside of the glass. Rain E said, "Look in the mirror." "OK, let me dust it off first." I eagerly said. I used the bottom of my backwards T-shirt and wiped it as best I could. I raised it to my face. There was just enough light to see my reflection. I was dead silent.

"Rachel, what do you see?" I stayed quiet. As I stared deep into the mirror, one tear fell on my cheek. Rain E softly spoke again, "Rachel, tell me what you see." I shamefully spoke, "I see my bruised eye, a bite mark, psoriasis rash, no smile, along with a sad, lifeless expression. I look. . . . .I look. . . . . Oh dear God, I look dead! Now I know why my mom cried all the time. Why are you now bringing up my injuries? Why not when they happened. You never mentioned them before. Why? And why now?" Tears flooded my eyes. I couldn't stop balling. Rain E wanted me to cry.

She finally answered my questions, explaining, "It was not the right time to bring up such pain. Now is the right time." "Right time for what?" I asked. Rain E stated, "The right time to face your demons and conqueror them!" "What if I'm not ready?" I asked. Rain E told me, "I believe you are."

She stepped right up beside me and said, "Take a closer look at the mirror." I inspected every part of the front with my fingers and eyes, from the stones, to the indentions, to the glass itself. I spotted, at the very bottom, two letters RR. Then I turned it over. It was another mirror. I never noticed it before. Rain E took my left hand that was holding the mirror, and raised it to my face. "Oh my goodness gracious!" I gasped.

Rain E calmly spoke, "Tell me what you see Rachel. Tell me what you see, NOW." I burst out, "I'm smiling Rain E. I see myself smiling. I'm happy. No sad eyes. No rashes, scars or bruises, at least not on the outside." I looked at Rain E and stared deep into her eyes. She contently smiled at me. That was the moment I truly began understanding why Rain E came into my life.

I sat the mirror down on the ground and gave my special friend a hug. I held on for a long, long time! I told her, "Thank you. From this day on, I am going to stand up to my evil dad "All" of the time, not just "Some" of the time. I will not be afraid, anymore! I will never take any of his "crap" ever again!" "Bravo Rachel, Bravo!" Rain E proudly exclaimed. "You conquered another "Self"." "What's a "Self"? I know

I know, you'll tell me later." I slightly chuckled. "Time to leave this cave for good!" Rain E announced with relief.

We walked towards the bright light that would lead us out of this "One of a Kind" cave. I left the mirror in the cave, on purpose. I saw what Rain E wanted me to see and I felt a hundred times better. It was hard to look at myself, but I now knew the reason why. We briskly walked through the rest of the cave. When we reached the end, I turned back around and said out loud, "Thanks for the truth, but goodbye for GOOD!" I turned back around and Rain E nodded one time. I did the same. I would never feel the same about caves, not anymore. Though they hold on tight to secrets, they hold on tighter to the dark truth!

Rain E led me to the edge of a cliff. She suggested we sit for a while. It was peaceful outside! I was peaceful inside! I looked up at the blue sky. The few white clouds rolling by were close enough to kiss. Among the clouds I heard, "Hello Rachel!" It was Bolt. He was riding on one of those clouds. I yelled back, "Hello to you. Hey I thought I wasn't going to see you until Christmas."

As Bolt drifted away, he shouted "You will!!! I'm still coming back at Christmas. Oops! I shouldn't have said that! Better float off fast before I divulge anymore special surprises! Oops! I shouldn't said that either! Bye my beautiful earth friend." As Bolt drifted away I heard him say once more, "Oops I shouldn't have said that!" I hollered, "Bye Bolt. See you whenever!" That Bolt! He was so comical and refreshingly honest! How incredible this place was, with friends just drifting by. I told Rain E, "I love Bolt!" Rain E said, "I love him too!" I added, "I love you Rain E. Thank you for taking me into the cave."

I remembered something Mom told me about the word "Thank." I shared with Rain E, "Did you know that there is only one letter difference in the words "Thank" and "Think"? If you remove the "i" in "Think" and replace it with an "a", you would have the word "Thank". My mom thought that If people would "Thank" God each day before they "Think", this world would be a better place to live in. If my dad would "Thank" God before he "Thinks", then he might treat me better knowing God was in control, always watching and listening. Anyway, I thought you would like to know. My mom's a writer and she looks at words all day long." Rain E said, "Your mother is a wonderful writer. She is also a wonderful mother."

Rain E added, "I forgot to tell you on our last visit, how much I love your name." I proudly said, "I love my name too! Mom told me

299

that when she was young and if she was blessed to have a daughter, she would name her Rachel." Rain E interrupted, "Your mother is blessed. Just like Rachel in the Bible, your mother couldn't have children, but God provided a way. She now has her Rachel, YOU! Rachel was a beautiful woman and so are you. Your mother wanted the best for you at any cost."

"Rachel, when you are older and more wiser, I hope you remember the sacrifice your mother made for you. Your mother was ready to leave your dad for good, until you showed up. God had other plans for her. She adopted you so you WOULD have a better chance at life. She endured ten extra long and painful years trying her best to protect you. She loves you that much! I believe there is no greater love than the love between a loving parent and their child and no greater sorrow than the loss of that child."

"Always remember how much your mother loves you! Well, now that the lecture is over, are you ready to go, my dear?" "No, I don't want to leave, not yet," I pleaded. "No silly, not back to the house, to the flowers." I stood up bursting with excitement. Rain E stood up and held out her hand. We were off, her right hand holding my left.

"Believers, look up-take courage.
The angels are nearer than you think."

Billy Graham

Chapter 31

I could see them! I could see the flowers! I kicked off my sandals and
tore out running. I barged through the entrance gate and ran right
up to the flowers. These flowers were beautiful. They sort of looked
familiar. I looked back at Rain E asking, "What are these?" Her back
was to me. She was standing near where that clipboard hung. It looked
like she was writing something. I asked again, "Rain E, what are these
flowers?" She whipped around so fast that 'mysterious' clipboard fell
out of her hands. I tried to peek at the secretive writing, but Rain E was
too fast picking it up. Something must have been awfully important on
it! She turned back around, hung the clipboard back on the hook and
walked towards me.

Rain E was standing at the gate when she said, "They are Irises,
but with a fun name attached to them." I jumped in, "What? Tell me!"
"They are Yellow Flag Irises." I loved that name. It was a happy name.
I was happy and the flowers were happy. I strolled down every path,
holding both hands out barely touching them, as I passed by. There
were short ones and some very tall ones. Some of the blooms were so
wide open a few petals fell off.

Two landed on my right toes. There was some sort of guck on
them, and now it was on my toes. I didn't mind. The flower was now
a part of me. I headed back to the entrance gate. Rain E was leaning
against it, just watching me. I waved as I approached her. She waved
back. I walked out and latched the gate. Rain E said, "Let's go to the
pond and rest a while." Off we went.

I was having such a happy time. It started with the ugliness of the
cave and it ended up at the beautiful garden. I ran and even skipped,
all the way to the pond. I got there before Rain E and walked over to

sit down on our bench. I saw a new color had been added. It was blue. The bench now had five colors. I sat down on the blue part. I needed to rest for a moment. Rain E caught up with me and sat down.

I told her that I noticed the blue color. I said, "This is my fifth time to visit. The bench has five colors. What's up with that?" Rain E chuckled, "What do you think it means?" I answered, "I'm not sure yet. I'm thinking it might have something to do with the rainbow." Rain E said her two famous words, "Imagine that!" Then she asked, "What do you think the color blue represents?" I thought for a few minutes and said "Two wonderful places, Heaven and the sky." I looked at Rain E. She was glowing. My answer must have pleased her.

Then I shared with Rain E "I love wearing the color blue, because I love blue jeans. My mom told me that blue was the favorite color among people, especially men. She added that more than 50% of flags in the world contained the color blue. Blue was nature's color for the beautiful sky and water, yet it is rarely found in fruits and vegetables. I believe blue symbolizes faith." Rain E was glowing more. She then said, "Blue is also found frequently in scripture exactly 50 times, which is no coincidence. I want you to read in the Bible, Numbers 4:5,6 when you get home. Another Biblical fact, the Ark of the Covenant was covered in blue cloth."

"Rachel, this visit has been a heart-wrenching one, but you made it through. Please remember, the color blue DOES represent Heaven and faith, but it also represents righteousness, truth and wisdom. You know about Heaven, you have faith, you understand righteous, and you found truth. Wisdom will follow," I smiled. Rain E was right. I found truth in the cave.

We sat there for a while then I got up and walked over to the pond. I was staring all the way across to the other side. The light was shining so bright that I couldn't even see the fish. Trees and bushes by the pond were reflecting off the water. I kept staring at it when an angel walked up beside me. I saw an angel! I quickly looked to my side. It wasn't an angel. It was Rain E. I looked back at the water. I saw the angel again! Once more, I looked to my side and Rain E was still standing there. I was very confused at this point.

As I was glaring at the water, the angel took my right hand and held on tight. I was too nervous to look straight at her. Instead, I slightly turned my head to get a sneak peek. I was about to glance up at the angel's face when one colorful pigtail brushed across our hands. It was Rain E's pigtail. As I reached to touch it, something blocked my view.

My comforter was covering my head. I impatiently scrambled to get it off. When I finally did, Rain E and the angel were gone. I was still on the floor, right by my bed. I must have grabbed my comforter off it last night during the storm. I stretched my back across the floor, brushed my hair away from my eyes and ears and just stared up at the ceiling. There was the sound of rain in the background.

I glanced at the window. It was closed without a branch stuck in it. Wow! That was some dream, but it wasn't a dream. I just knew it! I got up and went to the window. The screen was still in place and my sandals were sitting there. I thought, "What was going on? Did Rain E repair the window? Did I just dream about the broken branch and walking across it? Crazy! Maybe it was just a dream?"

I decided to go clean up. I got out of my sweats and backwards T-shirt. I turned the T-shirt inside out with the emblem back on the front. Mom had told me over and over to pull my T-shirts and socks off correctly. I decided to pay more attention now that Rain E noticed. I was still sleepy, so I just wet a washcloth.

I wiped my face, then my body. I sat on the side of the tub and wiped my feet, top and bottom. I placed the washcloth over the tub faucet. I brushed my teeth and hair, put on my pajamas and climbed into bed. I wasn't in bed very long when I heard a drip coming from the bathroom. "I guess I didn't turn the water completely off," I said to my tired self.

I slowly dragged my aching body out of bed and went back to the bathroom. I glanced down. The water wasn't dripping from the faucet. I turned to leave, when I looked at the washcloth, still hanging in the same place. I stopped to take a closer look. The drip was coming from the very bottom corner of the washcloth. I went over to squeeze out some more water. When I grabbed it, it was almost dry and very warm. Strange!!

I hung it back over the faucet handle and just as I was about to turn and leave the room, I saw something in the tub. It was yellow looking water, trickling into the drain. I touched it with two fingers. The yellow liquid was warm, extremely warm! I gasped! First the washcloth was warm and now the yellow liquid was warm. What was going on?

Oh my! It hit me. The yellow iris! The petals that fell on my feet! I didn't even notice the stain when I was wiping them. It wasn't a dream.

I was with Rain E. She was letting me know it was real. "Thank you Rain E" I quickly prayed, then jumped back into bed. I grabbed my comforter from the floor and tossed it over me.

I closed my eyes, trying to remember every detail when I was standing at the pond. I could see Rain E and the angel, but never at the same time. That blew my mind! I knew what I saw, even though it sounded crazy. My mind went over and over it. I could hardly wait to get home. "I will have fun drawing this on my pad," was my last thought before I crashed.

"You have enemies? Good! That means you've stood up for something, sometime in your life."

Winston Churchill

Chapter 32

I woke up happy. I got to see my Rain E and the reflection of an angel. In one year, I had seen a positive change in myself, because of my wonderful friend. I honestly had to admit, the cave woke me up. Dad would never again hurt me with his fist or his mouth! I meant it this time! No more hurting me!! Rain E showed me what I had become and I hated it. Mom had truly tried to help and I would always love her for that, but having someone my own age, really grabbing my attention, helped the most. It took someone outside the family to show me things I needed to see. Rain E showed me in a way I could understand, unlike all the doctors I was forced to talk to.

I got up and headed downstairs for some breakfast. Sissy was cleaning the house, as usual. Cleaning was her whole life. Maybe she just didn't want to get screamed at. I secretly poured a glass of milk, grabbed a banana, and raced back to my room. I wasn't going to follow those ridiculous rules. I was just not gonna let Dad know it. That made it more fun.

I didn't think Sissy even noticed me flying by or she just didn't care. At least she knew what I thought of her! Dad was at work, thank goodness for that. Peace and quiet for a few hours! I finished my milk and banana. I cleaned the glass in my bathroom. I wrapped up the peel in toilet paper and hid it under my bed, along with the glass. I would put the peel in my backpack the day I go home.

I found a note pad in my desk. I made a list of the stuff I saw at Rain E's. I did some reading from my required book for school. I kept looking at the scars on my arms. It was hard not to notice, when holding a book. My uncaring dad WAS the reason for my scars. Oh well, they were now a permanent part of my body.

I stayed in my pajamas all day. No need to change clothes until the monster returned! I quickly snuck downstairs and secretly put the glass, from under my bed, back in its exact place. I rushed back upstairs without Sissy ever seeing me. That was kind of dangerously fun, especially when breaking an insane rule, and not getting caught! I read some more then rested, then read some more. I must have read a long time, because when I glanced outside my window, the day was becoming night.

I heard the garage door slam. The monster was home. I could smell him from my bed. He must have already *steamed* before arriving at his castle (house). He yelled up to me to get ready to go eat. Oh brother, that was all we ever did! All those same 'ole boring restaurants! I wish just once something exciting and mysterious would happen during one of our dinners. Seriously just once!

I got ready and headed downstairs. I would ask where we were going to dinner, but why bother it was never any place I wanted to eat. Sure enough, it was Chinese. I was quiet in the car the whole way to the restaurant. I had my phone and text Mom just to say "Hi!" She quickly answered. I missed her so much.

I could hear the two of them whispering. Dad was upset his "travel" agenda was put on hold, because as he put it, "That "B" ex kept me from traveling, because of the "BS" trial. I didn't get to go out of town!" He actually said that "He" didn't get to go out of town, not "Them"! He was something else. I snickered a little. It was funny. Poor, poor Dad didn't get his way. Chalk one up for Mom!

I knew the final trial was in a few days, because my insane dad never shut up about it. He brought it up constantly. From the moment he came into the house, to the next morning, bitching about Mom's so called lies and threats and how it was interrupting his life. I even heard him demand a horrible thing from Sissy. Dad made it clear that she had her story straight, in case they call her to the stand. I could hear her saying, "Shhh", not in front of "you know who!" You know "Who" You know who was, *ME*! Did they think I was that stupid? I wondered what story he was talking about!

In the car, they continued to whisper until we pulled up at that same "Food Poisoning", "Non-Protecting Child" Chinese restaurant. Not informing me, we walked in and there sitting at a big round table was my ex-grandma, her sister and her daughter. We all sat down. Dad immediately started yapping to his mother about the trial. All of them, I mean every single one, started calling my mom ugly, hateful names.

This old sister of Martha had the nerve to call my mom a lying, selfish, idiot mother. She said it sitting right next to me. They all started laughing. They were laughing about the one person I loved the most. Just as I was about to ask why we were at such a big table, in walked "The Boys". So now I would be listening to even more people bashing my mom.

Enough was enough! I finally looked at Martha and said, "Why are you bad mouthing what a horrible mom I have, when you killed two of your sons!" It just came out and I was glad. There was dead silence. Martha finally spoke, "I "sawee". Is my Tweetie upset? We're just having some fun." "Fun! Fun! This is fun, talking bad about the only person I love," I blurted out. They were silent again. I said it. I finally stood up to all of them. I told them off! I was sure I would pay for it later. So what else was new!

After dinner, we were walking to the car, Mr. Evil said, "You're in trouble missy." I snapped, "No, you're in trouble!" "What did you say?" He growled back." I said, "You two will be in trouble if you ever lay a hand on me again! I will call the police and then Mom." I was glad said it! I was so mad at all of them, ripping Mom apart. We got in the car. Nothing more was said. That night, I went to bed without being yelled at or threatened.

Three days flew by. It was the day of the trial. Mr. Evil and Sissy got me up early. They had to drop me off at Martha's. When I got there, I went to the back bedroom to sleep. A few hours later I got up. I could hear talking coming from the living room. It was Sissy and Martha. I guess the trial was over. That was fast. Dad must have gone to work. I walked over to the door and cracked it open about an inch.

Sissy was telling Martha what happened. All I heard was evil Dad was being court-ordered to see a child psychologist. Sissy said Dad was "spitt'in blood", whatever that meant. Maybe he bit his tongue after the trial was over and blood came gushing out? Regardless if Dad had to talk to someone new, it didn't matter. He was NEVER going to listen to anyone. He would just lie and blame everything on Mom, like always. The only thing funny, Mr. Evil would be spending money on something other than himself. Come to think of it, I bet he was "spitt'in blood". I bet Mom was happy. Someone must have changed that worthless judge's mind. I bet it was the social worker.

When I talked with the lady social worker, she seemed genuinely concerned. As a matter of fact, she was mad!! She told me how sorry she was that no one had helped me. This nice social worker, Elizabeth, was the only human who had the guts to stand up for me. I was never going to forget her. I would be home in a few days. Mom would tell me what I needed to know. For now, I was positively going to keep clear from the monster.

Sunday finally arrived! Yea!! I was going home. I made it through the last fifteen days. School was starting in August in just a few weeks. I didn't mind starting school earlier, because I got out earlier. I loved my school. This year, there would be a new Latin teacher. Surely she was going to be better than the one last year. Last year's was horrible and mean! Every kid felt the same way about her, even some parents, including Mom.

I was already to go home. Dad was ready to take me. I think he was ready to get rid of me, because I was standing up to him. I did feel great about that. I packed all my stuff, along with the now 'black' banana peel. The ride home was a quiet one. No one said a word. While Dad was pulling into my driveway, I gathered up all my stuff. The car stopped.

I was getting out when I heard my dad spout off, "Good Riddens!" Can you believe that? In a sarcastic voice I replied, "Funny, I was thinking the same thing. Later dude!" My dad never truly wanted me around. In his sick mind, he thought he was hurting Mom, but he was really hurting me. I was home, thank goodness! No more grueling long visits until next summer.

I walked straight to my door. Mom was already standing there. The moment I reached her, she blurted out, "The judge believed the social worker!" I knew it! It WAS the social worker. We hugged for several minutes. This was the first time Mom had smiled big in over three years. I dumped all my stuff by the front door. I just had to hear all about the trial. Mom and I sat in the den.

She told me that the judge made a comment that someone was lying. She said that only two people testified, the social worker and the 'good' child psychologist, Gina. Mom said that the social worker testified that Dad was a mean and hateful bully and that he better change his ways, before his daughter walked away for good. She also added that it could already be too late. "Wow!" I thought. Mom said I was also to talk to the new child psychologist. I knew she hated me having

312

to talk to another doctor but that was what the court ordered. Anyway, I was home. All my stuff was unpacked including all the food trash in my backpack. Time to just rest! No more seeing Dad until after school started!

Mom and I spent the next few weeks shopping and eating out and just having a blast. I was ready for school. I never spent any time with the new court-ordered child psychologist. I guess Dad decided not to go. Oh well! School started. I was now in the sixth grade. The first day brought an uplifting and wonderful surprise in my Latin class. Like I said, I knew there would be a new teacher. I never dreamed it would be a man.

He was so nice and funny. He liked the TV show, *The Walking Dead* so the class nicknamed him "Zombie". When Mom picked me up, I jumped in the front seat and excitedly told her about our new man teacher. She was thrilled. I think because I always felt uncomfortable around most men, I guess because my dad hurt me so much.

Mom talked with me about that very uncomfortable subject. She told me that when a dad didn't spend the right kind of quality time with their daughter, a feeling of emptiness could occur. As the daughter continued growing and maturing she could either reject the males or worse, search for unhealthy male attention, because she never received the right kind of love and attention from her own dad. I know I felt rejected. Maybe that was the reason why I was so drawn to my Latin teacher.

I was glad Mom had talked with me about boys. It was an easy subject for her, especially since she grew up in a house full of only brothers. Mom's brothers, my uncles, had always been fun and safe to be around. I think the main reason it was an easy subject to discuss, because Mom was very close to her dad. They did stuff together all the time. He taught her how to play different sports and card games. They watched old movies together. Mom said Grandpa's favorites were *Ben Hur*, *Sailor Beware* and *It's A Wonderful Life*.

The night before Grandpa died, Mom had been shopping all day with her mom, my grandma. She decided to stay the night with them. Mom and her dad (my grandpa) stayed up late and watched *Ben Hur*, not realizing it would be their last old movie together. The next day Grandpa died. Since then, every Easter she would watch *Ben Hur* alone in her bedroom. I think Grandpa joined her because Mom was always quieter, and at peace, after the movie was over. I wished I had known him. I heard nothing but wonderful, funny stories about him. If Grandpa was alive today, he would let Dad have it and good!!

Another two months went by. Mom called her attorney wanting to know why Dad wasn't seeing the child psychologist. The attorney wanted to know the answer to that question too. So she called Dad's attorney and surprisingly the very next day, Dad had an appointment. Mom won again. Mom stayed on him constantly. He couldn't get away with anything. She even reminded him that if he did anything to harm me, she would have his "A" back in court and fast! That was one of the few times I heard Mom use a bad, but appropriate word.

Dad was now in what I called his "Scared Mode". I also believe it was because I was turning twelve in a few months. I could talk with the judge, at that time. Sad! You had to wait until you turned twelve to "Talk" Like I didn't know how to talk at age ten, nine, or even eight! What was wrong with these adults? I could have told the judge at age ten what was happening to me! It was happening to me!! I wasn't going to forget!

Anyway, I loved being at my Christian school, even though it was getting harder and harder. I spent lots of time studying, even on the weekends. It cost a lot to go there, but Mom paid for it, because of the extra courses offered, like Bible and Latin and because of the *strict*, but respectful rules enforced. If you ever thought my dad would pay, think again! He hated that I was even going to a Christian school. Christians made him feel uncomfortable. Dad took God's name in vain every day, all day, and he never read the Bible. He had never stepped inside a church, since I had been alive. Not kidding, NEVER! I wished he would go though.

Well, for now, things have calmed down. I was finally seeing the new child psychologist twice a month. Thank goodness it was a woman, even though she was a very old and tired woman, who sometimes dozed off during the sessions. She screamed a lot at Dad. It wouldn't help. He would never change. I even told her that many, many times. Only one single piece of the doctor's advice that helped my nerve-racking situation, just happened to occur during one of our intense sessions, when she was fully awake. She told my narcissistic Dad to respect my privacy and property and she indicated it REAL GOOD!

From that day on my dad tried, but not by much, to respect my privacy and property. Even Mom's attorney made sure of that! Dad didn't even try to take anything away from me, like he did before when he blatantly ignored the judge's ruling on the matter, like only allowing me to talk 5 minutes on the phone to Mom in front of them. Other than that, meeting with the old lady psychologist was the biggest waste of my time. All she kept telling me to do was just try to get along. That was it!! I was supposed to get along with a wacko, a mean and nasty wacko. Was I supposed to curl up with a devilish snake? Whatever! I could see now that she was also worthless. She was too old to be helping kids. If this was the best child psychologist the court could come up with, us kids were in trouble! Give me a break!

I had to continue seeing her, until Mom dropped the case or I talked with the new "Republican" judge. That irked Dad. He was a "Democrat" and thought all Republicans were Nazis, because that was what he told me. I was confused. I thought the Nazis lived in Germany, a long time ago. I learned about them in my reading class, last year. Why was my dad calling Republicans, "Nazis"? The Nazis were terrible human beings. They treated a specific group of people horribly just because of their religion.

Was Dad saying that Republicans treated our country's people horribly? To be honest, I wasn't quite sure what a "Republican" was. I did know they were part of our government. I didn't think our government hurt or even killed a lot people, because they went to a different church. That would have been on the news. My dad was the Nazi. He treated everyone badly. Crazy, crazy stuff I listened to, when Dad would speak!

Another month passed by. Back and forth to the new doctor! She wasn't helping much. I was so tired of going. I listened to nothing but screaming. She screamed. Dad screamed. She screamed. Dad screamed more. He lied and lied, mostly about Mom. That old lady started believing my dad. I couldn't believe it! Somehow, my dad could twist his words around and make other people think 'you' were the crazy one. Mom had seen it for years and now I saw it. Mom was right. Narcissist was Dad's middle name! He had this creepy, evil way of making you feel like you were nothing and he was the "King" of nothing (Me!) There was a time I felt as small as a bug. All I ever wanted to do was crawl under a rock and never come out. Now that I was out, I was never going back under that rock. Not anymore!

Age "12" concerned my dad. He never started fights with Mom anymore, because she didn't put up with his, pardon me, "Shit!" and I wasn't going to either. My dad had made me feel scared, guilty, and ashamed of myself for years. The last three years I had seen him do it to his mom, Sissy and "The Boys". I think the only reason they put up with it was because he bought them things. Not me. Not ever!

I had been rude to Sissy. She would try to order me around, pretending to be my mom. Sissy thought she had some kind of authority over me. Wrong!! My dad would stand there and tell me to be nice to her and I would just say, "Make me!" I had become tough like Mom. I learned from observing her. When I look back I wasn't just scared of my dad, I was TERRIFIED! I was scared of dad, like the boggy man.

Three and a half years later and I realized that I was living in a horror movie. Dad got kicks out of terrorizing me! Not anymore! Now if he even tried to hurt me, I would be calling call 911, in a flash! This was what our relationship had become. Dad didn't respect me and I sincerely didn't respect him!! We just tried stay out of each other's way. Sad! Sad! Sad!

*"O, What a tangle web we weave
when first we practice to deceive!"*

Sir Walter Scott

Chapter 33

It was nearing the holidays. I had to spend Thanksgiving with Dad and his dysfunctional family. I knew that word. I learned it in reading. The teacher said it meant, "Not functioning normally, a breakdown, like in a family." She also said it was related to the word "useless". Bingo! That was the best word to describe my dad and his family. Simple and to the point, "useless"! Thanksgiving with all of them, but Christmas with Mom! The first in three years!

School let out for Thanksgiving, Friday at noon. Dad was picking me up at school because Mom was out of town. It couldn't be helped. I understood. I said our "Stair Prayers" alone, on the steps inside my school building. Dad arrived and I quickly got in the car. I didn't want anyone seeing him. We stayed at the house all week. No traveling this year! I was so glad. I hated leaving town with those two! Thanksgiving morning, Dad's mom came over to show Sissy how to cook. Mom told me once, "That's the blind leading the blind." Now I know what that meant, one bad cook trying to teach a worse cook how to bake. It was awful!

The next day, Dad, Sissy and I went Christmas shopping. Dad even asked me what I wanted for Christmas. I thought I was going to faint. It was a first. I told him all I wanted was an IPad, and please no more rocks! He got it for me! I couldn't believe it. I think the only reason was because I was turning twelve in a few weeks and he knew I would be able talk to the "Republican" judge, alone. Wasn't that sad and wonderful at the same time! My evil dad was being nice to me because he had to be, not because he wanted to be. So from now on, for the rest of my life, I would never know which it was. Well, actually I did, that was what hurt the most!

After Dad bought the IPad we went to a clothing store. I hated shopping for clothes with him because of his ridiculous rule. I was given a specific amount of time to shop. No joke!! He would start the stopwatch on his phone. If time ran out before I had picked out something, he picked it out for me and that was that! If I started whining he would just tell me to zip it. Also, I could NEVER get a new blanket. I have always loved blankets especially fleece, since I was very young. I had at least ten at my *real* home. I have been collecting them for years ever since I got my first "Hello Kitty" blanket.

Dad's Rule; If I wanted a new blanket, I had to give 2 away. I have to beg Dad's mom to buy me a new one, because that was the only way I didn't have to get rid of any. I never realized how crazy that was until I mentioned it to Mom, while shopping a couple of weeks before Thanksgiving. I thought she was going to pass out from anger. I mean she stop dead in her tracks, she was so furious and in shock. I also told her about the "clothes shopping" rule too. She looked at me and said that she was so sorry for me having to put up with such nonsense. I think she wanted to say, "CRAP", but she was too polite, so I'll say it; it was "CRAP"! You know sometimes I would forget to tell Mom everything. She said I was so desensitized. I asked her what that meant. She said I was getting used to the craziness. I think she was right.

We all finished shopping and headed back to the house. When we got there, we ate Thanksgiving leftovers. There were lots of leftovers, because the meal was awful. I "left" the leftovers again and excused myself. I was tired and wanted to take a bath and go to bed, I guess from all the nonsense shopping with Dad and Sissy. As I was going upstairs, Dad said he was going to download some movies on my IPad. I nicely said, "Thanks." In almost four years he had never offered to do anything for me. It must be because I was turning twelve. What a magical, blessed number!

I took a long hot bath. It felt great. While I was in the tub, I was thinking again about Rain E and the angel. Maybe I would get to go back at Christmas like Bolt said? I got out and finished getting ready for bed. I put on my golden nightgown and thick fluffy red socks and climbed into bed. The only light on in my room was the lamp, by my bed. I reached over to turn it off, when Dad walked in. I wished he would knock? The new doctor even told him about my privacy over and over. Oh well! Like my grandma told me "Can't teach an old dog a new trick!" Not quite sure what that meant. Mom tired to explain that people were set in their ways and didn't like change. Not quite sure what she meant. Anyway, Dad just said that he was charging the IPad and would download the movies tomorrow. Then he left, never saying goodnight to me. I turned off the lamp and fell asleep.

The week flew by fast. I was finally back home, two days before school started. Dad kept the IPad. He said I had to wait 'til Christmas to use it. I understood, even though I really wanted to play on it. It was my gift from him. It was great being back home. Mom had made some of my favorite Thanksgiving foods, like cherry coke salad and broccoli rice. Even though Thanksgiving was over, I got to have a second, wonderful, quiet and "edible" holiday dinner. What a Mom! What a cook!

Now it was back to school on Monday. I had about a month before Christmas Break. My mid-term finals were going to be harder this year, especially in Latin. We had to recite The Lord's Prayer, in "Latin". Our Latin teacher was so nice and very helpful. Mom was so glad I felt comfortable around him. I think God sent him to our school on purpose.

Where did that month go? It was already the Friday before Christmas. I had to be with Dad through Christmas morning then home with Mom. My wonderful Mom packed for me some fudge and Christmas cookies to privately enjoy. We talked a while. She was happy I was coming home for Christmas, but I think I was happier than she was. I went upstairs to get my stuff.

I got to my room and partially closed the door. I went over to look at my drawing. I hadn't been able to work on it much, because of lots of homework and little secret time. I kept notes and I still had a good memory of my visits with Rain E. I would definitely work on it when I got back home on Christmas Day. I tucked it back under safe and sound. I grabbed my winter jacket and scarf. I had on jeans and a blue sweater. I just wanted to be extra warm. It was cold outside and there was no way I was going to get sick this Christmas.

I hurried downstairs and said my goodbyes to Grandma and our pets. Mom and I sat and talked a bit. She told me how proud she was of me. She could tell I was happier and stronger inside. She even noticed I was taking better care of myself than before by the way I looked. I had my self-esteem back, at least some. I did feel better inside.

The "honks" started. We hugged and I walked out bundled up and loaded down. I reached the car and turned to Mom. We signed and waved goodbye. All the way to Dad's I just rested. He said that we were just going to the house. When we got there, he ordered pizza. That was another first. Are you ready for this, when the pizza arrived, I ate at the table for the first time, ever! He must have been up to something. He was trying to be too nice to me. Even if it was the "fake" nice it was better than the hateful screaming!

After we finished eating, Sissy cleaned up everything. Wow what was up with her? I felt like I was in the movie *Coraline* and they were the fake parents. I went on up to bed. My brain was tired from a week long of finals. I just wanted to go to sleep. I changed and washed my face. I was too tired to bathe. The minute my head hit the pillow, I was out cold.

The next few days I hung around the house. It was the night before Christmas Eve. Dad was taking a bunch of us out to eat, of course, at a "Five-Star" restaurant. I now knew that meant "very expensive". I got ready and just sat around waiting for them. Finally everybody headed to the car. Right when I got in the backseat, Dad handed me my IPad. He actually said I could play on it until we reached the restaurant. He said that he wanted to make sure the movies were working correctly. I had to give it back when we got home. He said that it had to go back under the Christmas tree. Again, I understood.

At the restaurant, Dad had the young man at the entrance valet the car. Dad, Sissy and I got out. Inside waiting, were Martha, Delilah and the goofy boyfriend Tray. We sat at a large round table. This restaurant was lovely and dark. All the tables had lighted candles. I had just finished ordering, when I remembered I had left my IPad in the car. I panicked! "Dad, I forgot my IPad. Please let me go get it," I begged. He said, "It's in valet parking and they have the keys."

I begged and begged, reminding him it could be stolen. That was all it took. It would have been money down the drain, his money. He walked me to the lobby. Dad asked the attendant if he would go get the IPad. The nice guy politely said, "Sure, wait here. I'll be back in two shakes of a lamb!" I guess that meant he would be right back after he shook a lamb! Dad told me to wait there, because he had to go to the bathroom.

While I was waiting, I saw Sissy go in the bathroom. The nice man came back with my IPad. I decided to go to the bathroom too. I walked in and went to the last stall. While I was in there, I heard Delilah walk in. She asked if Sissy was in there. Sissy answered yes and said that she would be right out. I stayed quiet as a mouse. They were talking low, almost whispering, but I could still hear them. I covered my mouth with my right hand to keep extra quiet. I didn't want them to know I was in there. They were always so secretive, and I wanted to find out why!

Delilah started first. She told her mom, "Get me that job at his office. I will be handling his checkbook." Sissy said, "I'm working on it, patience." Delilah asked, "How's the "A" treating you?" Sissy smarted off, "I can handle him. I just play the meek and controlled, beaten down girlfriend. He's losing his memory. I've already gotten him to put me on his life insurance. I finally convinced him to take that stupid woman of a mother, Martha off. What can she do with all that money, she's almost dead?"

I tightened my hand over my mouth, because my breathing wanted to come out loud. Oh my goodness gracious! Those two were plotting to steal everything away from my Dad. I didn't know whether to feel sorry for him or applaud them for what they were planning. Then Delilah said, "What about the rotten kid?" She was talking about me. Sissy said, "I can't do anything about her. I've already tried. The law says she stays in his will." Delilah asks, "What if you can get him to put you in charge of his will?" Sissy added, "That "B" ex-wife would never let that happen. She'd come after me, with everything she's got. So what if the brat gets half, there's still plenty left for us. I just keep my mouth shut and let him think he's in charge. It's working. He's already bought me a new car and I'm taking money from his wallet every week. He's not even aware I'm doing it. What a schmuck! I'll just keep letting me treat me bad. Eventually we will be on "Easy" street."

Delilah said, "Keep up the great acting and get me that job!" They walked out together. I sat there on the toilet stunned and very confused. Dad didn't live on "Easy" street. His house was on "Maple". Maybe Sissy was the one who was losing it? Boy, did I get an ear full! I would be most certainly telling Mom all this in two days. No wonder Sissy had never tried to protect me! She could have cared less. She was only with my dad for the money, just like Mom told me last year. Mom was and still is "detective" smart!

I left the bathroom and went back to the table. Delilah asked if I got my IPad. Duh! Could she not see me carrying it? Then she asked what took so long. I looked straight at her face and said, "I had to go to the bathroom!" She directly looked at her mother with fear in her eyes. I started eating my salad, the waiter had brought while the bathroom scheming was taking place. Dad had ordered a large tray of different meats. It was good. Funny, Sissy and Delilah didn't have much of an appetite. Hummm! Wonder why?

During the entire meal, everyone pretty much stayed quiet, especially those two. Dad even asked Sissy if everything was ok. I leaned in and waited for a response. She put her head down and mumbled, "I'm fine. Just have a small headache! A lot on my mind." Yeah, a lot of deceitful stuff on your mind! Like the saying goes, "Oh what a tangled web we weave, when first we practice to deceive". Mom told me that saying. It suited the present conniving situation just perfect! I suspiciously watched Sissy and Delilah all during dinner. They looked worried and very tangled up, not knowing if I overheard "The Plot". I would never tell, at least not to them! It all made sense now. Sissy WAS in it for the money, period! I wondered if "The Boys" were in on it too? After all, they were the ones who introduced Sissy to my dad. Too close-knit creepy! Now, I really didn't want to be around any of them. What if they were also planning to hurt me? Mom WOULD come after them!

"Good people do not need laws to tell them to act responsibly, while bad people will find a way around the laws."

Plato

Chapter 34

We finished eating and everyone was ready to go. We waited for the valet. Dad and Sissy said goodbye to Delilah and Mr. Goofy. Martha was riding with us. She was spending the night to get an early start on the Christmas Eve dinner. There was not enough time in the night to get the kind of early start she needed. Sissy said that she didn't need to spend the night. She would come by in the morning to get her, but Dad insisted Martha stay.

I was kind of glad she was staying in the guest room next to mine. I felt a little safer having her there now that I knew all about "The Plot". We drove a while. Dad commented on how quiet I was at dinner. Martha agreed. Sissy said nothing. I said that I was a little sick to my stomach. I was and just needed a good night's rest.

When we got to the house, I hurried upstairs. I went to the bathroom and locked the door. "What am I gonna do, what am I gonna do?" I kept ranting. Then I prayed, "Dear Lord, help me with this problem weighing heavy on my brain. I'm a little scared. Help me make it home to Mom. In Jesus name, Amen." After praying, and took a bath.

I was getting out of the tub, when I heard a noise coming from the hallway. I quickly put my underwear on. I cracked open the door. There was a lot commotion going on. I patiently waited. The noise stopped. I grabbed my blue flannel pajamas and dove into bed. I got under my comforter and slipped them on. My head curiously peeked out. I lay there a little frightened, well more than a little, and looked over at the door.

All the lights were out. Everybody must have gone to bed. For some reason I kept watching. A moment later, a light came on outside my door. Then I heard footsteps. I started shaking. I was scared! Was it

Sissy? Was she coming to ask me if I heard anything in the restaurant bathroom? Was she coming to kill me? She wanted to get rid of Dad and now maybe me. I kept whispering, "Please don't come in, whoever it is. Please don't come in."

Then it happened. I could see some sort of shadow under my door. There was a pause. My heart started beating fast. I had to cover my mouth, I was breathing so loud. The doorknob turned. I froze! Then the door slowly opened just a little. I heard a voice. It was Martha. My door quickly shut. Martha started talking to Sissy. My door opened again, enough for the person to look in. I stayed completely still. It was Martha again. Whew! Thank goodness! She said goodnight and closed the door. I said goodnight to her. I hurried and put my desk chair under the doorknob and jumped back into bed. This was one time I wished I had a lock on my door. The chair would do the job! I learned it from Mom. The lights went out. I watched the door, until I fell asleep.

I woke up earlier than usual, because of last night. I nervously glanced at the door. The chair was still in place. This would become my door lock from now on. I got up, went to the bathroom and got ready for my Christmas Eve with the deceitful, dysfunctional family. What else was going to happen before I made it home tomorrow?

I changed into my sweats and the school T-shirt that I had worn backwards on my last visit with Rain E. I was just about to slip it over my head when I noticed on the front was a cross and a rainbow. Oh my gracious! I bet Rain E knew this! That was why she made such a point to tell me that I had it on backwards? I decided to wear the T-shirt all day, so I would feel closer to heaven, where I now believed Rain E lived. I grabbed a pair of my fleece socks. They were green and white striped. Kind of Christmassy! No shoes, it was one of those absurd "Rules". I had to follow them when Dad was around.

I headed downstairs. There was a lot of commotion going on in the kitchen. Dad was growling at Martha. I stayed quiet. He rushed by me, saying, "I have to go to the "GD" grocery store. That dumb "F" brain-dead of a mother forgot the corn bread mix for the stuffing. Only my mother, the "moron", would do that." He stormed out mad! I went over to the window to watch him pull away. Martha apologized for his behavior. I just looked at her and said, "Why are you apologizing to me? You should be apologizing to God for raising a monster." Wow! It just came out.

I walked back upstairs to Dad's office. I wanted to play *Minecraft* on his computer before he got back. I had just sat down in the swivel chair ready to turn it on, when I glanced to my left. I scooted over there. Sitting right on top of some folders was a check with lots of zeros on it. It caught my eye because of "who's" name was on it. It was made out to that judge Mom stood before all those times, fighting with Dad. I recognized the last name, because Dad constantly yapped about how he whipped Mom's ass in front of him in court.

Why did Dad whip Mom in court with the judge watching? Why didn't the judge stop it? I didn't know you had to pay the judge when you went to court. Maybe that was why Mom lost all the time! She forgot to pay him. It was now too late because that judge retired this past summer. I would still tell her about it, when I get home tomorrow. I put the check back exactly where I found it, I mean exactly! I didn't feel like playing on the computer anymore. I was nauseous. Instead, I went to my room and lied down.

I was almost asleep, when Mr. Evil barged in. "Did you go into my office," he barked. "You left the "GD" light on. I guess you don't mind burning up my money, since YOU don't pay the bills! Did you forget the "Rules"?" I tried to apologize, but I couldn't get a word in, as usual. I just knew what was coming next. The "check". He never brought it up, thank goodness!

He stormed out saying, "Hurry up and get your lazy ass downstairs and help the two morons with the dinner." Mr. Evil was downstairs, when he screamed, "I'm going to "steam". I want everything ready when I get back." I stayed on my bed for a few more minutes. I was thinking about what crazy Dad said, "Why would I want to burn money? Who would do that? Maybe Sissy was right. Dad WAS losing it!"

I got up and went to the kitchen to see if I was needed. Martha said that everything was under control. A couple of hours past. Dad was back. Dinner was ready. We ate. Well they ate! I could not eat any more bad tasting food. It reminded me of another saying from that funny lady Phyllis Diller. She joked, "The vet said because of my cooking, our cat has only three lives left". So funny! Mostly so true about Martha's cooking! After they ate, we opened presents. I got my IPad back for good, and some clothes. (Remember the "stopwatch" shopping?) I loved my new IPad the best! Everyone was sitting in the den, talking about different, boring adult stuff.

I got up and went to my room, with my new IPad. Sissy said good-night. She was strangely pleasant to me all evening. It was creepy! I would still place the chair under the doorknob tonight, after every light went off in the house. I took a quick shower and brushed my teeth and hair. I put on my sweat shorts and a different school T-shirt.

I was about to climbed in bed, when Dad walked in. He said, "You better remember I bought you that expensive IPad." I said, "Why would I forget." He continued, "Your ass is mine and don't you forget it. As long as I buy you expensive things, I'm in control. You got that! And another thing, don't you ever go into my office again without asking, unless you want the belt. Now get to sleep. I have to get up early to get you back to that "B" mother of yours." He stormed out, flipping the lights off.

I sat on my bed thinking, "What's wrong with him? He is so hot and cold. Gosh, I wish I could leave him right now, forever. I see it with my own eyes. He IS crazy! I wish now he hadn't bought the IPad. Mom was right. She warned me never to except expensive gifts from Dad. She told me that they come with a hefty price. I never knew exactly what that meant, until now." I had witnessed for over three years, Dad lavishing his mom, Sissy and "The Boys" with expensive gifts. Then he treated them like dirt, and they let him. I said it before "I will never become them!" I grabbed my chair and shut the door. I positioned it back under the doorknob. Maybe now I could get some rest!

Christmas morning arrived. I woke up thinking about the last few crazy days. I was going home in a few hours and getting out of this nut house, at least for a while. I thought I might have seen Rain E, but it didn't rain, but still I had hoped. Bolt said he was going to see me at Christmas and it was Christmas! Rain E always came when I was at Dad's. Oh well! I guess it was not going to happen. At least I will be with Mom and Grandma.

Everything was packed and in my arms, as I carefully walked downstairs. I sat my stuff by the den sofa and walked into the kitchen. Sissy walked in behind me. I was getting a bottle of water out of the refrigerator, when Dad came up behind me and pinched my left arm, hard. I screamed out, "Ouch! That hurt!" He just laughed, like the devil.

Then he had the nerve to grabbed the same arm and bite it. I mean he clamped his teeth down on me like some kind of wild animal and I was his prey. I jerked my arm back. He bit me so hard it bled. "Look what you did, that hurt!" I angrily screamed. I went over to the sink to clean the bite mark. I scrubbed it with soap, and dried it with my shirt. I turned around and screamed, "You're not supposed to bite me anymore. The court said so!" He gave me an evil look and said, "I don't give a damn what the law says, I'm the law. And while we're on that subject, I'm not seeing that child psychologist anymore, and neither are you. You think I'm going to let you continue telling more lies to someone new, then you must have rocks in your head."

I was so mad and upset. I tuned to Sissy, "Did you see what he just did?" Sissy didn't even answer me. Oh yeah, I forgot, her mind was on "plotting" and "stealing", nothing else! Dad poured a cup of coffee Sissy had made and sat at the table as though nothing had happened. I went and sat in the den. I was still shaking mad! I stared at my bruised arm. I grabbed my school jacket and put in on. I wasn't about to show it to Mom. It would ruin our long-overdue Christmas together. I wondered if that's why Dad bit me. He wanted to hurt Mom. He was that mean!

Sitting there, I held back the tears. I wasn't about to let Mr. Evil see me cry. He wanted me to be scared of him. I thought I wouldn't have to call him that name anymore. Guess I was wrong! This had been a bad, bad week! I wanted to be home worse than ever and be away from this loony bin. Sometimes, I felt like I was going to explode. Like I said before, my dad was hot and cold. One day he would be fairly decent and leave me alone, the next day he would be a screaming mad man, who looked for ways to hurt me. It was about to drive me insane. How much longer would I have to endure? I finally grasped why my mom divorced him. My dad was CRAZY! CRAZY! CRAZY!

Finally Mr. Crazy was ready to take me home. I gathered all my stuff. When I picked up my backpack, pain shot through my left arm. I kept myself from screaming. I headed to the garage and calmly sat down in the backseat. I stayed completely quiet. Dad and Sissy talked a little to each other. We pulled up in my driveway. Dad reminded me, once again, who bought the IPad. I got out and slammed the car door with my foot. It was Christmas Day and my mean dad hurt me, again. I walked to my front door, never looking back. I was home. That was all that mattered!

"To travel is to take a journey into yourself."

Danny Kaye.

Chapter 35

The front door opened. Mom was standing there waiting for a hug. She seemed down. Funny, she could tell I was upset. She always knew. Mom even asked me if everything was okay. I said that I was fine, just worn out. I was glad to be home. I felt safe. I would never truly feel safe again, at Dad's, after overhearing "The Plot". We walked to the bottom of the stairs, still hugging. I kept my arm covered. I wasn't about to bring up the bite. I would never ruin my Christmas with Mom and let Dad win. The bite incident could wait until after Christmas. There would be plenty of days to talk. We hugged and hugged. "I'm so glad you're home." Mom said smiling. I said, "Me too!"

I raced upstairs to change out of my stinky, perfumed clothes and boots. Mom would be washing all my laundry twice. I walked into my room. Mom had lying across my bed, a cool-looking Christmas long-sleeved T-shirt and black leggings. I wanted to cry it was so touching. So I did. I sat on my bed crying for at least five minutes. I had tears of joy being home with Mom and tears of relief being away from Dad. Tears were able to pour out of me both ways, at the same time! Tears of joy and tears of sadness!

I changed into my new outfit. I walked into my bathroom to brush my hair. Sitting on the counter was a beautiful Poinsettia. It was a soft cream color with sparkles all over it. There was a note on the stick in the pot. I pulled it out and read it. It said, "Merry Christmas my Love! We are finally together on this special day. Jesus is here in this home and now so are you!! I love you. Mom! PS: Hurry down, there are gobs of presents waiting for you to open!!" The note was so touching that tears refilled my eyes. Mom handmade it just for me! All over the card were different colored and sizes of drawn hearts, along with a Christmas tree and presents. I still have it to this day. I kept all my special notes in a secret box in my closet. All were from Mom!

I took the note and went and sat on my bed. I read it again. Tears were now falling from my eyes. All I could think about was how much she loved me. My dad had never done anything like this. Mom always made me feel so special. I dried my eyes. I went and brushed my hair. I looked at the poinsettia one more time and then up at the mirror. I stared at my face. Thoughts were racing in my head about how wonderful and kind my mom was and how rotten and evil my dad was. How did my mom stay with him for so long? Why did Dad hurt her so much? I guess I would never really understand the answer to either question.

I heard, "Rachel, hurry up dear," Mom called out. "On my way in five!" I shouted. I saw my slippers by the bed and put them on. I grabbed my stinky clothes and flew downstairs. I went to the utility and dumped them in the laundry basket. Walking through the kitchen, I saw Grandma and her best friend. I had forgotten she was spending Christmas with us. They were drinking orange juice in some kind of skinny wine glass. I think it was orange juice. They were sure laughing a lot. It was good to hear laughter in a home, instead of screaming.

Mom poured some coffee into a Christmas mug. I got out the orange juice from the refrigerator. I asked, "Can I have mine in a skinny wine glass too?" Mom said, "Sure. It's called a champagne flute." "Do Grandma and Sandra have champagne mixed in with their orange juice?" I curiously asked. Mom answered, "Yes, it's called a mimosa." I asked, "Why is the glass so skinny?" Mom replied "It has to do with the champagne itself. It's a grown-up subject." "Tell me, please. I've been in a bar and seen people drink," I stated. Mom nodded and pointed out, "That you have."

Mom explained, "There's carbonation in champagne and the shape of this glass helps it disappear faster than a standard wine glass. Also, it has a long stem to hold on to, without affecting the temperature of the drink." I still didn't quite get it, but at least Mom educated me. She knew interesting facts about a lot of different things. She never told me anything that I shouldn't know at my age, unlike Dad.

It was time to open presents. We all sat in the den. I got to hand out them out. Christmas time was fun with Mom, because of "The Twelve Days of Christmas." I briefly mentioned it earlier in the book. In more detail, starting on December 13, I would get to open only one gift each

334

day leading up to Christmas Eve. The presents had the numbers 1-12 on them so not to be confused with the others. They would be fun inexpensive gifts, like a special can of hot chocolate or a Beanie Boo, stuff like that. It had become a tradition. I believe Mom would still be doing it when I was in college. It had become a part of my happy memories tucked away for safekeeping.

After we finished unwrapping all the gifts, we sat around the tree and talked. Four generations of ornaments, from Grandma's side of the family, were hanging on our tree. Mom said that some were from the late 1800's to early 1900's. Grandma said that back then, the ornaments were made of glass. I asked myself, "I wonder how long people have been decorating Christmas trees? Maybe I should look in up on the computer?"

Every year on TV we have watched the lighting of the tree in Rockefeller Center in New York City. Mom told me it officially started in 1933, the year Rockefeller Plaza opened, but two years earlier, the construction workers put one up on Christmas Eve. They supposedly used tinfoil ends of the blasting caps, along with cranberries and paper garland. The Rockefeller tree now just displays an impressive forty-five thousand multi-colored lights. Mom also told me that the National Christmas tree in Washington D.C. had been lit every year since 1923.

After our interesting Christmas tree lesson, I helped Grandma and Sandra clean up. Mom started on the Christmas meal. Some of her family would be joining us. Everyone in Mom's family was a kind loving Christian. They never cussed, just laughed! I had been looking forward to this Christmas for such a long time.

The fun family arrived. It was time to eat. My uncle said the blessing. We served ourselves, buffet style. The food was fabulous! We all finished and everyone pitched in to help clean up. So different from Dad's family! Mom thanked me for helping and said I could go play. I went to the den sofa where I had left my IPad. I relaxed and played games on it. The rest of the family sat around the kitchen table, laughing and talking. It was getting dark, when everyone decided it was time to go. We all hugged and said our goodbyes.

Mom came into the den. She said she needed to talk to me. We went outside to the porch swing. We quietly sat down next to each other. Mom started first, "There's something I need to tell you. I wanted to wait until tomorrow, but I don't think I can hold back the tears, without you asking." "Mom, what is it, tell me, please?" I asked. Mom softly spoke, "Yesterday on Christmas Eve, of all days, the vet called and gave me some bad news. Our little Fluff Ball has cancer. The vet gives her maybe 4-6 weeks before it gets extremely painful. I will have to decide when it's time to let her go. As selfish as I would love to keep her alive until she goes on her own, I won't let her suffer."

Mom started crying. I started crying too. We sat there and held hands, gently swinging back and forth. I wanted to tell her all about what happened while at Dad's. I just couldn't. Not at this moment. She was already so sad. There was plenty of time, before I had to go back to him. Mom needed to take care of our dog, well, her dog. She was our last! Like Grandma mentioned when our male dog died last year, my mom has had our pets longer than she has had me.

I honestly didn't know how she would survive this. Three pets gone in less than two years an now number four!! This would be the hardest one of all! Mom would have to decide our sweet, precious female dog's last day on earth. That must be one of the most painful decisions ever! Anyone who had gone through this truly understood my mom's heart-breaking pain.

Mom finally got up and said that she was tired and ready to go to bed. I could tell she wanted to cry some more. We went in. I went straight over to our dog and gave her an extra-long hug. I whispered to her, "I love you!" I hugged Mom. We said our prayer, before I went upstairs. Mom went to her room. Fluff Ball followed. Upstairs, I said goodnight to Grandma and Sandra. I went to my room and took a bath. I cried in the tub over the news of our dog. After bathing, I put on my new pajama set and slipper socks Mom got me for Christmas. I crawled into bed and glanced at my bruised arm. You know, it didn't seem to matter as much, when a family member ends up getting cancer!

Lying there numb as could be, I was thinking about all our pets that have died and now our last dog was dying. I started balling. My hands covered my face. The tears stopped for a moment. Then I started thinking about my mean and hateful dad. It was the end of what should have been a wonderful Christmas Day. Our dog was dying of cancer and my mean and evil dad was hurting me again. Mom was sad. I was sad for her. She would be grieving the loss of another pet.

I prayed, "Please God, comfort my mom. I don't understand all the sadness in her life. She's losing her last dog while still grieving over the one that died in her arms. When will her heart get a rest? It needs time to heal before it's too late. Help me understand why this is happening to her." Then I cried out to Rain E, "Please help me Rain E. How can I get through this? My dad is hurting me again. Help me! I need to see you." I fell asleep in the middle of my cries, with plenty of tears still left in my eyes.

My body woke up me up telling me I needed to quickly get to the bathroom. I hated having to get out of my warm and cozy bed, but I couldn't hold it any longer. So, I rolled out. The floor felt extra cold, even with my socks on. Sometimes I would wear them to bed. Glad I had them on this time! I hurried to the bathroom because the floor was so icy cold. I mean it was freezing! I pushed back the bathroom door and went straight to the toilet. Finally relief! I washed my hands and headed back to my warm bed. My head hit the door, not hard. I guess I accidentally closed it when I rushed in. I opened it back up. "Hey, where's my bed," I yelled out. "Where is my bedroom?" I added. "What's going on?

My sleepy eyes opened to snow completely surrounding me. As I was rubbing them, I heard something far off in the distance. It was a sort of a swishing and jingling noise. Now with my eyes completely awake, I could vividly see how white and bright everything was, even without the sun shining. As I was looking all around, I noticed a forest of trees in the distance. I looked down and saw a fairly wide snowy road right in front of my feet. I glanced up and saw that the curvy wintery road faded into the thick trees.

I was studying the unique looking road when I heard the lovely noise again. As a matter of fact, the noise was coming from all the trees. It seemed to be purposely coming towards me. The Christmassy noise was such a delight to hear, after crying myself to sleep. I stood there freezing! Maybe I was dreaming and freezing at the same time? I didn't care because it was so peaceful and serene here. Then I saw something slowly moving. I kept my eyes on the trees. I finally could make it out.

It was two horses and some sort of sleigh. It WAS coming towards me! Closer and closer, jingling and jingling! Finally the horses were close enough to observe. They were as pure white as the snow around them. There was someone driving the sleigh. As the driver approached I heard, "Hello there!" It was Bolt. I yelled out, "Hi Bolt!" The sleigh pulled up and stopped right beside me. My mouth dropped as I gawked at those beautiful animals. "Bolt, it's really you! What gorgeous horses! What are their names?" Bolt answered, "The one closet to you is Cotton Ball and to her right is Snowflake. Both females, and sisters."

I walked up to both and said, "Hi there, Cotton Ball. Hi there, Snowflake" I gave them a soft pat on the head. "They are magnificent beauties! Bolt, you already know they're females, but you can also tell the sex by their teeth. I learned that at school. A male horse has more teeth than a female." Bolt just smiled. I bet he already knew that horse fact, but I still enjoyed sharing it with him. He said, "Rachel, my cloud partner, I love you filling my ears with knowledge." I chuckled. Bolt always said the darnedest things!

I was glaring at the gorgeous harnesses, perfectly balanced around the horse's necks. I couldn't take my eyes off of them! They were dazzling silver and gold color, with small red flowers intertwined within them. There were several long velvet green trims hanging down on the side of Cotton Ball. I stepped over to Snowflake's outer side. She was gracing the exact trim. My attention then turned to Bolt. He was wearing long, black, shiny form-fitting pants and a spectacular thick golden colored sweater. That blonde, curly hair of his, blended beautifully with his entire outfit! His short boots were solid white, matching the horses and not a bit of dirt on them! He looked cozy-warm and very stylish!

The sleigh was breathtaking! It looked like something out of a Christmas, family movie. It was a rich, sparkly-shiny red color with black outlining the red. I took a closer inspection. The glittering shine was coming from what looked to be real diamonds. Wow! I peeked inside the sleigh. It was all white, except for the red furry blanket lying across the seat. It looked warm and I was cold! Bolt told me to climb in. I gladly did just that! I wrapped the red fluffy blanket all the way around me. Oh my goodness! It instantly warmed my body like a heating pad.

I was facing forward. Bolt was slightly turned watching me. I think he wanted to talk, but was too scared information might easily leak out again! Some of the information he had accidentally shared helped lift my spirits. He let me know I was coming back at Christmas. Maybe that was why he was so talkative? But this time, he took his left hand and put it to his mouth and turned it. I knew that gesture. It meant: "Pick a Lock". He turned back around. I giggled. What a funny character!

I looked all around. The view was amazing! Then I glanced down. Inside this elegant sleigh across the front, were a bunch of brassy, gold-colored bells hanging in a row. I leaned forward to ring them and there was no sound. They were motionless. "They can't jingle," a voice called out. I looked to my right. "Rain E, I knew I would see you at Christmas! I just knew it!" I yelled back.

Rain E climbed in snuggling beside me. I couldn't help but notice the dress she had on. Fairly short, similar to a professional ice skating dress, with rainbow colors going in a vertical direction! It was elegant! She had on white gloves and a golden, crocheted scarf wrapped all the way around her neck, ending one big loop in the front.

I started shivering. Rain E politely pointed out, "Rachel can you feel around the blanket for two holes? Put your arms through them." I held it in front of me and found them. I put my right arm through then my left. As I brought the blanket in closer to my body, it became a coat fitting me just perfect! The funny thing was, when I first wrapped it around me, there were no holes. Well like I have said before, "It's a magical place!" Rain E then handed me a pair of white gloves, like the ones she was wearing. Now I was really toasty warm and comfy, like both of them.

I was staring at the bells again when I asked Rain E, "What did you mean, they can't jingle?" After a pause, Rain E began talking, "Rachel your life has been like these bells that cannot jingle. Do you remember when you were very young and your mother would sing you a song about a bell that couldn't jingle?" I quickly jumped in, "Yes, it's called "The Bell That Couldn't Jingle". I loved that song, still do! How did you know?"

Rain E answered, "I just do! Rachel, you have been blessed with a loving mother. She has always known how to make your Christmas times happy and memorable. She decorated your home every year with a manger sitting out along with many beautiful-looking angels. I really loved that! Even from a very young age, your mother has always cherished the true meaning of Christmas and taught it to you. When you were a child she kept Christmas magical. You are so blessed to have such a loving, kind mother. So many kids are not as fortunate."

There was a sad pause. Rain E then continued, "I want you to close your eyes and remember the first time your mother sang you that song. Take your time." I closed my eyes tightly remembering the first time Mom sang it to me. I was sitting on her lap in our living room next to the Christmas tree. Rain E quietly spoke, "Now open your eyes. Did you know you started smiling when you were thinking back? That was a happy time and it will be again. Now move your hand across the bells." I reached with my right hand and glided my fingers across them. They not only started jingling, they didn't stop. I looked at Rain E with my mouth wide open and all I could say was, "Wow!" "Your jingle is coming back," Rain E proudly stated. "Bolt, It is time go!"

Bolt grabbed the reigns. The horses glanced back, then straight ahead as though they were waiting for us to finish talking. They started trotting. The sleigh was moving to 'who knows where'. I didn't care. I was with Rain E and Bolt and now two very smart and beautiful white horses. The minute we started moving, I heard music in the background. It was the bell song. I guess Rain E loved it too!

"Music expresses that which cannot be put into words and that which cannot remain silent."

Victor Hugo.

Chapter 36

The sleigh ride was a blast! Bolt said it was only a short distance, before reaching our final destination. I lifted myself up, holding on to the sleigh. I could see the pond, now perfectly iced over. It was glistening! The air was still and crisp. I didn't feel as cold as before. My fluffy, furry red coat made all the difference. The white gloves helped too! I spun my head around in every direction. White snow covered the entire place. It looked like a painting.

The sleigh pulled up near the bench and parked. Rain E and I hopped out. I walked up to the front and gave each horse a hug and a kiss on the neck. While standing between their heads, I softly spoke, "Thank you for the wonderful ride, you beautiful creatures. I have seen white horses before, but not like you two." Catching me off guard, they both raised their heads and gave me a little nudge, pushing me back just a bit. I stared deep into their eyes. They blinked at the same time! They knew what I said to them. I was sure of it! Wow! They were thanking me. I gave them each a soft pat, then stepped aside.

I said goodbye to Bolt, thanking him for the ride and for keeping his promise. Bolt looked at me and said, "I told you I would see you at Christmas, even though it slipped out. No harm done. See you again, real soon. Oops! I better leave before I say anything else. Bye!" I giggled. He WAS a funny character! I stood there snugly warm. Bolt waved with both hands, while his teeth gripped the reigns. Cotton Ball and Snowflake gracefully pulled away. I giggled some more watching him. He really cracked me up! The horses sped up to almost a run. They seemed to be in a hurry.

Bolt slightly turned and waved a final farewell, this time, with his left arm straight up by his head. He did a long, slow arm wave the way down to his side. I waved back the same way. I thought to myself how everyone here was so kind, loving and amusing to me, including the horses. I watched them until there were completely out of sight.

I turned and looked for Rain E. She was sitting on our bench. I carefully walked over to join her. I was just about to sit down, when I noticed a new color. It was dark blue. Wow! That made number six! Rain E was already scooted to the left of the bench saving the new color, dark blue, just for me. She was aware that it had become a tradition for me to sit on the newest color each time.

Sitting there, I stayed very quiet. I didn't know what to say about my bruised arm. Rain E must have seen it when I was putting on the blanket coat. Bolt saw it. I remembered. He glanced at my arm, then at her. I still kept quiet. I few minutes went by. Rain E still hadn't spoken. Maybe she was upset that I didn't tell Mom about my bruised arm? She was just staring across at the pond in deep thought. I wanted to talk about everything that had happened since our last visit. I needed to speak! I just didn't know where to begin I was sure my compassionate friend already knew. She always knew!

Everything had been building up inside of me. I knew I needed to say it. I had to the get it all out. I was never going to move forward and heal until I got it all out. I was hurting inside. It was coming to the surface. I could feel it. I was now saying things back to my dad and standing up to all of his family. I would have never done that a year ago. I didn't want to cover up my heart anymore. It was time to start healing. Rain E had been teaching me that. I should just say it. I wanted to, but didn't. I kept my mouth shut.

I looked all around taking in the beautiful landscape. The snow was so thick and white. The whitest of whites! The pond had a spectacular gleaming shine coming from the ice. I looked to my right. I could see "The Flowers of the Week Garden" in the distance, just not the flowers. I wondered what they might be this time! I turned back around. Rain E finally spoke. Here it came. I just knew she was gonna pound me.

"Hey Rachel, do you know how to ice skate?" I surprisingly interrupted saying, "Excuse me." "Do you know how to ice skate?" I proudly answered, "Yes! Where are the skates?" Rain E leaned over the bench arm and picked up two pairs of knee socks, one red, one purple. "Which color would you like, my dear?" Rain E asked. I said, "I genuinely love both colors, but I choose red." Rain E handed me the red knee socks and said, "Red for you, purple for me!"

I pulled off my slipper socks, stuck them in my coat pocket and put on my magical red skating knee socks. Rain E slipped hers on too. They stretched all the way to my knees. My calves instantly started tingling. The bottom of my feet warmed within seconds. I curiously asked, "Are we going to skate in socks? They're snug tight and comfortable, but how can thin socks become skates?"

Rain E stood up and removed her golden scarf. She walked over to the edge of the pond and squatted. I leaned my head far to the right. I watched as she touched the top layer of ice. Instantly, a brighter gleaming light spread across it. My eyes bugged out. My bottom lip dropped. As Rain E came towards me, I looked down and noticed an indented straight line, right smack in the middle of each of her footprints. I immediately lifted my right foot. The bottom of my sock was smooth. I even rubbed my hand across it. Weird!

Rain E stopped right in front of me and smiled. I slipped off my coat. She reached out for my hands and pulled me up. We strolled right up to the edge of the pond. The snow never soaked through the socks. My feet stayed completely dry the whole way. Magical, just magical! Rain E started to step onto the ice, when I abruptly jerked her arm. "I've never skated with just socks on," I nervously expressed. "Stay with me. I will "guide" you. It is my "job"," Rain E confidently spoke. That was an odd, but comforting thought.

She took both my hands and slowly guided me onto the ice. You are not going to believe this, but the moment I stepped on the pond, the knee socks became skates! Rain E let go. I glided backwards, balancing my shaky body. I came to a complete stop then took off! I was skating like a pro, passing Rain E on the right, then on the left. Sometimes we skated together. It was a wintery blast! I was skating on knee socks, magical knee socks and loving every minute!

I could hear music in the sky. It was fun music, like the song Snoopy skated to in *A Charlie Brown Christmas*. I skated until I couldn't skate anymore more! I was pooped! I stepped off the ice and headed to the bench, sweating and breathing hard. I was exhausted from the skating and I was young! I plopped down on the colorful bench.

As I was catching my breath, Rain E walked right up to me. She took my chin and lifted it up to her face and simply said, "Watch!" She wrapped her golden scarf around her neck and stepped back onto the ice. She began circling the frozen pond. As I was watching, the golden scarf started unwinding and gracefully draping down her back, then around her waist. The scarf covered every inch of Rain E's body.

When it reached the dress hemline, it worked its way up, wrapping around her body and settling back on the top of her head. Her dress changed to one color. I was stunned watching this unfold in front of my eyes. Then all of a sudden, as Rain E was coming back around, her rainbow pigtails unraveled and all the colors left her hair, vanishing into the air. The golden scarf magically changed into golden hair.

Rain E abruptly stopped in the middle of the ice. Her dress and hair now both sparkling gold. My eyes were witnessing the most spectacular miracle. I was in a trance. Rain E paused for a moment. Still wearing her white gloves, she put them together, bowed her head and prayed. Next, Rain E looked up to the heavens and then at me. She was making sure I was watching.

The dance began. Soft piano music started filling my ears. Every movement purposely matched to the rhythm of the chosen song. I wondered who chose it? Rain E twisted and turned covering every inch of the pond. She started reaching her arms out to me, pulling them to her chest then raising them above her head. I felt a jolt inside me. She did it again. I kept my eyes glued on her. The magical skates easily glided her across the ice! They seem to be in charge.

The leaps in the air and difficult spins were exactly like you see on TV. She was skating like a pro, maybe better than a pro. All the twisting and turning, sharply cutting into the ice was most impressive. Rain E kept stretching her arms out towards me then pulling them to her chest, hands in a tight fist. Another turn, she would raise her arms up to Heaven, opening her hands. This routine continued throughout the duration of the dance. I was mesmerized! I didn't even feel the tears taking up space in my eyes.

Then one big tear landed on my thigh. I gasped for a breath of air. It was so difficult breathing. My insides were hurting. The pain was excruciating. Tears fell again. I held onto my stomach. I was gasping for more air to fill my lungs. Tears were now flooding my face. Then it hit me. Rain E was removing my pain and handing it to God!!

All the agonizing pain I had been living and struggling with for some time. The pain I had endured. I hated being hurt over and over by my dad and what was worse, I hated my Christian beliefs tormenting me. I was more terrified of hurting God than my dad hurting me. I loved God more. I had hate for my dad. I knew it was wrong to hate another human. I had been struggling with this for so long. It was the commandment "Honor thy father and mother" that was eating me up inside. Why would a loving God want me to honor someone who hurt me? I was hurting and just wanted it to stop.

While all this was swirling around in my brain, Rain E was swirling around the pond. More twists and turns. The dance must have lasted at least ten minutes. Even though my insides were hurting, I never looked away. Then another incredible thing happened. While Rain E was circling the pond once more, her golden hair became the scarf again. It swirled all around her dress.

She was half way around when out of the sky all the colors of her pigtails joined her hair. By the time she completed the circle and was back in the middle, her rainbow hair and dress returned. It was at that moment, I realized the dance was intended for me. All I could do was drop my head into my hands and ball like a baby. I was crying out loud and couldn't stop.

I could hear Rain E approaching. She stopped right in front of my knees. I kept my head down and said, "That was the most beautiful dance I have ever seen." I couldn't even look up. The tears were all over my face, neck and gloves. Rain E softly spoke, "Rachel, Rachel." I couldn't speak. Rain E squatted down. Her face was by my knees. "Rachel, are you ok?" I slowly raised my wet face. My eyes met hers.

She placed her hand on my right cheek. "My dear Rachel, I know you are hurting inside. Is there anything you want to say? Spit it out like a rotten piece of fruit!" I leaned back on the bench and looked up to God and exploded, "I HATE HIM!!!!!!! God forgive me, but I do. I HATE HIM! I HATE HIM! I HATE HIMMMMMMMM!!!! I know it's wrong, but I do, I hate my dad! I HATE HIM!!! Please don't hate me for hating! That's what has been tormenting me all these years."

Rain E moved to the bench and sat right beside me. "Rachel, I don't hate you and neither does God. God loves you. You are His child, His damaged child. He knows how much you have been hurting. Of course you hate the person who has hurt you. It is only human to feel that way. It is devastating when the person who is hurting you, is the one who should be protecting and loving you. Rachel cry! Get it out of your system. You have a great capacity for loving, but until you remove the hurt and pain, the love will stay buried. Let it out! Do you understand what I'm explaining?"

347

I wiped away the tears still on my face and said, "I think I do. It's hard to love myself and to love others as long as I still have hate in my heart. Is that right?" "Yes, my sweet Rachel," Rain E kindly answered. I yelled out, "Why did my dad hurt me so much? Why? It has been almost unbearable. There were times I wanted to just die, but I knew it would destroy my mom and I couldn't do that. I just tried to not let it bother me, but it did." I cried some more, and some more, and some more. It felt good to cleanse my soul. I realize this was supposed to happen. I now knew, 100%, Rain E was sent by God to help me.

The painful, but necessary crying finally stopped. I wiped my eyes, runny nose and wet cheeks. I looked at Rain E. She had tears in those gorgeous eyes of hers. Rain E was so kind and caring and very compassionate, just how you picture an angel. "Wait a minute. Oh gracious me!" I suddenly realized. "Rain E just had to be an angel, my angel!" It was all making sense. All those incredible, magical times I had been with her! All those many visits pondering about who Rain E really was. Pondering at home! All the uncanny ways and wonders of her! Should I ask her straight out? I didn't want to spoil it. I might not get to see her again. She would tell me when the time was right! Rain E always told me what I needed to know when I needed to know it, kind of like God.

We sat on the bench awhile longer. I was still sitting on the dark blue color. Rain E was on the green. I took a deep breath then one more. I was finally calmer. I wanted very much to change the subject so I said, "I like the dark blue color added to the bench." Rain E agreed, "Me too!" She asked me, "What do you like about dark blue? I answered, "Dark blue is rich like royalty. Maybe that's why it's called "Royal Blue".

"I think kings and queens love and adore this magnificent color. It also reminds me of the deepest part of the ocean where the rare fish and sharks hide. There's even a deadly octopus called the Blue-ringed octopus. Its venom is powerful enough to kill people within minutes. It's the most poisonous octopus in the world! I learned this in my science class and on the Discovery Channel."

This time I asked Rain E, before she shared with me her worldly knowledge. "What comes to your mind when you look at dark blue?" Rain E giggled and answered, "I love the color blue whether it is light or dark! To me, dark blue represents knowledge, strength and power. Dark blue is also referred to as indigo. God loved blue so much He made the sky blue and the oceans blue containing many shades of the rich color. God reminds us daily there is knowledge in the sky and in the waters and everything in between. Don't you think so Rachel?"

I told Rain E, "I never realized there was so much meaning behind each color. I think God created colors already knowing their meaning. My mom told me that colors are mentioned throughout the Bible. I'm glad we have so many beautiful colors in the world. I'm going to pay closer attention to them than ever before! Thank you for teaching me more about colors." "You're most welcomed! It is so rewarding to share knowledge with someone eagerly wanting to learn. You have been the best student," Rain E proudly spoke. She smiled with such warm satisfaction. I smiled too.

We stayed seated admiring the view. Rain E placed her hand on top of mine and spoke, "Rachel, I know it was hard to say those three words but you needed to. It had been bottled up in you way too long." I told Rain E, "There's a quote my mom has always shared with me. It says, "No one can make you feel inferior without your consent." A wonderful lady named Eleanor Roosevelt said it. She was married to President Franklin D. Roosevelt. I've learned a lot about presidents from school but mostly from my mom. I like this saying a lot! I will NEVER let my dad hurt me again! I WILL stand up him!" Rain E squeezed my hand. "Let's go see the flowers," she announced.

I put my furry coat back on, with my slipper socks still tucked away in the pockets. Rain E reached over on her left side again and handed me a pair of snow boots. Then she grabbed a pair. We put them on over the skating socks and stood up. I looked at the pond once more. It was probably the last time I would see it covered in ice. What a heavenly vision! We smiled at one another. Off we traipsed!

*"It's not what you look at
that matters, it's what you see."*

Henry David Thoreau

Chapter 37

It was difficult and very strenuous reaching the flower garden. The snow was extra thick making it harder to trudge through. As we were stomping, I was looking everywhere. One unique thing that stuck out in my mind, no footprints anywhere, not from animals or anything, just the ones we were making. As a matter of fact, after Bolt and those magnificent horses galloped off, the footprints disappeared when they did. Perfect snow, with no evidence of a visitor left behind.

I was a bit chilly. I felt snug and warm inside with my red furry coat. I kept my eyes roaming and my brain thinking. I had now visited, what surely must have been a part of heaven, six times! Wow! Rain E was real! I was real! I knew this couldn't be a dream but if it was a dream, it was MY dream, and God put this dream in my head. Rain E was part of my soul and mind and that made her "Real"!!!!

"The Flowers of the Week Garden" were a few feet away. I wanted to run, but my legs needed a rest. They were aching from skating and trudging. Rain E headed directly to the "infamous" clipboard. I went to the entrance gate. I yelled over to her, "I'm going into the garden." She yelled back, "Fine and dandy. Be there in a jiff." I walked in and right up to the flowers. I knew these flowers. They were Cyclamen. Mom beautifully displayed them in pots on our porches every winter. I knew they came in many colors, but this magical garden chose only pale pink, almost white. I gazed into one. Inside, was a red blotch right smack in the middle! The petals were emerging from the blotch. I looked back at Rain E. She was still working on that mysterious clipboard.

I patiently walked up and down every snowy path, like before. Had to keep the tradition! One weird thing I noticed. There was no snow on the flowers, only on the ground. That was very odd. How'd that happen? The trees and bushes were dusted with snow, but the flowers were clean and bright, as though they were supposed to be. Everything at Rain E's home was "supposed" to be!

I turned around to go meet Rain E, when she was already beside me. Spooky!! "So, do you like these flowers?" Rain E asked. "Yes, I love Cyclamen," I stated. "We have them at our home. Everyday I head out the back door to school I look at them. Mom has red and violet ones. They love the cold. Isn't it amazing how different flowers can live in specific temperatures! I think God did it on purpose, so people could enjoy only certain flowers each season."

"If you had all the same flowers every day of the year, you wouldn't appreciate them as much. I just finished studying all about flowers in my science class. I learned all the parts of the flower from the anther to the sepal and all the others in between. One thing my mom told me about Cyclamen is they are toxic to dogs and cats. That's why she keeps them in pots outside."

"Rachel, you are such an amazing, intelligent child. Your mother taught you all about the beauty of the world." I interrupted, "Yeah, and my dad showed me all the ugly. I have a beautiful mom and an ugly dad. I'm lucky to have at least one good parent. I've said before, some kids don't even have that." Rain E added, "I know. It is a sad shame, when God blesses humans with children and then they just destroy them."

We were standing by a bunch of Cyclamen in full bloom. Rain E bent over and picked one. She actually reached down and broke off one of her flower stems. I was a little in shock. She handed it to me and said, "Flowers are a thing of beauty, especially these! Cyclamen have been thought in reference to the Virgin Mary. The red spot at its center represents the sorrow she carried in her heart."

"Up close, flowers can show us many things. Take for instance this flower. From the naked eye, it looks almost perfect. No bruised or damaged petals. No pests wanting to eat and destroy its beauty. It is a perfect creation. The minute I removed it from its root, the life of the flower will now change. I will decide its future. I can either put it in water to enjoy a while longer, or wait until it withers and dies, from the lack of the special care it now requires."

"Even though I broke off one stem, the main part of the flower is still okay. The root is grounded and will continue to thrive, as long as it gets the nurturing it needs. Do you understand what I am telling you, my precious Rachel?" I said, "Sort of! I think you're saying I'm a flower or a root or something, is that right?" "Pretty much, but let me explain in more detail, so you can really grasp what I am saying." I stopped Rain E for a moment so we could sit and rest our legs.

A few feet away I saw a couple of large rocks. I walked over and brushed away the snow for both of us. It was nice, relaxing in a snow garden. Rain E continued, "Rachel, once a bloom dies it is gone forever. Sometimes you have to patiently wait for another one to appear. It can take anywhere from days to an entire year. Sometimes, it can happen overnight." I interrupted again, "Like the Hibiscus! It blooms for one day and falls off the next day. Mom told me that. At first I didn't believe it, so she told me to watch. A big bloom opened one morning. The next morning it was closed up. Mom was right. Sorry for the interruption." Rain E complemented me saying, "I love to hear about all the knowledge stored in your brain."

She continued on, "The most important thing to remember is not to neglect the entire flower, for if you do, it will completely die. If caught in time the damage can be repaired. You will have to feed, prune and nurture it back to health. A few blooms will fall off and wither away, but the root and the rest of the flower remains intact. Rachel, you are the "Rest of the Flower". It will take time for your bloom to come back, but when it does, it will be more beautiful, happier and alive than ever before. Your mother has kept nurturing and protecting you from all the elements that could have killed your roots. No matter what your dad tried to destroy, your mother was always able to keep it alive, even if it was just barely alive."

"Unfortunately many children never receive this early on. During the early growth in a child or flower's life, nourishment is the utmost of importance. You have to protect it from any harm that can and will occur. Your mother has continued in doctoring you back to health. She has always looked for any signs of trauma, and knowing when you needed extra care. These are the fundamentals in being a loving, responsible parent. Unfortunately, many never got this memo, because their parents never got this memo. It is a vicious cycle that repeats generation after generation. The end result: The innocent children suffer."

"With God, your mother and myself, we will make sure you blossom into the lovely, beautiful, spiritual Christian young woman God intended you to be. So the next time you pick a flower, remember how it became such a beauty." Rain E paused for a moment then chuckled, "Also, remember me!" I chuckled too. I told Rain E, "I could never forget you!"

We stayed seated on the rocks, admiring the garden. I removed my right-handed glove. I wanted to touch the flowers with my bare hand, like all other times before. It was soft. Not a fragrant flower, but a beauty like Rain E said. I put my glove back on and we stood. I started knocking the snow off my body, when Rain E told me not to worry about it. I asked why. She asked, "Ever done 'Angels' in the Snow?" "Yes, I love to do angels in the snow, it's just been awhile," I voiced with excitement. "Well my friend, "awhile" is upon us," Rain E announced with a huge smile. I think, "Awhile is upon on us" means "NOW"!"

We walked out of the winter garden. This time Rain E latched the gate. Slowly moving away from the pond and bench, almost immediately the snow became deeper. It became a challenge, lifting our feet up one step at a time. When we arrived at the thickest part of the snow, I was dogged tired, especially my legs. I was certain Rain E's legs were too, but I wasn't sure.

We were standing side by side. It was breathtaking. Solid white rolling hills as far as your eyes could see. If there were any bushes around, they were covered up. Rain E told me to, slowly and carefully turn around. She took my right hand in her left and shouted, "On the count of three; 1,2,3." We screamed all the way down into the snow.

Our hands were free. I looked at Rain E. She had already started flapping. I started flapping too. My arms were digging into the fluffy thick snow. We were both going as fast as we could. Rain E even shouted, "Dig in deeper! Let us create masterpieces!" I stopped for a rest. My arms were exhausted. Then one final round, cutting deeper and deeper, until my arms and legs couldn't do anymore.

We stopped and stared into the sky. Butterfly and Dove came out of nowhere. They flew right in front of us. Butterfly took her right wing and flapped it up and down extra slow. I think she was waving to me. I waved back. The cloudy, snowy sky made an opening for them. They disappeared just like that! Rain E stood up first. Her back was to me, standing next to my waist. I watched her stretch both arms up to the heavens. It was a long feel-good stretch.

I was getting ready to stand up, when my right hand moved down to my side. I gasped out loud! My hand went under Rain E's feet. I mean her feet were not touching the ground. She was a few inches above it, floating! I knew Rain E heard me. She turned, and politely helped me up. I looked down. Rain E and her feet were back on the ground. "Let us take a look at our masterpieces!" Rain E declared. I slowly turned balancing my feet. I first looked at my snow angel. It turned out nicely, with very smooth even strokes.

I glanced at Rain E's. I gasped out, even louder than before. The wing part of her angel had indents in them. They looked just like real wings. They WERE real ANGEL wings! I didn't say a word. I couldn't take my eyes off them. Rain E reached for my left hand and said, "Those are something else! They ARE masterpieces! Don't you think so Rachel? I am plum tuckered out. Let us go over to the edge of the cliff and relax our tired bodies." I was still speechless.

Rain E guided me to the cliff. The snow wasn't as thick making it easier to move through. I still was not talking. I wouldn't know what to say without sounding like a knucklehead. We helped each other's worn-out legs sit down. The view was heavenly. The clouds were moving away and breaking apart. The sun was now trying to peek through. I think this was the longest visit I had spent with my friend. I finally spoke, "Did you have a nice Christmas?" Rain E perked up and said, "Why yes I did. This will always be a memorable one because of you. Did you have a nice Christmas Rachel?" I answered, "I did. I got to spend it with my mom."

"It was happy and sad at the same time. I was happy to be home, but sad, because our female dog has to be put to sleep for good." I paused for a moment. I was choked up inside. Then I told Rain E, "Our dog has cancer. Mom has to decide her last day with us." Tears came rolling down my cheeks. I wiped them off with my gloves. These gloves that had held a lot of tears this trip! Maybe that was why Rain E gave them to me in the sleigh. They had accompanied me like a large Kleenex.

Rain E touched my left arm and said, "I am sorry about your dog. It is hard to lose them, especially so many in such a short time. Your mother will be strong. She will grieve along time for this pet, knowing she had to end her life. Remember this important statement, "Your mother would never let an animal suffer!" Rachel, your mother loves animals. Do you ever hear her say anything when you two see an animal that has died, like a squirrel or skunk, any animal on the side of the road?" I was stunned. I looked straight at Rain E's face. "Oh my goodness! My mom always says, "Rest in Peace". How did you know that? Please, no secrets, tell me who you are?"

I was staring deep into Rain E's eyes waiting for an answer, when she changed the subject. "Rachel, I know how much you love Christmas. Share with me what you know about the birth of Christ?" I dropped the question for now. She would tell when and if I needed to know, I hoped. I turned the conversation to baby Jesus.

I loved talking about Jesus. I think because I had learned so much about his life. Mom had been my main teacher, then school and church. Rain E passionately stated, "The word "Christmas" sounds so beautiful rolling off the tongue. Don't you think so?" I answered, "Yes! I love Jesus' other name. When I was very young, my mom told me what Christmas meant to her. She said that Christmas is a combination of Christ and "Mas". You have "Christ", His name and then "Mas". Mom said to her "Mas" first stood for "Mary's Adored Son" and then when Jesus became a man it stood for "My Anointed Savior". I knew Mom made it up, but I liked it and I will never forget it. My mom has enjoyed working with words most of her life. She will always be creative and very clever!"

Rain E was glowing, after I shared that with her. She looked right at me and said, "What your mother told you was beautiful, just beautiful." Rain E kept staring at me. "What is going on in that mind of yours?" she asked. I hesitated then reluctantly admitted, "I really want to ask you something, without sounding disrespectful to God. Rain E, what does God think of Santa Claus? I really want to know, if you know, because when I was very young, my mom would tell me to go to sleep, otherwise Santa wouldn't show up. It confused me. My mom's a Christian and taught me all about Jesus' birth, but I still believed Santa was real. As I grew, I realized he was only make-believe, or at least I thought he was. So one day I asked Mom. I still remember sitting next to her in our living room by the Christmas tree. She wrapped her arms around me and told me a wonderful true story."

She said, "A long, long time ago, there was a man named Saint Nicholas. He lived in another country across the ocean. He was a very much-loved bishop. He loved helping people. So one day he heard about this poor, but noble man who had three daughters who wanted to marry. Without money, they couldn't marry. So one night, Saint Nicholas put three bags of gold inside the man's window."

"Well, the next day, the poor man found out who did it, even though Saint Nicholas tried to remain anonymous. He never wanted to be praised for all his good works. From that day on, anytime someone received a secret gift, people assumed it was from Saint Nicholas. The story continued being told year after year."

"Soon it came to America through the Dutch settlers. Because this kind and caring bishop wore a red robe, that's how it became known as a 'red suit'. I believe Saint Nicholas gave out of the kindness of his good heart. He loved others and must have enjoyed giving gifts to all those in need." "I loved hearing about this real life wonderful man from my mom. But I'm asking you Rain E, "Does God think it's bad to celebrate Santa Claus on Jesus' birthday?"

Rain E seriously answered, "Saint Nicholas had a kind and generous heart. He did what God expected him to do. He was a true Christian! I think that today on earth, the true meaning of Christmas has gotten lost. Rachel, just always remember why Jesus came into the world and be a real Saint Nicholas, always giving to others in need." "I will. Thanks for explaining it. Mom pretty much told me the same thing," I gratefully said to Rain E.

The sky caught my attention again. The clouds were all gone. I was leaning back, when I accidentally landed on Rain E. She grabbed my arm and back. Her hands were extra warm, I guess 'cause it was winter. We stayed on our backs. I closed my eyes. When I opened them, Rain E was gone. I was back in my bed. My bed at home, with Mom, not Dad. That was a first. I glared at my ceiling thinking about my winter visit with my magical, very warm and professionally talented friend. It was so quiet and tranquil in my room. A soft voice whispered in my left ear to keep looking up. I knew it was Rain E.

I was staring at my ceiling, when out of nowhere, appeared the iced pond. I saw the snow and the colorful bench next to it. There was some writing on the pond. I rubbed my eyes, to get a clearer look. My eyes opened wide. The pond read, "HEAVEN LOVES RACHEL RENE". My eyes were now bugged out. Oh my goodness! That was what Rain E was doing when she skated by herself! All those remarkable twists and turns, she was writing a message, a message for me!!

For the first time, I saw her home from my home. I immediately crawled out of bed and got down on my knees. I prayed, "Dear God, Rain E is REAL! Rain E is my angel. She's my guardian angel! I just know it!" Tears gently fell from my eyes. "Thank you God for reading my letter and for sending Rain E." I wiped my face and climbed back into bed. What a happy change in my life, all because of my letter, all because of my letter, all because of my letter! I kept repeating those wonderful words over and over until I fell asleep.

"You can always tell about somebody by the way they put their hands on an animal."

Betty White

Chapter 38

The next morning, my eyes opened to a wonderful sight. My ceiling! My ceiling where a saw Rain E's home. This was the first time I visited Rain E, from *my* home. I wondered why? I was sure Rain E would tell me, if I asked. It was Christmas time. I was happy and sad to be home. Happy to finally be with Mom on Christmas Day in three years, and sad it would be our dog's last. I heard piano music coming from downstairs. Mom was playing her close friend's Christmas CD. So beautiful! Mom always listened to his piano music when she was sad. I knew why she was sad. It was our dog and the decision she had to make. Why did it have to be at Christmas? I got up and stretched in every direction. Sunbeams were coming through my windows. I think God was letting Mom know He was nearby for comfort.

I headed downstairs. Mom was getting ready to take Grandma's friend to the airport. Sandra was flying home today. I hugged her and thanked her again for the Christmas gifts. Mom came out of her bedroom, gave Fluff Ball a kiss, then she and Sandra left. Grandma stayed with me. I went to the kitchen and poured myself a bowl of cereal and then to the den to eat by our dog. She was resting on her favorite rug. I rubbed her tummy with my feet, while eating my cereal. When I finished, I put the bowl in front of her mouth. She licked up the leftover sugar milk. I was glad I did that! I will always remember it. It was sad looking at our pet, knowing she wouldn't be with us much longer. I went to get her brush. I must have brushed all her hair for over an hour. She fell asleep. I lay down by her and fell asleep too. I woke up to my Mom's voice. She said that she took a photo of the two of us. I kissed Fluff Ball on the nose and left to go change clothes.

The rest of the day was quiet. I had missed the quiet. I played games on the computer. Mom watched TV and Grandma did her puzzles, until dark. I got ready for bed. Mom came up and we said our prayer. She looked so sad. She kissed both my hands and told me how happy she was to finally have me home for Christmas. I watched her as she left my room, turning the light out. She walked down the stairs in the dark. I said an extra prayer to God to help Mom get through this very sad time. I closed my eyes with our sweet dog on my mind.

The next morning I woke up to an extra quiet house. I immediately wondered if everything was okay and if our dog was still alive. I stayed in my new pajamas and headed downstairs. I walked straight to Mom's bedroom. When I got to the door, she looked up, "Hi my sweet. Come lay down by me." I quickly climbed into bed. I got under her very warm comforter. The sheets were warm from her heating pad. I asked, "How is she?" Mom said, "Our Fluff Ball had a restless night, barking more than usual."

"I wish I could do more for her. I prayed over and over hoping she will be with us a bit longer, but I don't think that's possible. Her mouth is bleeding more often. The vet said to keep a close watch. When she starts having trouble breathing, it will be time. I wish I could remove the cancer, I really do. I believe my sweet Fluff Ball will tell me when she's ready to go. I will see it in her eyes. Pets hang on for us, so I will have to tell her it's okay to go, just like I did with all the others. This time will be the worst. I have to make the final decision. I have all the faith and trust in her. She will let me know when it's time."

Mom started crying. I joined in. I couldn't even begin to imagine what she was going through. I knew Mom was strong, but sometimes it was just not enough. God would have to pitch in. I knew He would. We watched some TV and started talking about my birthday coming up. I was going to be twelve. Yea!! It was a very important birthday to me because, I was almost a teenager and I could talk to the new judge in private, if I ever needed to.

The next two weeks, I just rested and secretly worked on my drawing. It was really looking good. I spent one weekend with my best friend. I helped Mom put up the Christmas stuff. I played a lot with our dog. I knew she wouldn't be with us much longer. What a sweetie pie she was! It was a special time for me. I took her for a short walk around the yard. This was one Christmas I would always remember.

School started back. I was turning twelve in three days. Those three days flew by. I woke up with a big smile on my face. My birthday had arrived! I was now twelve! One more year and I would I be a teenager. I had to go to dinner with my Dad on my birthday, court said, but first I celebrated at school. Mom brought three cookie cakes for all my classmates. She ate lunch with me. The cookie cake was a hit! When I got home, Mom had another cookie cake, just for me. It had the *Minecraft* decorations on it.

There was an enormous birthday card sitting on the kitchen table. I knew it was from Mom. Also sitting on the table, a dozen red roses in a beautiful vase. One rose for each year I had lived. I lit the candles, then Grandma and Mom sang happy birthday to me. I made a wish and blew them out. I'll tell what I wished for at the end of my story. I just knew it would come true!! I opened my huge card. There were twelve twenties taped inside. Wow! Mom gave me two hundred and forty dollars for my birthday. Grandma gave me gift cards to my favorite stores. We ate some cookie cake. I told Mom that was the biggest birthday card I had ever seen. I thanked her for the money and Grandma for the cards.

It was 5:30 pm and here came *the honks*. I hated having to go with Dad on my birthday. I had no choice. It was the law, a stupid law. Mom walked me out. She was standing on the porch as I got in the car. Here it came, "Happy birthday Tweetie, my Tweetie is a big Tweetie, isn't she? Ou looks so purdy," my ex-grandma said. Dad handed me a hundred dollar bill. Martha gave me forty. Thank goodness no more rocks or stuff animals!

Dad immediately asked, "What'd your mother give you for your birthday?" I proudly said, "Two hundred and forty dollars. One twenty for each year!" He was silent. I was glad. I loved putting him in his place, like Mom did! We went to eat Thai food on my birthday because that was what Dad liked. Oh well, some things never changed and never would.

When I got home, Mom was right at the door, as though she had been waiting there the whole time. I saw a look on her face, like I had seen before. It was the "Better watch out Dad" look. She sat me down at the table and said, "Rachel, I am so sorry for what your dad said to you when you were getting in the car." I quickly asked, "What did he say?" "Are you telling me you didn't hear him? I heard it from the porch and I am emailing him right now," Mom firmly stated.

I told Mom, "I tune Dad, Sissy and Martha out. I have for a long time. I'm serious. I haven't listened to them in months. What did he say? Please tell me." Mom said, "Your dad said, "Happy Birthday Stinky, get your fat ass in the car so I can go eat. I'm starving." I was in shock. I guess I HAD been tuning him out. Mom told me again that I had become desensitized.

I went to the kitchen. Mom went to her bedroom. She was in there a long time. She must have told Dad off. She came back out and we each had another slice of cookie cake. I asked if everything was okay. Mom said that everything was fine. She said that Dad never emailed her back. I guess he knew he was in trouble. I was so glad Mom constantly stayed on his case. It helped me stay strong.

I had to go to Dad's the following weekend. He was quiet the whole time. He was in his "Scared Mode" again. I decided to stay in my room and study. Mr. Evil left me alone the entire weekend. I think he REALLY was scared of the new "Republican" judge. Hey, whatever it took! Guess my age did make a difference.

When I got home Sunday night, I told Mom everything. She was thrilled to hear Dad left me alone. The next weekend I was home. Mom and I decided to go shopping. I wanted to use my gifts cards from Christmas and birthday. So, Saturday morning we got up extra early. I dressed and flew downstairs. Mom made her homemade biscuits. She went to change clothes, while I ate. Grandma was staying home. She said that she would watch our dog. Our sweetie was sleeping on her rug, so I didn't wake her. I was sure Mom gave the pain medicine to her. It made her sleep. We quietly left. We shopped at my favorite stores. I used two of my gift cards. We must have shopped for hours.

After we finished, we went to our favorite Italian restaurant. It was so crowded. The wait was over an hour, so we decided to eat in the bar area. After we finished ordering, Mom just stared at me and asked, "Are you going to tell me what's been our your mind since Christmas Day?" I answered, "I just hate being at Dad's. I'll be okay." Mom looked at me in disbelief and firmly said, "We'll talk when we get home." I quietly answered, "Okay." Throughout dinner, we occasionally chatted. I knew I had to tell Mom. I knew it would be tonight.

When we got home, I wanted to take a bath first before we talked. Mom said she would do the same. Grandma went up to her room. I think she knew something was going on. I stayed in the tub, long enough to go over in my head exactly everything I needed to tell her. I got out and put on my long blue and white plaid nightgown, robe and slippers. There was still a small bite scar left on my arm, that I had kept hidden.

I met Mom downstairs. She was in her black velvet robe and black UGG slippers. At first we were going to sit on the porch swing, but it was too cold. Instead, we sat at the kitchen table. I started first. I rolled up my sleeve. Mom gasped. "Rachel, my love, why didn't you show me this when you came home?" I nervously explained, "I wanted to, but when I found out about our dog, I just couldn't add to your grief. Mom, you already had a heart attack. Forgive me. It looks better now, even though the bite left some scaring."

Mom sharply stated, "Your dad will NEVER hurt you or me EVER again! Please never feel scared to tell me. He's worried about you getting older and that a new judge is on the bench." Mom kept looking at my arm. She raised her head up and worriedly asked, "Has he been pinching and poking you again." I wasn't about to lie, the way she was looking at me. I simply answered, "Yes!" Mom stayed calm, which was very unusual. She just said, "I'll take care of it." I knew that meant another screaming match on the phone. Mom asked if there was anything else I needed to talk about. I said that there were a couple of things.

First I told Mom all about what I overheard in the restaurant bathroom. Her mouth dropped open. I told her that she needed to tell Dad. Mom said, "I can't tell your dad about this for two reasons. First, he would never believe me and second your dad would just think I was trying to stir up more trouble. Rachel my love, this knowledge you have come by must never be repeated. It is of the upmost importance. Please, never ever share this information with anyone else. Never go anywhere alone with Sissy or her daughter. It's sad to admit, but you reap what you sow. Do you understand that?" I told Mom, "I think it means Dad has what's coming to him, is that right?" Mom snickered and said, "Yep! What goes around!"

The second and more important news came next. I simply asked, "Mom, is the judge's first name Raymond?" "How did you know that?" Mom asked. "Well, I was in Dad's office and saw a check made out to him. It had a lot of zeros on it." Mom got quiet. She sat there for several minutes without saying a word. I asked her if the check meant something bad. She stayed quiet. Then I asked her, "Mom were you supposed to pay the judge some money? Is that why you lost in court? Did your old attorneys not tell you this?"

Mom was sitting there slowly shaking her head back and forth in silence. Finally, she reached for my hands and quietly spoke, "Thank you for sharing this information. It all makes since now. I was never going to win in his court. It didn't matter what evidence I had. I'm just glad he and that other sorry lady judge are retired. God will get them."

"Rachel, do you remember which are my favorite books of the Bible?" I quickly answered, "Yes, Psalms, Isaiah and Romans." Mom replied, "You are exactly right. I know these 3 books almost by heart. Now that I know this disgraceful information, all I can do is what God wants me to do. It says in (Romans 12:19) "Vengeance is mine, I will repay, says The Lord." Rachel I will hand this horrible, disgusting news up to God, when I pray tonight."

I could see how devastated and livid Mom was. I was glad I told her. She asked me if there was anything else she needed to know. I said that was everything. Thank goodness I was done. I think Mom was too. We said our prayer then I went upstairs. I got in bed, feeling relieved. Mom seemed okay. I thanked God for helping me tell Mom everything. I asked Him to watch over all of us. I feel asleep saying goodnight to Rain E, my angel!

Another week went by. It was January 22nd. I woke up and got dressed for school. Mom was sitting at the kitchen table. I could tell she had been crying. I knew what was coming. Mom said, "It's time. Our sweet Fluff Ball is suffering. The vet is coming tomorrow while you are at school. I didn't want you to witness the procedure. I want you to remember the good and happy times." I started crying. Mom got up and we hugged for a long time. On the way to school we stopped for a breakfast burrito. When I got to my classroom, my teacher could tell something was wrong. I told her about our dog. My whole class said a prayer for her and our family.

When I arrived home from school, I took our dog on one last walk. We didn't go very far. I could tell she wasn't feeling well. At least she saw the outside one more time. Mom gave her the pain medicine. I got the scissors and cut a lock of her hair to keep forever. Mom did the same. She said that she wished she had thought of doing it with all our pets, but at least she had their ashes. That sweet precious dog never left Mom's bedroom all night.

The next morning, everyone stayed quiet. I was ready to go to school. I went over and gave our sweetie one last kiss. The whole way to school Mom never said a word. I got out and before closing the door, I said, "I'll be thinking about her. I will watch the clock until it gets to 10:00 am. Then I'll know she's in Heaven. I will miss her!" Mom was crying and I was crying. It was a sad day at school. One I would never forget! When Mom picked me up, we drove to the nearby park. I asked her if she was okay. I wanted to know some of what happened.

Mom, with her voice cracking, softly spoke, "Susan, our vet, arrived at 10:00 am. She saw how much the cancer had spread in her mouth and she said that I was doing the right thing. She added that there was no medicine strong enough to kill her pain. Putting her down was for the best."

"After Susan did a final examine, I told her I was ready. I sat beside Fluff Ball on her favorite rug, in front of the fireplace, and held one paw. I was stroking her head, when she looked up at me and blinked once. She put her head on my hand. It was as though she knew what was going to happen next. Are you sure you want to hear this?" I immediately answered, "Yes, Mom, I just didn't want to see it!"

Mom continued, "I placed my head on top of hers. I looked up and said I was as ready as I would ever be. Before she gave her the medicine, I whispered in that beautiful white Fluff Ball's ear, "Your brother is waiting. You can go now. I'll be okay. You are my first and last female dog. You will always be a part of me, just like all the others. I LOVE YOU!" The vet gave her the medicine to go to sleep. She was gone."

I told Mom I wanted to know what happened so I could share this in my story to everyone who has lost a pet. It is for those who have gone through exactly what my incredibly brave mom had to go through. We sat there in the car and cried. Mom told me that whenever I started feeling sad about our pets, to just remember the joy they brought us. I told Mom that I would always remember the park, the many car rides, swimming in the pool, the treats and all the fun games with all our pets.

Then I added, "I will also remember the "No Mores". They are; No more tummy rubs, playful bites, handshakes, purring, brushing up against you. No more chasing the fake mouse, (by the way, they know it's fake, but they chase it anyway). No more curling up with, or waking up to a furry tail wiping your face. No more endless entertainment. No more photos and the most important, No more staying glued to your side when you are sick, (they know that too). They are all gone, but NEVER forgotten!

In ten years, six pets have passed away, four in the last two. All died of natural causes, except for our female dog. Mom said that when a pet dies the grieving is bad enough, but having to choose when they die, the grieving becomes unbearable. I knew this day would stay with Mom, forever. I think the moment your furry family member dies, that love for them sky rockets even higher than before. Mom said that she thinks the love between a pet and a human is greater than the love between two humans. Pets love you unconditionally. I think she was right. Pets have made this a happier world to live in. I wish "certain" people could be more like the pets.

We still have two beautiful cats, the oldest and youngest. Go figure! I hope Mom gets another dog or dogs someday. She needs them as much as they need her. When the time's right, her sad and empty heart would be filled again with lots of licks and love. For all our furry family members who are no longer with us, thank you for years of happiness and unselfish love! It would take a lifetime getting over the loss of any loved one, furry or non-furry!

After Mom and I finished crying and talking and crying some more, we drove home. Each day got a little better, but not by much. A few days before the start of Spring Break, unexpected cold weather showed up. There was so much sleet and snow school closed early. I ended up getting two extra snow days. I didn't have to go to Dad's for several days. My Spring Break time with him was shortened due to the wonderful iced-over roads. That was another blessing from above!

Jesus answered, "I am the way, the truth, and the light. No one comes to the Father except through me."

John 14:6 (NIV)

Chapter 39

I survived!! My shortened few days of Spring Break time with Dad was coming to an end! For the most part, he was fairly decent to me. I bet Mom ripped him apart about biting me again. I never heard it, but I could always tell because Dad got into his "Scare Mode". Mom had gone out of town, but was coming home on the same day I was returning, just a few hours later. When Mom landed, she called to check on me. I told her I wasn't home yet. She hit the ceiling. I told her that Dad wasn't bringing me home until 10:00 pm, because it was his mother's birthday tomorrow and he demanded that I spend time with her. Mom said that she was calling Dad and she would talk to me when I got home.

At the restaurant were Dad, Sissy, Martha, her sister and me. We were waiting on our food, when I had go to the restroom. When I got back, I didn't know what was all said, but I did hear Sissy telling Dad, "You better get Rachel back home before that witch (Mom) takes you back to the new judge for violating the court order." I couldn't believe she said that! Big mistake! Dad got in her face. He screamed, "Shut the "F" up. Don't you tell me what to do! I'll keep my daughter as long as I want to. The "B" isn't going to run the show." I thought to myself, "We're not at a show, we're at a restaurant!" I think my dad WAS losing it. Everyone stayed quiet at the table. Nice birthday dinner! (I'm being sarcastic). I'm sure Martha was used to his screaming after all these years. I would never get use to it. Someday I wouldn't have to hear those bad words vomiting out of Dad's mouth, ever again.

It was just after 10:00 pm when I finally arrived home. Mom started in on me. I think because she was trying to teach me to stand up to Dad and not let him bully me. I told her that I tried to get him to take me home, but he wouldn't. I hated that Mom yelled at me. I knew why she did it. She didn't want me to marry a man like him. Honestly, Mom has told me that all the time. Gross, I never even thought about marrying, not at my age.

I knew she was just trying to prepare me for when I was older. Still, it grossed me out. I did understand why Mom was concerned. I only liked the men in my Mom's family and my Latin teacher. The rest made me nervous. I guess that was why I only saw lady doctors. Anyway, I was finally home. It would be summer before I was forced to spend another extended visit with Dad. After this mess, I think he will be treating me a little better. We would have to wait and see.

Easter was in four days. It had been three years since I spent Easter with Mom and her family. It always fell on Dad's weekend. I have missed three Easter services in a row. Once again Easter fell on his weekend. I had to go with Dad on Thursday evening because school was out on Good Friday. That was what the crazy family law said. A stupid law as far as I was concerned!

A week before Easter, I begged Dad to take me home Saturday night. I wanted to be with Mom on Easter Sunday. I made it very clear that it was not fair. I loudly told him that I was going to see Mom this Easter! I couldn't believe it. He said he would take me home Saturday evening. Wow Wee! What was up with him? I think it was those two very important 'turn' of events; I was older and I stood up to him, and he was scared I would talk to the new judge. Kind of a good place to be in!

Thursday around 5:30 pm Mom and I said our "Stair Prayers". Then we talked about Easter and Jesus. Mom passionately stated, "I love Easter. I am so glad we're finally spending it together. Easter means everything to me. It's the sole basis of our Christian belief. Jesus died for our sins and rose from the dead, just like the Bible says. Christians truly understand the suffering was not in vain. Jesus had to suffer and die for our sins. That is the most powerful event ever in the history of mankind, I do believe."

I told Mom "I also believe Jesus died for our sins and is the Son of God. Those who believe will get to live in Heaven. God must love us so much to sacrifice His only son. Why do so many people not get this? I would be scared not to believe in God and Jesus." Mom sincerely said, "I know Rachel. You have been fortunate in your young life to know and learn about Jesus. So many kids haven't been so lucky."

374

We got up and hugged. I told Mom, "Even though you've suffered so much in the last ten years because of Dad, I'm still glad you adopted me." Mom kissed me on the forehead and whispered, "I wanted you. You were meant to be my daughter, at any cost. I wouldn't have it any other way. Neither would have God! It was His plan."

The honks started. I was out the door. As usual, I turned and signed, "I love you." Mom did too. I yelled out," See you on Easter!" I got in and we drove away. Dad, Sissy and I stopped for dinner. We were sitting by a window, when I looked at the sky. There were dark clouds in the distance. Maybe rain was in the forecast? I guessed Dad saw me looking. He said, "We got a bad storm coming. Let's eat fast and get home." So we did. The car pulled into the garage.

I got out first and noticed the air smelt like rain. I went straight to my room and crashed on my bed. I hadn't been lying there very long, when a loud roar of thunder startled me. I jumped up and ran to my window. Sure enough, I could see the storm approaching. It was close. "I wonder if Rain E is in this storm," I hopefully thought! I hadn't seen her since Christmas. I had to see her at least one more time. There was so much I needed to tell her and ask her. I thought about her every day. Rain E helped me grow in so many ways. I stood by the window and prayed, "Please God let me see her one more time, please, just one more time!" I prayed it over and over, while staring at the dark clouds.

The lightning shot across the sky just like the first time. I kept watching for any sign of her. My eyes stayed focused on the dark clouds. Closer and closer, they were moving in my direction. The lightning was lighting up the sky. The thunder was roaring louder and louder. All of a sudden the lightning struck the ground. It was so loud I literally jumped straight up. I tried keeping my eyes focused on a specific group of clouds. Here came the rain. It started out just drops, then more drops, then a light shower, then lots of rain! Within minutes it was raining so hard, it was pounding on the roof! I glanced around my room.

My door opened and Dad was standing there. He stated that a bad storm was on its way. "Duh! No kidding!" "Has he even looked out-side?" I said under my breath. I kept staring at him with a puzzled look thinking who was the grown-up here. After that brain-dead remark, he didn't say another word. He shut the door. For the first time I thought about the words "Brain Dead" and about the person who started the ugly saying. Boy, I couldn't believe Dad was really leaving me alone.

Did he finally decide to not be a "meany"? Was he trying to be human after all these years? Too bad he didn't treat me nice, when it counted, and now it was too late. Maybe, his mind was going like Sissy and Delilah mentioned in their "Scheming Plot".

I turned back to the storm. It was violent and mysterious at the same time. The lightning was striking every few seconds. Within minutes, the thunder became loud, loud, loud, followed by an earsplitting booming sound coming from the backyard. The lights flickered several times then went out. My mind immediately went back to the very first storm when I met Rain E. These storms were identical! The house was now completely dark. The streetlight was also out! My body was trembling. This storm was violently scary. It was raging mad! I searched in the dark and found my pajamas, still in my overnight bag. I quickly changed and then covered up in my bed. Comforters hid you the best! I was fairly certain it WOULD protect me! Remember! They made the best and safest forts!

The noise wouldn't stop. There was knock at my door. I asked, "Who is it?" There was no response. I pulled my head out from under the comforter. The lightning crackled again. Sissy stuck her head in. She said that the power was out and then closed the door. Now I ask you, do I live with two idiots? Like I couldn't tell I was in the dark! She yelled from the hallway, "Stay in the house. Don't wander outside." Are you kidding me!! The answer to the idiot question was, "YES"! Like I was going to venture outside during bad weather and pretend to be a storm chaser as in the movie *Twister?*

I reached for my flashlight under my bed and clicked it on. Still pitch-black in my room and assuming throughout the house, even if Sissy hadn't realized it yet, I walked over to the window on the outside chance I might see Rain E. The storm was going strong. Couldn't see anything but rain and black clouds! I found some slipper socks to cover my cold toes. I went to the bathroom using my flashlight as my guide.

When I walked out, I glanced one more time at the storm. That was when I saw them. It was those angelic, magical rainbow pigtails! Even in the dark, black, violent thunderstorm, I saw them. Rain E was coming! The colors showed themselves, when the lightning lit up behind the clouds. She was coming to get me. I stood there for several more minutes, waiting for them to appear again, but they didn't. I climbed back in bed. I turned the flashlight off and placed it by my pillow. I threw the comforter completely over my entire body. I closed my eyes and fell asleep.

The storm passed without seeing my Rain E. Maybe I just imagined seeing pigtails, because I wanted to so very much. I heard Dad downstairs. Then I heard the car drive off. I jumped out of bed and ran to my window. Yep! He left. Sissy came up to my room. She knocked and asked if I slept okay during the storm. I said that I slept fine. I didn't really, but I wasn't about to tell her. I asked, "Where did Dad go?" Sissy answered, "To steam. Where else?" Then she added, "He's in one of his moods, so try to stay out of his way." I didn't respond. I guess he back to his "meany" 'ole self. Sure didn't last long! My only thought was, "He better take me home tonight like he promised."

I was a bit scared staying alone with Sissy. I put the chair under the door and never left my room. I had some snacks I brought from home. Dad stayed gone most of the afternoon. It was dark when he finally pulled into the driveway. I had been packed and ready to go from the time I woke up. I heard the door slam. He was coming up the stairs. I quickly pulled the chair away in time before he opened my door. I was sitting on my bed. He looked mad. I didn't ask. I didn't care. He paused for several minutes. It gave me the creeps. Then finally he said, "Let's go. I'm taking you home an hour early." He abruptly left.

I gathered up all my stuff and rushed downstairs before he changed his mind. This time it was just Dad and myself in the car. I text Mom I was on my way. She text only one word, "Yea"! You know, it wasn't that very long ago when Dad or Sissy held on to my phone until I pulled in my driveway. He treated me like a prisoner and he was the Warden. Even though that has changed, it will always stay in my brain because it was so cruel.

All the way to my home, Dad was quiet. I played on my IPad. When we pulled into the driveway, he barked, "Hey Missy, don't forget I did this for you!" He just had to say that. He was something else! I said, "I won't forget, NOW!" Right after I got out, I was about to slam the door. Dad barked again, "What do you mean by that sassy remark?" I slammed the door and walked away. I never looked back. Mom was absolutely right! Everything came with a price. Dad was incapable of loving. It was fake love and would never change. My dad was so "Hot" and "Cold" if he was an object he would be an ideal thermos!

I had just stepped onto the front porch when Mom opened the door. She must have been watching for me. She hugged and hugged me and hugged me some more. I never saw Dad pull away. Walking in, I couldn't believe I was finally home for Easter. Mom said to take a hot bath and just relax. I headed upstairs with all my stuff and did just that.

While I was soaking in the tub, I started thinking about Rain E. I thought for sure I was going to see her last night. Maybe my visits were over, "Completed". Mom knocked on the bathroom door and happily said, "I have a new outfit I bought you. Try it on and see if it fits. Tell me if you like it! It's one of your favorite colors, purple." "Okay, Mommy." I called her Mommy again.

I drew some more hot water and slid my head all the way under. I shot out so fast, spilling water all over the floor. I screamed, "PURPLE! The last color of the rainbow! The bench. It was all the colors of the rainbow, except purple. I saw them in order. I haven't seen purple. There was one more visit! The bench wasn't completed. That was it! I knew it! "Seven" colors, "Seven" visits!" Finally, it was all making sense to me. I would get to tell Rain E about my 12th birthday and how I 'stood up to evil dad'. I would be able to thank her for all the encouragement and guidance she gave me on every visit.

I got out of the tub. I tried on the top and matching skirt. It fit perfect. I decided to wear it for Easter. I draped it across my chair, and put on my fleece rainbow pajamas. I wanted to have them on in case I saw Rain E this weekend. I went downstairs to play on the computer. I hadn't been sitting there very long, when Mom walked in with some Easter sugar cookies and a glass of milk. What a wonderful and yummy surprise! I loved Mom's sugar cookies. They had been a family tradition, during the holidays, since she was a little girl.

The cookies were in the shape of chicks, bunnies and eggs. I thanked Mom for the new outfit and told her that I loved it. Someday she would eventually be told how much I loved it being the color "purple". I added that I wanted to wear it tomorrow. She hoped I would. Mom walked out reminding me that church service was early. She added that after church we were eating with her family. It was going to be a wonderful, happy, Christian day, three years in the waiting! I played a few more games until I was one yawn from falling asleep. I put the computer to sleep, before me.

When I walked out of the office, I called for Mom. She yelled out, "I'm up here in your room." When I walked in Mom was sitting on the material bench under the bay window. She looked up and said, "Rachel, come here, take a look at this. I want to show you something."

I hesitantly said, "What do you see?" I thought for sure she was going to say a rainbow moving in the clouds. "Come here silly!" Mom insisted. I sat right beside her. Mom said, "Now lean way over to your right as far as you can go." I did. I asked, "What am I looking for?" Mom pointed and said, "That! See the three stars in a row."

I looked at the clear sky. Mom couldn't have seen Rain E. "Hey, I see them. They're in a straight line, following each other, like marching soldiers." Mom told me, "They are in the belt of the constellation of Orion, also called "Three Kings". See that brighter star. That's Sirius. Regardless when it was first thought of, Christians named the three stars of Orion, The Magi, the three gifts brought to baby Jesus. Even in the book of Job (38:32) talks about the knowledge of Astronomy, like the zodiac."

I was so impressed with Mom's star facts. I said, "I remember studying about the three stars last year, but the teacher didn't tell me all this. Thank you Mom. You are so smart." "You're very welcome," Mom acknowledged. "I try to be extra smart for you! Remember you are as smart as you want to be. Knowledge is everything, so keep reading and learning. Now, my love, it's bedtime. We have a full day planned tomorrow."

Mom playfully touched my nose with her finger. I climbed into bed. She moved over by me. We said our prayer. After we finished, Mom affectionately said, "Rachel, it has been four hard and painful years, but God guided us all the way. There were times my faith was fading some. I'm sorry if you saw that. Now I know why I went through all of it. God wanted me to lean on Him. I did. I leaned so much, I must have knocked Him over time after time, but that's what He asked of me. I think about this special holiday. Easter is so important. I wanted you here with me, because Easter is not important to your dad. If it were, he would be in church. He only went once with me, and to this day I have never forgotten it."

"When they passed around the collection plate, I put a twenty in. Your dad glared at me and said "I'm gonna make you go to work, so you can throw away your own money." Grandma was sitting next to me, disgusted over what she heard. That was the last time I ever begged your dad to go to church with me. He's on his own now and look at what his life has become. When that shameful act occurred, you weren't even born. The church was just getting started."

"After we adopted you, I learned about your school and it was that same pastor who gave you his recommendation so you could attend there. In those very distressful days, his church was a needed part of my life. This pastor, our pastor, now has several churches, but the main one is still near us. I have always loved the way he and his dad preached. Remarkable men!"

"Every year around Easter, I look forward to the Christian movies. It's a very special, but sad time for me. Remember I told you about my Dad's death. Well it's Easter again. I will be watching *Ben Hur* tomorrow evening. Would you like to join me this year? I know Dad, Grandpa, would cherish it. He told me something on what would be his last night on earth that I want to pass on to you. I still remember that weekend like yesterday. I had shopped all day with Mom, Grandma. We were at the last store, when a strong feeling came over me to stay the night. So I did. Dad and I stayed up and watched the movie *Ben Hur*. After the movie we talked for some time. Your grandpa, my dad told me to never marry a man who would hurt me in anyway, but I did. On the day I filed for divorce, I thanked him for teaching me how to be strong. It can in handy living all those years with your dad."

"When I walked out of the courthouse, I looked up and saw a white dove fly by. I knew right then my dad was at peace. I got in my car in the parking garage and just sat in silence. I deeply felt inside that my dad was so proud of me and very much relieved I finally had the courage to walk away from so much unnecessary and intentional abuse. I thought I made a horrific mistake marrying your dad, but if I hadn't, you wouldn't be my daughter. God knew I was strong enough to survive living with your dad, because He knew you were in the waiting."

"I finally got away when the time was right. You know how hard and long I have worked trying to get you away from him too and I will still continue that crusade. My dad also shared with me that same evening that the most important message God wanted us to know was who Jesus really was and why He came to earth. I have never forgotten all of Dad's words that night. It will always remain the saddest, yet most memorable weekend of my life. I miss him so much!"

"It's taken some time Rachel, but things are getting better. I have finally found truth, happiness and quiet in my life again. Peace is following close behind. I want you to remember something I thought of. It's the word "TRUTH", a very powerful word. Jesus himself said, "I

380

am the way, and the TRUTH, and the life. No one comes to the Father except through me" (John 14:6 NIV). You learned this verse in Bible class this year. At Christmas, I was sitting at the kitchen table, doing some writing. I was staring at the word, when out of nowhere it hit me. I believe the word "TRUTH", T R U T H stands for "The Road Up To Heaven". Maybe that's why Jesus said it."

I saw something marvelous in Mom I had never truly seen before. Maybe I wasn't ready to see it until now. I kept staring at her beautiful, contented face. Everything she had been through and yet she never stops talking about God and Jesus. She has such a remarkable, resilient heart. It has been stomped on, broken, crushed, ripped apart and sewn back together, ripped apart again, hurt, deceived, let down time and time again and almost completely destroyed. I witnessed this time after time yet it was still intact because of her enduring love and strong faith in the one and only one that counted, Our Heavenly Father! My strong 'faith' not only comes from God, but also from the one who taught me the meaning of the word, my MOM!

I hugged Mom and whispered in her ears, "I will never forget everything you did trying to protect me. I will never forget what Grandpa told you and I will never ever forget your meaning of the word "TRUTH". This night will stay close to my heart, forever! I love you and I would love to watch *Ben Hur* with you and Grandpa!"

Mom kissed my forehead, then got up and turned the light out. She stood at the door and quietly said, "I love you too!" Mom left and went downstairs. The rest of lights went off. I closed my eyes. This was a wonderful night. I KNEW I would have a peaceful sleep, even if I didn't see Rain E. I had my Christian mom back, stronger now, than before filing for divorce!

*But small is the gate and narrow the road
that leads to life and only a few find it.*

Matthew 7:14 (NIV)

Chapter 40

I WAS in a deep and peaceful sleep, until the brightest light hit my face. I didn't want to wake up. I shoved my pillow and comforter over my head. I rolled over on my right side, away from the window. I tossed and turned for several minutes, hoping the light would move away. Nothing helped! Finally frustrated, I sat up in bed. The warm light was now sitting in my lap. My hands waved through it. This time it didn't just feel warm, it felt HOT! I moved my body to the left side of my bed and the light moved with me. I moved a little to the right. The light joined me again.

I slowly moved back to the middle of my bed, watching the light keep up with me. It was definitely following me on purpose. Strange and mysterious! This light became so blinding bright that I had to squint. I could feel the intense heat now on my legs. I opened my eyes a little wider and saw the light was coming from my bay window. I looked all around my room, twice. The light was completely covering me, and only me! I carefully crawled out of bed, searched with my feet and found my slippers.

I blindly walked to my window. With one hand over my eyes, I used the other to climb onto the fabric bench. The light was so bright I couldn't see which direction it was coming from. I was having no luck at all. Frustrated, I sat back on my knees to think. Then just like that, it was gone. I rubbed my eyes and leaned into the window. My mouth dropped open and stayed open. I couldn't believe what I was staring at. It was some kind of colorful road, right below my window and I was upstairs. It was floating in mid-air!

I grinned from ear to ear. It had to be Rain E, or some incredible dream. I raised the window and carefully removed the screen. As I was turning it sideways, it slipped through my hands. I watched it fall and land on a bush below. I would have to get it later. I looked back at the road. It was so unique and beautiful I just had to investigate.

I got up on my knees, close to the window ledge. Holding it with my right hand, I painstakingly stretched my left arm all the way out trying to touch the road. I was within an inch when my body smashed up against the frame. I wasn't going to give up. Not now! I leaned out a little farther. Now with my body halfway out the window, I was only a smidgen away from touching the road. I was trying to extend my left arm as far as it could go, when I lost my balance and fell out of the window. I was screaming so loud all the way down, I didn't care if Mom or the neighbors heard.

Then Boom!! I landed on my rear, right smack in the middle of this road. It was a soft and cushiony floating road containing all the colors of the rainbow, minus purple. Sitting there, I noticed the individual colors fanned-out, looking like a rainbow. I stood up, barefooted, looked around and found my slippers. Thank goodness they landed on the road with me. I was still in a daze. The funny thing was I didn't feel scared, just confused.

I was checking out my surroundings when I heard a familiar voice call out, "Rachel, stay on the outside and follow the road. We have so much to do in such a short time. Hurry, I can hardly wait to see you again!" It was my Rain E. "Stay on the outside! What did that mean?" I asked myself. I yelled back, "Ok. I'm on my way." Rain E hollered again, clarifying, "Start on red!" I looked down.

I was standing on the red, the color on the outside of the road. That's what she meant! I straightened my rainbow pajamas and hair and put on my slippers, then slowly started walking. I was watching my every step. There were deep indented creases between the colors, making it difficult to keep my balance.

I kept my eyes focused only on the colors and nothing else. I walked straight ahead. A few steps more and my feet were standing on orange. Then another couple of steps forward, I was balanced on yellow. At this point, I became very aware that after every few steps, not only were the fanned-out colors folding inward, they were shrinking in size causing the road to narrow. I stopped to rest. Then I nervously took another few steps and found myself standing on green. The road to Rain E WAS narrowing!

Taking only two more steps, forced my feet to squeeze together on light blue. Now close enough, I could to see the sky was a soft blue color with lots of fluffy white clouds everywhere. I bet Bolt was floating on one! I looked back at my home and screamed out, "Rain E, the road is gone!" Rain E calmed me by saying, "Remember the clock, do not look back only look forward. You are almost here."

I took a deep breath, then another one. By now the road was so narrow, I had to put one foot in front of the other to get out. With nothing to hold on to, I balanced myself like an acrobat. I have to tell you, I was shaking something awful! One more deep breath, I slowly and very carefully lifted my right foot and placed it in front of my left. As I was lifting up my left foot, the color changed to dark blue. I quickly planted it in front of the right foot. Whew! I made it. You know, that was kind of fun and adventurous. Slightly wobbling I didn't dare look back, only ahead.

There was a small step down below. I could see the thick, plush, green grass. I squatted down a little, then jumped with both feet flying high in the air. When I landed, I quickly looked up. There she was standing with arms opened wide. I cried out, "Rain E, it's really you! I prayed I would see you again!" Rain E smiled and said, "I know, I heard!" I ran to her. We hugged and hugged and hugged.

Then I abruptly took one step back because I realized Rain E had on rainbow pajamas, just like mine. I laughed out, "I love your pajamas." Rain E laughed too. Both our pajamas were long sleeved and flannel. Both tops had that same rainbow pattern going at an angle. The only difference, were the bottoms. Mine were red and hers were purple, just like the magic knee socks at Christmas! It felt wonderful to be back with my Rain E.

Looking all around, I saw in the distance that annoying bright light. I was glad it was annoying because it woke me up and brought me back to Rain E. I watched it slowly drift away along with all the clouds. I was now able to clearly see the entire place. I twisted my head around to look back at the unique road. It WAS completely gone. The front of Rain E's cottage had taken its place. Then I twisted the rest of my body around and found myself staring at the front door.

Rain E said, "Let's get going!" That sounded so urgent. I said, "Okay." We started walking fast. My mind started wandering. Something was different. I couldn't put my finger on it, but something was definitely different. I guessed it would come to me later. I could

385

see the pond and colorful bench, like always and just beyond that was "The Flowers of the Week Garden". We were heading in that direction.

The hills to my left and far right were loaded with trees and bushes. Rain E reached for my hand. We slowed our walk and strolled the rest of the way, enjoying the view. We were both quiet. The pond was within feet. When we reached the bench, Rain E said, "Let's sit a spell." I was just about to sit down, when I saw an extra color. It was "purple", the last color of the rainbow. "Wow! All the colors of the rainbow finally together! I was right. This was my seventh visit. I smiled big at Rain E. "Seven colors, seven visits!" I said with confidence.

We sat down covering most of the colors. I remarked, "I love the color purple. You don't even have to ask me what I think the color means to me. I know. Purple is referred to as the "Passion of Christ". I learned that at school and of course from my mom. It's a powerful color. Purple is associated with spiritual awareness and selfless love. I even love to write in purple! I know from my art class purple is a combined color of red and blue. Rain E, do you like the color purple?" Rain E genuinely answered, "Yes, I love everything about the color purple. It also represents wisdom, dignity and creativity. Most children prefer purple to all other colors. Rachel, I am overwhelmed and beyond impressed with your Christian knowledge relating to the color purple."

"Do you remember back when orange was added to the bench and I told you I would share extra information about it?" I eagerly responded, "Yes I remember! What else does orange represent?" Rain E was so serious when she said, "Orange also stands for "Separation". God separates from sin and evil. He cannot fellowship with sin. Please remember all of this I have shared with you." I answered sincerely, "I will."

We both took a deep breath and just looked out over the pond. Since our very first visit, over a year and half ago, we have always sat on this bench. "Wow! How time flies," I said to myself. That was how Rain E came to me, flying in the sky. All the colors of the rainbow were now on 'our' bench. All these visits were purposefully full of meaning.

The view was breathtaking. The pond was crystal blue and calm as could be. There was no strong wind, just a light breeze. The grass was thick and green as usual. The fluffy, puffy white clouds showed up again, gently floating across the sky. It was a perfect place. I sat there waiting for Rain E to speak next. Time passed by. Rain E reached for my hand. It was warmer than usual. "Rachel, my sweet Rachel, it has been quite a ride. I have laughed with you, comforted you, taught you and watched over you. You have blossomed beyond my wildest dreams. I am proud of you and proud of me. As I was helping you, you were helping your mom and your mom was asking God for help, then He helped me. What a complete heavenly circle! It has been a wonderful, productive journey."

"A journey that was filled with pain, heartache, joy, tears, sadness, patience, perseverance, and a lot of faith! It was the faith and your devoted prayers that brought us together. You asked for help and I was chosen to help you. When you called on God, God called on S TOR MY who called on me. Look at the remarkable change in you! You are now a stronger, full of life, beautiful Christian young lady. You hung in there and survived. Now you can survive anything, I am sure of it. Let me show you something."

Rain E reached on her side of the bench and grabbed that gorgeous clipboard. I finally got a close-up look. It was gold and silver, and very ornate, just like I saw from a distance. My eyes were glued to it, because my name was beautifully scrolled at the very top. Right under my name had the words "Seven Self-Helps" Down the left side was the numbers 1-7. Beside each number was a word with self in front of it. Rain E handed it to me. I felt like I was holding something holy.

The clipboard was warm, from Rain E's hands. My eyes filled with tears. I was reading a clipboard from Heaven. I felt a tear falling out of my left eye. Just before it hit the paper, a hand grabbed it. It was Rain E's hand. She looked at me and said, "Your tear is now a part of me and will never leave my body." I was choked up inside. Rain E wanted my tear. I composed myself and began reading out loud, "Number 1: Self-Esteem; Number 2: Self-Respect; Number 3: Self-Confidence; Number 4: Self- Awareness; Number 5; Self-Image; Number 6: Self-Love and Number 7." Number 7 was blank." I paused then asked, "Rain E, why is there nothing by number 7?" Rain E explained, "Number 7 visit is not completed yet."

"Oh, I get it, you have been like a teacher, and the subject was "ME". Right?" I asked. Rain E smiled and answered, "Yes and no. God has been teaching you. I was sent to show you those teachings and explain when needed." "Now I understand", I acknowledged. "I wrote to God for help. He's like the Head Master at my school and you are my classroom teacher. God gave you instructions and you did what He asked."

"Rachel you ARE so smart and wise beyond your years. Your mother taught you well. Listen very carefully to what I am going to tell. You have now been with me seven times. The number seven is a number close to God. It is mentioned in the Bible more than any other number. Seven is the symbol of completion."

I interrupted Rain E saying, "I know a lot about the number seven, from my mom. To be exact, the number seven is mentioned in the Bible 735 times, the most in Revelation, totaling 54. In (Genesis 2:2) God had finished his work creating everything. He was tired, so on the seventh day He rested. God made the seventh day holy. It says in (Revelation 10:7), the seventh angel is about to sound his trumpet and the mystery of God will be completed. Mom said that from the beginning of the Bible to the end, seven became the number representing completion, just like my time with you."

"When I saw the color purple added to the bench, I knew. There are seven colors in the rainbow. God gave Noah his promise never to flood the earth ever again. He gave him seven covenants and sent the rainbow as His promise. When God answered my letter, He sent you. You are my rainbow, Rain E Rainbow." Rain E proudly spoke, "You are an incredible child. Your biblical knowledge IS beyond your age level. Like I have told you many times, you have been taught well. My dear sweet Rachel, I came to assist, guide and teach you in the, "Helping Yourself" department. See on the clipboard, there are boxes checked beside the self-help you conquered."

"When we first met, you had little to no self-esteem. Look at you now. I loved teaching you the meaning of self-respect, concerning yourself and others." I remembered and quickly said, "Feeding the fish. They all ate together, sharing." Rain E then brought up, "Flying on our "alive" kites, scared you, but I knew when I deliberately headed into the storm, you would call on God to see you through. You did just that! That built up your self-confidence."

"Then came the "Dove Walk". You learned all about self-awareness, with a little self-assurance I threw in extra. When we reached the cave, I wasn't sure how you were going to handle looking at yourself in the mirror. Everyone has to face themselves, at some point in their life, whether they like it or not. Your self-image was greatly suffering! I am so sorry it was a hard experience for you. Now to let you in on a little secret! If you had not recognized what your dad had been doing to you was terribly wrong, the mirror on the other side would have stayed blank. The moment you broke down and said to me that your dad was never going to hurt you again, that was when I knew you gained a stronger self-worth and self-image of yourself. Do you remember that time?" I was quiet at first. Then I looked right into Rain E's eyes and stated, "I will never forget the cave. I know now how to stand up to my dad."

Rain E jumped right back in, "Just a few months ago, you finally let it all out. My heart ached for you Rachel, having to use the word "Hate". It goes against everything a Christian has been taught. I wanted you to know you had to release it. Your hatred and anger towards your dad had to come out. God understood. All those harmful emotions bottled up inside you for so long! It was destroying you. I know it was an unfair emotion you had to battle with. In time you will forgive your dad and the other adults that let you down. You are a kind and compassionate child. It is not your nature to hate."

I sat there and carefully took in everything Rain E was passionately explaining to me. She knew me so well. When she stopped talking I said, "I know I will forgive them all, because it's what God asks of me. It took a long time for me understand why I had to forgive people who hurt me. It was my mom who told me that I had to forgive them, even though they were not worthy of my forgiveness, because God wouldn't forgive me. She said to let God handle them because the Bible says He will." Rain E answered, "Your mother is absolutely right. Now here we are together again on your seventh and final visit! Let us go see the flower garden and all the other surprises I have in store. Then I will tell you about the last self-help." I smiled and said, "Like my mom always says, "Sounds like a plan"!"

We got up and headed to the flowers. Rain E kept the clipboard in one hand and the other hand in mine. Everywhere I looked was breathtaking. All the trees and bushes were full of either fruit or flowering blooms. The air was so sweet smelling. This must be Heaven. Everything here was perfect! When we reached the flower garden, Rain E walked over and hung the clipboard. I couldn't wait for her. I opened the gate and went straight to the flowers. Oh my goodness me! There were ten times maybe a hundred, more of this specific flower than all the other flowers combined! I mean, I had never seen so many of the same flower, growing all together. I knew this flower. I knew all of these were lilies!

Rain E walked up behind me. Usually she stood by the gate or startled me, but not this time. I looked at her face. She had an overwhelming look as though she was seeing her garden for the first time. I thought it was her garden. I always assumed it was. After seeing her face, I realized this was God's garden. Rain E was just taking care of it. I stated, "Rain E, this is the most beautiful garden of all. I have loved all the flowers on every visit, but this "takes the cake"! My mom told me that meant "Something Else"!

"These lilies ARE magnificent and "Something Else"!! Do they have a specific name, like the others?" "Why yes, my dear. They are called White Madonna Lilies," Rain E answered. I commented, "Maybe they were named after Jesus' mother, Mary. The lily is an Easter flower. It was the only flower Jesus ever spoke of. That's probably why it represents Him, as a part of Easter."

We stayed in the garden longer than all the other times put together. So much beauty to leave, but we finally did. Rain E took my hand and we walked out. This time the gate was locked. Rain E and I walked back to the pond. I turned my head back, waved and said goodbye to "The Flowers of the Week Garden" for the last time. Turning and twisting my body had to have bothered Rain E, but she never said a word. Quiet and polite like always!

We reached the lovely pond and bench. I thought we were going to rest a while. Instead, we walked right passed them. Up ahead was Rain E's cottage. Still as unique as always! I saw the lemon trees. This time they were packed with lemons. Some were already on the ground. I was going to pick one up, when a shadow covered the sky. I looked up and saw hundreds of doves flying by. I wondered if Dove was with them? I took Rain E's hand again and we kept walking. I never got a lemon.

We walked right passed Rain E's cottage. "That's it!" I screamed! "It's your door. It's white, not black! I knew something was different. Rain E why is your door now white?" Rain E stopped and of course I stopped too. She said, "So you noticed. Rachel, you never miss a thing. I will tell you about it later." She sounded so secretive. We walked to the right side of her cottage.

As soon as we turned, we were walking in the shade. I could barely see around her body. When we reached the other corner, Rain

E stepped aside. About twenty feet away was an enormous tree. I ran right to it. It was the exact kind of tree grown just for climbing. It had lots of thick branches. Two branches were low on purpose, begging me to grab them and hoist myself up into its home. So I did!

I started climbing when I noticed some ornaments hanging from the branches. I shouted down to Rain E asking about them. They were different colored, large-looking coins. Rain E shouted up, "Can you reach one?" I answered, "I think so. One more small step and I can grab the red one." I carefully balanced myself on to a sturdy branch then with my right foot I took one more step. I got it! Rain E said to pitch it to her. Then I slid over and reached with my left hand and grabbed the orange coin. I gently tossed it down. From there, I had to climb up two more branches to get to the yellow one. I slowly worked my way up.

As I stepped up to the next branch, my right foot slipped. I grabbed the branch above me with both hands and held on tight. Rain E yelled, "Be careful, it is a tricky tree!" Now she tells me. I yelled back, "I will. I've been climbing trees for years." I breathed deeply and pulled my body on up to the branch. I easily reached for the yellow coin and pitched it down. I was now pretty high up. In order to get to the green coin, I was going to have to climb in and around a couple of small winding branches. This had become quite an adventure!

I let both slippers fall to the ground. I needed to be barefooted to get a better grip. I squatted and worked my body around a twisted-up, pigtail looking branch. It reminded me of Rain E's hair. Twisting around a twisted branch! Pretty funny! "A couple of more steps to go and I'll be near the green one," I hollered." "Please be careful. You are way, way up there!" Rain E motherly yelled back. I took two small steps to the left, slowly leaned in, grabbed the green coin and dropped it. Whew! That one was tricky!

I glanced up to see where the last ones were. The light blue coin was only a step away. I scooted my feet across, holding on to the branch above me. "Got it! Here comes the light blue one," I yelled to Rain E. The dark blue coin was slightly to my left and up one branch. I grabbed the branch above me with my right hand. Then I positioned my left foot on a smaller branch near it and hoisted myself on up. Taking a longer much needed rest, I leaned my head up against the tree trunk and just enjoyed the view.

The dark blue coin was now close enough for me to just lift off. Cautiously looking down, I could see Rain E. Her arms were extended out, as I dropped it. The last one was near the very top. I pulled myself straight up and stood on the new branch for a brief moment. Then lifted myself up one last time. The moment my tired body reached the final branch I delightfully discovered I wasn't alone in the tree. My company was a beautiful white dove seating right beside the purple coin.

Never budging, I looked straight at the dove's face. The dove winked. "Olive, it's you!" I surprisingly spoke. She perched up on my shoulder. I gently petted her. She made a soft cooing noise then flew away. I watched her go upward into the sky until out of sight. I lifted the purple coin off the small branch and dropped and it below. I looked down. Rain E had the seven colorful coins all together.

Now at the top of this magnificent tree covered in green leaves, for the first time I wondered what kind it was. If I ever got back down, I'd ask my angelic friend. I was so tired! I was about to start my descent when Rain E hollered, "Rachel, you do not have to climb back down. Look to your right. See the rope attached to a seat. Climb on to it." I looked over and there it was. "Thank you," I gratefully shouted.

I worked my way over hugging the huge trunk and branches until I reached the rope. I carefully grabbed it, stepped onto the seat with my right foot, then left and cautiously turned around. "Now what do I do?" I shouted. Rain E hollered, "There's a green button on the left side of the seat. When you're ready, push it. It will quickly bring you to the ground."

As soon as I pushed the button, I was going fast, like on a zip line, only going down, instead of across. I reached the bottom in one piece. Rain E was waiting. I immediately told her what a blast that was and I wished that I could do it again. She said that I could one more time. I pushed the green button again and went straight up screaming with excitement, all the way to the top. I could hear Rain E laughing out loud. I got to the top and pushed the button again. This time it felt like I was going faster. I hung on tighter, screaming with joy all the way down. I stepped off and thanked my incredible friend for letting me ride it twice. She just smiled and giggled at the same time saying, "You're welcome my friend!"

I sat down on the grass by all the coins and collapsed on my back. I was pooped! My head landed right next to my slippers. The adventurous climb took a lot out of me. Rain E stretched out beside me. Finally rested, I sat up and stared at the coins. These coins were so cool looking. They look just like pennies, colorful pennies. Rain E sat up and handed me the red one. I held it close to my eyes studying every detail. The perimeter was indented. Across the front side, at the top read "In God We Trust", and to the left side the word "Liberty", just like a real penny. Abraham Lincoln's image was right smack in the middle. Amazing!

On the back had the words "E Pluribus Unum", meaning "out of many, one". I knew, because I learned it in my Latin class. It was on our American coins. I was going to inspect them even closer, when I got home. Mom told me that the traditional meaning of the phrase had to do with the original thirteen colonies: "Out of these colonies emerged a single nation". She also told me that the phrase "E Pluribus Unum" had thirteen letters in it, the same exact number of the original colonies. Thirteen letters, thirteen colonies! I wondered if other people ever noticed that?

"In God We Trust" was first put on the US coins, under President Lincoln. He was a good president and a good man. It was Benjamin Franklin who designed the first American penny. I also learned that at school and of course from Mom. I think Rain E already knew this, but she listened to me anyway, just like always. She didn't look at all bored. I liked sharing my history knowledge with her.

I sat there and admired the colorful pennies. The only things different from real pennies were the size, a small copper latch on the left side, and of course their colors. After a thorough investigation of the red coin, I decided to unlock the latch. Out fell a large letter. It was an "E". Rain E handed me another. It was the orange one. Out fell the letter "V". Then I was handed the yellow coin. It contained the letter "E". That made two "E's".

I was close enough to open the green coin. It contained the letter "I". Rain E politely handed me the light blue one. The latch was a little bent, probably from when I dropped it. So far, it was the only damaged coin. I finally got it open. Inside was the letter "L". Two left! Also near me was the dark blue coin. It was easy to unlatch. Out fell another "E". That made three. The last coin was the purple one. I asked Rain E if she wanted to open it, since I had opened all the others. She smiled and handed it to me and said it was for me to open, so I did. The last coin contained the letter "B". That was it!

Rain E said, "Now we have all these letters! Let us see what words we can spell." That sounded fun. I first spelled 'bee', then 'lie', then the name 'Eve' like Adam and Eve. Rain E asked if I saw anymore words in the letters. I spelled out the name 'Lee'. Then I spelled 'Live'. Then I saw it. The main word, "BELIEVE" That was it. Rain E looked at me and softly spoke, "Rachel, you found a lot of words in seven letters, but the most important one was, "BELIEVE". I love that word. It says so much."

"The word has seven letters, the same as the number of colors in the rainbow." Wow! I never thought of that. Rain E then said, "Close your eyes and make a wish. These round coin boxes look like pennies. So pretend you are tossing one into the pond." I told Rain E, "If I make a wish you will know it and it might not come true. You seem to always know what I'm thinking." "I will block it out of my mind, so it will come true. Now close your eyes and wish," Rain E added. I sat there with my eyes closed tightly. It didn't take long. I knew exactly what to wish for. I opened my eyes. Rain E leaned into my face and softly whispered, "I hope it comes true!" I whispered back, "Me too!"

We got up from under the tree. I put my slippers back on. Rain E said there was more to do. So off we went. As we were walking away, I asked her what kind of tree that was. She secretly said that it could be any tree I wanted it to be. I thought to myself. Then I said out loud, "I want it to be a Chinaberry tree, because that's what my grandma always climbed, when she was a little girl!" I looked back. It became a Chinaberry tree, just like that! Such a magical place!

We made it back at Rain E's cottage in no time at all. Rain E took my hand and walked me to her now WHITE front door. She said, "There are some people who want to see you." I opened the door. I could see the beautiful archway in the distance. I asked, "Are we going on the "Dove Walk" again?" Rain E nodded and said, "Come on! Let us get there fast!" She grabbed my hand and we started running. We ran across the thick, green grass. I stopped and took off my slippers. I wanted to feel the grass between my toes, just one more time. We took off running again, one hand holding the slippers and the other hand, just my pinkie, interlocked with Rain E's pinkie.

We finally reached the archway. I rested for a minute, so did Rain E. Running is fun and exhausting! I put my slippers back on. Rain E took my hand again. It was extra warm. Right when we reached the entrance, it lit up all by itself. We started walking through it. This was one time I was absolutely speechless. Now I know why I was blind-folded. Gracefully standing inside covering both sides of the archway, were real angels! These had to be the same celestial beings I saw in the clouds before the "Dove Walk" and while riding on Butterfly!

During the "Dove Walk", I felt feathers after I stumbled. Now I can confirm, it WAS a feathered-angel wing I grabbed. Tears filled my eyes and chill bumps covered my body. I realized I was part of a heavenly place. I didn't need to look up. All I had to do was look around then at Rain E. Her face sparkled. She gave me the most angelic, radiant smile. Even her long lustrous rainbow pigtails seem to grin. I contentedly smiled back at her and then turned to both sides and smiled at those pure, white heavenly angels. At the same time, they all smiled back at me. We finally reached the end of the archway. I turned and said goodbye to all of them. All at once, they nodded. I quickly glanced at Rain E to see if she saw it. When I turned back, the angels were gone. God must have called them home.

I turned back around and Stormy was standing there. "Stormy, it's really you. I didn't think I would see you again," I happily cried! Stormy greeted me saying, "Rachel what a wonderful difference a year makes. You look so much happier and stronger than ever before. I am so proud of you my child!" I sincerely answered, "Thank you. You look as beautiful as ever. Thank you for letting me finally see the mysterious and very secretive "Dove Walk" archway. I even got to see Olive for a brief moment." Stormy just smiled.

As we were standing there I noticed right past her, all the doves resting in the same spot as before. I wondered if Olive was among them. I didn't want to disturb their sleeping, so I gently and quietly stayed glued to Stormy's side until we passed by them. Now standing near the cliff, she softly spoke that she needed to talk to me. I followed her to a nearby sitting area, I had never seen before.

There were three large whitish-brown, flat stones. Stormy and I each sat on one. Rain E stayed behind. Stormy began, "Rachel, I have been carefully observing your visits. I know how much Rain E has helped you. We are awfully proud of her, but even more proud of you. You and your mother have had many difficult times and that has burdened my heart and God's. You never gave up on your faith. Absolutely remarkable for such a young age with so many obstacles!"

"My time has come to an end with you. I want to leave you with one last thought. Always remember these words "All authority in

Heaven and on Earth has been given to me." Do you know who spoke those words?" I smiled big and shouted, "YES!" It was Jesus. I just learned that Bible verse this year." Stormy continued, "You are 100% right! So remember my sweet Rachel, Jesus has all authority, not those bad judges and adults who did not protect you."

"I am so deeply sorry your mother stood before those two very harmful, uncaring judges. You and your mother suffered greatly from their decisions. Remember, just like your mother told you "Beloved, never avenge yourselves, but leave it to the wrath of God, for it is written Vengeance is mine, I will repay, says The Lord" (Romans 12:19). So keep leaning on The Lord and remember what I told you before, to never think of taking your life." I said, "I won't. (Wow! Stormy even knew what Mom told me). Thank you for caring so much and an extra thank you for telling me all about the "Dove"! I love my pet, "Olive". Thank you for her too!"

Stormy tenderly held both of my hands in hers warm hands. We stood up, staying close to one another. I really studied, even more than last time, what she was wearing. It was a solid white, full-length flowing gown. I could see the fabric was silk. Even with her long sleeves covered with crystal sequins, I could still see she was wearing her gold and silver bracelet. The neckline scooped in the front. I couldn't see her back. I never saw if she was wearing the toe ring, but I bet she was.

She released my hands then with her left hand she touched my cheek. I stared right into her eyes. I was getting choked up. I felt some tears coming on. Stormy was saying goodbye. I could feel it. This was it! I reached up and touched her hand that was still on my cheek. As one of my tears rolled down touching her fingers, I tried to wipe it off but the heavenly warmth of her entire hand instantly dried the tear. I looked up at her face. She was glowing so much she was almost lit up.

My eyes looked up above her head. I gasp! There was a golden halo over her. Stormy was an angel! I took several deep breaths, then several more. Stormy took both her arms and lifted them up to God. I gasped even bigger. Out from her back appeared two enormous white, feathered wings. She blew me a kiss. It was warm when it hit my face. I blew one back. I called out, "Goodbye S TOR MY !" Oh my goodness! I pronounced her name correctly! I smiled as she disappeared into the clouds. I stood there in shock.

As S TOR MY disappeared, Bolt appeared on a cloud. He floated down to me. I smiled big and called out, "Bolt, how are you? How are Snowflake and Cotton Ball?" He happily replied, "I'm fine. Snowflake and Cotton Ball are great! You look wonderful. No more black eyes, I see. Just that beautiful smile and happy look!" I timidly said, "I didn't know you saw my black eye. I tried to hide it. I was so ashamed, but now I'm stronger and DO stand up to my dad." Bolt proudly answered, "I knew you could do it. You have had a great teacher in R A IN and a wonderful, caring mother at your side. I had to come say goodbye, before your special time continues with R A IN. Take care stylish girl!"

Bolt turned his cloud around and started floating away. Just before he disappeared, he loudly said, "Rachel, you have a lot to share with others, SO DO! Bye my sweet. I will miss you!" I waved back and yelled out, "I will miss you too and your stylish rainbow-colored suit you're wearing. Love your white boots." I kept my eyes focused on him. Just as he was disappearing Snowflake and Cotton Ball joined him. Flying high in the sky, they both looked back at me and nodded their heads, just like before. I nodded back. They were all gone! I will never forget them! I will never forget S TOR MY!

I stood there staring at the sky in hopes of getting one last glimpse of all my departed friends, when Rain E walked up. I turned and said, "When I drew you two years ago, I never in my wildest dreams thought you were real. Now here I am, standing by my drawing! Thank you for coming to my rescue. I know God sent you. I wrote Him and finally my prayer was answered." Rain E sincerely answered, "Yes, I knew you drew me and prayed to God for help. I was sent to help you because I am your "Guardian Angel". You realized early on who I was because of your strong Christian beliefs, but it was not my place to tell you, just yet." It was an emotional moment. We stood there and just stared at each other.

Then I remembered the doves sleeping. I asked Rain E, "Why they haven't budged with all the commotion going on?" She commented, "Maybe they are in a deep sleep. Bend down and wake them." I quickly remarked, "I don't want to disturb them." Rain E said, "Go ahead." I reached down expecting them to fly away, like the first time. They didn't move. My hand touched something cold. It wasn't doves, it was snow!! I whipped my head around to where Rain E was standing. She was smiling big. She declared, "The first time you wanted snow and a snow cone. This time I delivered. Come stand by me."

I got up and stood right in front of her. "Think of your favorite snow cone flavor. Close your eyes and turn around once." I thought of strawberry. It WAS my favorite. I quickly spun around. When I opened my eyes, Rain E was holding the biggest strawberry snow cone I had ever seen. She handed it to me. You know, this was the only time, in all my visits I was given something to eat. What a great choice of food!

We sat back down on the large flat stones. I was enjoying every bite of my snow cone. I told Rain E that my mom said there was food in Heaven (Mark 14:25). She giggled. I asked Rain E if she had ever enjoyed a snow cone. She said that she hadn't. Rain E asked if I knew how this icy cold treat came about. I explained, "This man named Samuel Bert invented a snow cone making machine in 1920. He sold them at the largest State Fair every year until he died in 1984. That's a lot of snow cones! I wished I could have met him and thanked him for inventing one of my favorite snacks." Rain E sat there, hopefully enjoying my story. She just patiently waited for me to finish my snow cone. It was good! I completely ate every bit of it, including drinking the juice.

After I finished my delightful snack, I looked up at Rain E. She looked so serious. She said, "I am so proud of you. I HAVE been watching over you for a very long time. You have been through sad times, and I am sorry for that. God knew you were hurting, and yet you never truly gave up on Him. I know it was hard to understand why it took so long for help to arrive. Your mother told you the truth. God is not on your time you are on His. God has a plan for you and your life. You will continue growing stronger in every way. I love you Rachel Rene and God loves you too." The tears started again. Rain E's words were comforting and beautiful.

It seemed to be getting a bit colder, maybe because my insides were freezing from the snow cone. Snow cones DO produce temporary, but yummy chill bumps! Rain E got up and said it was time to go. She said she wanted to show me something else. We backtracked through the archway. The angels were gone, but the wonderful smell of honeysuckle was still present. Rain E walked in the middle. I on the other hand, stayed right up against the archway dragging my hand across the 'now' vines all the way to the end.

When we reached the entrance, I took one last look to burn it into my brain. I wanted to remember every detail, from the vines, the honeysuckle, the ground, to the angels. I smelled my hand. It smelled of honeysuckle. It smelled heavenly. I took my slippers off again, so I could walk in the grass all the way back.

We were back at the cottage, standing two feet away from Rain E's "white" front door. Rain E simply said, "Open the door." I turned the extra-large knob. It felt like the large knob that was on my bathroom door. I opened it and there was another door. It was red. In the middle of the door, in very large letters the words, "Self-Esteem". I opened it and on the back was the outline of a large box. I turned to Rain E. She handed me an over-sized check mark. Rain E said, "Place it in the box." I did. The door lit up.

I turned back around. I was standing in front of an orange door. It read in large letters the words, "Self-Respect". I opened it and there was another outlined box. Rain E handed me another check mark like before. Then I turned around to a yellow door. It read "Self-Confidence". I went through it. The check mark was sitting by the side of the door. Rain E handed it to me. I put it in the large box on the back of the third door. This was fun!

I turned to a green door. It read "Self-Awareness", along with smaller letters "Self-Assurance". Rain E handed me another big check mark. I remembered when she told me about the extra "Self" help. I wanted to make it more fun, so I spun around twice. I was now looking at a light blue door. It read "Self-Image". I will never forget this one. It was the cave visit. We both went through like before. This time I asked if I could pick up the check mark. Rain E told me that it would be absolutely fine. I told her this was one check mark I wanted to apply extra hard so I would always remember the mirror.

Next I decided to spin in the opposite direction. I stopped right in front of a dark blue door. This door read "Self Love". The ice pond! The visit where I let it all out! It will be a part of me forever. I opened it and we stepped through. Rain E handed me the check mark. I placed it in the box and quickly turned. This door was the hardest to deal with, but easiest to leave.

I was now facing the purple door. It was the last color in the rainbow, the last door. I read in even bigger letters," SELF-BELIEF". I went to open it. Rain E wasn't near me. As I turned the knob, I heard her say, "I am waiting on the other side." I opened it and there she was holding the last of the check marks. It was the biggest of them all. Rain E said, "Before you put this one on the final door, I want say again how proud I am of you. You have self-belief in your life now. Never lose sight of that. Your "Seven Self-Help" chart is complete! Now apply the check and watch!"

I gladly took it from her hands and then firmly pressed it into the box. The final door lit up like the first door. Once applied to the door, the door itself began to tremble! A little uncomfortable at what I was witnessing, I quickly stepped back. Within seconds, the whole door was wildly shaking. Then all of sudden the purple door shoved into the dark blue door and kept shoving into each door until reaching the red door. The door became a rainbow-colored door. All the doors became one. Rain E told me to open it.

I was a little afraid at first, but with Rain E at my side, I bravely did what she requested of me. All of a sudden, the rainbow door lifted to the sky and bled back into a rainbow I saw in the distance. I bet it was the rainbow I slid down on my first visit. Now here at my last visit, the rainbow door returned home, probably preparing for a visit from another sad child. I did hope so!

As I looked around, I saw everything I had seen on all my previous visits, all together. I stepped through where the door had been standing to take a closer look. Rain E stayed behind. I saw the pond, the bridge and the "rainbow" bench. I looked to my right and saw the cave. The whole entrance was now completely filled in. I saw all the beautiful hills and the valley where we rode our 'live' kites. Straight ahead was the archway. I walked towards the pond. I could see "The Flowers of the Week Garden". It was the only thing that looked different. I raced to it. When I arrived to the entrance gate, I realized for the first time in my life I knew what it felt like to be blessed with sight. I will never take it for granted again. I stood there mesmerized witnessing the most spectacular, breathtaking, heavenly garden ever imagined!

All the flowers I had seen before were now beautifully blended together. The unlocked gate had already been purposely pushed back inviting me in. It was as though the flowers were waiting for me. So of course, I accepted the invitation and rushed into the garden to join them. I just had to be a part of them! I briskly walked up and down all the paths several times admiring all the individual, brilliant colors, when suddenly I abruptly stopped! Goodness me! I had forgotten about Rain E! I went back to the entrance. She was standing there smiling, holding the clipboard and the lock. I watched her walk over and gently place the clipboard back on the hooks. My sheet was gone, leaving only a new blank sheet. Maybe ready for another hurt kid!

I walked through the gate and looked up. The sign now read, "The Completed Journey Flowers Garden". MY journey had come to an end. Rain E told me to turn and face her. I did and gasped again! I've been gasping a lot this visit. My mouth dropped open. Rain E spoke, "I love you Rachel Rene." Then I spoke, "I love you Rain E Rainbow. I will keep you in my heart forever. You rescued me and helped me in so many ways. Thank you."

I was now staring at the most beautiful angel, my guardian angel! Rain E was no longer rainbow colors. She was draped head-to-toe in a gorgeous white dress similar to what S TOR MY was wearing. Her hair was golden again, like when she iced skated by herself. Rain E blew me a kiss. It traveled so slow I could see it moving in the air. It landed over my heart. I blew one back. I watched it float through the air, until landing above her head. Then it circled around forming a golden halo. Wow! I made a halo!

The halo raised Rain E off the ground. She was leaving me. We said goodbye to one another. As Rain E was disappearing in front of my eyes, she shouted, "I'm only a wink and a pinkie away!" I screamed out, "No Rain E come back. I forgot to ask you something. Rain E come back!!!!!" Come back. Come back. Come baaaack."

I opened my eyes and was back in bed, staring at my ceiling. I got up and ran to the window. The screen was still attached. I crawled back in bed thinking it was all just a dream. At least it was a wonderful dream. I closed my eyes remembering it all. God must have put Rain E in my thoughts and soul, because she seemed so real! She just had to be real! I forgot to ask about the nice black man at the hotel in California and why the road was narrowed. Oh well, guess it was too late!

I was about to doze off when whispered in my ear were the words, "The road to Heaven is narrow, but wide enough for you, my special child. Keep living the Christian life. You are on the right bridge to that everlasting road! Also one last thing, Always be kind to others, you never know when you are talking to an angel." I grinned ear to ear. I firmly announced, "It was you!" Rain E giggled "No. It was STOR MY."

I whispered back, "Imagine that"! Rain E answered, Yes, you didn't just "Imagined that", you "Lived That"! I fell asleep saying goodbye to R A IN. I said her angel name, just like S TOR MY. I finally could pronounce both of their names on the same day, the last day. This would be the most happiest, peaceful sleep of my life!

"Out of difficulties grow miracles."

Jean de la Bruyere

Chapter 41

I woke up a few hours later. I lay there thinking about my angel, R A IN. It was sad to say goodbye, but I knew it was time. She and the others had helped me so much. I couldn't wait to tell Mom all about them, but first my drawing had to be completed. The surprised look on her face would say it all. The gratifying event would be taking place on Mother's Day next month. I looked over to my left and realized the narrow rainbow road that had just been outside my window, was my final way of reaching R A IN's heavenly home! I was beyond thrilled that my last time two visits with her happened while I was at home.

Mom came up to wake me. She touched my shoulder, thinking I was still in a deep sleep. I rolled back over and said, "Boo!" Mom took a step back and stated, "You silly! You scared the 'dickens' out of me!" Mom fell on the bed pretending to pass out. I leaned over and looked at her face. She quickly opened her eyes and scared me with, "Boo!" We giggled.

Mom pulled up on her elbows and remarked, "You look rested. Did you have wonderful dreams all night?" I didn't even know how to truthfully answer that question. All I said was, "I had the best dreams ever!" Mom added, "You know, I did too, "Imagine that". I loudly gasped! Mom asked if I was okay. I quickly responded, "Oh, I just had something in my throat." Mom said, "Better start getting ready for church, then it's lunch with the family! We'll share dreams later on tonight. How's that sound?" "Okay Mommy." I cheerfully said. I called her mommy, again. Still feels good! I had forgotten it was Easter morning with all that was going on in my dreams. Mom headed downstairs. I secretly checked under my mattress. The drawing was still there. I went to get ready. I put on my purple outfit and silver sandals. I looked very "stylish", as Bolt would say.

When I was walking out of the bathroom, I noticed an elegant antique-looking box with a purple bow tied around it. I hurried to open it. It was white gloves, just like the ones R A IN gave me. I immediately thought, "Wonder if she left them here for me?" I carefully slid the gloves on, one at a time, individually dressing each finger until the extremely soft fabric was perfectly in place. I turned the lights out and headed to Mom's bedroom. Grandma was coming out the same time. She said, "Don't you look lovely! So grown up!" I smiled big! I guess I did look grown up.

Grandma had on a vibrant pink dress, with white trim. She also looked very nice. She even had on silver looking shoes similar to mine. When we got downstairs Mom was just coming out of her room. She looked amazing. She had on a slender skirt with blue and yellow flowers all over it. Her top was a white button-down with a short blue sweater over it. Her sandals were a silver-gold color. We all looked pretty 'spiffy'.

Mom stated, "Oh, I see you found the box of gloves." "Did you leave the box on the table?" I asked. Grandma answered, "No, I did. Your mother and I believe you are now mature enough to wear something very old and treasured!" I remarked, "The gloves don't look old!" Grandma continued, "They are not only old, they are yours to keep. They have been in the family a long time. Your great, great grandmother passed these down to her daughter, my mother, and I passed them down to your mother. Look the inside."

I took the gloves off and turned the fabric slightly. I felt a textured, raised part near the base of where the thumps go in. The tiny initials RR were beautifully embroidered. I was stunned. Grandma then stated, "See, you have the same initials as my Grandmother Rainy Rachel. Your Mom always loved the name Rachel, from the Bible, and from her ancestors. So you see, the gloves were destined to be yours." I hugged Grandma and Mom. I told both of them how much these gloves meant to me and that I would cherish them forever.

As we were leaving, I spotted our two cats sleeping in the den chairs. They never budged. They're cats, what can I say! We all piled in the car. Before pulling out, Mom turned to me and said, "Rachel, I am so thankful you are here with us on this Easter. I am so proud of you standing up to your dad! It's the beginning of a great day!" I was happy for many reasons. My special gloves were an added touch! Off we drove.

The church was decorated with hundreds of lilies. They were everywhere. Sunday school was first. I saw all my school buddies. They were thrilled to see me on Easter. Even the youth pastor came up and hugged me. Mom and Grandma met me after Sunday school ended. We all headed into the sanctuary. It was stunning! More lilies everywhere! I wanted to sit up front. So we did. The service was emotional. Our pastor was amazing! He talked all about the resurrection. He read from John as I followed along in my Bible.

My favorite part was when Mary Magdalene went to the tomb and the heavy stone was rolled aside. I got emotional reading when she was weeping for Jesus and saw the two angels. That must have been something else to witness! I loved that Jesus spoke to a woman first, because someday I will be a woman. This was the exact Bible story Mom told me last Easter. This time our pastor shared it with his congregation, which included me. He did a great job! I have always loved hearing all about Jesus and Mary Magdalene. She saw angels and didn't realize it and I saw angels and finally realized it. Mary saw Jesus and someday I will too!

After the service was over, we had to leave fast in order to get to the restaurant in a nearby city. I said goodbye to all my buds. Mom said goodbye to our pastor and thanked him for a wonderful service. It felt so good finally celebrating Easter with my mom in church, after three years. It took about an hour to get to the restaurant. We parked and headed on in. One of my cousins and her husband were walking in at the same time. We all sat at a large table. I counted eighteen of us. Everyone complemented my outfit and told me how glad they were to see me. I just blushed. The food was fantastic. One of Mom's brothers paid for everybody. That was nice of him. We all said our goodbyes. I could hardly wait to get home to finish my drawing.

On the way, Mom was listening to her piano friend's music mixed with other piano music. This song came on. It sounded just like the one, when I was skating with R A IN. Then the next song that played was the same song R A IN skated to by herself. How weird was that! I bet R A IN had something to do with it! She wanted me to know she was always close by. I reclined my chair. Grandma always let me sit in the front, because my legs were longer than hers. I asked Mom if I could play the last two songs again. She said that I could enjoy listening to them over and over all the way home. As I closed my eyes, my mind traveled back to the iced pond. What a visit that was! It relaxed me so much I fell asleep. I didn't wake up until Mom nudged me, after the car was in the garage.

We walked in together. Grandma had already gone in. Sitting on the kitchen table was the biggest Easter basket. It was filled with "Goodies". I hugged Mom so hard. What a difference from the awful baby egg hunt last year with Dad and the dysfunctional crew. I carried it upstairs. I wanted to look at it for the rest of the day. I changed into a T-shirt and jogging shorts.

Mom came upstairs and we watched *Ben Hur*. We enjoyed a couple of chocolate eggs during the movie. I even ate a few yellow marshmallow chicks. I really liked the movie. Mom pointed out that the man who played *Ben Hur* also played Moses in *The Ten Commandments*. What an impressive actor! I was glad Mom asked me to watch the movie with her. Grandpa was there too. I just felt it! Mom got up to go get ready for bed.

It was getting dark outside. The wonderful day flew by way too fast! I didn't get to work on my drawing, but I would have all week and next weekend. I took a quick bath and changed into my rainbow pajamas. Just as I was slipping the top over my head, I smelled something familiar. I removed it and closely sniffed it some more. I fell back into my vanity chair. It was strawberry!! I must have spilt some on my top, when I drank the juice from the bottom of my snow cone. I put my top completely over my face. I could smell Heaven!

I heard Mom coming up the stairs. I quickly pulled the pajama top all the way on and climbed into bed. She walked in and sat beside me. "How did you like your basket?" Mom asked. "I LOVE IT! You don't treat me like a baby," I proudly stated. Then Mom quietly asked, "How did you like the movie?" I smiled and said, "I loved it and I loved having Grandpa there." Mom contentedly smiled and added, "I loved having him there too!" We said our prayer and talked about the day. Then Mom said, "Tell me all about your dream last night. Was it adventurous?" "You go first. Tell me what you dreamed?" I eagerly asked. I knew it would either be exciting or scary.

Mom got in bed beside me. She took my hand and started, "I woke up in the middle of the night and looked over at my door to the backyard. I could see vivid colors trying to sneak their way in through all the cracks. There was this one tiny space near the doorknob where more colors were peeking through. They were able to reach my bed. I took my left hand and passed it through them. The colors were warm, almost hot."

"I moved my fingers back and forth watching the colors circle around my entire hand. Then twirling and swirling the colors wrapped themselves up into a bow. I was mesmerized. I couldn't take my eyes off the traveling colors. Then they were tugging on my hand, wanting me to follow, so I did. I was near enough to see the colors circle the doorknob on purpose. I unlocked the door, turned the knob and carefully opened it."

"More colors instantly filled my room. It was amazing and incredible. The colors let go of my hand and floated up. I stood at the door and watched them join a rainbow road. It was above me floating in mid air. Isn't that odd?" I interrupted Mom and asked, "What time did this happen?" Mom continued, "I'm not sure. It felt like morning, because everything was so bright. I kept my eyes on the road. It went way, way up into the sky! I walked out all the way to the pool, and noticed an unusual, tilted dip in the road. I was able to touch the bottom."

"The moment I did, I was pulled all the way through. I ended up landing on a star. I looked above my head. Two gold ropes were attached to the pointed part of the star. I was sitting on a star! It began slowly swaying. It reminded me of Frank Sinatra's song, "Swinging on a Star". A few moments later, music started coming from behind me. It was that exact Frank Sinatra song. I was in total shock to say the least. Nothing else to do except sing along. My dad used to sing it to me and when you were little, I sang it to you. I stopped Mom again and remarked, "I know. I remember. It had animals in the song." Mom gladly stated, "I'm glad you remember. It has always been a special song to me."

"Anyway, I kept swaying back and forth. I was scared at first, but swinging helped calm me down. I just figured it was a wild dream and I would eventually wake up, but I didn't wake up for a while. Just like on the song, I saw a mule drifting by me. Next I saw a pig. They circled around me then disappeared. I kept looking straight ahead. I saw a large rainbow striped fish leap into the air. I watched it splash in a small pond and disappear. I kept telling myself that this was the craziest, yet the most colorful dream, I had ever had."

"As the swinging star started floating down, several monkeys ran by. Passing through the rainbow road, the star landed outside my bedroom door. Just before I stepped off, the mule and pig ran by. They both gave me a wink then vanished into thin air. I stepped off and the star lifted up into the sky. I looked back up and the road was gone. I was opening my door, when I heard a splash and quickly turned around. That same fish came flying out of our pool then vanished. Never saw the monkeys but that one time!"

"I walked in my bedroom and locked up. I crawled back into bed. A few hours later I woke up when my phone alarm went off. I lay there for a few minutes reliving the entire dream. Funny thing, it didn't seem like a dream. It was so real, but why didn't the home alarm go off when I opened the door? I climbed out of bed, turned off the home alarm, and opened the back door. No road was there, just a clear sky! I glanced across the yard and noticed the pool cover was still attached. It hadn't been removed yet! That's when I realized it was a dream, even though it sure felt real."

I was stunned to hear that Mom dreamed about the same road I was on. I curiously asked, "Mom, what do think your dream meant?" Mom specifically told me, "Dreams can relate to our daily lives. Sometimes we relive traumatic events while dreaming because they made such a lasting impression. For me it was when the shark bumped me while I was floating in the ocean. I still have nightmare shark dreams to this day."

"In my dream last night, I believe the mule represented the importance of learning and the pig was to remind us to always take care of ourselves." I asked her, "What about the fish, the monkeys and the star?" Mom said, "I think the fish leaping out of the water was a way of escaping, even if it's just for a brief moment. The monkeys were just having fun. The swinging star, that's an easy one: To me it represented feeling carefree and alive!" Mom asked me about mine. All I told her was I dreamed I was in Heaven and it was beautiful. Mom said that must have been a wonderful dream. I told her that it was.

She got up and gave me a kiss on both cheeks, tucked me in and told me to have more sweet dreams. Mom turned the lights out and went downstairs. I rolled over and stared at my bay window. My eyes were getting heavy. I could still see R A IN. I will miss her. I yawned myself into a contented, peaceful sleep.

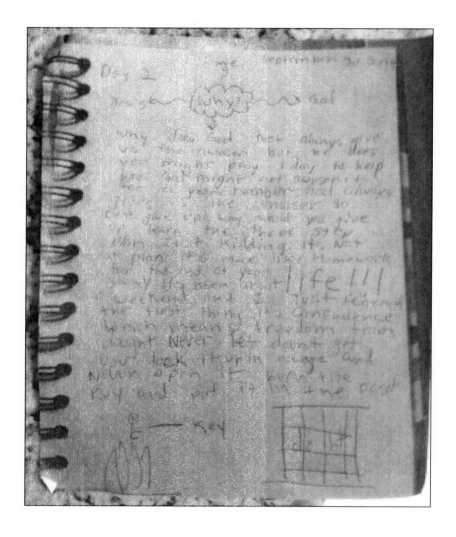

"Don't cry because it's over.
Smile because it happened!"

Dr. Seuss

Chapter 42

Easter was gone 'til next year! R A IN, S TOR MY, Bolt, Dove, Butterfly, Snowflake, Cotton Ball, Olive and my angel dreams also gone. I would miss them all. I knew they would return someday. Mother's Day was around the corner and school was almost over. Back to Dad's for those two extended visits and dreading every minute of it! Dad had calmed down for now. Sissy stayed out of my way. Goofy Tray married Delilah. They seldom came around. Dad DID hire her as his bookkeeper. Wonder what was next on their "Plotting Agenda"?

"The Boys", each had a baby girl with women they never married. I overheard Dad tell Sissy he hired Ronny. I guess this way he could still spend extra time with him. Sick! My ex-grandma has kept her distance from me. I hadn't seen my ex-blood sister and that ex-prisoner boyfriend of hers, James, since they went into drug rehab. Mom finally told me some of what he did, causing him to spend a lot of time in jail. I now knew why the courts protected me from him.

I still had a lot of anger towards the judges and family members who didn't care enough about my happiness and safety. I would never have any good feelings about them again. Mom told me "Forgiveness can't change the past but you can work on changing the future." She was right! What would the future hold for me? So many decisions would be mine! I would eventually forgive Dad and all the others, I just wouldn't forget. The day would come when I could legally walk away from all of them for good!

It was the Friday, one weekend before Mother's Day. I know, because I had been counting down the days. That important day when I handed Mom her gift, "the drawing"! Mom came down sick that morning. It was the first time she had stayed in bed, since her heart attack. My best friend's mom drove me to and from school.

When I got home that afternoon, I headed straight to her room. Grandma stopped me dead in my tracks. "Grandma, I want to see Mom!" I urgently requested. "I know you do, but your mother is very sick and contagious. Her fever was so high this morning, I had to drive her to the doctor, and you know I don't drive much anymore," Grandma explained. "Your mother has pneumonia, and she doesn't want you to get it again. Remember how sick you were in Florida? She needs plenty of bed rest."

I was scared for Mom. I DID remember how bad I felt! I stood at her door and was about to leave when I heard, "Hello my sweet." "Mom!" I yelled out. I started to go in. Mom immediately said, "No, no Rachel, don't come any farther. I hate to say it. The words even feel nasty rolling off my tongue, but this is one time I'm glad you will be at your Dad's. I'm too contagious right now. When you return Sunday, we'll be able to hug, I hope." "Okay Mom. I'll go finish my homework and wait for *the honks*." I stayed quiet as I walked away, closing the door behind me. I immediately prayed, "God, heal my mom, in Jesus name, Amen." That was the shortest and to the point prayer I think I had ever said, except "Help me"!

I diligently worked on my homework, at the kitchen table. Grandma helped me with grammar. My mind kept drifting, thinking about Mom. Grandma noticed my worried look on my face and gently spoke, "She will be fine. God is watching over her and us." I smiled a little and then went back to my homework. I finished around 5:00 pm. Dad would be here in an hour. I raced up stairs to change. I had some time to work on my drawing. No chance of Mom walking in! I got it out from under the mattress, along with the pencils and some crayons.

I started first on the "Coin" tree. I could still remember where each hung. Next, I drew the angels in the archway, and S TOR MY with her halo. I placed Bolt, Snowflake and Cotton Ball in the sky around some clouds. I had time to add to the garden putting all of the flowers together, to remind me of my last visit! I looked at my phone. It was 5:45 pm. As I was holding it, a text dinged. The message was from Mom. It said, "Now I lay me." I started crying. I text back, "Down to sleep." Here came, "A bag of peanuts." I sent, "At my feet!" Next came, "If I die!" I text, "Before I wake!" Mom finished, "Give them to my brother Jake!" I cried and laughed out loud.

The next text came, "I'll be fine. Don't worry. I just need rest. I love you!" I quickly text, "I love you too Mommy!!!!!" I put everything back in hiding and headed downstairs. Grandma was making Mom some hot tea. She took it to her while I stayed by the door. Mom blew me a kiss and I returned one.

I heard *the honks*. I sadly spoke, "Bye Mom. I'll text you again tonight." Mom replied, "Bye my love!" Grandma walked me out. I hated leaving Mom, but I knew Grandma would take good care of "Her" daughter. I got in the backseat. Something was odd, no Sissy in the front. Dad said that she was resting. He had to take her to the hospital because she passed out from her diabetes. Mom told me last year, "Sissy has 'Juvenile Diabetes' and if not controlled, results could be deadly."

I guess I didn't realize how bad it was until Sissy slipped into a coma, while we were on vacation. She didn't have much feeling in her feet and couldn't see well. No wonder Mom refused to let her drive me around! I now had a better understanding of Sissy's disease. I wish I understood the mental disease that plagued Dad!!

I stayed quiet in the car. Dad on the other hand looked mad. Maybe because he had to take care of someone other than himself! Who knows? He started talking about having a party for Sissy's birthday, which was following week. He demanded me to make her a birthday card and write all over it, "I Love You" and "You are Like My Mom" and to sign it "To Sissy Mom, Love Rachel". I wanted to heave. Three years later and Dad still wouldn't drop it. I couldn't stay quiet any longer. I flat out said, "NO!" He started calling me a mean and hateful brat. He demanded me to make Sissy a birthday card and write all that "crap" on it. I said even louder, "NO! You can't make me!" Then my dad said the most hurtful words ever.

He smarted off, "Fine, just be a hateful "F" n brat. As far as I'm concerned, you are nothing but a piece of trash I can throw away in the garbage. You've been replaced anyway. I have a NEW daughter!" I was shocked! Was my dad THAT mean and cruel? I had my answer, before even finishing my thought. I WOULD NEVER forget this car ride. That was it for me. I looked at Mr. Evil and said, "You'll be replaced too! As my friend R A IN said "Watch"! I never said another word. Mr. Evil didn't even bother to ask who R A IN was or what I meant. I knew because someday Dad will "WATCH" me walk away!!

415

Words! Words! Words! So many wonderful words to choose from each day, kind and loving words to be said! NEVER did any of them come out of Mr. Evil's mouth! Where did these hurtful words even come from? Did he just have an evil dictionary along with his evil heart? Did he enjoy hurting me? Did he still want to kill me? It was like in the movie *Austin Powers*. Dr. Evil went to 'Evil' medical school and wanted to kill his son. Maybe that was how my dad really thought? I came up with his nickname watching that movie. Dad was not a doctor, so I substituted "Mr. for Dr." It was a funny and sad feeling rolled up into one!

One thing I did remember from watching that funny movie was the scene in Las Vegas. Mom told me that the man playing the piano on top of a car was Burt Bacharach. He wrote many songs, including *The Bell That Couldn't Jingle*. A wonderful song! I would sing it to my kids someday. I would love my kids so much. I would never hurt them!

"Why would anyone want to hurt or even worse want to kill a child? Why? Why do people have kids if they don't want to take care them?" I sadly thought. Too much to comprehend! There were times my brain just couldn't handle my two different worlds. I would go to the dysfunctional, distasteful and demonic house of horrors, then back to my marvelous home full of morals and manners.

The weekend was "tiptoe" quiet. Dad stayed at the hospital most of the time. I didn't go. I didn't care. So I studied, watched movies, talked to friends and text Mom. Early Sunday morning, Dad barged in and said he was taking me home now. Sissy was coming home at noon. Dad said she needed peace and quiet in the house. I asked, "So where are YOU going?" He just glared at me. Again, who cared! He deserved everything I shoveled his way. I was ready in a jiff. Yea!!! I was going home early! I text Mom I would be there shortly. She was thrilled!

Dad had just pulled out of the garage, when he called Martha. He had it on speaker. At first she didn't pick up. Dad started cussing about that. He called back. A different voice answered the phone. I thought Dad had dialed the wrong number until I heard the voice shout, "What do you want NOW?" It wasn't a wrong number, it WAS Martha! I was in total shock. I didn't make a sound! I kept my head down, pretending to play on my IPad. This was too juicy, not to listen in on. Dad screamed, "You stupid mother "F" r. If you had a brain you'd be dangerous." (This time I said it along with him under my

416

breath, with my head tilting back and forth). I'd heard it so much I had it memorized. Dad continued his violent speech, "I told you to get your worthless ass to the house yesterday, before Sissy comes home. You are the sorriest of the sorriest!" What did that mean? Another confusing question for Mom!

Out of nowhere, Martha said two of the most wonderful, long over-due words, "SHUT UP!" Dad abruptly stopped screaming. Martha yelled, "I am sick and tired of the way you treat me and ashamed of myself. I command you to stop cussing at me. I should have never lied in court and protected your ass. Rachel has suffered greatly from your hands and mouth, and I could have stopped it. God will never forgive me, because I lied in court and didn't tell the truth about your abusive behavior. I have seen you harm Rachel and still did nothing because of my fear of you, my own son. I can tell how much she hates me and rightfully so. She will never forgive me. I will NOT be in your life if this is how you will continue treating your daughter and me."

"I am almost eighty. You NEED medical help, if it's not too late. I blame myself for not whipping your butt when you were young. I knew something was wrong the day you came home from the Boys' Scout retreat. You dropped out one week before becoming an Eagle Scout and have been punishing me ever since. When your troop leader died just a few years ago from AIDS, I mentioned it to you. You totally changed the subject. What ever happened back then, I didn't cause, yet I was blamed. You need professional help to work through whatever is eating you up inside. Stop blaming and hurting all those around you! Rachel WILL walk away someday. You can bank on it!!!" Martha hung up.

Silence immediately engulfed the car! I couldn't believe what I heard. I didn't understand what Martha was talking about with the Boy Scouts and AIDS. Wasn't "Aids" other helpers? What was that all about? I would definitely ask Mom. Dad never said a word. It was as though a deep dark secret was revealed. I didn't say a word either. After the screaming match, I recognized not only are my visits with Dad depressing and disturbing so are my car rides with him. He pulled into the driveway. I quietly got out and watch that beautiful, but tortured new car drive off. A car that held so many uncomfortable secrets! If only it could talk! Dad slowly drove away, which was also weird.

As I was walking to the front door, I realized I had the same school T-shirt and sweats on all weekend. Grandma let me in. I rushed to

Mom's bedside. She was sitting up watching TV. Mom turned the sound down and asked how I was. I told her I wanted to talk when she felt better. I couldn't wait to tell her about Martha's conversation. She was going to die! Mom said she felt better, but still needed to stay in bed until Wednesday, doctor's orders. I went to my room. There was a note on my bed saying my best friend's mother was taking me to and from school all week. She's a great Mom too. I unpacked and headed to the refrigerator. There was leftover pizza. Cold pizza! Yum!

Grandma had slept on the den sofa all weekend to care for Mom. She looked exhausted. I told her I would watch Mom for a while and that she needed to get some rest. Grandma did just that. I checked on Mom. She was asleep. Grandma came down around 9:00 pm to give Mom her medicine. I also went in. I sat with her a while.

Mom had on a Doris Day movie. I've loved her movies since the first time I watched with Mom, *The Glass Bottom Boat*. Most kids probably don't know who she is, but I do plus a lot of other movie stars from Mom's generation. Some of my other favorite movies from along time ago, that I haven't mentioned are, *Butch Cassidy and the Sundance Kid*, *Singing In The Rain*, and *It's A Mad, Mad, Mad, Mad World;* That one's hilarious, especially the small plane scene and the couple locked in the paint store.

Mom let me watch *The Birds*. I liked that one too! My all-time favorite movie that came out when Mom was young would always be, *That Darn Cat*. I guess really good movies have been made in every generation. We finished the funny movie.

Mom looked tired. I said goodnight. Mom said the same. I went upstairs and took my shower. I said our prayer for the both of us. I jumped in bed and got out my drawing pad. I finished all the trees and plants, R A IN skating and what she wrote in the ice! I fell asleep working on it.

Monday morning arrived. I woke up with the pad still on top of me. Grandma knocked on my door. I hollered I was up. I hid everything in the mattress and got ready for school. I heard the doorbell ring. It was my best friend. Grandma said Mom was still asleep. So, off to school! Mother's Day was Sunday. I secretly worked on my drawing every night, after everyone was asleep. By Wednesday, Mom was up and moving around. All the boxes were packed and ready to go Saturday.

We were moving to a new home the same weekend of Mother's Day. I think that was why Mom came down sick, packing for a month.

It was a busy week. Friday evening, while in my room, I carefully pulled out my drawing. A satisfying smile took over my face. The drawing was finished, from the Rainbow slide to R A IN saying goodbye. Staring at it brought back sad and happy memories. So sad that I had to say goodbye to R A IN, but happy that she came into my life! I slid the drawing back under my mattress. Tomorrow I would wrap it up beautifully!

"Try to be a rainbow in someone's cloud."

Maya Angelou

Chapter 43

The movers were there at the crack of dawn. I crawled out of bed and removed my drawing pad. I didn't want them moving it. I kept it by my backpack to secretly carry to the new home. I got ready and headed downstairs. Mom was in the kitchen. She had donuts for everyone. It took all day to load the furniture. Grandma stayed at the old house. Mom was heading to the new home, when she asked if I wanted to join her on the first trip. I did. The movers followed. When we turned on our new street, I saw lots of kids in the neighborhood. Maybe that was why Mom bought a home here? We parked in the street, so the movers could easily unload.

I went upstairs to my new room, carrying my pad and backpack. Mom never suspected a thing. I stretched out on the floor and played on my IPad. When the movers needed my room, I just moved to another. I helped Mom carry in all our personal stuff that had been loaded in the car. The movers finally finished! Mom went back and forth several more times. I got to guard the new home! The last car trip Grandma and our two cats arrived. Everyone was pooped! It was a long tiring day! Moving was HARD!!

It was after midnight when Mom came up to check on me. She had on her long-sleeved red nightgown and UGG slippers. I had on my rainbow pajamas, just like the ones R A IN wore on our last visit. I wanted her to feel a part of our new home. Mom tucked me in and we said our prayer. Then she said, "Everything is going to get better. I promise. Even though you have to keep seeing your dad, it won't last forever. I'm stronger and I KNOW you are stronger too. If anything happens to you, we can and will go back to court. There's a new judge on the bench." I rejoiced, "I know. He's a "Republican! I'll be okay."

I paused for a moment then said, "Mom, there's something I want to ask you. What's AIDS?" Mom looked at me strangely and asked, "Where did you hear that word?" I said, "From Martha." Mom asked, "Why would she be talking about that to you?" I explained, "She wasn't talking directly to me. She was screaming at Dad over the speakerphone in the car. I know I'd heard of AIDS. I know it means helpers, like the teacher aides at school, but isn't it also a bad disease?"

"Martha was screaming and screaming at Dad about a Boys' Scout camping trip. Something about Dad blaming her for something that happened at camp. Martha yelled that she was not going to take his cussing anymore and to seek help. She kept yelling at Dad to stop punishing her for something she didn't cause." I absorbed Mom's expression. She had a stunned but contented look on her sweet-revenge face. A look as if she already knew about the Boys' Scout trip! Mom never revealed what she knew. I didn't inquire.

Mom then asked me, "Did Martha say anything else? What did your dad say?" I remembered, "Oh yeah, she admitted she lied in court and didn't protect me, then hung up. Dad stayed quiet." Mom boldly remarked, "YOU ARE KIDDING!!! Too bad you didn't record it!" Mom looked at me smiling. I grinned like the sneaky "Grinch" and said, "I DID!" Mom was beyond elated.

She listened to the whole conversation and instructed me to never erase it and never let Dad get into my phone. I promised. Mom kissed me on the forehead and remarked, "You have become quite the little detective! I'm proud of you for taking such smart and clever, almost dangerous risks." Wearing a gratifying smile, I replied, "You said you needed "Hard" evidence. I guess this was it!" Mom got up and turned out the lights as she left my room. I crashed! My body was "spent" from the move, but my mind was overjoyed from recording Martha. Mom was so proud of me. I HAD become a detective, a professional detective!

The next morning I was awakened with the sun shining on my face. I struggled out of bed and turned the blinds the other way. I glanced through the window to a beautiful sunny day. Maybe the bright light was Rain E letting me know she was nearby! (I still like calling her Rain E) I actually loved both names. Wonder if she felt the same? I climbed back into bed. The time on my phone said 7:00 am. I easily fell back to sleep.

The next noise I heard was Mom. She hollered to get ready for church. I dragged myself to the bathroom and got ready. I forgot to get the wrapping paper before it was packed. I had a purple satin ribbon I always kept in my desk. The drawing pad was still resting under my bed. I lifted it out and tied the ribbon around the whole thing. This way the drawing wouldn't tear. Mom could rip it out after returning home from church and lunch. I was wearing my floral sundress Mom bought a month ago. I had on black glittery sandals. I was ready to go. I took one last "lady" glance in the mirror before heading downstairs.

I snuck the pad all the way out to the garage and secretly put it in the car. Grandma helped distract Mom. Ten minutes later we were out the door. Church was wonderful. I saw all my buds! Lunch was at the wonderful resort. It was crowded because of Mother's Day. It was a buffet like before, except with extra food and tables in several rooms. We, of course, helped ourselves. The food was *delish*! Mom and Grandma had one of those mimosas. I had iced tea. This nice man walked around and handed all the mothers a yellow rose, Mom's favorite.

Then, I reached down and handed Mom her gift. Grandma had helped me sneak it into the restaurant. With excitement and anticipation going on inside me, I watched as Mom untied the purple ribbon. My eyes were glued on her face, as she lifted the hard cover. Mom's mouth dropped open. "Rachel, my goodness! This is the most beautiful drawing you have ever done. The colors! All the different landscapes, people and animals! How did you ever come up with so many interesting and unique things?"

I proudly said, "I had seven dreams about this place!" "You did!" Mom excitedly stated. "Was that the dream you told me about at Easter?" I hem hawed around then answered, "Sort of, well yeah, but there's more." I politely asked if we could talk in private when we got home. Mom said that would be absolutely fine. We finished eating and headed out.

All the way home, the drawing rode beside me in the back seat. Like I said, usually Grandma let me sit in the front because I had longer legs, but I wanted to sit with my drawing. It was around 2:00 pm when we got home. I went up to change. Mom took the drawing to her room. I said I would be right down. I hurried and changed into a pair of jean shorts and T-shirt and raced to her room. Mom was sitting up on her bed just resting from the lunch and from of course, the hard move. I climbed up beside her.

We carefully lifted the top covering together. Mom was really studying the drawing. She looked at every detail. "Do the numbers on the different flowers represent something of importance?" Mom curiously asked. "Each time I dreamed about my angel's home, she had a different flower in her garden. I put a number by the flower I saw in the order of my dreams, so I wouldn't forget when I'm older." Mom interrupted, "Your dream was about an angel?" I told Mom, "Yes. My angel's name is Rain E. Her angel friends are Stormy and Bolt. There is so much I want to tell you, especially how Rain E and I met."

"Mom, do you remember when I wrote to God asking for help?" Mom immediately answered, "Yes! That's when I found your letter under your pillow, after you had to go with your dad for fifteen days. That will always be a memorable day tucked away in the sad part of my brain." I continued, "The second night of that grueling visit, was when dad punished me over cutting a triangle brownie. I had been sitting at the kitchen table doing my homework, when I got up to take a look at the storm. I saw something moving in the clouds. I'm not kidding!"

"When I went to bed that night, I cried out to God worse than ever. I even asked if he received my letter. Well, that night after I fell asleep, I was awakened by the violent storm. I went on the balcony and fell off." Mom interrupted again. "You never told me that!" "I didn't really fall off, I dreamed it. Mom, I met a wonderful angel named Rain E, after coming off a rainbow slide and landing on the grass in front of her home. I visited her seven times over the course of two years. She's the one that helped me survive my times at Dad's. She's the one who taught me how to stand up to him, because I was a human being and didn't deserve being abused. Mom, Rain E's not just an angel, she's my angel! I found out on my last visit, even though I started suspecting it sooner."

I looked at Mom and she stated, "Rain E had to have been your angel. The change in you IS something else! God DID answered your letter! Rachel you know everyone has a guardian angel. All you have to do is ask God for their assistance. They are there watching us 24/7." I told Mom, "I know. Rain E knew everything about me, even before I told her. I hope someday she returns and you can meet her. I want to share more with you about my dreams and the drawing, but I'm kind of tired. Can I go lay down for a while? I think it was the move that did me in." Mom said, "Of course. I'm a bit tired too." We hugged and I excused myself. I went upstairs to lie down. I passed by Grandma's room. She was resting too.

About an hour later, the doorbell rang. I heard some commotion going on downstairs. Then I heard, "Rachel honey, Can you please come down here? We have company." I rolled out of bed. I mean I rolled out of bed landing on the floor. I was turning the corner stair when I heard voices. I reached the bottom and standing there was a woman, a teenage girl and a little boy. Mom said, "Rachel, these are the Ashby's, our neighbors next door. This is Mrs. Susan Ashby, her oldest daughter Angela and this little fellow is Colt." I shook their hands. "Did you say, oldest daughter?"

Mrs. Ashby replied, "Yes, my younger daughter, Pinkie will be right over. She forgot something and also badly needed to clean up. She and her paints have been playing outdoors all afternoon." I remarked, "Pinkie's an unusual name." Colt jumped right in, "I named her that!" Mrs. Ashby stated, "Her real name is Penelope, but when Colt was a toddler he used to hang on to Penelope's pinkie, following her throughout the house. He loved the attention his sister gave him. Colt had a hard time pronouncing her name. It kept coming out "Pinkie". The name just stuck! Pinkie never minded. To this day those two, pinkie-lock fingers before getting out of the car for school."

The doorbell rang again. I went to open it. I gasped out loud. Mom asked if I was okay. I quickly turned my head and said, "I'm fine." I whipped my head back around to the new neighbor. This girl loudly said, "Hi there, friend. I'm Pinkie." Pinkie confidently strolled on in. I was in shock. Her mom scolded her, "Pinkie, I told you to wash up!" She stated, "Pinkie loves to paint and chalk on the sidewalk, driveway and sometimes on herself. She is always getting the entire colors of the rainbow in her pigtails. I call her my "Rainbow Pigtail" mess." Pinkie embarrassed, whined "Mom!!" I gasped again. Mrs. Ashby said the words "rainbow" and "pigtails" in the same sentence. I needed to sit down, but didn't. I just kept staring. Pinkie asked, "You gotta name?" "Uh, yeah. I Uh I'm Rachel," I stuttered. "Hi there Rachel. I just turned thirteen. Do you like to paint?" I cautiously answered, "Yes."

I couldn't stop staring! This girl was about my height, a little more slender than me, fair-skinned, with freckles only around her nose. I think her hair was a reddish-brown color. Not sure with all the paint splattered on top! She had on jean shorts and a tie-dyed short sleeve

425

T-shirt and no shoes. She dressed like me! "You like my T-shirt?" Pinkie proudly asked. "I made it myself with one of those kits. It's easy and messy fun!" I said, "I made one too! My mom bought me the kit last year." Pinkie excitedly asked, "Can you find it amongst the boxes?" I happily announced, "I know exactly where it is. I'll be right back!"

Pinkie quickly called out, "Wait, first take these. They're still warm!" Pinkie handed me this foiled-covered plate that she had carried in. It WAS still warm on the bottom. I peeled back the foil and gasped again. It was brownies cut in the shape of "TRIANGLES". I fell back onto the sofa. Angela said, "We always cut brownies and other foods into different shapes. Today Pinkie chose triangles. Hope you like them? They're from scratch. My mom's a fantastic cook. She's been teaching me. I'm 17 years old and very much want to learn. Pinkie sometimes takes part in the cooking lessons, but she prefers the outdoors. Colt is 9. He sits on the counter and just watches us cook." I handed the brownies to Mom. She took them to the kitchen.

After I went upstairs and changed shirts, Pinkie asked if I wanted to go outside and do some chalk and paint drawings. I said that I would love to. I was intrigued with this unique individual and NEEDED to get to know her better. We politely excused ourselves and headed to Pinkie's "art studio" (the sidewalk). While we were walking, I kept eyeballing Pinkie's hair, stumbling a few times, before we reached the art supplies. "Are you going to stare all day? Let me fix this!" Pinkie voiced.

She reached down and grabbed her watercolors. "Now stand perfectly still. I'll make your hair "rainbow" like mine." I stood still, straight and as tall as a board. I watched as Pinkie painted my hair. She dipped her paintbrush into all "Seven" colors of the rainbow. "There! We're Twins!" My new interesting pal announced. She handed me a small mirror. Pinkie was right. My hair looked exactly like hers. "We've got masterpieces to do. No time to waste!" Pinkie loudly proclaimed.

I gasped again. (Pinkie just said the same phrase, like Rain E). Pinkie asked, "Are you alright? Do you have acid indigestion in your stomach? I've seen that on TV commercials. Is that what's making you gasp? Come on, sit a spell and rest your insides. Crisscross applesauce! Been saying that since kindergarten!" I surprisingly added, "Me too!" Pinkie was funny and clever with words, just like Rain E.

We sat right beside one another legs crossed, and started chalking. Pinkie inquired, "Do you have a dad?" I said, "Yes, but he doesn't live with us." Pinkie said, "Oooh! The big "D"." I asked, "What's the big "D"?" She said, "You know, "Divorce". It's going around like the plague. Half the kids I know have divorced parents. I'm telling you, it's the plague!" I asked, "Are your parents the big "D"?" Pinkie dropped her head and kept drawing. She never looked up and abruptly stopped chatting. I stayed quiet. A few minutes passed. Then she sadly spoke, "No, my dad died in Iraq." I saw a tear drop out of her eye and land on the colored sidewalk. The blue color bled. As a second one was falling, I caught it.

Pinkie looked up. Tears were now showering her cheeks. She cried out, "It's not fair. I hate war!!! Why did we have to send troops to another country? Why? My dad was coming home a week before my fifth birthday. Colt was just a toddler. He doesn't even remember him. Mom said Dad was killed when a bomb exploded. Most of the men with him were injured or killed. Dad was closest to the explosion. She didn't go into any specific details. I guess too hard for us kids to hear! I just miss him so bad. I was too young to lose a dad over a stupid war. I'm sorry, but that's how I feel. I know the president was protecting our country, but my dad was the one who was supposed to protect me!"

Pinkie leaned her head into my chest and just bawled. I put my arms around her. I understood that kind of sorrow. I felt it when my mom almost died and when all our pets passed away. This was her dad. I could tell she loved and adored him. That warming, bonding love, I didn't understand. I never had it with my dad.

We continued hugging. I cried with her. It was at that moment we became instant friends. She leaned back and said, "Thanks my friend. That's the second time I have cried since the news of Dad's death. I needed to get the hurt out. It had been bottled up for so long. I know it was worrying my mom. Thanks for pulling it out, my new best friend." I smiled, "You're welcome, new best friend." I knew I already had a best friend. I think it was just fine to have two.

I then remarked, "It's sad. You miss your dad and I don't. Doesn't seem fair. Your dad protected and loved you and my dad never protected me and NEVER, EVER loved me! We have each other now. That's all that matters!" We both smiled big and proceeded with our drawing, of all things, "A Rainbow".

As we were drawing, something brushed up against me. I heard, "Stormy, get out of here, before you get paint on your paws again!" I whipped my head around. "Is that your cat? Did you say her name was "Stormy"?" Pinkie said, "Yeah she's been with us, gosh, at least eight years. I still remember swinging in my backyard when she came over the fence. She was a "MESS"! Matted hair and dirrrty! She moseyed right up to me and started rubbing against my leg, like she was home."

"Mom saw her from the sliding glass door and came running out. The cat went right up to her, as though she knew her. Mom broke down in tears. I stopped swinging and asked what was wrong. Mom picked the cat up and held that pathetic creature, right in front of her eyes and spoke, "Now I know you are with us!" She took the cat inside for a bath. I followed. Mom bathed that "mess" in the utility sink, then handed me a towel to do the drying. Sis and little Colt sat in the living room. I joined them holding the cat. Mom said that she would be right back. We all waited a bit. I kept the towel-drying going. The cat never tried to scratch or claw me. Strangely sat calmly in my lap."

"Mom finally returned from her bedroom, caring a photo. She stopped dead in front of us three and held it in front of our faces. We all gasped. It was my dad in uniform holding a dark gray cat that looked identical to the cat wrapped in the towel. At the bottom of the photo read "My new pal "Stormy". On the back was a note that read "Found her roaming in the bushes, during a storm. My troop took her in. Seems to fancy me at bedtime. Curls up at my feet. Hope she can continue warming my toes back home. Named her "Stormy", because of her colors and, of course, the storm. Miss and love everyone, Dad".

"As far as I know, that "Stormy" never made it back to the states, but our "Stormy" found her way to us. She's been a part of the family ever since." I heard a "meow" and turned around. Here came Sugar. Sugar and Stormy sniffed each other then ran off playing. I guess they were now best pals.

We went back to our drawing. My back was to the sun when Pinkie said, " "Rach" (that's what she now calls me), look at that! I know we have doves in our state. I've just never seen one that snowy white! Rach, turn around!" I turned around and sure enough, the dove was headed our direction. Pinkie added, "It's carrying something in its mouth." We both watched as the dove moved closer and closer towards us. I gasped again! Pinkie commented, "You should really have that stomach checked out!" I said, "Oh, I'm fine."

The dove was now within feet of us. To get a better look, I put my hand above my eyes to block some of the sun. Pinkie continued, "Rach, I think the dove is coming straight to you! Don't let it poop on you!" I giggled. Pinkie was as funny as Rain E, maybe just a bit more. My eyes stayed focused on the dove. It was circling above us. All of a sudden, the dove dropped what was in its mouth. It landed right in the middle my lap, as though I was the intended destination.

Then the dove circled over us once more, ending directly in front of my face. It winked! I gasped, this time, covering my mouth (Pinkie thinks I'm ill). It was Olive! I watched her circle one more time, flapping down just her right wing. She was waving goodbye. I yelled out, "Bye Olive!" Pinkie asked, "Who's Olive? You know that dove?" I smiled and said "Kind of. Tell you about it later." Pinkie firmly stated, "You better! No secrets between best friends!"

I looked down in my lap. It was one red rose, with the bloom half opened. There was a note tied to the long stem. Pinkie impatiently shouted, "Rach, read it out loud!" I untied the string and unfolded it. It read: "Your life is now blooming. It will continue to bloom, until it blossoms. Thanks for the promotion! Remember: I am only a prayer and a pinkie away," signed, "RR". I looked up to the Heavens. Pinkie said only, "Wooooooo! Somebody up there likes you!" I corrected her, "No, somebody up there LOVES me!"

Mrs. Ashby, Angela and Colt came outside. Mrs. Ashby said, "Time to go in Pinkie. School tomorrow. It was a lovely day getting to know your mother. Hope to meet your grandmother tomorrow. Your mother said she was resting from the move. Moves are HARD! It was only two summers ago we moved in, though seems like yesterday. How time flies! My dear, it was especially delightful meeting you!"

Angela headed on in politely saying goodbye. Pinkie got up and helped me up. We gathered up all the art supplies and placed them back into Pinkie's red bucket that had been sitting between us, while we were drawing. Colt carried the bucket on into the house. We dusted ourselves off and spontaneously gently slapped our hands together. Pinkie then gave me a double wink with her left eye, crossed her middle finger over her index finger on her right hand, and held it in front of my face. I returned the same comical facial and hand gesture.

I watched as she brought her crossed fingers closer to mine and we gently clanged them together like two swords, then Pinkie quickly switched the crossed fingers in the opposite direction. I did the same.

We clanged them together again, then made a fist and clanged the fisted knuckles together. That day, it became our secret greeting! We were going to think of a name to call our greeting when we got together again. Pinkie had stated earlier that we were "TWINS", and two winks and two crossed fingers could represent "Twins". It was going to be fun having a "named" secret greeting. Never had one before!

As Pinkie headed in, she loudly stated, "Tomorrow after school Rach, we'll talk and chalk some more. Let's draw with our left hands. It'll be adventurous. See ya!" I chuckled. Talk and Chalk! Pinkie WAS funny! She went inside with her mom. Walking to my front door, I hollered back, "See ya!" Before I went in, I turned and took one last look at the sky. The sun was gone, but the rays graciously allowed me a final glimpse at Olive in the distance. I watched until she was completely out of sight. What a heavenly creature!

I was turning the doorknob, when I realized I had forgotten my rose and note. I hurried over to retrieve it. They were gone. I frantically walked all around Pinkie's yard and driveway. The rose and note were nowhere to be found. Pinkie never picked it up. She went in empty handed. I stood there in a daze. I guess it was meant for me to see only once, yet Pinkie was allowed to see it. I thought to myself. "My new curious and funny best friend will be asking me all about "Olive" and the "note" tomorrow. I can count on it. I do believe I would enjoy telling her!" I chuckled.

While standing by myself, I realized there had to be a heavenly reason we both saw it! Maybe because my time had ended with Rain E, and now it was beginning with Pinkie! Who knows? Only two I could think of, God and Rain E! I knew Rain E would always be near. I think meeting the Ashby's was planned. Wait a minute! Mrs. Ashby said they moved here two summers ago! Two summers ago I met Rain E! Wait another minute! R A IN said she was a wink and a pinkie away, then in the note she was a prayer and pinkie away. Pinkie! My new friend!!

I got choked up inside thinking all about it. I called out to God, "Thank you!" That was all I could say. No more words could get passed the cracking throat and voice. I quietly stood there a few more minutes, gazing at God's sky. I went in, locking up behind me. Mom was in the kitchen. She said that Grandma was upstairs doing crossword puzzles, unpacking, resting, or all. I gave Mom a big hug and then planted a bigger kiss on her cheek. I thanked her for choosing this home.

I raced upstairs, took my tied-dyed T-shirt off and laid it across my material chair. My jeans, I left by the door. They definitely needed washing. Lots of paint everywhere! I took a long shower, washing the paint out of my hair, even though I wished it could have stayed in. I got out to finish my bathroom routine and toweled dried my hair. All the paint came out. I jumped into bed.

Mom came up and we said our prayer. I said to her, "I hope you had a wonderful Mother's Day. Mom responded, "It was the best Mother's Day ever. I will cherish my drawing!" Then I added, "I love the new neighbors. Pinkie is quite a character. We're gonna be great friends! Mom, can I ask something? Was Angela adopted?" Mom said, "No love. Angela is from Mrs. Ashby's first marriage."

"Her dad had cancer and died soon after Angela was born. Susan, Mrs. Ashby, grieved for years, then she met Pinkie and Colt's dad. It was such a horrific tragedy how he died. She has now lost two husbands." I remarked, "I know Pinkie sure misses her dad. I wonder what that feels like? Angela is beautiful. Her skin color reminds me of my very special friend Stormy, the one in my drawing. Colt's a cutie pie." Mom agreed, "Yes, Angela is beautiful. She could be a model. Colt is adorable. Looks like how you would picture a cherub. I do believe Pinkie is going to be a life-long friend of yours. Something or someone is telling me that!"

"Maybe Pinkie would like to sleep over this weekend. I'll tell the both of you the "Spooky" story I promised you! It's about the ghost in Matt's apartment. It will give you goose bumps all over your body! Your cousin, my nephew told me about it the night it happened." "Yea"! I cheered and added, "I bet Pinkie likes scary and spooky stories like me. I just sense it. I'll ask her tomorrow after school. Thanks Mom for being my mom. I love you! I also love your stories. Will you tell the shark story again this weekend? Pinkie is gonna die!!"

Mom kissed me and said, "I WILL! Now close your eyes before you scare yourself and can't go to sleep. Maybe your angels will visit again soon. Night my love." "Night Mom." I turned on my side and said goodnight to R A IN, S TOR MY, Bolt, Dove, Butterfly, Snowflake, Cotton Ball, Olive and (Pinkie). I prayed, "Thank you God for sending all of them, and thank you for bringing Pinkie into my life. To you Rain E, "R A IN", thank you for helping me with my life. It was "DARK" because of my dad, but because of God, you made it "LIGHT" (7times)!!!!!!!

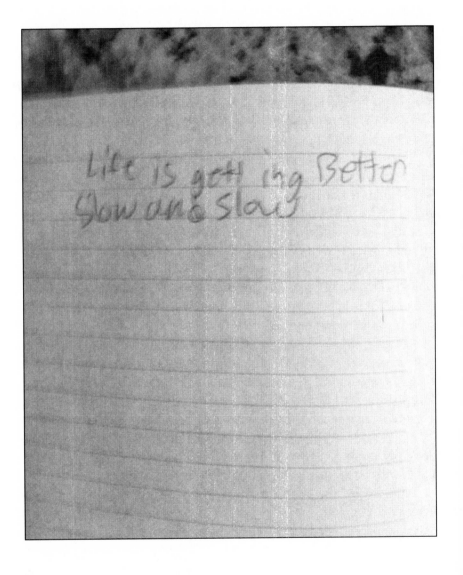

Epilogue

They say time heals. I think that's a dumb thing to say. Why do I want to wait for time to maybe heal me and help me feel better, when God can help me feel better right now. Time will go on, dragging with it my painful and detailed vivid memories. These memories tangled up inside of me forever. Time only puts distance between those memories and me. That's all it's good for. I believe time will even have trouble getting rid of the painful scars left on my heart. Scars from my dad and all those "26" worthless adults, who didn't help me at all!! God will have to help me deal with this too. How long it will take to erase these memories? I honestly don't know.

I still cannot believe so many adults failed me! Here's the list I promised:

- Two (2) - (worthless) Judges;
- Three (3) - "original" (money-grubbing) Attorneys, (that's how Mom described them. I quite agree!)
- One (1) - (non-caring, daddy-friendly court-appointed) Therapist;
- Two (2) - (one who only wanted to talk, the other one fell asleep during sessions) Child Psychologists;
- One (1) - (who just wanted to medicate me) Psychiatrist;
- Five (5) - (who gave up rescuing me) Policemen;
- One (1) - (just said document everything) Detective;
- Six (6) - (the worst out of the whole bunch) CPS women; (including the first social worker Mom spoke with)
- Three (3)- (never reported the abuse to authorities) Doctors;
- One (1) - Ex-grandma and *finally*

My only blood sister who is now my ex-blood sister! "26" adults and not one of them stood up for me! It took almost *three* years before someone actually tried to help. Mom's new attorney tried and the wonderful social worker I told you about. It still wasn't enough to permanently get me away from my dad. I do, from the bottom of my heart thank both of them for trying. My wonderful, caring teachers and new doctor wanted to testify but were never allowed. Thank you also for trying.

When I look at this list, my blood sister and ex-grandma by far hurt me the most. My own family! So devastating! How do you live with yourself knowing you lied to God, while testifying in court? All I can say to each and every one of you disgusting adults, I hope your final destination is HOT, REALLY HOT!!!!!!!! It will take time, but like I said, I will forgive every last one of you miserable human beings, I just won't forget. How much damage was done? Time will tell.

I thank God every day for my devoted, loving Mom. A mom who had a frightening encounter with a shark, struck by a car when she was a child, survived a F5 tornado, had a horrific car wreck as an adult, lived through an abusive marriage, dealt with the loss of pets (four within two years), battled numerous times with the uncaring family court, many surgeries, and a heart attack. God protected her early on in her life and to this day, because He knew she was meant to be my mom.

One time I asked Mom about her life. You know what said? After everything she has been through and then some, Mom told me that others still have it worse off than her. She added that one of the ministers she watches on TV commented that in this country, our worst day is someone's best day living in a poverty country. He's a wonderful minister from San Diego, California. There are other awesome pastors we enjoy watching. They are, a father and son in Georgia, a husband and wife and three dynamic-speaking men, including our pastor's dad, all from Texas. Mom also loves to listen to a powerful-speaking lady evangelist. I've heard her. She is good! We watch all of them, and others, on TV when we are unable to go to our church. I'm glad there are lots of good pastors throughout our country. They have all helped my mom heal inside. Mom once shared with me a quote by a lady she admires. Her name is Oprah Winfrey. She said, "Where there is no struggle, there is no strength." WOW! That lady knows what she's talking about. No wonder Mom memorized it. I did too! I'm glad I have a strong Mom and I'm glad she chose to adopt me! Mostly I'm glad she got away from my dad! Throughout the book I gave you several reasons why I believed Mom finally left Dad. I can sum them all up in 2 words: "Abusive Narcissism".

I thank God for answering my letter and sending Rain E and the others. My heavenly help! I will miss seeing Rain E, Stormy, Bolt, Dove, Butterfly, Snowflake, Cotton Ball and Olive. I know they were part of my dreams, but they WERE real, because God put them in my dreams and my dreams are a part of my soul. That's what made them REAL!

Now an important announcement! My birthday wish and coin wish came true! It was the same wish. I wished Rain E would show me a sign that she would always be near. That sign came in the form of a girl named "Pinkie". Thank you God!

I will deeply miss all our pets that have passed on. I never did tell you, four months before our loving male dog died in Mom's arms, he hurt his back leg causing paralyses. Mom chose a series of laser treatments for him that lasted weeks. He was finally able to walk again, after the final treatment. Then a month later he had his heart attack. I told Mom that she was the reason he was able to walk into Heaven. That's the kind of human being she is!

Now four years later, everything Mom and I have been through, we are still surviving and hang'in in there. All those years and no matter how hard Mom fought to protect me I still have to see my dad. That's the downside of my life. The upside, my faith continues to grow stronger each day. I'm growing up and my dad cannot change that. As I get older and older, my dad is aware of what's coming. He should know, Mom has told him enough. I WILL walk away!

During those horrific, terrifying, painful years, my dad TRIED to take from me: my self-esteem, self-confidence, self-worth, self-respect, along with my phone, my friends and even my favorite blanket, not to mention my mom, but he never succeeded. God and Mom wouldn't let him!! What kind of human being does that to a child? A monster!! A monster in the form of a dad!! A famous writer Mark Twain said it best: "Of all the animals, man is the only one that is cruel. He is the only one that inflicts pain for the pleasure of doing it." So true! My dad was and still is cruel! He DOES inflict pain for the pleasure of doing it! He's not just an animal he IS a monster! He will NEVER change, but the law can.

Now that I'm older, I watch the news with Mom. She encourages me to be aware of what is going on in our world. I saw our country's White House lit up with rainbow colors. Mom said that a group of passionate people worked a long time to get the law changed. I asked what they needed changed. So let me get this straight, our government took a long time helping them, but can't help kids being abused daily, over and over, year after year, by the same mentally ill parent or caregiver. Wow! If it took years to change that law, I guess the wait will be even longer before the president displays the colors BLACK and BLUE letting the country know the law finally decided to help us abused and mistreated kids. PLEASE HELP US!!!!!!! NOW!!!!!!!

Final Acknowledgements

To my loving Grandma: For taking care of Mom and me when we were sick. To my friends, Mom's family, wonderful school and church: For their support. To Mom's wonderful and patient editor Debbie Mitchell and family friend and typist Susan Williams. We love and thank you ALL!

To all our pets who have died, which now includes my Sugar. She died of cancer a month after Mom and I finished writing this book. WE WILL MISS YOU ALL! I WILL MISS YOU SUGAR!!! Our oldest, sweet elderly cat is still with us. She out lived them all!

Twelve to Eight

Now I am Twelve
Life's still not swell.

Fours years gone by
Not a blink of an eye.

Sad and depressed, added to fears
All I remember were lots of tears.

Though Mom showed me love, with gobs of attention
There was always Dad's belt, along with detention.

I did my best to try to please
Impossible living with a narcissistic sleeze.

My life was far worse, than insane
The monster, the evil man was to blame.

But God gave me Rain E. and my Mom
Along with my Bible, especially Psalms.

My dad needs help, but not from me
It can only come from Heaven and He.

I want to go back to when I was eight,
Before my young heart was full of such hate.

There will be scars, that I can say
Longing them to go, instead they just stay.

Whether Eight to Twelve or Twelve to Eight
It all came down to one last debate.

Nothing changed, no human stepped in
To help my life, to help me win.

So life goes on, it never sits still
Tick, tock the clock, so I just chill.

It is what it is, I've been living in Hell
Thank goodness for time, it's nearing Farewell!

C. T. Ford and R.R. Ford

Coming in 2016 "The Twin Club"

T he adventures of Rachel and Pinkie in: The Haunted House
   The first, in a series of six books about Rachel Rene's life! Each year, one book will deal with the on going struggles she continues having concerning her relationship with her dad. Plus her budding friendship with Pinkie and the rest of the neighborhood gang! The kids are faced with challenging aspects, situations and mishaps in their lives that are funny to down right scary!